Crystals • Jewels • Stones

and

Crystals and the New Age

Crystals
Jewels · Stones
Magic & Science

Isidore Kozminsky

and

Crystals and the New Age

Stuart Weinberg

Edited with a Foreword by

Hannah Finne

IBIS PRESS
Lake Worth, FL

Published in 2012 by Ibis Press
An imprint of Nicolas-Hays, Inc.
P. O. Box 540206
Lake Worth, FL 33454-0206
www.ibispress.net

Distributed to the trade by
Red Wheel/Weiser, LLC
65 Parker St. • Ste. 7
Newburyport, MA 01950
www.redwheelweiser.com

ISBN: 978-0-89254-171-3

Library of Congress Cataloging-in-Publication Data
Available upon request.

Book design and production by Studio 31.
www.studio31.com

Printed in the United States of America (vg)

"Another, ere she slept, was stringing stones
To make a necklet—agate, onyx, sard,
Coral, and moonstone—round her wrist it gleamed
A coil of splendid color, while she held
Unthreaded yet, the bead to close it up—
Green turkis, carved with golden gods and scripts."

Edwin Arnold—*The Light of Asia*

Contents

Crystals, Jewels, and Stones: Magic and Science
by Isidore Kozminsky

135

Part One
Crystal and Stones in the Bible and World Mythology

*Inspiration and Knowledge: Experiments on Sensitives: Gems and Color
Attractions: Ancient Gem Classification: Science Hermetic Among
Ancient Nations: Punishment of the Peach Tree: Modern Classification.*

PART TWO

PRECIOUS AND SEMIPRECIOUS GEMS ARRANGED
IN ALPHABETICAL ORDER

Hyalite, the Eye Opal: Hydrophane, the Magic Opal: Menilite, the
Liver Opal: Opal Jasper: Rose Opal: Semi-Opal, the Forest Opal:
Tabasheer: Marco Polo's Account of the Expedition of the Great
Khan: The Opal of Invulnerability and Remover of Dread: The
Marvel of Transformation: The Opal In Myth and History: Petrus
Arlensis Describes the Opal: Pliny's Poetical Opinion: The Paederos
Child Beautiful as Love: The Orphan: Roman Senator and his Opal:
Ophthalmios The Eye Stone: Opinion of Medieval Writers: The Bay
Tree: Albertus Magnus and the Opals that Sparkled in Darkness: The
Zodiacal Sign of Royalty and the Opal: Keraunios or the Thunder Stone:
The Beauty Stone: The Stone of Hope, Achievement and Love: The
Large Hungarian Opal: Australian Opal Fields: Sir David Brewster's
Theory of Colors in Opals: Dr. G. F. H. Smith's Explanation:
Sensitiveness of the Opal: Superstition Against Opal: The Plague at
Venice: The "Burning of Troy": The Crimean War: Scott's Anne of
Geierstein: Combinations of Diamonds and Opals: Destruction of the
Vanities at Florence: Story of the Opal of Alfonzo XII of Spain: A
Cholera Stone Fatal to the King and to All Who Received it from Him
According to Astrological Science: The Baron's Opal of Fortune: The
Great Australian Opal —The Flame Queen.

Pearl: How Produced: Symbolic Stories of the Ancients: Boethius and
the River Pearls: Vishnu Creates Pearls: Pearls on the Ramayana:
Sandius' Contribution to the Royal Society of London in 1673: Sir
Everard Home and Darwin on the Formation of Pearls: Mr. Kelaart's
Reports to the Government of Ceylon: Researches of Professors
Herdmann, Hornel and Seurat: The Time of Pearl Maturity: Home on
the Luster of the Pearl: The Form of a Pearl: The Process of "Skinning":
Jerome and the Story of the Doves: The Pearl of Prince Imenheit: The
Great Persian Pearl: The Hope Pearl: The Austrian Imperial Pearl: La
Pellegrina: The Great Southern Cross: The Pearl of Phillip II of Spain:
The Pearl of the King of Maabar: The Tibetan Prayer of Victory: King
Jaipal's Necklace: The Famine in Egypt: Ebu Hesham's Account of the
Tomb of Princess Tajah: Benvenuto Cellini and the Pearl Necklace of
the Duchess of Florence: The Pearl Rope of Marie Alexandrovna: Pink
Pearls: Red Pearls: A Death Rite Mentioned by Marco Polo: Pearls
Used in Buddhist Ceremonies: Julius Caesar, an Expert in Pearls: The

of Boiling Water: A Charm Against Drowning: A Modern Illustration: Rabbi Benoni: "Book of Winds": Topaz Charms.

PART THREE
STONES IN ASTROLOGY, MAGIC, AND HERALDRY

*The Way of the Spirit: Destiny, the Law: Point of Union of Forces
Known to the Hermetic Philosophers: Universal Order and Harmony.*

ILLUSTRATIONS

Foreword

by Hannah Finne

Isidore Kozminsky's classic study, *The Magic and Science of Jewels and Stones*, was first published in 1922. This greatly expanded edition—retitled *Crystals, Jewels, Stones: Magic & Science*—will serve as an invaluable resource to anyone seeking knowledge of the spiritual and mythic properties of the mineral world.

Isidore Israel Kozminsky was born in Melbourne, Australia, in 1870 to a family of Prussian Jews. His father, Simon Kozminsky, immigrated to Australia by way of London. The Kozminsky jewelry store, which he established, today remains one of Australia's best-known and most respected jewelers. Raised amidst the late nineteenth-century Australian gold rush, Isidore Kozminsky was knowledgeable and passionate about gemstones of all varieties—and, in particular, the wealth of beautiful specimens being produced in his homeland.

In addition to his expertise with stones, Isidore was exceedingly well-informed concerning occult and esoteric tradition; he was a prolific author and a reputed member of the Hermetic Order of the Golden Dawn. Among his many well-respected works are *Numbers Their Meaning and Magic*, *The Paths of the Kabala*, and *Zodiacal Symbology and its Planetary Power*. In the latter work, he describes symbolic images for each degree of the zodiac. Although less well-known than the similar Sabian symbol set, Kozminsky's symbols remain an important tool for many modern astrologers.

In *Crystals, Jewels, Stones: Magic & Science*, Kozminsky offers a well-rounded and thorough resource for the study of gemstones. He draws from a variety of sources and multiple traditions to address every facet of his topic, giving the reader a wealth of information on the history, uses, and qualities of stones both mythical and real.

Kozminsky begins by considering ancient philosophy concerning stones—in particular the relationships between crystals and astrological symbolism. He addresses Biblical gemstone lore with an in-depth discussion of the stones upon the Breastplate of the High Priest of Israel as described in the Book of Exodus. He weighs contrasting accounts of which stone sat in which position on the Breastplate in order to present a thorough and well-reasoned case for his own interpretation, as well as an explanation of its astrological and symbolic significance.

A variety of myths and legends concerning stones follow, drawn from all parts of the world. Kozminsky carefully examines the relationship between mineral fact and fiction. Whenever possible, the author—ever a relentless academic—cites the probable background of legends, drawing comparisons across cultures and through time to explain the evolution of societal beliefs about particular crystals. Though he is deeply respectful of these ideas, Kozminsky consistently dispels superstitious beliefs about cursed stones. This is particularly notable in his fascinating section on the histories of various famous (and infamous) diamonds. Beautifully rendered birth charts for many notable individuals whose lives were affected for better or worse by the jewels they wore provide concrete examples of the astrological effects of gemstones.

An alphabetical listing of significant stones includes information about the chemical and physical properties of important gems, as well as mythical, medical, and magical lore accrued through the ages. This well-researched, carefully organized, and thorough section is an invaluable reference, particularly when paired with the straightforward lists of stones' properties and astrological associations found in the appendices.

Addressing the cultural and magical context of stones, Kozminsky examines the heraldic and national associations of gems, and provides material excerpted from esteemed magical texts. From *The Book of the Sacred Magic of Abra Melin the Mage*, Kozminsky includes several symbolic Magical Squares related to various stones. From Charubel's work, *The Psychology of Botany, Minerals and Precious Stones*, he shares invocations and sacred seals used to unlock the occult virtues of assorted jewels. Finally, he offers a guide to mentions of gemstones in Shakespeare's works, organized by stone and cited by play, act, and scene.

* * *

Ibis Press is delighted to offer you this new edition of Kozminsky's work, which has been edited to improve its clarity and accuracy without altering or abridging its content. Spellings have been modernized, Americanized, and made consistent through the text, and every effort has been made to correct typographical errors from the original. Although some changes have been made to the structure of the book to improve clarity, all of the original material remains.

We have replaced the color images from the original edition with updated photography in order to provide the reader with the highest-quality visual references for the crystal and stones Kozminsky describes. Several of the unique black and white photographs of rare collector pieces that Kozminsky provided have been retained.

Most importantly, we have included *Crystals and the New Age* by Stuart Weinberg, a noted expert on crystals and gemstones, and the owner of Seven Stars bookstore in Cambridge, Massachusetts. Calling on knowledge gained through his years of buying and selling crystals in the New Age market, Weinberg examines the many ways in which gemstones have become a powerful magical and economic factor in the contemporary spiritual movement. He introduces several traditions within which crystals are commonly used, and offers a list of suggestions for further reading.

Weinberg's primary contributions, however, are his biographies of those legitimate channels who have shaped the New Age as we know it. Channels are individuals who act as a conduit for knowledge from an invisible source, often spiritual or angelic. Weinberg's essay explores the question of what makes a channel credible by looking at the lives of five individuals whose work shows the greatest evidence of authenticity. The work of these five channels—Emmanuel Swedenborg, Helena Blavatsky, Alice Bailey, Edgar Cayce, and Jane Roberts—built and expanded upon the foundations of the New Age, and heralded the expansion of human consciousness.

Weinberg considers what sets these individual apart from the myriad others who claim spiritual inspiration for their writings. His intimate biographies of their lives and work offer fascinating and illuminating accounts of revolutionary spiritual thinkers who have stood the test of time.

By tracing the lineage and legacy of channeling from the eighteenth century to the modern day, Weinberg also offers a new perspective on the often confusing associations of certain stones within astrological, planetary, and magical systems. Psychic wisdom, conveyed through a human agent, is responsible for many of the associations of certain crystals within astrological, planetary, and magical systems. However, the proliferation of such channels through the ages has led to disagreements over the "correct" lists of signs and stones. Where Kozminsky addresses this multiplicity of lists by examining their historical contexts to determine those most likely to have an authentic, ancient source, Weinberg looks at the problem in terms of the authenticity of the channels who created them. His suggested reading list gives his personal recommendations for those crystal channels he finds most accurate.

Weinberg's portrayal of the New Age as an evolving, vital movement helps show why crystals are as relevant today as they were when Kozminsky's book was first published nearly a century ago.

Crystals, Jewels, Stones: Magic & Science is a must-have for anyone who, like the authors, is captivated by the variety and beauty of the mineral realm. As a scientific and magical sourcebook, it is beyond compare. We hope you find it to be an enjoyable and accessible read, and a useful reference volume.

CRYSTALS AND THE NEW AGE

STUART WEINBERG

The New Age is a both vision and a market place. In each case it is vast and encompassing. The vision encompasses a multiplicity of religious and spiritual traditions, intersects scientific thought, and integrates an array of tools and techniques for analysis and strategy: personal, social, global, and interplanetary. It tends to modulate its vision; its interface with traditional creeds is nuanced and selective. It tolerates diversity and disagreement within and for the most part ignores critique from without. It is targeted by a few, notably evangelical Christians, scientists, and skeptics. It generates literature, products, and services on a large scale. And while traditionalists and the disinterested significantly outnumber its adherents and devotees, it is nevertheless a cultural and economic force.

Crystals emerged in the New Age market in the 1980s, changing the demographics of New Age retail. During this period, Occult bookstores gradually morphed into New Age gift shops with books. On the one side the tight mark-up of new books, a growing dominance of screens in our culture, and an aggressive market share strategy of Amazon and Barnes and Noble squeezed the Independent Bookseller. On the other side, an array of products with retail-friendly profit margins evolved in the metaphysical arena. In this regard Crystals were very retail-friendly.

The precedent for the sale of crystals and mineral specimens was the rock shop. The clientele were collectors and rock hounds; the program was search and display. The New Age pragmatized the Mineral Kingdom. Crystals were integrated into healing modalities, meditative frameworks, and shamanic techniques. Traditions utilizing crystals were rediscovered and reconfigured. These renewed traditions caught miners' attention, offering them a new market for their product, especially the numerous stones found in Arkansas and Brazil. Retailers competed for early looks at distributors' shipments. As demand grew, what had been friendly competition developed a commercial edge.

* * *

Within the context of the modern New Age, three elements were crucial for the developing body of crystal literature which in turn expanded the volume of crystal sales, and increased the prominence of crystals and minerals in the New Age market. These three elements are the chakras, astrology, and channeling.

Much contemporary crystal literature integrates chakra and astrological associations for specific crystals without any discussion of the two systems. The following includes rudimentary discussions of the chakras and astrology to introduce the reader to the reasoning behind these associations. As some crystal literature relies on channeling to assign properties, meanings and functions to specific crystals and minerals, biographical sketches of five channels who helped to establish the paradigm for channeling for the modern New Age era are also included. Finally, a selected bibliography of crystal literature provides suggestions for further reading in the field.

The New Age Spins on Chakras

Chakra, from the Sanskrit, translates as *Wheel, Disk, Vortex,* or *Center.* Wheels turn, disks rotate, and vortices spin. Chakras are centers of energy configured through the etheric body—a body of light, rarely visible, which reflects and infuses the physical body. This etheric body is composed of strands and streams of light, converging and diverging. Intense convergences, interlacing strands and streams of light, create wheel-like configurations within the body of light. These are the chakras.

The seven chakras are located in line, from the base of the spine to the crown: base, sexual/sacral, solar plexus, heart, throat, the third eye (in the forehead,) and the crown. The glands in the physical body express chakra activity in the etheric. From base to crown, the corresponding glands are: adrenals, gonads, pancreas, thymus, thyroid, pituitary, and pineal. As the influence of the glands plays through internal organs, the chakras' résumé grows.

The floral metaphor works well with the chakra system. Each chakra is represented as a core surrounded by petals. The cores hold distinctive geometrical configurations, and the petals vary in number. From base to crown, the numbers of petals are: 4, 6, 10, 12, 16, 96, and 972.

Color, too, forms a spectrum: infrared to ultraviolet. From base to crown, the chakras reflect this spectrum; the chakras are, respectively, red, orange, yellow, green, light blue, deep blue, and purple. The borders of the chakras are black at the base, ranging to white to translucent at the crown.

Crystals express the vibrancy, aesthetic, and range of color very well; color and geometry are two keynotes of the mineral kingdom. As such, from chakra to color to crystal and back, crystals can be set in an etheric framework with therapeutic applications. Crystals heal, and in specific ways based on chakra-gland correlation.

The strands and streams of light of the etheric body form three prominent channels flowing through and linking the seven chakras. The central channel is called the *sushumna*; the *ida* and *pingala* are subsidiary channels intersecting the *sushumna* at certain chakra points. A serpentine flow of energy, *kundalini*, moves through these channels, vitalizing the chakras and causing them to spin. Spinning chakras are a gauge of personal transformation.

The vibratory alignment of crystals through color to chakras, may enhance vitalization and spin. Crystals hold dimensions of power in a framework of personal development and spiritualization.

The New Age Knows your Sign: Astrology

The zodiac is a circle drawn in space, surrounding our Solar System. The 360-degree wheel is divided into twelve 30-degree arcs. These are the Signs of the Zodiac, Aries through Pisces. Astrology is geocentric. From the earth, an astrologer views the Sun, Moon, and 8 planets as moving in orbit within the Zodiac wheel. To chart a birth, astrology stops the orbital movement of the Sun, Moon and planets, locating each within a 30-degree arc or Sign, and more precisely each in a degree of that arc or Sign.

Moreover, for a given birth time and place, astrology assumes another division of the circle drawn in space. This division, twelvefold as well, overlaps the Zodiac wheel. There are two axes: one from east to west, called the ascendant-descendant, the other from north to south, the zenith-nadir. These lines intersect, creating four quadrants with three segments each. These segments are known as the Houses. Starting from the eastern axis point, the ascendant, the Houses number one to twelve. The beginning point, or the cusp, of each of the Houses aligns with a degree of an arc or Sign, as do the planets. Therefore, the Sun, Moon and planets are located within a House as well as a Sign.

The twelve meanings of the Signs and Houses are sequential (Aries through Pisces, one through twelve,) and shared: Aries aligned with the First House through Pisces aligned with the Twelfth House. The sequence suggests personal evolution through socialization. The Solar System reflects the twelvefold set of meanings as well. The distribution and sequence, however, have some nuance. The Sun, Moon and eight planets—ten in all—link to twelve Signs and Houses. Moreover, the order of association is not linear.

Sign	House	Planet
Aries	1	Mars
Taurus	2	Venus
Gemini	3	Mercury
Cancer	4	Moon
Leo	5	Sun
Virgo	6	Mercury
Libra	7	Venus
Scorpio	8	Pluto
Sagittarius	9	Jupiter
Capricorn	10	Saturn
Aquarius	11	Uranus
Pisces	12	Neptune

From another perspective, astrology offers a linear division of the Solar System. In proximity to the earth, with relatively fast orbital movement, are the Sun, Moon, Mercury, Venus, and Mars. These bodies are intimately linked to persona through Sign and House location. The dualities resonate: Sun and Moon, will and emotion; Venus and Mars, attraction and aggression. Mercury represents attunement and manipulation in the proximate environment. Though further away, Jupiter and Saturn, another duality, are principles of expansion and contraction.

The outer triad—Uranus, Neptune and Pluto—express dynamics of change. Uranus is a lightning bolt; Neptune, gradual and fluid erosion. Pluto is orgasmic, representing transformation from inside out. The slow orbital movement of these outer planets suggests generational influence through Sign location. House position, on the other hand, is personal.

Astrology is deeply geometric. At a given birth time, the locations of the Sun, Moon, and planets at specific degrees on the 360-degree wheel in space measure variant degree or arc separations from one another. Certain arcs, in approximation, create angular relations between planets. Prominent angles for Astrology are, in degrees of arc: 0, 60, 90, 120, and 180. These relations, called aspects, are respectively known as: conjunction, sextile, square, trine, and opposition.

An approximate arc of 90 degrees creates a side of a square; the dynamic between planets is blocked, or excessive to overcome the block. An approximate arc of 120 degrees is a side of a triangle; the dynamic between planets is fluid and benign. Squares and oppositions tend to express challenges, while trines and sextiles express skills, gifts, and opportunity. Aspects are the core of Astrology, integrating the three systems of Sign, House, and Planets into the complexity of character and experience.

Crystals and Astrology

Specific crystals and minerals are linked to each of the twelve signs. From the vantage point of marketing, an individual generally buys the stone associated with his or her sun sign, or perhaps one's partner's sun sign. The decision to purchase a particular crystal because it lines up with the sign one's Mars is in, or the sign of one's ascendant in the western astrological system is unlikely.

Crystal literature varies in aligning minerals and crystals with each of the signs. In some books, the list of stones for each sign is long, with some crystals linked to multiple signs. The rationale for associating minerals with signs is frequently not given. There are planetary links to specific minerals as well, which may have an alchemical and hermetic rationale. The alchemical planetary links tend to have more depth and consistency than the general sign correlations.

Crystals are integrated into Vedic astrology with specificity, detail, complexity, and consistency. Moreover, they function therapeutically on physical and emotional levels, and are commonly prescribed by Vedic astrologers. In the Vedic system, purchasing a particular crystal because it lines up with the sign one's Mars is in, or the sign of one's ascendant, is not a stretch.

CHANNELING: PARADIGMS AND PRECEDENTS, FORERUNNERS AND PRECURSORS

The New Age Changes Channels.

Crystal "cookbooks" offer recipes for physical well-being, emotional balance, and spiritual growth. The complexity of the physical, emotional, and spiritual is served by the diversity of the mineral kingdom. Sorting out the alignment of a diverse set of crystals with the complexity of a person is a speculative and intuitive art. In the eighties, this speculative, intuitive artistry was preeminently Channeling.

Channeling is intuitive communication from an invisible Source through a human conduit. The Channel speaks in the name of the Source to a receptive audience. Hopefully, for the Channel, the audience grants both the Source and its Channel credibility and authority.

Emanuel Swedenborg

Dining in a London tavern in the spring of 1745, Emanuel Swedenborg had a vision. A vaporous emanation began to exude from his pores. These vapors, falling to the floor, transformed into crawling creatures which ignited in a flash. A male presence appeared in the corner of the room. As Swedenborg's friend Carl Robsahm relates, the male in the corner said "Eat not so much," and disappeared.

That evening in Swedenborg's lodging, the same male appeared. Identifying himself as the Lord, he commissioned Swedenborg to an expansive spiritual reinterpretation of Scripture. The presence opened up a panorama of an inhabited spirit world for Swedenborg to view. Because of these compelling spiritual experiences, Swedenborg's creative and literary focus shifted; he was on the path to becoming the first major channel of the New Age.

Emanuel Swedenborg was born in Stockholm in 1688. His father, Jesper Swedberg—at the time of his son's birth a chaplain in the Swedish Royal Court—was later appointed professor of Theology at Uppsala University and Bishop of Skara. The family's wealth derived from the mining interests of Jesper's father, and the property of Swedenborg's stepmother, Sara Bergia.

Upon graduating from Uppsala University in 1709, Emanuel traveled the European continent expanding his intellectual base. This was the first of eleven such European trips, the last of which would end with his death in London in 1772.

Swedenborg was an intellectual giant. Early in his adult life, he established himself as a scientist, engineer, and inventor. In 1714, Swedenborg designed a fixed-wing aircraft, with viable wing surface, landing gear, and cockpit. He invented a hoisting apparatus to raise ore safely and efficiently from mines. He anticipated the anatomical relevance of neurons in the organization of the nervous system, and suggested the prominence of aspects of the endocrine system. Swedenborg was the first to develop a nebular hypothesis of planetary evolution in the solar system. During this scientific phase, Swedenborg authored and published volumes on chemistry, mineralogy, and biology.

With the designation of nobility for families of Swedish Bishops in 1719, Swedenborg gained a seat in the Swedish Parliament. In the political arena he functioned actively and diligently. In 1724, he was appointed to the Board of Mines, serving for twenty-three years. Rising from assessor to councilor, he played a significant role in modernizing the Swedish mining industry.

Even before the turn from Science to Spirit marked by his London vision in 1745, Swedenborg's dream life intensified. A journal he kept details twenty-one months, from 1743 to 1774. It includes a description of a vision in Delft, after Easter 1744. In this vision, Swedenborg is cradled in Jesus' arms. The Lord inquires about a bill of health.[1] Such a symbolic credential would be interpreted as establishing Swedenborg's ensuing mission of spiritual discovery. In another dream, Jesper ties Emanuel's cuffs with ribbons.

In the following years, Swedenborg, conversing with angels and spirits, charted the demographics of Heaven and Hell. He communicated with spirits and inhabitants of Mercury, Jupiter, Mars, Saturn, Venus, the

---

1 The Bill of Health was a certificate documenting the health status of crew and passengers leaving port on a ship.

Moon, and five worlds beyond. With sources in spirit and extraterrestrial, Swedenborg was a prolific channel.

Between 1749 and 1756, Swedenborg published eight volumes anonymously. Titled *Arcana Coelestia: Heavenly Mysteries*, these volumes were an expansive spiritual exposition of Genesis and Exodus. Unfortunately, their massive nature proved a deterrent on the commercial market. In 1758 five shorter works, more accessible and eclectic, were published. These included *Heaven and Hell, Life on Other Planets* and *The Last Judgment*. This last was an interpretation of Revelation. For Swedenborg, the second coming was a spiritual reorientation of Christianity which took place in 1757. Six more books were published in 1763, and a series of six more between 1764 and 1771. The final book, *True Christian Religion*, was preceded by a work on the interface of soul and body, and another, *Conjugal Love*, on intimacy in marriage.

In the summer of 1758, Swedenborg embarked on his seventh European trip. His agenda was the London publication of the five shorter works which followed the *Arcana*. He left England in June of 1759, landing in Gothenburg, on the coast of Sweden, 300 miles west of Stockholm. In Gothenburg, Swedenborg accepted a dinner invitation at the home of William Castel, a merchant of note. Fifteen guests attended the dinner party. At the dinner, an agitated Swedenborg announced that a dangerous fire was, at that moment, sweeping through Stockholm. Sodermalm, the locale of Swedenborg's house in Hornsgaten, was threatened. Several hours later, Swedenborg, with relief, announced that the fire had been extinguished three doors from his house, which remained intact. Swedenborg's account proved accurate in all details, and was widely publicized.

In 1716, Swedish King Charles XII attempted to invade Norway, but was forced to retreat. He tried again in 1718. While inspecting trenches on the perimeter of the Fredriksten fortress, Charles XII was killed by a bullet through his skull, entering through the left and exiting right. Whether the fatal shot came from grapeshot launched by a Norwegian cannon; a round fired from the musket of an assassin working for Frederick I (the husband of Ulrika Eleanora, sister and successor to Charles XII); or an accidental discharge from an improvised "button-bullet" he is reputed to have worn, King Charles' death had major political ramifications. Ulrika Eleanora's claim to succeed her brother was challenged by their nephew Charles Frederick. In spite of the opposition, she gained the crown in 1719, ceding power to the Riksdag, an aristocratic parliament, and ending an era of absolute authority for the Swedish monarchy. A year later she abdicated the throne in favor of her husband, Frederick I.

The Riksdag elected Adolf Frederick Crown Prince of Sweden in 1743. His selection was strategic: in domestic politics, one political party, the Hats, trumped another, the Caps; internationally, a Swedish-Russian treaty was in play through family links of the Crown Prince. When Frederick I died in 1751, Adolph Frederick was crowned King. However, Adolf Frederick's willingness to be merely a figurehead contrasted with the disposition of his Queen, Louisa Ulrika. Ambitious, arrogant, and elitist, her disposition was toward absolute power in the state and manipulative control in her marriage.

Sister of Frederick the Great, King of Prussia, Louisa Ulrika was cunning and ruthless. In 1756, she strategized a coup to regain absolute power for the monarchy. Replacing 44 diamonds of the crown with glass, she pawned the true gems in Berlin. Supplementing her funds with royal jewels and jewelry, the Queen financed the coup. Unfortunately for Louisa Ulrika, the drunken talk of conspirator and pub owner, Ernst Angel—a nephew of Frederick I—exposed the plot. Ten decapitations later (Angel included,) the Queen was reprimanded and the King put on notice.

In the fall of 1761, Louisa Ulrika received correspondence from her sister which mentioned Swedenborg's ability to converse with the dead. Swedenborg's psychic abilities were documented in his publications of 1753, and had been well publicized in detailed accounts of clairvoyant episodes, including the Stockholm fire of 1758. Intrigued, the Queen invited Swedenborg to the royal court.

Seeing the invitation as an excellent opportunity to spread his message, Swedenborg offered the royal couple copies of his publications. In time, the conversation turned to spirit communication. Swedenborg affirmed his ability, describing it as a gift from the Lord. The Queen asked Swedenborg to contact her deceased brother, Augustus William, the former Crown Prince of Prussia, who had died in 1758.

Swedenborg accepted the commission, and returned to the royal court several weeks later, publications in hand. Louisa Ulrika was playing cards as Swedenborg entered. Interrupting the game, he requested a private audience. Though her initial response was that privacy was unnecessary, Swedenborg tactfully persisted and the Queen agreed. They moved to another apartment with witnesses at one end of the room.

Louisa Ulrika's reaction to Swedenborg's communication was palpable—witnesses described a distinctive change in the Queen's demeanor. She was heard exclaiming that only her brother could have been the source of the communication.

There was a complex geopolitical backdrop for the spirit communication between the royal siblings through Swedenborg's mediumship. A seven year war, beginning in 1756—two years before Augustus William's death—had been initiated by a third sibling, Frederick the Great, King of Prussia. Frederick faced an alliance of Austria, Russia, France and Sweden; thus, the interests of the Prussian King and Crown Prince were in opposition to the interests of Sweden. The interests of their sister Louisa Ulrika, on the other hand, were another matter.

In the spring of 1761, Mme. de Marteville, widow of the Dutch ambassador in Stockholm, was approached by a goldsmith named Croon. The goldsmith asked for payment of an outstanding debt incurred by her late husband. De Marteville had purchased a silver service from Croon, for a price of 25,000 Dutch guilders.

Knowing her late husband to have been meticulous in financial matters, the widow had doubts about Croon's claim. She could not, however, locate the receipt. The Russian ambassador, a family friend, suggested contacting Swedenborg, whose reputation for bridging the gap between living and dead had grown. Mme. De Marteville visited Swedenborg and requested his assistance.

There are divergent accounts of the further developments. In one version, Swedenborg contacted de Marteville in the spirit world and was simply assured that the matter would be sorted out. Eight days after this assurance, the widow had a vivid dream in which her late husband appeared, and showed her a hidden compartment in an upstairs bureau where the receipt was located. In the other version, Swedenborg visited the widow three days after her request. He informed Mme. De Marteville that the bill had been paid seven months before her husband's demise. The receipt, he told her, could be found in a secret compartment behind the left hand drawer of the bureau. Swedenborg, the widow, and her guests went upstairs and discovered the secret compartment in the bureau and the receipt for the silver service. In either version, we have a happy ending for the widow, an unhappy development for Croon, and an enhancement of Swedenborg's résumé.

These three anecdotes—the fire in Stockholm, the correspondence between Louisa Ulrika and the late Augustus William, and the de Marteville receipt—were highly publicized in their time. Swedenborg's psychic gifts are merely one facet of an impressive résumé. His scientific genius, expressed through his inventions and theoretical constructs, and his public service, as Assessor of Mines and member of the Riksdag, are other facets. Multi-faceted genius of this sort is rare, and unfortunately, not always appreciated. Da Vinci defined his era; Swedenborg did not.

What Swedenborg did accomplish, for our purposes, was the inauguration of the New Age in its contemporary expression. While his spiritual filter was predominantly Christian, his skills set the paradigm for spirit communication as expressed through the mediumship of the 19th century and the channeling phenomenon of the 1980s. Emanuel Swedenborg was a prolific conduit for a variety of sources to a varied audience; he was the first channel for the modern New Age.

Helena Petrovna Blavatsky

The seminal figure for the modern era of New Age spirituality was Helena Petrovna Blavatsky. Born in the Ukraine in 1831, she was the author of two masterworks: *Isis Unveiled*, published in New York in the fall of 1877, and *The Secret Doctrine*, published in London in the fall of 1888. Madame Blavatsky was the focal point for the dissemination of evolutionary frameworks encompassing cosmic, planetary, and human development. Integrating diverse religious and occult traditions, some reaching back to antiquity, her set of teachings was termed Theosophy, and an organization of aligned individuals—the Theosophical Society—was established around her work.

Blavatsky's authorship represented a collaboration which was, in part, psychic. A clandestine group known as the Brotherhood of Masters and Adepts was introduced as an overarching source for material in *Isis Unveiled* and *The Secret Doctrine*, as well as other publications expressing themes of Theosophy. In this respect, Madame Blavatsky's work represents a major step in shaping the traditions of channeling in the New Age.

Lineage

Helena Petrovna's father, Peter von Hahn, was an artillery captain in the Russian Army, who would rise to the rank of Colonel before retiring. His heritage was German and military; Peter's father was a decorated General. Counts and Countesses also figured in Helena's paternal line, providing an aristocratic context for the early lives of Helena Petrovna and her siblings. At the time of Helena Petrovna's birth, Peter was deployed in Poland.

Her mother, Helena Andreyevna von Hahn, published her first novel at the age of 23 under the pen name Zuneida B-va, six years after giving birth to Helena Petrovna. This work and the novels that followed portrayed the plight of women of strength in challenging contexts. Unfortunately, a successful literary career for this George Sand of Russia was eclipsed by an early death from tuberculosis in 1842.

Both before and after the death of their daughter, Helena Petrovna's maternal grandparents played a significant role in her life. Helena Pavlovna de Fedeyev, Helena Petrovna's grandmother, had a lineage of nobility through the Dolgorusky clan of princes and princesses with links perhaps to ancient Persian royalty. Fluent in five languages, Helena Pavlovna was recognized for her scholarship in natural science, in particular botany and geology. Her expertise included archeology. Her husband Andrei Mihkailovich was a high-level government administrator, whose appointments included provincial governance.

Helena Petrovna's early and formative years, before and after the death of her mother, involved various living arrangements, due to shifting military deployments for Peter von Hahn and periods in which she, her sister Vera and her mother lived in comfort and affluence with their grandparents Helena Pavlovna and Andrei de Fedeyev. This affluence provided for governesses, education, and training in French and English.

The three Helenas—Pavlovna, Andreyevna, and Petrovna—each exhibited literary and intellectual prowess in dramatic fashion. The drama set in motion by Helena Petrovna continues to play out.

Marriage

After being taunted by a governess, seventeen-year-old Helena Petrovna enticed a proposal from the plumeless raven—a distinctively bald forty-year-old Nikofor Blavatsky, then Vice-Governor of the newly formed province of Yerivan. Though she had second thoughts, young Helena was nevertheless caught in the betrothal.

The wedding was in July of 1849. The reluctant bride allowed Nikofor no intimacy. Conjugal tension increased in the months that followed, until a resourceful Helena Petrovna escaped on horseback to her grandparent's home in Tiflis. Arrangements were made to send the recalcitrant bride to her father, who would meet her in Odessa. However, Helena worried that her family's strategy was to reunite her with Nikofor. Devious Helena Petrovna—with her new and enduring surname Blavatsky—managed transport on an English sailing vessel to Constantinople instead of boarding the steamer to Odessa. This was only the first of many international travels, including journeys to Greece, Egypt, Eastern Europe, the Americas, and perhaps even Tibet. She did not return to her homeland, Russia, until 1858.

Master

Throughout her childhood and youth, Helena had visions and dreams of a tall Hindu; turbaned and bearded, he was a benign and powerful presence. There are two accounts of London meetings with this protector and teacher which defined her alignment with the Brotherhood of Masters and Adepts.

From May to October of 1851, London hosted the Great Exhibition, a display of nineteenth century scientific and technological advances and inventions. The Crystal Palace, an expansive glass structure housing the international exhibits, was erected in Hyde Park. Over six million viewed these exhibits. Among the notable guests was the Prime Minister of Nepal, General Jung Rannerjee. Helena was in London at this time, staying with her godmother, the Countess Bagration, at the upscale Mivarts Hotel. While walking in London in August, Helena noted a group of Indian princes moving in the crowds. A six-foot-eight-inch Rajput was among them. She recognized him as the vision of her childhood, and he acknowledged her in turn. The following day they met privately in Hyde Park.

Several years later, in 1853, Dulap Singh, the deposed Maharaja of the Punjab, the Sikh empire in India, arrived in England. His territory on the Indian continent, had been annexed by the East India Company in 1849, at the close of the second Anglo-Sikh conflict. Converting from Sikhism to Christianity in 1853, Dulap Singh was exiled to Britain. The teenaged Maharaja, however, was embraced affectionately by Queen Victoria and the royal court at the inception of his life in exile. Helena references meeting her mysterious Hindu in London as he accompanied a dethroned native prince in 1854.

In these meetings, Helena's role in the global agenda of the Brotherhood of Masters and Adepts was specified. From this point, her life path converged with the goals and strategies of her masters.

Family Reunion

Christmas of 1858 marked Helena's return to Russia after adventures spanning continents. She arrived unannounced during the wedding celebration of the sister-in-law of her widowed sister Vera. The event was held in Pskoff, at the home of Vera's father-in-law, Nikolai Yarmontoff. Helena's psychic compass in locating her family suggests the intuitive skills that she displayed throughout her life. For a time, she remained with her father, siblings, and in-laws at the house in Pskoff. During this period in the Yarmontoff home disconnected rapping sounds were frequently heard and furniture moved mysteriously. Helena acknowledged psychic links to these strange phenomena; she attributed them to goblins that were drawn to her.

In the months that followed, Helena displayed her psychic skills in dramatic ways to overcome the skepticism of her father and step-brother. By controlling the strange rapping, she was able to spell out *Zaitchik*, the name of Colonel Hahn's favorite war horse in an early Turkish campaign, which he had covertly written for the experiment. For her step-brother Leonid, she supplemented the gravitational force of a three foot high, one-legged chess table. Her disconcerted sibling was unable to budge the small table.

Helena's sister Vera had inherited property and a home from her late husband in the province of Novgorod. Helena described in detail deceased members of the family that had owned the house. One—a tall, gaunt, elderly man with black headgear—had dramatically long nails, his hands resembling claws. Serfs living on the property identified the strange figure described as a deceased master of the house who had contracted a rare blood disease for which cutting nails or hair had dire ramifications. These distinctive abilities played a significant role in Helena Petrovna Blavatsky's link to the Brotherhood of Masters and Adepts.

In 1862, Helena briefly reconciled with her husband Nikofor. Though there was no intimacy in the reconciliation there was, however, the joint adoption of an infant, Yuri. Indications were that the baby was the illegitimate son of Nikofor's sister, Nathalie, and the married Baron of Estonia, Nikolai Meyendorf. Helena cared for the sickly and hunchbacked child until his death in 1867.

In November of 1867, Helena was involved in the Battle of Mentana, aligned with the progressive forces of Garibaldi against the Papal Army of Rome, which had been supplemented by French brigades with sophisticated rifles. The French technology was decisive; Garibaldi was defeated and captured. Helena suffered bullet wounds to her leg and shoulder, as well as a broken arm. There were hints of geopolitical threads in Helena's global adventures. Moreover, her antagonism toward the Roman Catholic formulation of Christianity is well documented in *Isis Unveiled* and *The Secret Doctrine*.

Tibet: Morya and Koot Hoomi

In the summer of 1868, Helena received a message from her Master. She was to meet him in Constantinople, and then accompany him overland to Tibet. The land route from Constantinople to Shigatze, their destination in Tibet, was about 400 miles; it would be a rugged journey of three to four weeks on horseback. Fortunately, Helena was an expert rider, with or without a saddle.

Helena remained in Tibet through 1870. Her Master, known through the Theosophical literature as Morya, had a particular alignment with a colleague known as Koot Hoomi. The two oversaw the dissemination of metaphysical and spiritual teachings under the heading of Theosophy. Each had a residence bordering a stream in a ravine with proximity to Shigatze and the Tashilhunpo Monastery, residence of the Panchen Lama and his court. Access to the resources of the monastery library indicated a particular link to the court of the Panchen Lama, who was a young teenager at this time. Within the theocratic hierarchy of Tibet, the Panchen Lama represents the Gelugpa lineage, the Yellow Caps, who trace their spiritual roots through fourteenth- and fifteenth-century Buddhist reformer, Tsong-kha-pa, to the archetypal figure of the Buddha Amithaba.

Training and study were the keynotes of Helena's time in Tibet. The training was geared to the refinement and amplification of her inherent psychic abilities; the studies ranged from the assimilation of Eastern religions and metaphysical systems to achieving fluency in Senzar, an esoteric language used by adepts, as well as English. Evidently, the Masters' plan for Helena necessitated a command of English beyond the tutoring provided by the governesses of her childhood and youth

Middle East

The Suez Canal was opened in 1869; Helena sailed through it in December 1870. The Middle East was the backdrop for Helena's next few years.

In July of 1871, en route from Athens to Cairo, Helena boarded a merchant ship, the SS *Eumonia*. An explosion of gunpowder and fireworks sunk the vessel. Four-hundred were on board the ship; Helena was one of sixteen who were rescued. The Greek authorities provided assistance and passage for the survivors. Helena sailed to Alexandria, where the number 27 proved fortuitous in a casino. She used her windfall to continue on to Cairo, taking rooms at the Hotel d'Orient. Here she first met Alexis Coulomb, the son of the hotel's owner; he and his wife Emma Cutting—then a member of the hotel staff—would become notorious during Helena's time in India, as we will see.

Helena's time in Cairo was marked by a failed enterprise; a Société Spirite, a society of mediums investigating Spiritualist phenomena and providing links to the deceased for the living. Unfortunately, she hired badly; her mediums were frauds and cheats. The Société lasted barely a month.

The Brotherhood had a near-eastern contingent, headquartered in Luxor. The names Hilarion and Serapis Bey surfaced, as well as Greek and Coptic teachers, and a Venetian; all provided further instruction for Helena as well as access to the Pyramids and Karnack.

After traveling through Syria, Palestine, and Lebanon, Helena returned once more to Russia in the summer of 1872, meeting her aunt Nadya in Odessa. In November of 1870, an Asiatic man had hand-delivered a letter to Nadya. The letter, written in French, assured her that her niece was well and would return to visit her in 18 months. Upon delivering the note, the unusual letter carrier became stranger still, vanishing mysteriously.

In the spring of 1873, Helena was settled comfortably in the Paris residence of her cousin Nikolai von Hahn and his wife. In June, however, a communication from Morya directed her to America. Though her funds were limited at this time, she was able—barely—to cover a first class ticket. At the docks, however, she encountered a mother with two children, distraught over being swindled in the purchase of counterfeit tickets. Helena rebooked her passage, crossing the ocean in steerage with the woman and her children. She landed in New York on July 7, 1873.

America

A primary objective of Morya in directing Helena to America in 1873 was establishing a bond with Henry Olcott, an American journalist whose work chronicled the contemporary phenomenon of Spiritualism. The core belief of Spiritualism is that death is a door to a spirit world, a world which can intersect with the world of the living. The dead can communicate with the living, and, taking on subtle and ethereal form, can manifest. Select individuals, called mediums, can facilitate this communication and manifestation.

Henry Olcott was studying scientific agriculture at Columbia University in New York when his father's business crashed. He left school to work a thirty acre farm in Ohio on a sharecrop basis. By the age of 23, he had gained an international reputation for expertise in agriculture. By 1859, he had co-founded an agricultural institute in New York State, had two volumes of his lectures on agriculture published, and been hired as an agricultural correspondent for the *New York Herald Tribune*.

Henry's moral compass led him to volunteer to cover the hanging of abolitionist John Brown for the *Tribune*. On December 2, 1859, he witnessed the execution in Charleston, Virginia. Henry enlisted in the Union Army in 1861. He fought in the North Carolina campaigns; however, malaria and dysentery limited any further role in combat.

Instead, Olcott was assigned to investigate illegal profiteering in the Army. Uncovering extensive corruption, the scope of his investigation expanded to the other services. Commissioned by the War Department, he was promoted to Colonel. When Lincoln was assassinated in 1865,

Olcott was appointed to the three man commission charged with investigating the conspiratorial aspect of the murder. Interrogations and raids led to the arrest of a major conspirator. Later that year, Henry resigned his commission.

In 1868, Olcott was admitted to the New York Bar. He established a law practice in New York City. His clientele grew to include the New York City Treasury, the Stock Exchange, steel manufacturing, railroads, insurance companies, and banks.

In July of 1874, Olcott impulsively purchased an edition of the *Banner of Light*, a Spiritualist journal. The issue documented the phenomena surrounding a pair of mediums, William and Horatio Eddy of Chittenden, Vermont. His interest piqued, Henry's impulse purchase led to a trip to Chittenden, and an article on about phantoms materializing at the Eddy farmstead for the *New York Sun*. This initial article attracted national and international attention. The *New York Daily Graphic* suggested a set of follow-up articles, sending a sketch artist to accompany Olcott. They stayed in Vermont for three months, the articles appearing twice weekly in the *Graphic*. Later, Henry expanded them into a book, *People from Other Worlds*, published in 1875.

Olcott's résumé of success in uncovering fraud in the military, coupled with his systematic and thorough investigation of the phenomena at Chittenden, established his credibility. His well-documented accounts describing and crediting the Eddy mediumship and phenomena supported Spiritualism, whose dramatic growth in popularity in America and Europe had engendered a skeptical backlash. Supporting Spiritualism, at least for the short term, was another objective of the Brotherhood.

After reading Olcott's follow-up articles in the *Sunday Graphic*, Helena decided to visit Chittenden. Olcott was at the Eddy farmstead when she arrived. At the dinner table, the vivid red shirt Helena wore—a remnant of the Garibaldi campaign and the Battle of Mentana—caught Olcott's eye. After the noon meal, Henry lit Helena's cigarette and the two began a conversation that lasted a decade and a half.

Materialism provided a philosophical base for skeptical efforts to debunk spiritual phenomena. Energized by impressive scientific advances, materialists were outspoken in their criticism of Spiritualism. For the Brotherhood, the materialists' worldview was limiting. Furthermore, it was antagonistic to their philosophical and spiritual teachings. Helena represented the Masters interests, countering the skeptics efforts to debunk spiritual phenomena. Her brilliant and incisive piece published in the *Daily Graphic* defending the Eddy phenomena against the harsh and unsubstantiated claims of fraud by the New York physician Dr. Beard was acclaimed. She expanded her journalistic role with articles in the *Spiritual Scientist*, a Boston-based Spiritualist publication unusual for depth of scholarship and absence of sensationalism. Helena played a more direct role as well, using her psychic skills to introduce exotic ethereal figures into the Eddy panorama of phantoms.

In November of 1874, Olcott left Vermont, returning to New York City. He relocated Helena to an apartment at 16 Irving Place in lower Manhattan. Her father had died in June of 1874, and her inheritance provided financial respite.

Early in 1875 she went to Philadelphia to investigate a controversy regarding Nelson and Jennie Holmes, mediums accused of fraud by Liza White, who claimed she had been hired to impersonate a spirit named Katie King, known for manifesting in various Spiritualist circles. The Holmes circle included Robert Owen, former U.S. Congressman and ambassador. Owen appealed to Olcott. He joined Helena in the investigation.

Whatever the integrity of Jennie Holmes as a medium, Helena chose to support the phenomena by using her psychic skill to manifest the ethereal form of Katie King as well as the form of one known as John King, in the last of a series of séances held by the Holmes to validate their mediumship. Jennie Holmes, knowing that she had no role in these manifestations, was startled. Helena, as she had in Chittenden, took a direct role in supporting Spiritualism as a movement.

Another Marriage

Helena remained in Philadelphia and inexplicably married Michael Betanelly, an entrepreneur who had emigrated from the Georgian province of Russia. Helena's celebrity had grown as she published more articles. Betanelly was impressed, and pursued Helena. Though initially resistant, she eventually acquiesced with the stipulation of no intimacy. At that point, she had received communication that Nikofor Blavatsky was dead.

The wedding was on April 3, 1875. Olcott did not attend. In fact, he remarked that the ceremony should have been held two days earlier—April Fools' day. The troubled marriage lasted barely four months. In spite of his promise, Betanelly had begun to grope Helena. His import business was failing as his debt increased. And, finally, it turned out that Nikofor was not dead. Helena left Betanelly, returning to New York. Henry found Helena another apartment; this time at 46 Irving Place.

Helena's profile rose as her journalistic career developed. Her articles, published in the mainstream press as well as in the *Spiritual Scientist* and other specialized journals, were reprinted as pamphlets, selling for 10 cents each. She was providing translations and original commentary on social and spiritual subjects for the Russian press. Her magnetic personality and brilliant conversational skills expanded her social milieu. An intellectually elite and growing contingent visited the suite at 46 Irving Place for discussion and lively conversation.

The Theosophical Society

The earliest expression of the impetus to form an organization is an entry in Helena's scrapbook dated July 1875, noting a directive from India to establish a philosophical-religious society and to choose Olcott as another founding member. On September 7, a group of seventeen gathered in Helena's suite at 46 Irving Place for a lecture on Egyptian sacred geometry by architect and engineer George Felt. The lecture was followed by discussion. During the discussion, a note was passed from Henry to Helena or Helena to Henry. In either case, the note was passed through William Quan Judge, a young lawyer of Irish descent. The note suggested forming a society for the study of subjects akin to the one presently being discussed. The principals agreed. Henry rose with the proposal. General agreement among the gathering followed.

Within a week, officers were chosen, with Henry as president, Helena as corresponding secretary and William Judge—destined for a prominent role in the future of Theosophy in America—as counsel. Their name, the Theosophical Society, was agreed upon as well. *Theosophy* derives from the Greek; *sophia* is wisdom, *theo* is God (or in this case, perhaps, gods, elevated but not supreme). In any case, a defined group sharing core spiritual values and dedicated to the study of diverse religious and philosophical traditions was a preeminent objective of the Brotherhood.

Isis Unveiled

In the summer of 1875, Helena showed Henry sheets of manuscript she had composed under orders. Unaware, she had begun writing what would become *Isis Unveiled*.

In the fall of that year, after the September gatherings in which a philosophical-religious organization was proposed and before it was publicly constituted as the Theosophical Society in November, Helena spent several weeks with Cornell professor Hiram Corson in Ithaca, New York. Corson, a distinguished professor of English literature, had been drawn to Spiritualism after the sudden death of his daughter at age 16. The Professor extended the invitation to Helena with the expectation that she would utilize her mediumistic abilities to contact his deceased daughter. Helena, however, was disinclined. Her interface with Spiritualism was shifting. She now viewed séances and mediumship as regressive exercises, interfering with progressions that should follow physical death. Instead, Helena spent much of her time at the Corson home adding to the *Isis* manuscript. The professor estimated that she was composing twenty-five closely written pages a day. And this without reference material, as his library was extensive, but limited almost wholly to English literature.

By the end of November, Helena and Henry were sharing a set of suites at 433 West 34th St.; hers was the first floor suite, his the second. The work on *Isis* continued. In the summer of 1886, they moved to an apartment at West 47th St. and 8th Avenue. This was to be their last American residence. Dubbed the Lamasery, the décor included a stuffed baboon with white collar and tie, glasses, and a manuscript of Darwin's *Origin of Species* in hand; a lioness; an owl; several lizards, stuffed as well; an upright piano which Helena played expertly; and a dramatic mural of a jungle scene with an elephant, tiger and serpent. Most important was a long desk, centered in the sitting room. Here Helena and Henry sat, facing each other, unveiling Isis.

Isis Unveiled was a collaboration. The bulk of the text came either from or through Helena. As Olcott expresses it in the first volume of *Old Diary Leaves*, she was the channel through which this tide of fresh, vital essence was being poured into the stagnant pool of modern spiritual thought. The channeling took different forms; she might write to a spirits dictation, or alternatively, clairvoyantly view and then copy pages of text and references. Other intelligences would use her body directly as a writing machine. Members of the Brotherhood inhabited her body, displaying variations in mannerisms, demeanor, and writing style—both expression and script—which indicated distinct Masters and Adepts. While Helena's intelligence and skill in using the English language must be acknowledged, much material in *Isis* displayed scholarship superior to hers as well as textual references beyond the resource material at her disposal.

Henry's role in the collaboration was crucial. The text produced by Helena was a disjointed collection of segments and passages, reflecting the various adept personas using her body as a writing machine. The subject matter was diverse as well, as the authors addressed a range of contemporary thought, scientific to theological. Olcott created the two volume division, under the headings of Science and Theology. He organized and reorganized the pages Helena gave to him, creating the table of contents and chapter division and headings for volume one. Emily Kislingbury composed the table of contents for volume two. Alexander Wilder, physician and self-taught Greek and classical scholar, wrote the initial part of the preface to volume one, excluding the glossary. He was also contracted to work up the index. Some of the text may be attributed to Olcott and Wilder as well.

In its final form, *Isis Unveiled* consists of two volumes, each exceeding 600 pages. The first volume is titled *Science*, the second, *Theology*. It was published in September of 1877 with serious cost overrun, due to late alterations and adjustments to the text. The publisher, J. W. Bouton, disconcerted over the increased expense, was pessimistic. His pessimism evaporated, however, as the first edition of 1000 copies sold out ten days after publication.

The broad theme of the first volume is the limitations of materialism as advocated by Thomas Huxley and John Tyndall, leading scientists of the nineteenth century. Using the phenomena of Spiritualism and magical traditions, some stretching back to antiquity, the authors of *Isis Unveiled* argue for a perspective which transcends Huxley's protoplasmic matter as the ultimate reality. In the polemics directed against the Huxley-Tyndall contingent, elements of the eastern teachings constituting the Theosophical framework of the Brotherhood are introduced.

In the second volume, the hegemony of Christianity as spiritually authoritative doctrine is challenged. Alternative religious traditions, including the Egyptian, Pagan, and Eastern, are explored as revelatory doctrines. The Gnostic teachings of Christianity, marginalized to say the least by the Roman church, are shown to be in alignment with the expansive and inclusive Theosophical teachings.

The critical acclaim and spectacular commercial success of *Isis Unveiled* magnified Helena's celebrity. However, the schism between Theosophy and Spiritualism widened with the emphasis at the end of Volume Two on the lack of any coherent philosophy in the Spiritualist literature. Helena further noted that much of the current mediumship attracted astral remnants, decaying ethereal figures and forms without real intelligence. The expression of these spirits was generally limited and repetitive. This critique adversely affected the Theosophical Society as prominent Spiritualists withdrew. Indeed, the organization had hit an American wall as other early supporters disconnected as well. The momentum from the initial gatherings slowed as public meetings stopped. The Society was in a holding pattern.

India and Arya Samaj

On July 8, 1878 Helena was naturalized an America citizen. Before the end of the year, however, she departed from her adopted homeland and, with Henry, headed east. For Helena, the decision to travel to India followed a directive from Morya. For Henry, the request came in an astral visit, the Master leaving a materialized turban for emphasis.

The doldrums of the American Theosophical Society did not extend to England. En route to India, Helena and Henry stopped for several weeks in London, attending a meeting of the British Theosophical Society. On January 18, 1789 Henry and Helena embarked from Liverpool on the S.S. *Speke Hall*. The ship docked at Bombay harbor on February 16.

Their liaison in India was Mooljee Thackersey, a wealthy mill owner Henry had met on a voyage from England to America in 1870. Mooljee was a member of Arya Samaj, a dynamic and growing Vedic society led by Swami Dayanand Saraswati. Mooljee provided a link to the president of the Bombay branch of the Arya Samaj, Hurrychund Chintamon. Helena began a correspondence with Chintamon early in 1878. Enthused with the Hindu connection, she and Henry proposed an alignment of the Theosophical Society with Arya Samaj. The Theosophical Society would gain thousands of new members, establishing a presence and identity in India. In the spirit of the proposed merger, revenues from subscriptions and contributions to the Society collected in New York were sent to Chintamon in Bombay. Further, Olcott was prepared to defer presidential authority to Swami Dayanand.

Deciphering the rules of the Arya Samaj—sent in Sanskrit without translation to New York by Chintamon—tempered the Theosophists' enthusiasm. Sectarian and exclusionary, Swami Dayanand narrowed spiritual authority to Vedic literature. While the anti-Christian, anti-missionary chord was struck by both organizations, for the Theosophists, the abuses and corruption of the Roman church and the devaluation of the Eastern religious traditions by the missionaries were the issues. For Swami Dayanand and the Arya Samaj, everything outside the Vedas was an issue. The relationship between organizations was reconfigured by the Theosophists, the link becoming more tenuous as separate identities and lines of authority were maintained.

Chintamon, as requested, provided simple lodging and minimal staff for Henry and Helena. Adjacent to the lodging was a photography studio. Both were owned by Chintamon. A reception for Henry and Helena was held at the studio the evening following their arrival in Bombay. About 300 attended the vibrant event. The next morning, Henry and Helena received an exorbitant bill from Chintamon. The tab included fees for the lodging and studio, chair rental, food and refreshments, and building repairs. Moreover, it came to light that Chintamon had personally held on to the revenues sent from New York. Helena demanded restoration of the funds to Arya Samaj. Chintamon acquiesced, but was eventually expelled from the Vedic society.

Over time, the relationship between the Theosophical Society and the Arya Samaj deteriorated.

A. P. Sinnett

On February 25, 1879, Henry received a letter from A. P. Sinnett, editor of the *Pioneer*, one of the more influential English newspapers published in India. While in England, Sinnett had investigated Spiritualist phenomena. Intrigued, his interest in occult themes deepened. In his correspondence with Olcott, he extended an invitation to visit. The Sinnetts lived in the northern city of Allahabad. Henry and Helena left Bombay for their initial visit to Allahabad on December 2. They arrived two days later. Sinnett and his wife Patience were gracious hosts; furthermore, Helena and Patience had an instant rapport.

Along with her acclaim as the author of *Isis Unveiled*, Helena's remarkable skill in the production of spiritual phenomena was a major component in her celebrity. Fascination with phenomena accounted for much of the rising interest in Spiritualism. The phenomena produced through Helena's agency had a similar effect in attracting students to Theosophy. Moreover, the Theosophical framework offered an exposition of levels of realty beyond the limits of the materialism of science. Within this framework, the magic of phenomena was clarified and validated. The Sinnetts, fascinated as so many were by phenomena, made many requests of Helena. On a number of occasions, she complied. Several dramatic episodes stand out.

On October 3, 1880, Helena, Henry, the Sinnetts, and two acquaintances were up early for a picnic. The servants prepared for six, packing accordingly. As the party was leaving, they were joined by another gentleman; however, there was no adjustment in the provisions. While the party had a destination, they had not decided at the outset which of the various possible routes to take. On the route they chose, they stopped after a while for breakfast on a flat, grassy slope. Six cups and saucers had been packed. Someone suggested that Helena manifest a seventh cup and saucer for the late arrival. The request may have been light-hearted, but after some hesitation Helena said that she would try.

Moving six or seven yards from the picnic cloth, she marked a spot on the ground and asked one of the men in the party to dig. The spot was on the edge of the slope, covered by thick weeds and grass. Digging was difficult as the roots were dense and intertwined. First the cup, then the saucer, was excavated. A network of roots had surrounded both and had to be cut away. The seventh cup and saucer matched precisely the six that had been brought. Three matching sets had been left at the Sinnett home. All three were there when they returned. The patterns on the sets, purchased years before in England, were unique and peculiar.

The second episode develops from a promise to Sinnett by the Master Koot Hoomi. On October 20—two and a half weeks after Helena produced the cup and saucer—there was another excursion. On this occasion, the party proceeded up Prospect Hill in Simla. The women were carried on jampoons, standard vehicles for ladies traveling short distances in India. At lunch, Helena asked Sinnett where he would like to receive a materialized object. At first, Sinnett pointed to the jampoon pillow of one of the female guests on the picnic. His wife Patience immediately interjected, asking that the cushion be hers.

Patience placed her jampoon pillow under a rug as Helena requested. After a minute she uncovered the pillow. Sinnett cut the sewn border of the velvet and cloth pillow cover, stitch by stitch. Then he cut the stitching of an under layer of cloth. Finally, he ripped through the feathers inside the cushion, finding a brooch that Patience had left on her dressing table that morning. The brooch found within the cushion, however, had the initials KH scratched on its surface. And next to it was a short folded note from the Master to Sinnett.

October of 1880, during which the phenomena described as well as a variety of others were produced, was the month in which Sinnett proposed a direct correspondence with a member of the Brotherhood. His proposal was accepted. The correspondence began that year and continued until 1884. The letters Sinnett received were composed for the most part by Koot Hoomi, and on occasion by Morya. They were delivered in a variety of ways—some were precipitated, some channeled through Helena, some came by ordinary post, and others by extraordinary post. The teachings and doctrines presented in the letters were integrated by Sinnett into two books: *The Occult World*, published in London in June of 1881 and *Esoteric Buddhism*, published in June of 1883.

In *The Occult World*, various Theosophical themes are introduced, and a number of phenomenal episodes are described in detail. The letters from Koot Hoomi are acknowledged as a primary source, lengthy excerpts forming part of the text. In *Esoteric Buddhism*, a systematic exposition of the Theosophical framework is offered with more extended excerpts from the correspondence. The impact of these books was significant. Their accessibility expanded the Theosophical audience, continuing the trend of introducing Eastern Spirituality into Western consciousness.

The Coulomb Affair

When she visited Cairo in 1871, Helena lodged in the Hotel d'Orient. While there, she made the acquaintance of Emma Cutting, an employee of the Hotel, and future wife of Alexis Coulomb, son of the owner. Upon his mother's death, Alexis inherited the hotel. Known for his quick temper, toolbox, and glass eye, Alexis could not maintain the d'Orient, and the hotel closed. Their fortunes deteriorating in Egypt, the Coulombs traveled east. In India and then Ceylon, their attempts at business—farming European vegetables and revitalizing an old hotel—failed utterly. Nothing grew in the stony soil, and another hotel went bankrupt.

Henry and Helena's arrival in India was well publicized. The Theosophical Society represented the recognition and elevation of the Hindu and Buddhist traditions. The Indian press celebrated the presence of the Society's founders. The response of the Anglo press was tempered. In Ceylon, the story generated great interest in the Buddhist communities. Funds were raised to sponsor a visit. In May of 1880, the Theosophists traveled to Ceylon and stayed for two months. They were greeted in the Buddhist country by large and enthusiastic crowds. Henry returned for more extended visits in 1881 and 1882, establishing Theosophical lodges throughout the country while embracing Buddhist doctrine.

In Ceylon, Emma had followed the news of Helena's arrival in India, noting the funds raised in Buddhist communities to finance a visit from the Russian adventuress she had known in Cairo years before. In August of 1879, Emma wrote to Helena describing her and Alexis' financial plight, and requesting assistance in finding an employment situation for the couple in Bombay. Empathetic and grateful for Emma's kindness in Cairo, Helena extended an invitation. Five months later, in January of 1880, the Coulombs arrived in Bombay.

In March of 1879, Henry and Helena had moved to a compound in the native quarter of Bombay. The address was 118 Girgaum Backroad. Their household included Rosa Bates, a former schoolteacher, and Edward Wimbridge, an artist and architect. The two had accompanied Henry and Helena on the voyage from England, forming a Theosophical committee of sorts. Rosa's role in India was generally domestic, as Helena's dysfunction in this area was extreme. In addition, Mooljee Thackersey had found a fifteen year old gujatri boy, Babula, to serve the Theosophists. Babula, conversant in several languages including English, remained with Henry and Helena throughout their time in India.

By the spring of 1879, Henry and Helena had published articles·in the *Bombay Gazette* and the *Indian Spectator*. In July the two decided to publish their own magazine, *The Theosophist*. By October they had 381 subscribers, the print runs increasing from 400 to 750 with the first two issues. The periodical provided needed revenues, and with Helena as editor, functioned as the official organ of the Theosophical Society.

The Coulombs had barely managed transport from Ceylon. A charitable French Consul paid their fare, but the couple came in tattered clothes with only Alexis' toolbox as luggage. The Theosophists gave them temporary shelter at Girgaum Road, with the understanding that they would relocate as their fortunes improved. Henry found employment for Alexis as a machinist in a cotton mill; however, Alexis had a poor attitude toward the mill owner, and the job did not last. A skillful carpenter, he began doing odd jobs in the compound, while Emma shared the household chores. They received no wage, but room and board were provided.

In May of 1880, Henry and Helena embarked on their first voyage to Ceylon. Wimbridge accompanied them, along with Damodar Mavalankar, a young Brahman who had given up his caste status and inheritance to join the Theosophical mission. The Society's objective of universal brotherhood was antithetical to the caste system in India and had engendered a Brahman backlash. The Coulombs and Rosa Bates remained in Bombay. Rosa's domestic skills were, as it turned out, limited; conversely, Emma was energetic and competent in the household. Henry gave domestic authority to Emma and, to placate the former schoolteacher, assigned a sub-editorship of *The Theosophist* to Rosa.

The Theosophists returned to Bombay in July. Henry had lost 15 pounds in Ceylon and now weighed 170. Helena had gained 8 pounds, tipping the scales at 237. A volatile chemistry had developed between Rosa and Emma, turning the atmosphere on Girgaum Road toxic. Rosa alleged that Emma was poisoning her. Emma lashed back. Skeptical of Rosa's charge, Henry tried to arbitrate. Helena sat back, nervously chain smoking and occasionally interjecting remarks that tended to exacerbate the conflict. Eventually a truce of sorts was consented to. The tension, however, was barely masked. Reconfiguring the living arrangements did not help. In August Wimbridge and Bates left the residence. Wimbridge accepted the financial backing of a friend of Henry and developed a lucrative furniture business. Rosa Bates disappeared.

At the end of August, Henry and Helena left for the north of India. Visiting the Sinnetts at Simla was one of the priorities of their trip. By Emma Coulomb's account, she and Alexis were instructed to locate a new residential headquarters in Bombay for the Theosophists. They succeeded in finding an excellent house with an elevated view of the sea from its hilltop location on Breach Candy. Crow's Nest, as the new bungalow was called, had spacious rooms, large verandas, and a location less congested than Girgaum Road. A rumor of haunting reduced the rent to a third of its market value. By mid November the Coulombs and Damodar were settled at Crow's Nest. After spending Christmas with the Sinnetts at Simla, Henry and Helena returned to Bombay. They were delighted with their new home and headquarters. Henry sensed a ghostly presence one evening, but was able to dispatch it quickly by pronouncing a magical Arabic word that Helena had taught him in New York.

Two years later, Henry and Helena celebrated the seventh anniversary of the Theosophical Society. On December 7, 1882, delegates representing branches throughout India convened at Framji Cowsji Hall in Bombay to mark the anniversary. A large and enthusiastic audience attended the event. Ten days later Henry, Helena, Damodar, Babula and the Coulombs left Bombay for Madras, a city on the southeastern coast of India. On the outskirts of that city, Huddlestone Gardens, a 25 acre estate along the Adyar River had been purchased with the help of local Theosophists. The estate, with a mansion and extensive grounds, would become their new residence and the permanent headquarters for the Theosophical Society.

Helena chose the rooftop apartment above the mansion at Huddlestone Gardens. Henry settled in a bungalow on the estate 100 yards from the main house. From the veranda on the roof, Helena could see the Adyar River intersecting with the Bay of Bengal. Within her quarters, she separated her sleeping area from a sitting room with a curtain. Upon Helena's request, Alex Coulomb began constructing an additional room bordering her bedroom wall on the western side. This would be the occult room, a charged space, with a vibratory quality suitable for astral visitation. On the occult room wall adjacent to Helena's sleeping area a cabinet was hung. Designated the Shrine, the cabinet functioned as a teleportation device: correspondence to Masters and Adepts placed in the cabinet disappearing quickly, responses materializing in the shrine in a timely manner. On one occasion, two vases with a note materialized in the shrine for Henry.

Several months later, pieces of a broken saucer dropped by Emma were wrapped in cloth and placed in the cabinet by Major-General H.R.

Morgan, a friend of Helena's who, on business in Madras, stopped at the Adyar compound to view portraits of Masters. A few minutes later, Damodar, in the occult room with the Major-General and Emma, reached into the cabinet and removed and reopened the cloth. The saucer was whole. A letter accompanied the reconstituted china. Both General Morgan and Emma gave written testimony of the phenomenon.

In the early evening of December 26, 1883, five letters appeared in the Shrine. Four were addressed to individuals; the fifth was a message from Koot Hoomi to the delegates attending the 1883 Theosophical convention at Adyar. Among these delegates was a wealthy Raja, Prince Harisingh Rupsinghji of Bhavnavar. Harisingh was one of the benefactors whose financial support sustained the organizational growth of the Society in India.

The Coulombs received no wages for their service to Henry and Helena in Bombay and Adyar. Their compensation was room and board. The limitations of this arrangement did not suit Emma. She approached Prince Harisingh during his December visit to Adyar. Noting Harisingh's gentle demeanor and aware of his generosity towards Henry and Helena, Emma requested a personal loan of 2,000 rupees. The Prince was noncommittal.

Tensions at the London Theosophical branch provided the impetus for Henry to plan a visit to England early in 1884. An escalating conflict between Lodge president Anna Kingsford and A. P. Sinnett had to be sorted out. Sinnett had returned to London in May of 1883, and published *Esoteric Buddhism* two months later. His proximity to the founders and the Masters, as well as the success of his two Theosophical books, elevated his status within the London Theosophical community. This did not sit well with Kingsford. A schism developed between Kingsford and Sinnett, each having a devoted following.

It was decided that Helena, for reasons of health, would travel with Henry to Europe. On February 7, with a small party including Franz Hartmann, Helena began the trip north to Bombay port. Emma, aware of plans to visit Prince Harisingh en route, asked to accompany her mistress to Bombay. On February 10, the party visited Harisingh at his mansion. Emma privately revisited her request for 2,000 rupees. The Prince felt that Helena should be apprised of Emma's loan request. Helena was upset with Emma's efforts to improve her personal finances using access to wealthy benefactors of the Society, and expressed her displeasure to

Emma with intensity. The loan was out of the question. Emma adopted an apologetic demeanor. Though she would not budge on the loan, Helena was conciliatory toward Emma.

Henry and Helena sailed for Marseilles on February 20. Emma's sorrowful response to Helena's tongue-lashing proved to be barely skin-deep. Less than two weeks after Henry and Helena left India for Europe, the Coulombs, holding the key to Helena's apartment in her absence, blocked access to the second story quarters at Adyar. Members of a Board of Control, appointed as an executive committee during the founder's time in Europe, were refused entry to the Occult Room by Alexis on March 2. Several days later, Damodar, also denied the use of Helena's quarters, was told by Emma that Helena had directed Alexis to construct trapdoors in the apartment. Board members, particularly Franz Hartmann, a German-born, naturalized American medical doctor from Colorado, and St. George Lane-Fox, an electrical engineer, became increasingly suspicious of the Coulombs motives and machinations at Headquarters. While Henry and Helena accommodated the Coulombs' problematic behavior patterns as a trade-off for domestic order and service, Lane-Fox and Hartmann, in particular, viewed them as liabilities for the Society.

The Board, reflecting Lane-Fox and Hartmann's critical view of the Coulombs, was poised to evict the couple. A letter from Koot Hoomi to Damodar counseled compassion and patience. Six weeks later, a communiqué from Morya noted trap-doors and tricks and an ongoing alignment of the Coulombs with a Christian missionary contingent dedicated to undermining the influence of the Theosophical Society in India. Morya, suggesting that the Missionaries would reward sabotage of the Society, called for prudent but decisive action. On May 14, the General Council of the Society served notice to the Coulombs. The keys to Helena's apartment were handed over on May 18. A week later, Emma and Alexis left the Headquarters at Adyar.

Upon their exit from the Adyar compound, the Coulombs received immediate support from the Missionary community. Living quarters were arranged for the couple. Prior to the eviction, Alexis told Franz Hartmann of a promise of 10,000 rupees for help in undermining the Theosophical efforts in India. While perhaps inflated, this offer does provide context for the attacks on Helena's credibility that ensued.

The clergyman of note in the strategic attempts to sabotage the

Society that followed was Wesleyan Methodist Minister George Patterson, editor of the *Madras Christian College Magazine*. In its September
1884 issue, Patterson published the first installment of an article entitled
"The Collapse of Koot Hoomi." This installment included excerpts from
fifteen letters supplied by the Coulombs, which they claimed had been
written to them by Helena. The letters detailed effective efforts in the
production of fraudulent phenomena to gain attention and support for
the Theosophical Society. The Coulombs, according to the correspondence, were Helena's confidants and confederates in subterfuge during
her time in India. The plotting included a series of trap-doors and sliding panels in Helena's quarters at Adyar. These trap-doors and panels
accounted for the letters and objects manifesting in the Shrine. Also
described was a cloth sewn costume, with head and shoulders, nick-
named Christofolo. The costume was either held up by bamboo poles
for viewing astral appearances at a distance or worn by Alexis for closer
encounters with Koot Hoomi in astral form.

The published letters, written in French, were clumsy forgeries.
While Alexis' handwriting resembled Helena's, the grammar, syntax,
and spelling were flawed. Helena's French was refined and expert, her
writing style elegant. Moreover, the letters integrated many odd Italian
elements, suggesting a primacy of Italian underlying substandard French.
Emma's resume included teaching Italian.

William Quan Judge, upon arriving at Adyar in August, investigated
Alexis' handiwork. Judge found a ragged hole in the wall behind the
Shrine. Plaster debris was still on the floor beneath the hole. The panels
and trap-doors, while planned with ingenuity, were unfinished. Mallets
and files were necessary to force them open. A few days later, a group
including Reverend Patterson visited Adyar. Patterson asked to see the
shrine but was refused. Hartmann then asked the Reverend how much
he had paid Alexis. Evidently caught off guard, Patterson replied that he
had paid 100 rupees. Christofolo was, by all accounts, destroyed.

The Coulomb–Missionary alliance, flawed and clumsy in its efforts
to undermine the Theosophical Society, was nevertheless effective. Helena's celebrity and the Society's accelerating growth guaranteed international coverage for the Coulomb account in the *Madras Christian College
Magazine*. The public fascination extended to the Masters or Mahatmas
as portrayed in Sinnetts *Esoteric Buddhism*. Koot Hoomi was acknowl-

edged in Sinnett's dedication in *The Occult World* and extensive excerpts from his correspondence with Sinnett were included in both books. Thus, "The Collapse of Koot Hoomi" resonated for an audience, familiar with *Esoteric Buddhism* and *The Occult World*, in Europe and America.

The Society for Psychical Research

In January of 1882, English physicist William Barrett initiated a conference in London for scientists, academics, and Spiritualists interested in a range of paranormal phenomena. This meeting led to the establishment of the Society for Psychical Research (SPR). The SPR's leadership included Henry Sidgwick, Professor of Philosophy and Economics at Trinity College in Cambridge; Frederick Myers, poet, classical scholar and lecturer at Trinity; and Edmund Gurney, a student of music at Trinity. Sidgwick's academic stature and his role as mentor to Myers and other prospective members of the SPR led to him being chosen President of the newly formed organization.

Sidgwick, Myers, and Gurney had been investigating mediumistic phenomena since 1871. They had been hopeful of validating phenomena at the outset of their investigations; their results, however, either exposed clever conjuring or were inconclusive. Sidgwick's interest had begun to wane early in 1877. Myers continued investigating mediums until 1879. Barrett's particular interest in thought-transference or telepathy intrigued Sidgwick. While pessimistic, the Trinity contingent reengaged their interest in spiritual phenomena through the newly formed SPR.

Sidgwick's reputation attracted elite support and expanded membership for the SPR. The Spiritualists, however, began to balk at the critical approach of the investigations and over time withdrew. Sidgwick and a cadre of close associates were predominant. This group included Sidgwick's wife Eleanor, sister of Arthur Balfour, future Prime Minister. Eleanor was a rigorous investigator, playing a prominent role in testing and evaluating phenomena.

At a January 1883 meeting of the London Branch of the Theosophical Society, Frederick Myers enrolled as a member. The Sinnetts returned to England from India several months later. A. P. Sinnett, interested in the work of the SPR, met with Sidgwick, Myers and Gurney. Their intellectual strata appealed to Sinnett's elitist disposition, leading him to develop the connection. Myers involvement in the London Branch furthered the relationship with Sinnett.

Henry and Helena arrived in London in April of 1884. On April 15, a dinner was given for Henry by an American member of the SPR. Myers, Gurney, and Barrett were invited. Henry felt that reaching out to the SPR with accounts and displays of the phenomenal skills of Helena and the Masters would benefit the Theosophical Society. *The Occult World* and *Esoteric Buddhism*, with their profiles of the Masters or Mahatmas as they were referred to in India, suggested areas outside of Spiritualism for the investigators of the SPR. The leadership of the SPR was amenable, and a series of meetings and interviews from May to August with Henry, Sinnett, and Mohini Chatterjee, a Theosophist from India who accompanied the Founders to Europe, were held.

On July 5, Myers, Gurney, Barrett, and F. W. Thurston visited Helena. They were treated to a phenomenal auditory display of bell tones and chimes that synchronized with gentle hand movements from Helena. The four described the experience in written testimony. They returned on July 26 and Helena recreated the musical phenomena. The accounts, particularly Myers', are detailed and reinforced the conclusion that the sound displays were authentic phenomena.

Helena was invited to Cambridge to meet Henry Sidgwick and his wife Eleanor on August 9. Sidgwick's journal notes Helena's fine intellect and humanitarian disposition. The interface of the Theosophists with the SPR through 1884 was generally friendly and positive. The only discordant note in the relationship with the SPR had been struck on June 30. On that evening, Henry, Helena and Sinnett attended a meeting of the SPR. There, Henry delivered an extemporaneous speech during which he displayed a toy tin Buddha mounted on wheels. For whatever reason, Henry delighted in his little Buddha on wheels and did not hesitate in showing off his little toy. The audience that evening did not share his delight. By Sinnetts's account, Henry's performance with props played badly at the gathering, irritating everyone. Later that night, Helena seconded Sinnett's upset, giving Henry an incisive, loud and lengthy rebuke. Both Helena and Sinnett felt the evening would have unfortunate ramifications.

Richard Hodgson

In November of 1884, the SPR leadership dispatched Richard Hodgson to India to investigate the phenomena associated with Helena, the Masters, and the Theosophical Society. Sidgwick financed the trip.

Hodgson was born in Melbourne, Australia, in September of 1855. Graduating from the University of Melbourne in 1878 with a degree in law, he traveled to England to continue his academics, shifting from law to philosophy. He studied at St. John's College in Cambridge. While in Melbourne, he had attended a Séance with a friend, sparking an interest in Spiritual phenomena and the afterlife which upset his Methodist family and derailed a romance with a cousin. He never married. In Cambridge, Hodgson joined in the investigations of Sidgwick and Myers. When the SPR was formed in 1882, he enrolled as a charter member.

At Cambridge, Hodgson progressed in his academic career. He also displayed a set of personality quirks noted by friends and associates. After taking honors at St. John's College, he was initially unwilling to kneel to the Vice-Chancellor in the ceremony proscribed for graduation. He was eventually persuaded that the gesture was worth the degree. He always wore brown suits rather than the standard black in formal contexts. This pattern of expressing individuality, however, had no career ramifications. Finally, Hodgson habitually interjected unsolicited opinions on a wide variety of subjects in a booming and authoritative voice.

These bombastic and opinionated outbursts reinforce Hodgson's pattern of socially discordant egocentric behavior. Emotional imbalance and bipolar tendencies may well have affected Hodgson's paranormal investigations.

Helena returned to Madras on December 20. 1884. En route, she stopped again at the Hotel d'Orient in Cairo. While in Egypt, she uncovered a history of fraud and financial deceit involving the Coulombs. She brought affidavits and written testimony to India. Henry, however, would not support litigation, citing legal problems with Helena's evidence. Helena insisted. Henry threatened resignation from the Society. When prominent members agreed with Henry, Helena deferred.

Meanwhile, Hodgson had already arrived in Madras. During this period, the SPR had formulated a preliminary report regarding Helena and the Masters. While not critical of Helena's claims, the report called for further investigation. More significant, there was no mention of the musical bell phenomenon that Myers, Gurney, and Thurston had witnessed and attested to. There is indication that another member of the SPR committee, J. H. Stack, had influenced Sidgwick to delete the accounts of this phenomenon from the first report.

Hodgson, arriving at Adyar two days before Helena and Henry returned, requested entry to the upstairs apartment to view the occult room and the Shrine. Damodar, however, would not admit Hodgson to Helena's personal quarters in her absence. Moreover, Damodar and the other Indian Theosophists were reticent in relating anything pertaining to their Mahatmas to the SPR investigator. When Henry and Helena finally reached Adyar, Hodgson, upset with being denied access, was brash and insistent.

Furthermore, when the party did go upstairs there was no shrine. Helena, home for the first time in ten months, was surprised. Damodar then acknowledged that he had removed the shrine from the occult room in September and in Hartmann's presence, burned it. And Alexis Coulomb's handiwork, the hole in the wall behind the cabinet's placement had been patched up. There was, in fact, no physical evidence related to the shrine phenomena, other than the room itself, for Hodgson to evaluate.

On January 2, 1885 Hodgson revisited Adyar to interview Helena. The next day, he met with the Coulombs. Emma and Alexis offered their account regarding the Shrine, Occult Room, and Koot Hoomi costume, detailing the roles they played in the associated phenomena. The costume, which would have been significant physical evidence supporting their account, Emma claimed to have destroyed in a fit of disgust. The only physical evidence they presented to Hodgson were the letters, allegedly written by Helena, that were published in the *Christian College Magazine*. Hodgson believed the Coulombs' narrative and credited the letters as genuine.

Regarding the Shrine and Occult Room, Hodgson measured the space and drew a lot of diagrams which supported his acceptance of the Coulomb's account. Later analyses, however, reveal inaccuracies in Hodgson's configurations which were necessary for his indictment of Helena.

Samples from the letters were submitted to a handwriting analyst, F. G. Netherclift. However, Hodgson never allowed Helena to view the collection of letters provided by the Coulombs. The only acknowledged sample by Helena was an empty envelope addressed to Emma. Scraps of correspondence or notes Emma may have collected from Helena's discards may have been part of Netherclift's analysis. There is, however, a lack of transparency in Hodgson's maneuvers with the written evidence. It was unclear what Netherclift compared with what. Moreover, Netherclift's expertise and judgment has been questioned by contemporary experts.

Hodgson was invested in proving that Helena authored the Mahatma letters received by Sinnett.

Sinnett had shown him samples of the correspondence, allowing Hodgson to trace the writing. Hodgson made copies of his tracings to submit with samples of Helena's script. Neither Netherclift nor Sims, an expert from the British Museum, believed the samples to be the work of one individual. Hodgson, however, emphasized what he thought were similarities in the scripts, and for some reason the two analysts rolled over for Hodgson. A contemporary SPR investigator, Vernon Harrison—himself an expert graphologist—seems to have been dumbfounded by the second judgment of Netherclift and Sims supporting Hodgson's predisposition. Harrison as well as a number of later analysts concluded that Helena was not the writer of the correspondence to Sinnett.

Hodgson departed from India at the end of May, arriving in England on April 16. Helena resigned as corresponding secretary of the Theosophical Society on March 29 and sailed for Naples two days later. She would not return to India.

On May 29, Hodgson summarized his investigation at a meeting of the SPR. At June 24 meeting, he read a part of the report. In December, the full report, 200 pages in length, was published. His conclusion was that Helena was one of the most accomplished frauds in history.

Perhaps the most bizarre aspect of the Hodgson Report was the assignment of motive. Acknowledging that financial gain was not part of Helena's agenda, Hodgson came up with a geopolitical theory in which Helena was serving Russian interests by spying on the British in colonized India. Hodgson's speculation assumed that Helena masterminded fraud and subterfuge on a grand scale, duping untold numbers of intelligent and accomplished individuals, producing massive volumes of sophisticated philosophical and spiritual material as a cover for espionage.

The Hodgson Report was repudiated by the SPR in 1986. Vernon Harrison noted Hodgson's bias and his selection and manipulation of data to support that bias. Hodgson's prejudgment raises questions. Perhaps Helena was on the wrong pole of Hodgson's bipolarity, a victim of his emotional imbalance. Perhaps Hodgson was paid off by the same Missionary interests that financed the Coulomb's deceit. Perhaps Hodgson was enlisted in a British strategy targeting Russian interests in Asia. One way or another, Hodgson was askew. Regardless, he was now a celebrity in his own right, established as a leading investigator of psychic and spiritual phenomena. If he had validated Helena, Hodgson would have been a minor footnote in the story.

Accounting for the support of the Sidgwicks, Myers, and Gurney for the report is another matter. Why did Henry Sidgwick delete testimony from Myers and Gurney crediting Helena's musical phenomena from the preliminary report while signing on to Hodgson's blatantly flawed conclusions later on? Why did Myers, who had built a relationship with Sinnett, Henry, and Helena, allow his, Gurney's, and Thurston's testimony to be discounted?

The Sidgwicks were indeed the power couple in the early years of the SPR. Increasingly, they were dealing with fraud and manipulation in the majority of their investigations. They may have grown to view their role in the SPR as skillful debunkers. Debunking is the common approach of skeptics. Rather than expose the sleight of hand or the mechanics underlying deceptive phenomena in the act, debunkers offer a theory of how the phenomena investigated could be conjured through sleight of hand and mechanical technique. Debunking, however, proves nothing. It simply offers an alternative explanation which in many cases is more convoluted and strange than a straightforward acceptance of subtle powers working on spiritual levels affecting physical reality.

Regardless of its weakness, the Hodgson Report was, in its time, effective. It created doubt on a large scale. Given Helena's celebrity, it was a sensational story, creating ripples of dissatisfaction within the Theosophical community. Some prominent members of the Society distanced themselves from Helena, while others were steadfast in their support. Helena, battered emotionally by the report, relocated to Europe. There she entered the next phase of her service.

Hodgson also relocated. He moved to America, eventually living in a small apartment at 15 Charles St. in Boston. In the US, he was charged with running the American chapter of the SPR. He befriended William James and his family. James was involved in Psychic research as well.

Hodgson's skepticism was challenged through the mediumship of Lenore Piper. At first, Hodgson postulated a dissociated personality for Lenore. However, a close friend of his, George Pellew, an author and poet, died of injuries suffered when he fell from a horse. Lenore channeled Pellew in trance.

Hodgson was amazed and transformed. He began receiving spirit communications himself. Spending much of his time isolated in his small flat, he would allow no one access in fear of vibrational disturbance. Stranger yet, eight days after he died playing handball in 1905, a discarnate Hodgson began to communicate through Lenore Piper. This communication continued for three years. Through Lenore, Hodgson said that he had seen the deceased Myers. He also contended that Helena (who had died in 1891) was in the depths of hell, suggesting bipolarity in death as well as life. Accounts of Hodgson's communications were reviewed by Eleanor Sidgwick in England. True to form, Eleanor—the consummate debunker—did not find them authentic.

Moving on: *The Secret Doctrine*

Helena sailed from India on March 31, 1885. She landed in Naples on April 23. Leaving Italy August 8, she reached Wurzburg, Germany several days later. Helena remained in Wurzburg for ten months. In May of 1889, she was situated in Elberfield, Germany. In July she left Germany and settled in Ostende, Belgium. A year later, Helena was living in London.

On October 20, 1888, the first volume of *The Secret Doctrine*, Helena's second masterwork, was published simultaneously in London and New York. The second volume appeared in December. In spite of a notable lack of newspaper coverage, the first printing was immediately scooped up. A second printing followed before the end of the year.

The earliest projection for *The Secret Doctrine* was Helena's mentioning a new book on Theosophy to Henry in May of 1879. The two then worked marginally on an outline and a preface for the new project. Establishing the Society in India and developing a Theosophical magazine, however, superseded work on the new book and the project receded for the time being.

Four and a half years later, in the January supplement to the Society's magazine, *The Theosophist*, *The Secret Doctrine* was advertised as a new version of *Isis Unveiled*—reconfigured, revised, and accessible. *The Secret Doctrine* would be published in installments of 77 pages, beginning in March. An April advertisement pushed the starting date to June. In June the date was pushed to August. Then to September. In September, there was no *Secret Doctrine* and no advertisement.

While installments of *The Secret Doctrine* never appeared in *The Theosophist*, the manuscript was nevertheless developing. There are references to chapters completed in the revised *Isis* during Helena's time in France in the spring of 1884. Indeed, the final phase of Helena's service, a seven year cycle in Europe, interrupted by a short and difficult hiatus in Adyar early in 1885, was the backdrop for the composition of *The Secret Doctrine*. In April of 1885, Helena, returning west, received occult transmissions, pages of manuscript, on the voyage to Naples.

The Secret Doctrine was initially projected as a reformulated *Isis Unveiled* for which Helena would lean heavily on T. Subba Row, a Madras lawyer, whose erudition and link to Morya elevated his status at Adyar. However, as the project developed, Subba Row expressed an unwillingness to support the release of hitherto secret aspects of doctrine, eventually disengaging. Moreover, the *Isis* connection became more nuanced as *The Secret Doctrine* emerged as a distinctive text, with a lineage including *Isis* and the two Sinnett books, *Occult World* and *Esoteric Buddhism*.

As Helena traveled Europe from 1886 through 1888, the manuscript expanded. Though it was primarily a collaboration between Koot Hoomi, Morya, and Helena, several others played crucial roles in shaping the text. Constance Wachtmeister, a Countess and widow of the Swedish Ambassador to England, transcribed text and helped care for Helena. Physician Archibald Keightly and his nephew Bertram—born only a year apart—had both been raised in families sympathetic to Swedenborg's rendition of Christianity. They were drawn to Spiritualism and mesmerism, and joined the Theosophical Society after discovering Sinnett's *Esoteric Buddhism*. Like the Countess, the Keightlys helped care for Helena, and did much to organize and edit the manuscript as it developed. These four individuals comprised the household at Helena's final lodging, on Lansdown Street in London.

Both *The Secret Doctrine* and *Isis Unveiled* were published in two volume editions, and were similar in length. In *Isis*, the first volume was Science, and the second Theology; in *The Secret Doctrine*, the volume division reflects an overarching evolutionary framework. Volume one was entitled Cosmogenesis, volume two Anthropogenesis. Sections on science and symbolism, the theological component, are included in each volume.

The evolutionary framework is grounded in a series of stanzas drawn from an ancient text, *The Book of Dzyan*. This archaic manuscript was found in a monastic library at Shigatze during Helena's lifetime. Access was controlled and limited. The stanzas are a literary and metaphorical account of the evolution of the cosmos, solar system, and planet. Our planetary narrative unfolds the development of species, civilizations, races, and individuals.

The Secret Doctrine, like *Isis Unveiled*, was in large part channeled material. The Masters were Helena's sources, and she their primary conduit. For the most part her modality was visual: she would view clairvoyantly and transcribe pages of written material. As difficult and challenging as these masterworks were, they were commercially successful. With their publication an expanded audience became focused on the Brotherhood and its use of conduits in communicating knowledge.

In the evolutionary context of *The Secret Doctrine*, a variety of themes and references were integrated. Witnessing Helena's process, Constance noted the meager reference library—yet, an extensive log of sources were quoted in the manuscripts. Helena viewed the pages composed by her Masters in the astral light and transcribed them. Constance, in turn, copied Helena's transcriptions. The quotations from source material were later verified. The rare discrepancy was a reversal of numbers, indicating a mirror reversal for images in the astral light for which Helena, on occasion, did not compensate.

For the modern era of New Age Spirituality, Helena Blavatsky was the second major channel. In her case, the sources of her teachings were identified and, although elevated, personified. With Helena, the paradigm of channeling developed its own narrative to an extent that generations in the centuries following easily accepted the process and—in many cases—too easily accepted the product of the process.

Final Years & Legacy

In 1889, Helena published *Key to Theosophy* and *The Voice of the Silence*. The former was an accessible expression of Theosophical themes in dialogue form; the latter, a collection of excerpts from *The Book of Golden*

Precepts, a text drawing from various eastern traditions. An epidemic of influenza swept through London in the spring of 1891. A weakened Helena fell victim to the disease; on May 8, she died.

At the beginning of the nineteenth century, Western culture barely acknowledged the existence—much less the legitimacy—of Eastern spiritual traditions. By the end of that century, however, the spiritual climate had been transformed. Helena's magnetic celebrity played the primary role in this transformation. With her phenomenal psychic skills, literary gifts, and depth of scholarship, she attracted attention on a large scale. This attention highlighted a spiritual impetus for inclusivity and tolerance, and a vision of the unique potential for personal development.

The Blavatsky channeling paradigm developed against the backdrop of Spiritualism. The Spiritualist bias toward deceased sources, however, was antithetical to Theosophy. Morya and Koot Hoomi, channeled sources for *Isis Unveiled* and *The Secret Doctrine*, were men who lived and died. While Theosophists and Spiritualists shared the supposition of death as transition, neither Morya nor Koot Hoomi had made that transition prior to the composition of Helena's masterworks.

The next generation of Theosophists mythologized the Masters, elevating the Brotherhood into a hierarchy of demigods. This boost over and above the résumé of remarkable psychic skills, intellect, and selfless humanitarian goals, tweaked the channeling paradigm into the twentieth century.

Besant and Leadbeater

The mantle at Adyar was passed from Henry and Helena to Annie Besant and C. W. Leadbeater. Besant, a socialist reformer, union organizer, and feminist known for her oratorical skill, was asked to review *The Secret Doctrine* by W. T. Stead, editor of several periodicals. Though she had been aligned with materialists and secular thinkers prior to this assignment, reading *The Secret Doctrine* affected Besant. She asked Stead for an introduction to Helena. The two bonded, and Annie Besant joined the Theosophical Society in May of 1889. Following Henry Olcott's death in 1907, she would succeed him as President.

Leadbeater's entry into the Theosophical universe preceded Besant's by five years. Ordained into the ministry of the Church of England in 1878, Leadbeater—despite his conservative protestant alignment—was drawn toward investigations of hauntings and ghostly phenomena. A fascination with Spiritualism and its phenomena followed. In 1883, Leadbeater met an old friend who had been second officer on a steamer that transported Helena from Bombay to Calcutta. Leadbeater's friend narrated two anecdotes of Helena's psychic prowess: she lit a cigarette in gale force winds, and accurately predicted the friend's appointment as captain of the vessel before it docked in Calcutta. Leadbeater, unfamiliar with Theosophy, was intrigued, and later that year read Sinnett's *Occult World*. Contacting Sinnett in London, Leadbeater began attending meetings of the London Theosophical Lodge. By the end of 1883, Leadbeater was a member of the Theosophical Society. Volunteering to assist Sinnett in responding to an increasing number of letters inquiring about Theosophical topics, Leadbeater diligently composed replies which led to further inquiries. These correspondences grew, well served by Leadbeater's fluid and accessible communication skills.

Leadbeater's first contact with Helena followed the drama of the April 7, 1884 meeting of the London Lodge. Helena appeared unexpectedly at this meeting, which had been convened for the election of Lodge officers. The antagonism between A. P. Sinnett and Anna Kingsford, the current Lodge President, had reached new levels of hostility in the electoral context. Considering herself an angelically appointed incarnation of Hermes and Joan of Arc, Kingsford found her elected replacement—G. B. Finch, a candidate representing Sinnett's faction—unacceptable.

As tensions peaked, Helena, dressed in black, rose and exited the room. She then reentered, Sinnett introducing her to the audience. Wild and chaotic adulation followed. Helena walked to the front of the room, taking over the platform. She expressed her dissatisfaction and closed the meeting, calling candidates from both factions into a private conference. Kingsford was diplomatically offered her own Lodge, designated the Hermetic Lodge T. S., distinct from the established London Lodge.

At his residence after the meeting, Sinnett introduced Leadbeater to Helena. Though he was awed by her presence, Leadbeater's devotional inclinations extended beyond Helena to the Masters. He had documented this in a published letter to a Spiritualist journal. Helena noted Leadbeater's efforts, as well as his problematic status as Anglican clergy. Leadbeater's spiritual and vocational path, however, was at this point emphatically Theosophical. Indeed, in November of 1884 he left

England, meeting Helena and her party in Egypt, joining the group en route to India.

Leadbeater and Besant were prolific authors, adding multiple titles to the Theosophical canon. The accessibility of their publications contrasted with the intellectual challenge of working through *Isis Unveiled* and *The Secret Doctrine*. They were the first Theosophical authors to detail the chakra system. Leadbeater's developing clairvoyance, rather than a channeled source, was the basis for much of his published material. During the Besant–Leadbeater tenure of leadership, the Adyar-based Theosophical Society expanded dramatically.

However, controversy erupted as well. In 1889, Helena had established in London a framework for a level of instruction beyond *The Secret Doctrine*. An inner group, select and limited, assembled for this teaching. This elite group was designated the Esoteric Section, and had its own set of rules, as it was geared to the path of the *chela*—that is, discipleship and access to the Masters. Henry, though he was displeased with the creation of an inner, elite subset within the Society, received a communication from Koot Hoomi suggesting he allow Helena to proceed with the specialized instruction.

After Helena's death in 1891, Annie Besant assumed leadership of the Esoteric Section. In 1894, however, William Quan Judge—claiming a seminal influence in the formation of the Section, possession of extensive instruction from the Masters for the group, and Helena's blessing—declared himself leader of the Esoteric Section, relegating Besant to secretarial status. Besant rejected Judge's declarations. The controversy continued to spin until Judge, at the American Convention in April of 1895, severed the links between the American section of the Society and Adyar. An independent Theosophical Society in America was announced, with Judge as president; however, Judge died the following year. While the Adyar- based Society reestablished its dominance in America, Judge's lineage continued in a Point Loma-based Theosophical Society, claiming direct alignment with Helena.

Leadbeater created another set of problems. He had shown a propensity to take young boys under his wing, ostensibly for clairvoyant training and spiritual guidance. Sexuality played a major role in his instruction. His enthusiasm for masturbation as a strategy for controlling illicit intimacy included hands-on training. In January of 1906, Helen Dennis, Corresponding Secretary of the Esoteric Section in America, sent a letter to

Annie Besant detailing Leadbeater's sexual strategy in his tutelage of her son and another boy, Douglas Petit. A letter from Leadbeater to one of the boys surfaced. In the letter a portion is composed in code. Deciphered, it offers direction for increasing the pleasure of ejaculation. The coded segment ends: "Glad sensation is so pleasant. Thousand kisses darling."

Henry formed a committee in London to assess Leadbeater's conduct. While he defended his actions, contending that masturbation was a viable solution to sexual frustration, Leadbeater offered to resign from the Society. Henry accepted the resignation. Besant, in the background, at first defended her colleague, but later withdrew support. She then shifted again, reaffirming her support. Leadbeater began to reference black magicians insidiously working for his downfall. In 1907, following Henry's death, Besant was elected President; by the end of 1908, Leadbeater was reinstated.

Alice Bailey

On Sunday morning, June 30, 1895, fifteen-year-old Alice La Trobe-Bateman, while visiting a favored aunt in southern Scotland, had an unexpected visitor. A gentleman—tall, impeccably dressed, and wearing a turban—walked into the drawing room. Sitting down beside her, he spoke of work in the world planned for her. Emotional maturity and self control were requisite. She would travel globally, doing her Master's work.

Born into British aristocracy and wealth, the teen-aged Alice was petulant, self-absorbed, and habitually depressed. She had nevertheless internalized a disciplined regimen of Bible study with a strong classical education. In her twenties, Alice was drawn into evangelical work, her service and ministry directed through the Elise Sandes Soldiers Homes and the YWCA, initially in Ireland and then in India. In her evangelical ardor, Alice tended to display the type of spiritual arrogance peculiar to Christian fundamentalism.

In 1907, she met and converted Walter Evans, a British soldier stationed in India. Alice noted Walter's intellect and education, his exceptionally good looks, and his common lineage. The class-conscious Alice was disconcerted and infatuated.

When Walter's military commitment in India was fulfilled, he traveled to the United States to study for the Episcopalian ministry. Health concerns, meanwhile, brought Alice back to England. Though she returned for a short stint in India, physical and emotional exhaustion caused her evangelical zealotry wane. Eventually, she returned to Scotland, and in 1907 married Walter. Alice's class consciousness had always been acute, and her descent in class strata was disorienting. Walter's progress toward a clerical appointment elevated him somewhat. The couple visited Walter's family en route to America.

In America, Walter was ordained, and Alice discovered housework. She also discovered her husband was prone to violent fits of rage, generally directed towards her. Three children—Dorothy, Mildred, and Ellison—were born. While Walter impressed his congregation, at home, Alice was getting knocked around.

On the pulpit, Walter blossomed. At home, he was disengaged, autocratic, unsupportive, and increasingly brutal. In a California parish, the church warden's wife visited a day after the abusive cleric had targeted his wife's face with a pound of cheese. His accuracy undid him; Walter was talked to and transferred. At the new parish, however, Walter's violent pattern continued. After the birth of Ellison, their third daughter, the attending physician discovered Walter's marks of abuse on Alice's body. Walter was removed from the pulpit, put on probation, and monitored by the church community. Alice put her husband on notice. Though still disengaged and unsupportive, the violent outbursts ceased. Six months later, Walter was reassigned to a Montana parish. Alice, choosing to remain in California with her daughters, would not see him again. She found employment in a Del Monte sardine cannery, where she progressed from labeling to packing, handling ten thousand sardines a day.

While living in Pacific Grove in 1915, Alice overheard two women with British accents conversing, and made their acquaintance. The ladies, former students of Helena Blavatsky, invited her to attend a lecture. Though Alice found the lecturer inept and the Theosophical presentation both dull and bizarre, Alice valued the friendship of her compatriots, and thus accepted the literature they offered. Within a short period, Alice, mentored by two other elderly women, was reading *The Secret Doctrine*. Alice joined the Theosophical Lodge in Pacific Grove. Her studies progressed, and in 1917 she moved to Krotona, in

Hollywood, California, the location of the National Headquarters of the Theosophical Society.

In 1918, Alice was admitted to the Esoteric Section of the Society. Entering the shrine room at Krotona, she was surprised to see a portrait of the turbaned gentleman who had spoken to her in the drawing room of her aunt's residence in Scotland twenty-three years before. When she was told the image was of Koot Hoomi, Alice alluded to her bond with the Master. The response was skeptical and dismissive.

In January of 1919, she met Foster Bailey. The two actively aligned while working for the Society. Foster was appointed National Secretary later that year, while Alice became editor of the Theosophical Magazine, *The Messenger*.

In November of 1919, Alice was spending a quiet afternoon on a hill near her home. Suddenly, a musical note sounded, followed by a clear voice. The voice spoke of books that Alice might write; Alice responded aloud, expressing her unwillingness. The voice persisted, speaking of her special telepathic gift, but Alice again refused. Finally, the voice suggested she reconsider, promising to return in three weeks.

After the promised interval, the voice spoke again. Alice heard it in her sitting-room that evening, but was still resistant. The voice repeated its request. Her curiosity finally piqued, she acquiesced. Within several weeks, chapters from a book that would be titled *Initiation, Human and Solar* were transcribed. The process was straightforward: Alice heard and wrote. A month later, a fearful Alice retreated from her work; the voice requested that she reach out to her Master to discuss the collaboration. Employing a telepathic technique she had been taught, Alice linked with Koot Hoomi. He assured her that there was no risk in the process. He told her that working along these lines would have great value and that he himself had suggested her role. Reassured, Alice complied.

The collaboration, beginning in the spring of 1920, spanned forty years and produced eighteen books. The voice, designated in the works that followed as the "Tibetan," belonged to Djwal Khul, a disciple of Koot Hoomi during Helena's lifetime. Djwal Khul was credited with significant contributions in the efforts that produced *The Secret Doctrine*.

Alice's channeling process evolved as she continued writing. The clairaudient model, in which she would hear the voice of her source and simply transcribe, was succeeded by telepathic linkage in which content impressed on her psyche was decompressed in writing. This decompression manifested in volumes of metaphysical teaching, the complexity and depth of which validated its source. For the transcription of symbols and glyphs, a clairvoyant technique was employed.

The first transcriptions were shown to B. P. Wadia, who had been sent to Krotona in 1920 as a representative of Annie Besant. Wadia had joined the Society in Bombay in 1904, and moved to the Adyar headquarters in 1907. Besant, seeing Wadia as a rising star, put him in charge of the Theosophical Publishing House. Impressed with the manuscript from Alice and the Tibetan, Wadia published the early chapters in *The Theosophist*, the official Adyar journal. Though he indicated his willingness to publish any further material from this source, conservative elements within the Society reacted poorly to Alice emerging as a viable channel. Nothing else was printed.

The core of conservative opposition to Alice and Foster Bailey was the Esoteric Section. Originally configured by Helena as a model for an elevated level of instruction from a teacher with specialized training and a unique link to the Brotherhood, the Section had devolved after her death into a political cadre invested in the manipulation and control of status and power within the Society. Indeed, the first major schism in the Society was created by the Judge–Besant dispute over leadership of the Esoteric Section.

In the summer of 1920, American Theosophists convened in Chicago. Foster Bailey, National Secretary, and Alice, editor of the American Theosophical magazine, represented a progressive trend. Their conservative opposition, however, triumphed in an election of national officers. The new national president, L. W. Rogers, was openly antagonistic to Foster and Alice. They were expelled from the Esoteric Section and nearly evicted from Krotona grounds. Besant, evidently finding the latter move a little too cold, blocked the eviction.

Wadia, in the background, was troubled by this consolidation of power in the Society as well. Like Alice, he had issues with Leadbeater and the direction of the second generation of Theosophical literature. He adopted the slogan "Back to Blavatsky," representing a movement within the American Theosophical community opposed to Roger's autocratic administration. Foster Bailey joined Wadia's opposition, forming the Committee of 1400, a group organized to reestablish the primacy of Helena's writings.

Both at Adyar and in America, however, the conservatives prevailed. Foster and Alice relocated to New York City and married. Wadia resigned from the Adyar Theosophical Society and joined the United Lodge of Theosophists, which had been established by Judge's protégé Robert Crosbie in 1909.

Alice continued to channel the Tibetan. She and Foster formed the Lucis Trust, an organizational framework for publication of her collaborative work with Djwal Khul. Their first book, *Initiation, Human and Solar*, brought the Brotherhood—now designated the Hierarchy—into focus. The Masters were identified and positioned in a configuration indicating levels of authority and areas of responsibility. *Letters on Occult Meditation*, the second published book, was followed by a massive text, *Treatise on Cosmic Fire*. Alice described the latter book as the psychological key to *The Secret Doctrine*, offering more stanzas from the ancient text Helena accessed.

Alice authored some works of her own as well. While these were published in the same format as her channeled material, the demarcation between the Tibetan's texts and her own is clear. *Treatise on Cosmic Fire* was followed by an instructive and practical volume, *Treatise on White Magic*, geared to the refinement and control of the emotional or astral body through mental practice.

A five volume set, *A Treatise on the Seven Rays*, expanded a teaching barely alluded to by Helena. The Ray template can overlay historical cycles as well as entities, individual or collective, within those cycles. While this concept is discussed elsewhere in the second generation of Theosophical Society literature—as are other themes and subjects developed by the Tibetan—the difference between the two versions is as extensive as the gap between pre-school and post-graduate studies.

Alice acknowledged the foundation had Helena provided her in *The Secret Doctrine*. However, she also emphasized the problems and challenges of the text. Unlike Helena's channeled material, Bailey's is highly organized, polished, and displays continuity. Moreover, the fact that she identifies a single source for her writing—the Tibetan, Djwal Khul—supports the cohesive quality of the body of work. Indeed, the clarity of the channel-source process in the Alice Bailey–Djwal Khul collaboration may be unparalleled in the genre. Between her redefinition of the relationship between source and channel, and the significant amount of material she produced, it is clear that Alice Bailey was the third major channel of the New Age.

Edgar Cayce[2]

Edgar Cayce was born in 1877 on a farm in Christian County, Kentucky, in close proximity to the city of Hopkinsville. The Cayce clan raised dark tobacco, an elite crop for pipe smoking and chewing. Edgar's grandfather, Thomas Jefferson Cayce—astute, highly organized and exceptionally intuitive—had expanded the family's farming interests. Tom Cayce was noted for skills including extraordinary dowsing ability, the greenest of thumbs, and telekinetic displays involving dancing brooms. The genetic lineage for Edgar Cayce's remarkable psychic ability can be clearly traced through his grandfather.

In May of 1880, Edgar fell onto a board with a protruding nail. The nail punctured his skull, entering the brain cavity. Witnessing the accident, Edgar's father Leslie ran to his son and removed the nail. Turpentine was poured on the wound. Edgar recovered with no apparent effects; there are, however, precedents for random head injuries—perhaps stimulating the pineal gland—leading to unusual psychic abilities.

A year later, Edgar and his grandfather were riding to visit an uncle when Tom's horse, startled by a snake, bolted across a river. In the tumult Tom was thrown from the saddle, and stomped upon by the horse. He did not survive. Edgar, calm through the incident and its aftermath, was overheard conversing with his grandfather in the months that followed.

The families of Edgar's parents, Leslie Cayce and Carrie Majors, had long dominated tobacco farming in their region of Kentucky. Carrie inherited 166 prime acres, but Leslie's ineptitude in farming lost the land to creditors. Leslie then leased a general store, a fine platform for his communication skills and love of political banter. Over time, the dry goods store failed as well; Leslie's penchant for alcohol and a retail policy of providing a free drink from a barrel of whiskey for every dollar spent on dry goods did not help his bottom line. Leslie returned to farming in

---

2 Much of the data presented here on Edgar Cayce comes from the excellent biography *Edgar Cayce, an American Prophet* by Sidney D. Kirkpatrick

1880, but involvement in financial schemes led to an erratic professional life. Nevertheless, father and son had a strong bond, Leslie playing a role at various points in the evolution of Edgar's psychic gifts. Edgar's posthumously published memoirs include several narratives provided by Leslie of events and circumstances in his son's life.

Edgar was precocious and reclusive in his childhood. By his tenth year, he had developed an enthusiasm for reading the Bible and a commitment to attending church service. The congregation in Hopkinsville belonged to the Christian Church, later called the Disciples of Christ, an ecumenical protestant group stressing biblical rather than clerical authority. Edgar committed early on to read through the Bible every year. He played an active role in his local church, initially as a teenaged sexton and later as a Sunday school teacher. In 1889, Edgar was overwhelmed by the appearance of a luminous angelic figure in the doorway to his bedroom. The figure acknowledged Edgar's prayer to be of service, and spoke of faith, integrity, and healing.

While Edgar's focus on Bible and his Church flowed into the prayerful attitude leading to his luminous vision, it did not extend to the classroom. At the Beverly Academy, with his uncle Lucian as teacher, Edgar could barely concentrate. For the thirteen-year-old, even spelling *cabin* proved too great a challenge. While Edgar remained after school filling the blackboard with cabins, Lucien visited Leslie and apprised him of his son's academic disconnect. After dinner that evening, Leslie drilled Edgar on spelling. Edgar would study the page, hand the book back to Leslie, and then space out, unable to spell the word.

This pattern repeated through the evening. Infuriated, Leslie struck his son after each failed attempt, buffed and rebuffed in Edgar's words. Eventually Leslie knocked Edgar off the chair. Father and son were both exhausted from the exchange; a distraught Edgar asked for a short recess. He laid his head on the spelling book as Leslie left the room. Soon, Leslie returned and recommenced the drill. A refreshed Edgar, with no hesitation, spelled the four words Leslie pronounced. Edgar continued, spelling the entire lesson for his father. After that, Edger spelled words Leslie chose randomly from the text. Then as Leslie pronounced a word, Edgar related its page, line and the words preceding and following. Strangely disconcerted, Leslie struck Edgar once more. This would be the last time he hit his son.

Edgar's academics were transformed. His suddenly phenomenal memory enabled him to move through three school grades in a year. His idiosyncratic skills were displayed in an episode involving a Kentucky congressman Leslie knew from childhood. The congressman, recently appointed Ambassador to Peru, delivered a lengthy speech before Congress. Leslie read a copy of the 110 page speech to Edgar on two consecutive nights before sleep. On the third evening Edgar, alone on a podium, flawlessly recited the hour-long speech to a large audience including the congressman. There were newspaper accounts of this remarkable feat, and Leslie won a $10 wager with the newly appointed ambassador.

While Edgar evolved as a student, his ineptitude in athletics created distance from his classmates. Attempting to bridge this gap, Edgar took part in a playground ball game called Old Sower. His incompetence in the game, however, led the penalty of standing with his back to the other players as balls were thrown in his direction. A ball struck him hard in the back, and Edgar blacked out. Witness accounts indicate that he did not lose consciousness, but began behaving in a bizarre manner, speaking rudely and out of turn in the classroom that afternoon. The strange behavior continued on the walk home from the schoolhouse, as Edgar rolled on the ground and jumped into ditches. As riders and carriages approached on the road, he would jump in front of them with hands outstretched.

At home he threw food at his sisters with evident delight. Then he grabbed a hot pan of coffee beans that had been cooking on the stove. Without flinching, he began planting the beans in the yard. Leslie was angry; Edgar was sent to bed. While Edgar slept, he spoke of an intimate relationship between his teacher and the school superintendent. Through the night, although the votes were still being tallied, he intermittently cheered Grover Cleveland's victory in the 1892 presidential election.

While he could not have known of his teacher's intimate affair, he was in fact accurate. More importantly Edgar, although sleeping, recited instructions for fixing a poultice to place on the back of his head. The ingredients—corn meal, onions, and herbs—were gathered, and the poultice was applied. In the morning Edgar was fine, and Cleveland was President. In the years of his life that followed, Edgar offered diagnostic medical direction in more than 10,000 cases while in similar sleep or trance states. This poultice, with himself as the subject, was the first.

In 1893, Edgar quit his studies at the Beverly Academy to work on his Uncle Clint's farm. An infatuation with a popular classmate that had ended with a humiliating rejection may have been a factor; his mother's seventh and final pregnancy certainly was. The family finances had been decimated by Leslie's badly timed investment in a crop of dark tobacco. Furthermore, his father's behavior had become erratic; Leslie was absent from home for days at a time, and lethargic when he returned. Edgar, unlike Leslie, had the temperament and capacity of his grandfather, Tom Cayce, for farming. The income from the employment was welcome in the family.

Edgar matured significantly during this period. His tall frame filled out with the rigors of farm work. In early August of 1894, Edgar returned to the field after dinner to repair a damaged plow. Sensing a presence approaching from behind, he turned to see the luminous figure from his childhood. Edgar was told to leave the plow and return to his mother. His year of work on the farm was over. Edgar arrived at his parent's home in Hopkinsville that evening.

Bookselling

At this time, Hopkinsville was an expanding metropolis in southwest Kentucky. With the economic foundation of a growing tobacco trade, Hopkinsville grew as well. It had an opera house, a variety of specialized retail, a baseball field for Hopkinsville's own team, the Moguls, and three funeral parlors. Edgar found employment at Hopper Brothers' Bookstore. He was initially told that there were no openings by Will Hopper, one of the brothers who owned the shop. After making employment inquiries at a dozen shops and businesses along the urban main street, Edgar returned to the book shop. Focused and persistent, he offered to work for a month without compensation to prove his value. The brothers accepted Edgar's proposal. His diligence and extraordinary memory, enabling to easily locate books in the large inventory, endeared him to the brothers. At the end of the first month, he was presented with a new suit; after the next month, ten dollars. He worked for the Hopper brothers for three years.

The bookstore provided textbooks for classes at two public schools, a private military academy, and two colleges. It supported the intellectual needs of a growing and increasingly sophisticated urban population. The inventory included classic and contemporary literature, an array of popular dime novels, office supplies, stationary, picture frames and molding, wall paper, umbrellas, and more.

Hopper's Bookstore was a cultural center in Hopkinsville. Bookselling, a social art, was a fine expression for Edgar's natural intelligence and sensitivity. As it was a meeting place for the students of the various colleges and academies, Hoppers' widened Edgar's circle of acquaintances. As a destination for the social and intellectual elite of Hopkinsville, the Bookstore was an early platform for the young man's spiritual work. Edgar's involvement in church activity deepened. His passion for scripture, coupled with his remarkable recall, was recognized by the Pastor. Edgar's role as Sunday school teacher expanded and he was asked to play a significant part in the development of a local branch of Christian Endeavor, an interdenominational and international outreach program for youth.

Gertrude Evans

Ethel Duke was a Hopkinsville elementary school teacher, and had known Edgar at Beverly Academy. She was also familiar with his particular skills, having witnessed his recitation of the lengthy congressional speech that had so astounded the community. While visiting the bookstore to purchase school supplies, she renewed her acquaintance with Edgar and extended an invitation to a social gathering at the home of Samuel Salter, an architect and builder. Salter, originally from Philadelphia, had been contracted to build houses and buildings in Christian County, Kentucky. He eventually married and settled in Hopkinsville. Samuel's buildings were known for their aesthetic design, intricate woodwork, and solid construction. The Salter estate was called the Hill. Trained as a doctor, Samuel grew herbs and medicinal plants. His interest in the arts and history was reflected in a large library. Progressive and intellectual, he represented the cultural aristocracy of Hopkinsville.

The invitation to the Salter social had, in fact, come from Samuel's granddaughter, Gertrude Evans, who was Ethel's cousin. Leslie Cayce, conservative, petty, and jealous, forbade his son from attending the gathering. A disappointed Edgar nonetheless acquiesced to his father. Ethel later returned to the Bookstore, this time accompanied by Gertrude, and the two were formally introduced. Edgar had noticed her buying college textbooks at Hoppers on previous occasions, but they had not spoken.

The ladies extended an invitation to another moonlight gathering at the Salter's that Friday; this time, Leslie was kept out of the loop. By the end of that Friday evening, Edgar had met much of the Salter clan; an array of businessmen, politicians, and clergy from Christian County; a large portion of the student body from South Kentucky College; and most important, had spent quality time alone with Gertrude. Edgar was smitten.

As the relationship developed, Edgar spent more time on the Hill. The younger members of the Salter clan—particularly Gertrude's brothers Hugh and Lynn, and their cousins—loved him, as did Carrie Salter, Gertrude's aunt. The older family members had reservations. Carrie, Ethel, Hugh, and Lynn were fascinated with Edgar's psychic skills and the strange occurrences of his childhood and youth. He displayed his abilities for them, identifying card after card of an unturned deck and locating a variety of lost objects. Gertrude was less enthralled with this aspect of Edgar's persona.

Nevertheless, the courtship proceeded, and on March 7, 1897, Edgar proposed . Five days later Gertrude accepted. Their kiss was Edgar's first. A week later, Edgar showed Gertrude a small diamond. By the end of the summer the precious stone, cut and set in Romania, was on Gertrude's finger.

Summer's end in 1897 brought another development. The Hopper brothers sold their interest in the bookstore. With the new ownership, Edgar's services were no longer required. He spent a month as a clerk in a dry goods store, followed by a year in sales at a department store. Edgar had loved selling books; he was not happy in other roles. Carrie Salter suggested looking to a larger city. By the summer of 1898, Edgar was in Louisville.

Louisville

The John P. Morton Company was a major wholesale and retail book outlet in Louisville, Kentucky's largest city. Edgar applied for a position. Though initially rejected, he accumulated letters of recommendation from former customers of Hoppers and flooded the J.P. Morton mailbox. This evidence had the desired effect—Edgar was hired. He had memorized the large Morton catalogue of books and merchandise, and recited the entire list to his fellow employees on his first day at work. Edgar was soon recognized at J.P. Morton's as a remarkable resource—grudgingly, perhaps, by coworkers, who knew nevertheless that through Edgar anything in the massive warehouse could be located. There was no ambiguity in the management's attitude.

One day Edgar was assigned to the Morton showroom to wait on a young woman from a family of wealthy tobacco merchants. Margaret, the tobacco heiress, was impressed with Edgar's demeanor as well as his expertise in describing a range of items from the Morton inventory. The sale to Margaret that day was substantial; Edgar's boss was delighted. The next day Edgar and his employer received an invitation for dinner at Margaret's family residence.

Soon after arriving in Louisville, Edgar had joined the local First Christian Church. The minister in Louisville, Edward Powell, had known Edgar from a brief tenure in Hopkinsville. He invited Edgar to teach a Sunday school class, and to work for the expanding Louisville branch of Christian Endeavor. That evening, at the dinner table in a palatial mansion located in an exclusive section of Louisville, Edgar discovered that Margaret attended the First Christian Church and was a dedicated participant in Glad Hands, the Christian Endeavor program of the Louisville church. Edgar and Margaret began to work in concert in the outreach program, conducting prayer services at hospitals and the county jail every week. Margaret began to attend Edgar's Bible classes on Sunday.

There was an intimacy to Edgar and Margaret's developing relationship. While not likely sexual, their emotional bond grew in the months that followed. Back in Hopkinsville, Gertrude sensed that something was amiss, as Edgar's correspondence and visits became less frequent. Emotionally distraught, she stopped attending classes at college. She was losing weight, her health deteriorating. When Edgar arrived in Hopkinsville for Christmas, just as the century was about to turn, Gertrude's condition was dire, physically and emotionally. After New Year's, Edgar returned to Louisville to work a final week for J.P. Morton. He received an envelope with forty dollars inside, a considerable monthly wage in 1900. Then, he returned to Hopkinsville to heal Gertrude and their relationship.

Speechless

Edgar needed an income. He joined his father as a district agent for Woodmen of the World Insurance, a company based in Omaha, Nebraska. The company sold reduced rate life insurance policies to groups organized for the purpose of buying their insurance. The appeal of the groups, established as fraternal orders, was an aggressive policy of discrimination. This racist attitude worked well for Leslie; it did not for Edgar. Perhaps reflecting this discomfort, Edgar began to experience migraines which diminished his ability to concentrate.

In April, Edgar was on a business trip in Elkton, a town twenty miles east of Hopkinsville. He went to a doctor there for a sedative to relieve his headache. That evening Edgar swallowed the prescribed white powder and went to sleep. He awoke the next morning in bed in his parent's home in Hopkinsville. A friend had found him the previous evening, wandering around the Elkton train station and acting in a bizarre manner reminiscent of the Old Sower episode of his youth. Although Edgar was coherent when he woke, he was unable to speak above a whisper. As the weeks passed, the condition did not improve. The insurance partnership, which had relied on Edgar's adept recall of rate tables and policy options, failed. Leslie, true to form, blamed his son. Barely audible, Edgar's prospects for employment were dim. He was despondent.

A reprieve from the hopelessness and despair enveloping Edgar came from William Bowles, a friend of the Hopper brothers. Bowles operated a photo studio in Hopkinsville. He offered Edgar a salaried apprenticeship at the studio. While Edgar's funk remained, he accepted the position. Bowles trained his apprentice, financing a trip to Louisville for Edgar to attend a brief course on the rudiments of photography. In addition to being a rapidly growing trade, photography was a vocation of sorts for Edgar. He quickly displayed an aptitude and a sense of artistry. His studio portraits were superb, as were his perspective shots of local events.

Edgar's vocal dysfunction, however, continued to plague him. His condition was common knowledge in the community. A touring hypnotist—Stanley Hart, known professionally as the Laugh King—was performing in Hopkinsville. Hart had tried unsuccessfully to hypnotize Edgar during an engagement at the Opera House in 1895; he had, however, been hypnotized on two occasions after Hart's initial failed attempt.

During Edgar's employment at J.P. Morton in Louisville, the performer Herman the Great had come to the showroom to purchase decks of playing cards—props for his touring vaudeville act, which involved sleight of hand and hypnotic demonstrations. Edgar waited on Herman. When Herman invited Edgar to be a subject of hypnosis, Edgar accepted the invitation. With the staff of J.P. Morton looking on in the showroom, Herman easily put Edgar under. When Edgar awoke, he was lying on a countertop in the showroom. He had been, according to his co-workers and Herman, an excellent subject.

A second episode unfolded several years later in Madisonville, Kentucky. A local outbreak of smallpox left Edgar and Leslie quarantined in a Madisonville hotel during a business trip for Woodmen's Insurance. One of the guests was a hypnotist, who offered to provide entertainment during their isolation with a display of his skills. Edgar was one of the subjects chosen. While in hypnotic trance, Edgar was directed to play the piano. He played beautifully, to the astonishment of the hotel guests and the hypnotist.

Hart, impeccable in his black tuxedo, invited Edgar onto the stage of the Holland Opera House. This time, Edgar slipped easily into trance. When Hart spoke to him, Edgar responded in a clear voice. The audience was elated. Their elation, however, was short-lived; upon being brought out of the hypnotic trance, Edgar could once again only whisper. After the performance, Hart talked about stages of hypnosis, and offered, for a $200 fee, a permanent cure for Edgar's condition. With a contribution from the local newspaper, the *Kentucky New Era*, the money was raised. Hart's repeated efforts with post-hypnotic directives, however, had the same result. Edgar spoke clearly in trance, but could only whisper when awake. Hart, unable to make any progress with his treatments, left Hopkinsville to continue his tour.

The drama surrounding Edgar's condition continued to play out in Hopkinsville. Dr. William Girao, formerly Gertrude's psychology teacher at South Kentucky College, expressed a clinical interest in Edgar's case. An agenda of self-promotion motivated Girao's interest; the professor eagerly gave a barrage of press interviews and arranged a public display of Edgar being put under in the front window of a Hopkinsville funeral parlor. Girao also sent newspaper clippings detailing Edgar's story to a leading New York hypnotherapist, Dr. John Quackenboss, who was intrigued by the accounts and traveled to Kentucky to work with Edgar.

Quackenboss proceeded with integrity and compassion, but was unable to effect a cure. He was, however, able to give Edgar a successful post-hypnotic directive—the doctor asked Edgar, while in trance, to remain asleep for 24 hours. Exactly 24 hours after the suggestion, Edgar awoke. After Quackenboss returned to New York, a persistent Girao turned to Al Layne, a local osteopath who had worked with hypnosis in his practice.

Layne continued his hypnotherapeutic efforts with Edgar in the months that followed. During that time, even whispering had become so painful that Edgar began to use a pad and pencil to communicate. His weight, as a consequence of his despondence, had dropped to under 100 pounds. Layne noted, however, that Edgar was increasingly conversational in trance. Moreover, in that state, he would follow directives flawlessly.

Girao had kept Quackenboss apprised of Edgar's condition. In their correspondence, Quackenboss suggested that Layne ask the talkative trance Edgar for a healing strategy.

Layne complied, and the response changed everything. Edgar spoke of a partial paralysis of the inferior muscles of the vocal chords produced by nerve strain, and a psychological condition producing this physical effect. Referring to himself in the third person, Edgar directed Layne to suggest an increase in circulation to the affected parts while the subject remained unconscious. Layne did as he was told. Edgar's neck began to swell with blood; his upper chest turned first pink, then red. After twenty minutes Edgar, still in trance, told the onlookers that the condition was removed and the vocal chords were normal. He directed Layne to suggest the circulation return to normal, and after that to awaken his body. Layne followed instructions. Edgar woke up spitting blood, soaking through a handkerchief. Then he greeted everyone in the room in a loud, clear voice.

The dramatic recovery nevertheless required monthly treatments with Layne, as Edgar's voice would periodically fail. These sessions continued for a year. During this period, Layne proposed expanding the scope of Edgar's trance diagnostics to provide assistance for others in need. Edgar did not refuse.

Layne set up a small office, with a cot, chairs, a desk, and file cabinets above his wife's hat shop. A stenographer was brought in to record some of the trance sessions. The first case was Layne's own gastrointestinal disorder. In trance, Edgar confidently diagnosed Layne's condition, prescribing specific medications and a regimen of exercise. Layne diligently followed the advice and was cured. Word spread; family members and friends approached Edgar and Layne, seeking diagnoses and cures.

Once or twice a week, Edgar would lie down on the cot in Layne's office. In that first year, more than eighty trance readings, generally medical, were given. As a rule, if the treatment recommendations were followed, health was restored. The language of the diagnosis was sophisticated. In one case Edgar pinpointed the location of a swallowed celluloid button lodged in a child's windpipe. The button, which had caused breathing problems, had not appeared on X-rays. The patient's presence was not even required; in one session, he located a patient in the root cellar of a farm house in real time, while her husband was sitting with Edgar and Layne in their office.

Edgar, gaining weight and confidence, began to put his life back on track. In 1902 he contracted with William Bowles to set up temporary photo studios in some of the smaller townships in Christian County. Bowles supplied the equipment and assisted in scheduling appointments. Ambivalent in regard to his trance sessions and uncomfortably dependent on Layne to know exactly what information he was providing when put under, Edgar was fine with creating some distance from the Hopkinsville osteopath. He set up a studio in Pembroke, ten miles southeast of Hopkinsville. After his time in Pembroke, Edgar moved to Lafayette, eighteen miles south of his home.

Bowling Green

Soon after arriving in Lafayette, Edgar was contacted by Lucian Potter, owner of Potter's Bookstore in Bowling Green. Lucian needed a manager for his bookstore. Edgar agreed, on the condition that he be allowed his own studio space in the rear of the shop. Lucian was happy to accommodate him.

Bowling Green and Potter's Bookstore were fine fits for Edgar. The city, with a population of over 10,000, was poised for growth as an economic and cultural center in southern Kentucky. Students from Ogden College and Bowling Green University frequented Potter's. Edgar's accessible demeanor and immediate mastery of the inventory endeared him to both the longstanding clientele and the youthful student population.

Edgar set up his photo studio in the back of the shop. Even with a competitor in the building—Clark's photo studio, located on the floor above the bookstore—Edgar was active. His portraits and school photos provided him with additional income, and he soon began working with landscapes. His ability to frame images and manage the interplay of light and dark in the scenes created some stunning photos. One brilliant shot of Fountain Park, the city center, after a snow storm was published by Lucian on a Christmas card. Thousands were sold, and Edgar received a bonus.

Edgar found lodging at Hollins' Boarding House, a short distance from Potter's. His fellow boarders included three young medical professionals: his roommate Hugh Beazley, a throat specialist, and the Blackburn brothers, John and James. An older boarder, O. A. Roup, a circuit judge and newspaper publisher, stayed several nights each month. Edgar enjoyed their company and camaraderie with the group sharing the Boarding House developed quickly.

Joining the First Christian Church of Bowling Green, Edgar became active in the local Christian Endeavor program and was asked once again to teach a Sunday Bible study group. His classes were quite popular, and he was acknowledged by being appointed a deacon in the church.

During this period, Edgar developed a card game for recreation at a local YMCA. Sixty-four cards with images of various commodities traded on the options market of the stock exchange were designed; the object was cornering markets. The game, which Edgar called "Pit," was very popular at the YMCA socials, and decks were printed for the YMCA members. Edgar sent a sample to the game company Parker Brothers, of Salem, Massachusetts. Parker Brothers sent him a letter of thanks and a check for six dollars; within a short time, Pit was being marketed nationally. Edgar received a dozen decks and a complimentary note from the game company. Edgar requested a percentage of the game's profits from Parker Brothers—a request the company refused. He considered, but did not pursue, legal action. The game, still under Parker Brother's copyright, is today still being sold. Edgar had better fortune with the prize of a gold watch, won in a national competition to solve a New York newspaper crossword puzzle. Perhaps sleeping on the newspaper, Edgar nailed the puzzle in record time.

Edgar was on a roll. Life in Bowling Green clearly suited him. Al Layne would visit occasionally, but only to treat Edgar's voice and follow up on patients that Edgar had previously diagnosed while in trance. Edgar allowed Layne to conduct the sessions at Hollins' House, but insisted they be done clandestinely. He did not want to attract the attention of his housemates. Edgar's inclination was to leave this aspect of his life in Hopkinsville.

Al Layne, on the other hand, was ambitious and calculating. His training and certification in osteopathy was from a mail-order course. He understood clearly what controlling Edgar's trance diagnostics meant for his career. In August of 1902, Layne approached Professor Charles Dietrich on a street corner in Hopkinsville. Dietrich, an eminent educator and administrator, had been hired as superintendent of schools in Hopkinsville. He had transformed and elevated the Hopkinsville school system; it was now considered a model of progressive education in the south.

In 1898, Dietrich's daughter Aimee, then two years old, had contracted a debilitating case of diphtheria. While she recovered physically from the disease, her mental and emotional development stopped. At the age of six, she behaved as if she were two. The Dietrichs consulted doctors in New York and Florida. Unable to offer any remedy, they could only designate Aimee retarded. In Cincinnati, a specialist diagnosed a rare and fatal brain disease. The Dietrichs were distraught. When Layne offered his and Edgar's services, Dietrich was and remained skeptical, but ultimately accepted the offer. Edgar, aware of Dietrich's status and accomplishments, took a train to Hopkinsville. Dietrich had Layne and Edgar use a back entrance so as to not attract the neighbors' attention.

Edgar lay down on the sofa in the Dietrich's living room. Waking twenty minutes later, he found Mrs. Dietrich in tears and her husband in a state of shock. In trance, Edgar had diagnosed their daughter's condition, described its cause, and provided a strategy for treatment. When she was two, Aimee had slipped stepping down from a carriage and injured her back; the diphtheria germs had settled into the bruised area of her spine. Her body had formed a membrane around the bruise which thickened over time, reducing the flow of blood to her brain, resulting in her retardation. Osteopathic manipulation would soften the membrane, allowing the blood to circulate freely. With treatment, Edgar had explained, Aimee would recover.

In the three days that followed, Layne performed a series of manipulations on the girl. After the third set of adjustments, Edgar, again in trance, was satisfied. The next day he returned to Bowling Green. Three weeks later, an ebullient Mrs. Dietrich called him at Potter's; a week after he left, Aimee had spoken her parents' names for the first time. A week after that, she was adeptly cutting out paper shapes with a pair of scissors. Within three months, Aimee was behaving like a normal six year old.

Edgar was reticent about bringing attention to his psychic skills in Bowling Green. While Mrs. Dietrich had acclaimed him in an article published in the Hopkinsville newspaper, the story, to his relief, did not reach Bowling Green.

Edgar's life in Bowling Green had stabilized. His finances improved with the salary from Potter's Bookstore, supplemented by earnings from his photography studio. It was time for Gertrude to join Edgar in Bowling Green. Their wedding took place in June of 1903 on the Hill. Family and friends attending numbered three hundred. In their wedding photo Gertrude looked radiant; Edgar looked disoriented. The newlyweds took a room in a boarding house across the street from Hollins' House.

Gertrude had never been comfortable with Edgar's trance work, but his vocal dysfunction was recurrent and needed treatments. Yet for her, the sessions were at best intrusive; at worst, they were threatening and destabilizing for their relationship. Edgar saw the good: the healing that came from the trance diagnoses and remedies, healing that had been called for by the luminous presence in 1893. A part of him was drawn to the trance connection. The overt psychic skills he willingly and astutely integrated into his life; his remarkable memory had served him as a student at Beverly Academy and as a teacher for Bible study classes. It was invaluable for his career in bookselling. The trance states were another matter, as was Al Layne. Layne advertised himself on the sign above his office door as a doctor, stretching the truth. His persistent efforts to induce Edgar to return to Hopkinsville and enter into partnership in a medical practice were bothersome. Yet, particularly after the Dietrich case, Edgar was disinclined to give up trance and end his association with Layne.

Just days after the wedding, Layne walked into a Sunday dinner at Hollins' House. Gertrude and Edgar were dining with his former housemates. O. A. Roup, the circuit judge and newspaper publisher, was curious about the frequent visits during which Edgar and Layne would retire for hours to Edgar's shared room when Beazley, his roommate, was not present. Layne told Roup he was providing therapy for Edgar's recurring voice problems. Roup noted that while Layne was an unlicensed medical practitioner, Beazley, Edgar's roommate and friend, was an accredited throat specialist. Feeling slighted, Layne countered, talking about hypnosis, trance states, diagnoses, and cures. He spoke of Edgar's own case and others.

The dinner party, Roup, Beazley, James and John Blackburn, listened intently. Gertrude, infuriated, fled the room and the house. Edgar did not follow her. The dinner party had many questions, to which Edgar and Layne responded. Layne suggested a demonstration. In trance, Edgar diagnosed cases for Layne and proposed treatments. His medical terminology was sophisticated and his tone professional. The treatment strategies were diverse and, in one case, state-of-the-art. His friends from Holland House were astonished. They had known Edgar for a year; his integrity was unassailable. He was a good man. Layne and the dinner guests continued to talk, while Edgar left, crossing the street to be with Gertrude. She had begun to pack her clothes. They had been married less than a week. Gertrude did not leave Edgar that evening, but this conflict represented a deep conflict in their relationship.

On June 24, 1903, a front-page story by O. A. Roup was published in the *Bowling Green Times-Journal*. The strange dramas of Edgar's youth were described, as were the details of the Aimee Dietrich case. Edgar's employment at Potter's Bookstore and his membership in the First Christian Church of Bowling Green were noted in the article. Nashville papers quickly picked up the story; by the next week, it was running in newspapers throughout Kentucky and Tennessee. Lucian Potter, kept in the dark about this aspect of his manager's life, felt he could no longer trust Edgar, and asked him to seek other employment. Members of the First Christian Church saw demons. Edgar was no longer welcome in Bowling Green. The newlyweds were asked to vacate their room in the boardinghouse. Layne was investigated and charged with practicing medicine without a license; his office in Hopkinsville was shut down.

The young couple retreated to the Hill, where Gertrude's three aunts were their support system. Her aunt Carrie had married Dr. Thomas House. Carrie House loved Gertrude and believed in Edgar. She and her sisters mortgaged the Hill to finance a photography studio in Bowling Green for the couple. Edgar and Gertrude formed a partnership with Lucian Potter's brother Frank, former assistant county clerk. Tall, blond, and gregarious, Frank knew many people. Edgar, Gertrude, and Frank purchased the Harry Cook Studio on College Street, facing Fountain Square, the city center. While Edgar took a course in modern techniques in McMinnville, Tennessee, Frank redecorated the studio, adding modern technology: adjustable shades on rollers, painted canvas backdrops, and an overhead projector.

The studio was an immediate success. Edgar was a brilliant photographer, personable and sensitive with the customers and skillful with the subjects. Edgar's portraits won awards. The remaining competitor was Clark's Studio, located on State Street above Potter's Bookstore. Clark's could not compete with Edgar, and offered to sell their space. Edgar and Gertrude brought Lynn Davis, Gertrude's brother, and his friend Joe Adcock into the partnership to finance the acquisition. The Cayce Studio adapted well to the spacious new space, ironically located above Edgar's former studio and place of employment. The College Street studio became the Cayce Art Company.

Al Layne rebounded as well. The Blackburn brothers had intervened, and secured Layne admission and advanced placement in the Southern School of Osteopathy in Franklin, Kentucky. A degree from the well-established school would legitimize Layne's practice. Edgar traveled to Franklin for therapeutic sessions whenever his voice would sporadically fail. After several months, however, Edgar decided to find a facilitator for the trance work in Bowling Green. He chose his friend and former housemate, Dr. John Blackburn, to guide the therapy. Edgar gave Blackburn a notebook with verbal directives for inducing trance, and specific suggestions to generate healing that he and Layne had composed.

Blackburn took advantage of their first session to ask questions of a personal nature as well as deal with Edgar's vocal disorder. The impact of this session on Blackburn was evident to Edgar upon awakening. Blackburn's commitment to the process was also evident. Further, Blackburn proposed that a group of doctors be assembled to witness and investigate Edgar's remarkable abilities. Edgar agreed. A stenographer was engaged to transcribe the sessions. The team of seven would study Edgar for the next year and a half.

Though members of Blackburn's team were initially skeptical of Edgar's abilities, a series of early tests converted them. Edgar was able to read in trance the contents of randomly selected documents sealed in envelopes placed in buttoned pockets. For nine pregnant women— all patients of local doctors—he accurately predicted the gender of the

coming newborns. On one occasion, a priest walked into one of the medical team's office during a trance session, carrying a sealed and unmarked
package that had just been delivered. The priest did not know the contents of the package. Edgar, in trance, was asked. His reply was altar
candles. The priest opened the package. Dumbfounded, he quickly left
the room.

Blackburn, following Al Layne, referred to the intelligence communicating in Edgar's trance state as the Source. Members of his committee,
their skepticism dispelled, began to consult the Source for their patients.
Dr. Fred Stone, inquiring about his mother's health, asked for a description of her bedroom. In trance, Edgar began with the wall colors, then
details of the pictures hanging on the walls and arranged on the window
sills, and finally the bed; he even reported where the steel springs had
been manufactured, and where the cotton in the mattress was grown
and processed. Blackburn accompanied Stone to his mother's house on
the outskirts of Bowling Green. Her room was exactly as described. They
dismantled the bed to inspect the manufacturer's stamp. Edgar's remote
view had been flawless.

Blackburn's committee began to give press interviews and arrange
public demonstrations, raising Edgar's profile. During a public session at
Potter College, in response to a woman's question about financial dis-
crepancies in her family's business, he identified the embezzler. A public
demonstration at Bowling Green Business College was requested by a
Professor Lambert; while Edgar was in trance, Lambert inquired about
a murder in his home town in Canada. A woman has been shot on the
stairs of her home. The police had no motive and no weapon. Edgar
related the pistol's make, model, serial number, and place of purchase—
Roanoke, Virginia. He also gave the number of empty chambers in the
cylinder, and its current location, at the spot where the roof gutter from
the house connects to the sewer. The victim's sister, exacting revenge
for a sabotaged relationship, was the perpetrator. The weapon was subsequently found at the place described, and the sister confessed.

An executive from the Southern Railroad was referred to Edgar. He
inquired, through correspondence, about an accident that had occurred
on his division of the railway. Edgar identified the worker responsible and
advised terminating his employment. The executive did not act on the
advice, but did request a second reading. In this session Edgar predicted

another accident, with the consequent death of the official ignoring the warning, in Virginia and West Virginia. Nine months later, the railroad executive was riding in a private rail car. The same employee again failed to throw a switch. Another train, now on the wrong track, smashed into the private car, pushing it over the state line—from Virginia to West Virginia. The executive did not survive the crash.

Joe Dickey, a Professor at Bowling Green Business University, approached Edgar for readings for himself, his wife, and his daughter. Dickey, who would be appointed President of the University, befriended Edgar, and conducted a number of sessions with him between 1905 and 1907. He did not hesitate to share information about Edgar's amazing skills with his many contacts in the academic and business worlds. As part of a University lecture series on modern scientific inventions, Dickey invited Nikola Tesla and Thomas Edison to Bowling Green. The inventors met with Edgar and took part in trance sessions. Tesla acknowledged an intuitive source underlying his own genius: technical data and images of blueprints received in dreams. Edison, grounded in the business applications of his inventions, had a keen interest in measuring the connection between electricity and psychic phenomena.

In April of 1906, the Blackburn committee scheduled a final demonstration of Cayce's abilities. Leading physicians from the county were invited to a Guild Hall to witness a session. Edgar, in trance, diagnosed a patient being treated at Potter College. The man, he said, was recovering from typhoid fever. His pulse rate was 96 and his body temperature 101.25. The patient's diet needed to change. Doctors were sent to the College to assess the reading. They returned to the hall and verified the diagnosis.

The audience was amazed. Some were incredulous, believing they were being hoaxed. An osteopath from Chicago ran onto the stage and drove a surgical needle into Edgar's arm to test the trance; when Edgar did not react, the osteopath pushed the needle into the sole of his foot. Still, there was no reaction. Another doctor pushed a hat pin through Edgar's cheek, while a colleague inserted a pen knife under the nail of Edgar's left forefinger and lifted. Edgar did not flinch and blood did not flow. The doctors, sadistic tendencies satisfied, were dumbfounded. Blackburn brought Edgar out of trance. He groaned in pain and blood flowed from the wounds. His finger was permanently disfigured. Leslie, who had attended the demonstration, took Edgar home. While Edgar did not express any anger over the episode, Gertrude was livid. In the aftermath, Blackburn's committee disbanded.

In December of 1906, days before Christmas, a fire in the Cayce Studio on State Street burned the building to the ground. A consigned collection of paintings, carbon prints, and watercolors from Franz Von Hanfstangl, a New York dealer, were destroyed in the blaze. Insurance covered Edgar's property and equipment, but not Von Hanfstangl's art. Edgar was now $8000 in debt, a significant sum in 1906. He continued to do business on College Street.

On March 14, 1907, Gertrude gave birth to nine and a half pound Hugh Lynn Cayce. Blackburn was the attending physician. Disaster struck again in September of 1907, when a fire decimated the College Street studio. Equipment was lost and negatives destroyed. The insurance adjustors were generous, and Edgar quickly rebuilt the studio. Gertrude and baby Hugh Lynn moved back to the Hill to save money. Edgar began sleeping at the College Street studio, working to pay down the debt from the State Street fire.

Gertrude's aunt Carrie and her husband, Dr. Thomas House, took another loan on the Hill to buy Frank Potter's interest in the Cayce Studio. Thomas moved to Bowling Green to manage the studio. His contribution in this capacity was negligible; he did, however, conduct trance sessions with Edgar. Thomas' focus, however, was not health. He began a trend in which financial concerns, strategies, and schemes were explored in the readings. Thomas asked about a stash of gold rumored to have been buried in the vicinity of the Hill during the Civil War. In trance, Edgar narrated the circumstances in which a Confederate soldier hid the gold. Unhappily for Thomas, the treasure had been recovered by members of the soldier's family after the war.

Continuing this trend, Edgar's father Leslie visited Bowling Green. The victim of a bond theft in Western Pennsylvania was offering a sizable reward for information about the thief. In trance, Edgar spoke about the victim's wife, her affair with his business associate, their absconding with the bonds, and their current location in Columbus, Ohio. He described a hidden birthmark on the unfaithful wife and two deformed toes on her left foot. Leslie wired the information to the victim. When the thieves were arrested in Ohio, he received the reward.

However, Leslie wasn't finished. His plan now was to invest the reward—along with funds from associates in Hopkinsville—in the commodities market, trading according to information provided in trance sessions. Edgar would receive a percentage of the profits to pay off his debts. The first week was lucrative, and the second even better. Then Edgar spoke about a man named Leiter cornering the wheat market, and fluctuations in value: it would rise to a $1.19 trading price, and then suffer a sharp drop. Leslie and his associates from Hopkinsville, feeling this information was counterintuitive, failed to act on it. That turned out to be a mistake; their holdings were lost.

In the midst of the Leslie's commodities adventures, Joe Dickey, the professor from Bowling Green Business University, added his own financial scheme to the mix. A friend—Paul Cooksey, an attorney and businessman from Bowling Green, now living in New York City—was well-connected in financial circles. Dickey spoke to Cooksey about Edgar's unusual gifts. Though Cooksey was intrigued, he needed further validation. Dickey and Thomas House conducted a session. In trance, Edgar viewed Cooksey remotely and was able to describe in detail his movement and circumstances on a particular day. He named the tune Cooksey was whistling as he walked up the stairs to his office, identified the client who was waiting, the real estate deal they discussed, and the court appearance at three o clock to address the property issue.

Edgar then described in sequence three letters Cooksey opened after the meeting his client: a bill, a business letter, and a personal note from his girlfriend. Edgar added that Cooksey received a phone call while reading his girlfriend's note. Dickey wired Cooksey a transcript of the session. Cooksey, impressed, wanted Edgar, Dickey, and House to come to New York. Edgar was not inclined to make the trip. Cooksey decided to come to Edgar instead. In Hopkinsville, Cooksey asked for a reading. Edgar, uncomfortable with Cooksey, declined. Finally, when Cooksey persisted, Edgar agreed to one reading, on the condition that Cooksey return to New York after the session. Leslie conducted the reading. Cooksey made $20,000 in the stock market from the information Edgar provided in trance. A portion of this went towards paying down Edgar's debt.

From the stock market, Dickey moved to horse racing. Edgar agreed to a trial reading. In trance, he picked six winners in seven races, noting that the seventh race was fixed. Dickey was thrilled. He and Edgar traveled to Cincinnati and went to the track. Edgar named winners in four races, and Dickey laid down the bets. With his share of the winnings, Edgar was finally out of debt.

The materialistic impetus that drove Thomas House, Leslie Cayce, Joe Dickey, and Paul Cooksey in this cycle of readings was out of balance with the spiritual equation linking Edgar to the Source. Dickey had a breakdown two months after returning from Cincinnati, spending the next two years in therapy. For Edgar, any effort to induce trance left him with a headache or asleep. Depressed, he closed the Studio in Bowling Green and returned to the Hill.

After three months of introspection, self-doubt, bible reading, and gardening, Edgar found work as a traveling photographer based in Gadsden, Alabama. From Gadsden he moved to Anniston, Alabama, having been offered a better salary by the Russell Brothers Studio. Leslie traveled to Anniston, accompanied by a family from Bowling Green whose twenty-one month old son could barely move his legs. Leslie succeeded in inducing Edgar's trance. Osteopathic adjustments were prescribed; Dr. Tom Posey treated the boy, following Edgar's direction. The child was cured, and Posey duly impressed. He referred more patients to Edgar.

Leslie stayed in Anniston to facilitate the readings. In July of 1910, Edgar and Leslie moved to Jacksonville, Alabama to open a branch studio for the Russell Brothers. Later that year the two relocated in Montgomery, Alabama, to work for the Tressler family, eminent photographers from Nashville who owned a chain of studios throughout the South. Edgar had continued his readings in Anniston and Jacksonville, his reputation again growing as more doctors requested his unique services.

Wesley Ketchum

Dr. Wesley Ketchum, a homeopath from Hopkinsville, had used Edgar five years earlier to assess a leg injury that George Dalton, a wealthy contractor, had suffered while attempting to jump a space of four feet at a construction site. Dalton had broken bones above and below his kneecap. The doctors he consulted maintained that he would not walk again, and prescribed amputation. In trance, Edgar proposed boring a hole in Dalton's kneecap and attaching the bone to the cap with a nail of dimensions specified in the session. Though the use of nails or screws to attach bones was, at that time, unheard of, Ketchum followed the instructions. After two months in traction, the bones healed; in time, Dalton walked.

Ketchum was unapologetically progressive in his approach to medicine and did not hesitate to use creative and nontraditional therapeutic models. He enclosed round-trip railroad tickets in a letter to Edgar, requesting his assistance for three patients in Hopkinsville. Edgar arrived home in late August to work with Ketchum. After working on Ketchum's cases and spending precious time with Gertrude and Hugh Lynn, Edgar returned to Montgomery.

In early autumn, Ketchum presented a paper to a National Conference of Homeopaths at Cal Tech in Pasadena. The subject of the presentation was an unnamed psychic with limited formal education who provided remarkable and sophisticated diagnoses and therapeutic strategies while in trance. Cases were detailed. Ketchum gave the text of the paper to a Chicago colleague who presented it at Harvard during the annual meeting of the Clinical Research Society, an elite group of 500 physicians. The response to the presentation was overwhelming. National syndication picked up the story and it ran in newspapers throughout the country. The Associated Press sent a reporter to Hopkinsville who identified Edgar as the illiterate trance healer. More reporters arrived. Edgar's life was researched and recounted in follow-up articles; Leslie Cayce was happy to supply photographs and details. While Edgar was in Alabama, Hopkinsville was overrun by newspapermen, curiosity seekers, and many in need of medical help.

Ketchum telegraphed Edgar in Montgomery. He proposed that Edgar return to Hopkinsville and enter into a partnership in the business of giving health readings with himself and Albert Noe, manager of the Latham Hotel. The revenues from the readings would be split between Ketchum, Noe, Edgar, and Leslie, who would conduct the trance sessions. Ketchum and Noe would subsidize the office setup, pay all overhead costs, and hire a stenographer. Edgar responded, insisting that Ketchum and Noe finance a photography studio in Hopkinsville owned by Edgar and family as part of the arrangement. Ketchum agreed. Two days later, Edgar was in Hopkinsville. He found patients standing in line at Ketchum's office, eager to receive readings. In the first month, Ketchum received 10,000 letters and $2000 in cash.

On the afternoon the contracts for the partnership were to be signed,

Edgar, Leslie, Ketchum, and Noe were sitting in a room in the Latham Hotel. Spirits were high, and a fine celebratory dinner was proposed. There was a knock on the hotel room door; Noe rose to open it. An East Indian, stylishly dressed in a light colored suit and wearing a turban, walked into the room. The uninvited guest greeted the men, shaking hands with each. He told them that he come to ask Ketchum, Noe, and Leslie about their plans for Edgar. The gentleman with the turban put the question individually to each and gave each a specific warning. He spoke of the destructive nature of greed and self-interest for the partnership. Then he spoke of spirituality and the higher purpose of Edgar's gift. As he was leaving the room, the Indian promised to join the partners at dinner, but never appeared. In fact, no one in the hotel other than the four partners recalled seeing the visitor at all.

The new Cayce Photo Studio was on the top floor of the building adjacent to Hopper's Bookstore. A suite of rooms in the back of the studio were set up for Edgar's trance sessions. The sign on the door leading into the suite read PSYCHIC DIAGNOSTICIAN. Edgar scheduled an hour in the early morning and another in the late afternoon for readings. The sessions began on the day the legal documents were signed. Nine readings were given in the first week. Edgar did not set a fixed fee, although a guideline of $25 was adopted, as was the stipulation that no one be turned away for lack of funds. Ketchem's fees for prescribed treatments were at his discretion. His calm demeanor and balanced disposition interfaced well with Edgar's sensitivity. Ketchum, in this phase, brought intellect, insight, and professionalism to the service. When Leslie broke his kneecap, Ketchum began to conduct the sessions.

In December of 1910, Frank Mohr, a businessman from Columbus, Ohio, requested a reading for a niece with polio. Edgar had located an underground deposit of coal in Nortonville, Kentucky for a man who had later sold the mining interest to Mohr. Expanding the mining operation, Mohr built the highly successful Norton Coal Corporation. Edgar's recommendations for treatment of Mohr's niece were dramatically successful. Mohr was so impressed that he made Ketchum and Noe an offer for Edgar's contract. They declined.

The persistent Mohr adjusted his proposal—the partnership agreement would be expanded to include Mohr, who would build and staff a hospital to serve the specialized treatments prescribed in the readings. This move would solve what was becoming the crucial stumbling block for Edgar and his partners: finding medical professionals who would accept the trance diagnostics and perform the specialized treatments. Ketchum and Noe liked the new proposal. The principals reached a verbal agreement.

Believing the agreement would be honored, Mohr purchased land in Nortonville, hired architects, and began construction. Ketchum and Noe began to hedge; they likely wanted to adjust the financial framework of the agreement to their benefit. During this phase, Mohr suffered a serious spinal injury in a mining accident. In a reading, Edgar recommended surgery, but stated that Mohr would lose his sight if specific corrective measures were not taken after the operation. Mohr's doctors were incredulous about the possibility of blindness, and Ketchum did not support Edgar's directives. This was strange. Something was amiss in the partnership. Construction on the hospital stopped. Civil lawsuits followed, but came to nothing as Mohr returned to Columbus to recuperate. Edgar was not happy—Ketchum's integrity was, for the first time, in question.

On March 28, 1911, Gertrude gave birth to a second son, Milton Porter Cayce. The baby died on May 17. Edgar, preoccupied with readings and the studio, had been disengaged throughout Gertrude's pregnancy. Gertrude did not like Ketchum or Noe, and she distrusted Leslie. She took no interest in the partnership or the trance work, which she saw increasingly as a barrier between her and her husband. She did not ask for a reading, although the baby suffered through a case of whooping cough followed by colitis. By the time Edgar addressed the failing health of his second son in a session, the baby was too far gone. In her grief and guilt, Gertrude contracted tuberculosis. In trance, Edgar gave his most detailed reading to date. He prescribed a complex regimen and an unusual compound of drugs. Gertrude slowly recovered.

In December of 1911, Dr. Hugo Munsterberg, Dean of Psychology at Harvard, arrived in Hopkinsville. A large man, well over six feet tall and weighing 250 pounds, Munsterberg had a forceful, intimidating personality, and spoke with a German accent. He had traveled from Cambridge, Massachusetts to debunk Edgar. Ketchum and Edgar answered questions, provided transcripts to read, and invited the professor to witness a reading. After interviewing Carrie House and the Dietrich family, Munsterberg prepared to leave Hopkinsville. His conclusions now supported the trance work; his observations, however, did not support the partnership. While Munsterberg encouraged Edgar to continue the readings, he suggested a reevaluation of the alignment with Ketchum and Noe. The professor's advice was astute.

Edgar began to look more closely at Ketchum. After Leslie fractured his kneecap, Ketchum had conducted the sessions. Frequently he would dispense with the stenographer, taking notes himself and transcribing them later. Suspicious, Edgar discovered that contracted readings had not always been conducted. Edgar confronted Ketchum, who admitted using the trance sessions for tips on horse races. Ketchum claimed that profits from well-placed bets were going into a fund for building a hospital. A recently purchased farm with a stable of race horses and a new automobile—one of the first in Hopkinsville—suggested otherwise. Moreover, Ketchum, although married, was known to be supporting a mistress—Katy deTuncq, a French teacher at a local woman's college. Exposed, Ketchum consolidated his assets and left Hopkinsville with his mistress. He enrolled in a refresher course at Harvard Medical School, and made a futile attempt to engage Munsterberg. Ketchum and Katy deTuncq would eventually marry in Hawaii.

Edgar walked away from the remnants of the psychic partnership and a studio full of equipment. Gertrude was still recovering from tuberculosis. With his wife and young son remaining in Hopkinsville, Edger left for Selma, Alabama.

Selma, Alabama

Selma, a growing river city with a population of 20,000, suited Edgar. It suited the Tressler Company of Nashville as well. The Tressler family was actively extending its chain of photography studios through the south. Edgar had worked briefly for their studio in Montgomery before returning to Hopkinsville to partner with Ketchum. In January of 1913, he opened a branch Studio for the Tresslers in Selma. Edgar chose a spacious second floor suite in the business district. He rented a three room apartment on the floor above the studio. Hugh Lynn and Gertrude would join him when her recovery from tuberculosis progressed sufficiently to allow travel.

The First Christian Church in Selma embraced Edgar. He was appointed Deacon, and was asked to teach a Bible Study class and to organize the local branch of Christian Endeavor. The Bible class attracted students from a range of denominations: Baptists and Catholics; Presbyterians and Episcopalians; Methodists and Disciples of Christ, i.e. members of the First Christian Church that sponsored the class. The success and popularity of the class, which published its own magazine, was unparalleled in Selma. The class was called Class No. 7, after the number of the meeting room. The magazine, which Edgar edited, was the *Sevenette*.

Edgar resumed trance work in April. A conversation with a customer in the studio led to his first session in Selma. The customer's young daughter had suffered from infantile paralysis. Her leg and foot had warped as a consequence of the disease. A friend from the Bible Study Class, Alfred Butler, conducted the reading. Butler's sister Flora had been committed to an asylum as the result of an emotional disorder which had developed suddenly. Edgar diagnosed an impacted wisdom tooth. After the tooth was extracted, Flora's behavioral symptoms gradually dissipated.

In December, Edgar received a letter from Amanda Fay Delaney, wife of William Delaney, a wealthy lumber baron from Lexington, Kentucky. An automobile accident ten years earlier had left Amanda Fay paralyzed. She had heard of Edgar's work through the Dietrichs, and hoped he could help. Edgar accepted an invitation to come to Lexington. He wired John Blackburn, who agreed to accompany him and conduct the session. However, Blackburn unexpectedly had to perform an emergency operation and could not leave Bowling Green. Edgar traveled to Lexington alone.

Amanda Fay was, in Edgar's words, pitiful. Her swollen body was brought into the room on a stretcher. At 5'5", she weighed over 200 pounds. She could barely move her limbs. Her sensitive skin could not even tolerate being covered by a bed sheet. Delaney's doctors' prognosis was severe arthritis, for which they could offer no remedy. William Delaney's physician was present as was a stenographer he hired to transcribe the reading. However, Delaney refused to conduct the session, as his Catholicism did not allow him to call spirits.

A Jewish neighbor, Dave Kahn, was asked to facilitate. Edgar handed Dave the small black notebook that he and Layne had put together, and gave the young college student a short course in trance guidance. As the couch in the room was short and Edgar was long, he lay down on the floor. In trance, Edgar spoke of a horse and buggy accident in Fort Thomas, Kentucky; Amanda Fay had jumped from the carriage, injuring the base of her spine on the carriage step. Seven years later, the automobile accident exacerbated the earlier injury. Paralysis was the result. The treatment was osteopathic adjustments and various medications and compounds taken orally. A particular osteopath in Lexington was recommended. Dave Kahn went to the pharmacy to fill the prescriptions, and Edgar returned to Selma later that afternoon. Seven months later, Amanda Fay was sitting up and combing her hair. Nine months after that, at her birthday celebration, she walked. Eventually, she even drove.

Edgar and Dave Kahn bonded. Their friendship would span decades. Edgar read for the Kahn family often throughout 1914 and 1915. Dave's brother Leon was an epileptic. Unfortunately, the family could not find doctors willing to follow Edgar's directives for treatment, and Leon died. Dave's sister Eleanor contracted scarlet fever; this time, the Kahns found cooperative physicians. Eleanor recovered.

Once again, Edgar was succeeding as a photographer. With a series of commercial assignments including promotional shots for the Southern Railroad and layouts for a variety of grocery products, Edgar was doing well enough to buy his studio from the Tressler Company. Edgar's success was reflected in Gertrude's optimism as she and six-year-old Hugh Lynn arrived in Selma. Moreover, she would begin to play an active role in the trance work, although the circumstance which led to this was a family crisis of high magnitude.

On a cold January afternoon in 1914, a mischievous Hugh Lynn was playing with matches and flash powder in the studio. The prank he was planning took an explosive turn when a lit match head fell into a box of flash powder. Hugh Lynn screamed; his hair and face burned, and the boy could not see. The doctors converged. Vision in the right eye was gone, and the left was problematic at best. Specialists advised removal of the right eye.

In the aftermath of the accident, Gertrude conducted her first session. In trance, Edgar said that tannic acid should be added to the solution the doctor had applied to Hugh Lynn's eyes. He then specified a schedule for changing the dressings and a timeline for removing the bandages. Hugh Lynn would recover sight, Edgar stated, in both eyes. Though the specialist had reservations about the tannic acid, Edgar and Gertrude ignored him. In two weeks the bandages were removed, the burnt flesh fell away, and Hugh Lynn could see.

Not all of Edgar's sessions during this period were related to health. The Kahn family business was food warehousing and distribution; they had contracts to supply a number of schools and universities in the region. When Dave asked in a session about improving business, Edgar directed him to a Chicago warehouse which, in a production breakthrough, was packaging food in one gallon cans. Only one, two, and three pound cans had been available previously. In 1915, there were no mechanical can openers; opening cans to feed hundreds of students was time consuming and labor intensive. The Kahns, in a profitable arrangement, become distributors in Lexington for the Chicago company.

Dave's line of inquiry led to the question of his future in the family business. In response, Edgar spoke of a mighty change in the country. Dave would leave Lexington. It would not be voluntary, and the Kahn family would be unhappy with his leaving the flock. He would wear a uniform, going and returning in honor. In 1915, this made no sense; in 1917, its prophetic nature became clear.

In April of 1917, Dave Kahn was indeed in uniform. As conflict in Europe escalated, Dave was recruited for the U.S. Army in New York City. Edgar would provide trance counsel for Dave that would outline assignment options: one in the states, the other overseas. Edgar suggested Dave choose the European front, so Lt. Kahn went to France.

During the war years, Edgar received many requests for readings related to the conflict, including one from the wife of the American Counsel General in Italy. The reading was well received. Perhaps as a result of the Counsel General connection in Italy, Edgar was called to Washington D.C. Two trips were made to the nation's capital. Edgar would only refer to these trips as top secret and for someone high in authority. Years later, Dave Kahn identified President Woodrow Wilson as that someone. The subject of the readings for the President may have been the war, the League of Nations, or Wilson's own deteriorating health. In any case, the readings for the President were part of a dramatic trend, as the number of readings grew and Edgar's profile rose in the second decade of the twentieth century.

On February 9, 1918, Gertrude gave birth to a third son, Edgar Evans Cayce. The delivery was easy and the baby was healthy.

Oil

First Lieutenant Dave Kahn returned from Europe energized and exuberant, only to find an unfortunate situation. The family business, which had been solid when he enlisted, was now in debt. Recalling the reading in 1915, Dave began looking in other directions for his livelihood. Perhaps unsurprisingly, his line of sight went right through Edgar.

Dave invited Edgar to Lexington in April of 1919 to propose a partnership. They would offer psychic consultation for business interests. Though reluctant, Edgar nevertheless listened to his friend. Edgar mentioned a letter he had recently received from D. M. Thrash, a principal of the Sam Davis Petroleum Company in Cleburne, Texas. Thrash had read about the trance work in a New York Times article and inquired whether Edgar's skills could be used to locate oil underground.

Edgar had reservations and was inclined to disregard the request; Dave suggested he reconsider. The lieutenant's commission in France had been in the supply network for the war effort. Petroleum had been crucial for the transport of supplies, weapons, and troops during the conflict. Its importance for the developing peacetime industry of the twentieth century could not be overstated. Moreover, the number of automobiles in the United States was increasing exponentially. Several thousand cars had been on the roads at the turn of the century; by the end of the war, there were two million. Demand for oil reflected this exponential growth. Edgar again listened to his friend.

Thrash and his partners had drilled to a depth of 3,500 feet at a well site in Desdemona, Texas. While oil flowed at adjacent sites, it did not flow at theirs. Sam Davis Petroleum had spent $21,000 with no return. Edgar agreed to read for Thrash. The hole, he said, was not dry; he gave detailed instruction for opening the well and tapping oil. He provided precise geological data and placement position for explosives. Edgar quantified the quart measure of nitroglycerine needed for the breakthrough, as well as how many gallons of oil would flow. Dave Kahn was impressed. Thrash and his partners were impressed as well. The geological data regarding rock and sand formations was accurate; the rest of the reading made good sense. While the financing to resume drilling at the site was not, at that point, in place, the inclusion of Edgar and Dave in the Sam Davis Petroleum group was discussed. Dave proposed a trip to Texas. Edgar had hired a capable assistant for the studio in Selma. Gertrude did not object, and in July of 1919, Edgar and Dave left for Cleburne, Texas.

The imposing size of D. M. Thrash belied his accomplishments as a writer and local historian with an eclectic interest in Spiritualism and astrology. He had, for this reason, asked for Edgar's birth data in their correspondence. Thrash and his associates treated Edgar and Dave as touring celebrities. In the Sam Davis Group were Davis himself with holdings in land and cattle; Brown Douglas, factory owner for dry goods production; and Martin Sanders, veteran oil driller. Cleburne was a busy industrial city, twenty miles west of Dallas and Ft. Worth. Its population was 15,000 and growing. Thrash and his partners were part of the Cleburne economic and cultural elite. Their financial interests included newspaper publishing, banking, and urban transportation as well as oil.

Edgar and Dave traveled overnight by train to Comyn, known for its brothel and saloon. In the morning they traveled by buckboard wagon to Desdemona. Originally called Hogtown, due to its proximity to Hog Creek, this town was renamed in 1877 after the daughter of a local justice of the peace. The oil boom in Desdemona began in September of 1918, when oil was struck on land owned by Joe Duke. The well, named Joe Duke #1, caught fire. It burned for three days. Then, it gushed. Pumping was not necessary; it soon produced three thousand barrels a day. More than twenty other wells followed. Within a year, seven million barrels of oil had flowed, and Desdemona was booming.

Edgar and Dave saw rows and rows of metal shacks and tents, as well as a large mess hall. In the landscape were lines of drilling rigs, wooden derricks up to eighty feet high, pump jacks, and freight wagons. Smoke and steam clouded the air. Arriving at the site Edgar had read for the Davis group, they found only a wooden stake marking a capped drill hole filled with cement.

Before he returned to Alabama, Edgar read for another Cleburne oil interest. Joseph Long, executive for the Home National Bank, was a principal of the Lucky Boy Oil Company. Long requested a reading for Lucky Boy #2, another site in Desdemona that had not produced. Drilling had stopped at 3,500 feet. Edgar advised plugging the hole at 3,000 feet and exploding 150 quarts of nitroglycerine at that depth. The flow, he said, would stabilize at 600 barrels a day. In November, Long—frugal but short-sighted—shot fifty quarts of nitro into Lucky Boy #2 at the specified depth. Though there were traces of oil, the promised gush did not come to pass. Long asked for another reading; Edgar obliged. The message was to follow instructions. Another hundred quarts of nitro were shot into the hole. This time, the gush was spectacular.

Months before Joseph Long made Edgar a legend in Desdemona, he and Dave had returned to Alabama. Kahn astutely maintained his military commission. Through a connection to the Army Chief-of-Staff's office, he was able to secure an assignment to investigate the oil industry in Texas and the South in the interests of the Military. Dave then contacted Major Edwin Wilson, with whom he had served in Europe.

The Major, a cousin of President Woodrow Wilson, had decided to resign his commission and seek a position in the private sector. While Edwin had no experience in the oil industry, his brother Alf had been an executive for Sigma Oil, which had been bought out by Standard Oil. During the war, Edgar had read for Edwin who in turn may have played a role in Edgar's clandestine trips to Washington, D.C. While Dave was working to raise capital, Edwin traveled to Cleburne to examine the business records and lease agreements of Sam Davis Petroleum and begin discussions of a new partnership configuration. Edwin's family connections were not lost on Thrash and company. While Edgar chose not to be contractually included in the reconfigured partnership of Sam Davis Petroleum, his role as psychic consultant continued and was indeed crucial. Moreover, in the aftermath of Lucky Boy #2's gushing success, Edgar's return to Cleburne and Desdemona was triumphant.

This triumphant return was in January of 1920. Dave Kahn had raised sufficient funds to get himself appointed vice-president and managing director of the Sam Davis Petroleum Company, which was thus able to make a large capital investment in modern equipment. Edwin Wilson accompanied Dave and Edgar to Ardmore, Oklahoma, where they purchased a rotary drill, a steam-driven motor, a drill head, thousands of feet of pipe, and enough explosives for twenty wells. Dave was looking well beyond one Sam Davis well. Next on the agenda was finding a veteran driller. In trance, Edgar provided a name, a town, a hotel, and a room number. Cecil Ringle was dumbfounded when he opened the door of his hotel room in the small cattle town of Sprawn, Texas. He and his family were traveling from Illinois to Desdemona to look for work. Dave hired Cecil, his father, and his son. His wife, Leona, would cook. Profit-based incentives were part of their work contract.

The group reached Desdemona in February; by March the derrick was built. Edgar, recalling his time at his Uncle's farm, enjoyed taking part in the physical labor. With everything in place at the Sam Davis site, challenges began to proliferate. Equipment brought from Oklahoma disappeared. The cable from the motor to the drill broke. Pipes running water to the drill broke. Replacements took time and were costly. At 2,500 feet, the rotary drill bit hit an obstruction. An electromagnet brought up a barrel of nuts and bolts, chains, and a twisted drill bit head. Sabotage was not uncommon in the Desdemona oil fields. The Sam Davis site was evidently a target.

After a period of steady progress, a cable broke and a set of drilling tools plummeted to the bottom of the well hole. While Ringle succeeded in recovering the tools, tension permeated the site. Thrash and his partners suspected Dave Kahn of hidden agendas and misappropriation of funds; Kahn, disillusioned with the partnership, had been considering separate oil ventures. A trance session to sort out the projections and animosities did not work; Edgar fell asleep and did not wake until morning. On the following night, however, Edgar's reading was clear. Kahn was not mismanaging funds; rather, greed and self-interest had undermined the drilling operation. The alignment that supported the Sam Davis oil enterprise had been fractured by selfishness and the mental turbulence that followed. This reading restored neither calm nor harmony. Cecil Ringle accused Dave Kahn of hitting on his wife Leona, and drew a gun. Edgar stepped between the men. Though no shots were fired, the tension and animosity remained.

Edgar and Dave chose to disengage from Sam Davis Petroleum. Thrash and his partners were left with Cecil Ringle managing their well sites, and Cecil's contract had a generous profit-sharing clause on the first page. While Cecil was working late at the site, a partner visited Leona and asked to borrow their copy of the contract, telling her that the office copy had been misplaced. Leona was gullible, and handed it over. The partner returned with a rewritten first page. The next day Cecil was paid for services rendered and dismissed. He had no recourse; Thrash and his partners were City Fathers in Cleburne. The Ringle family left Desdemona.

The Edgar Cayce Petroleum Company emerged from the ashes at Desdemona. Edgar, Dave, and Edwin Wilson regrouped with the help of a small capital investment from Martin Sanders. A reading sent Edgar and Dave to Luling, a small town 40 miles south of Austin. They were driven by Joe Rush, a Desdemona driller. Years before, Rush had worked in Luling for Morris Raynor, a partner in a Detroit based oil company. Raynor, a Spiritualist, had been guided to Luling by a Detroit medium.

Raynor worked the Luling fields for years, but his persistence did not pay off; after a decade he relinquished the lease rights.

The information from Edgar's trance session was as sparse as Luling. They would find a man at the county courthouse in Lockhart, twenty miles north of Luling, and he would direct them. The Caldwell county judge was sitting on the courthouse steps when Edgar, Dave, and Joe Rush arrived. The elderly judge told them that oil was likely under land owned by an impoverished group of black farmers. A white woman, Minnie Phillips, was the farmers' protector. Leading with her shotgun, Minnie represented the black farmers' interests.

As Edgar, Dave, and Joe approached the farmhouse, a raised shotgun barrel peered out the door. Holding the gun, Minnie expressed her disinclination to speak to oilmen. Dave responded that he was in the Army and had come from Kentucky. Minnie's brother was a pharmacist in Lexington. The name of the pharmacist that filled Fay Delaney's prescription for young college student Dave Kahn had been Phillips; the synchronicity was not lost on either side of the door. Lowering her shotgun, Minnie invited them in.

After telegraphing her brother in Lexington, receiving a health reading from Edgar, and serving dinner, Minnie began to talk about oil in Luling. Oil, as it turned out, was there in abundance. On rainy days it permeated the ground and cattle would not drink from the shallow pools of water. In trance, Edgar corroborated Minnie, speaking of a sea of oil covered by a dome of salt underneath them. He described the two-pronged trunk of a nearby dead tree; thirty feet from the tree would be the drill site, three hundred feet down would be the oil. Edgar Cayce Petroleum purchased the lease rights to 5000 acres in Luling. The lease expired in 14 months. Oil profits would be shared with Minnie and the farmers. If they did not break ground in six months, however, the lease rights would be forfeited. The sad story for Edgar and Dave was that they could raise only enough capital for the lumber to build the derrick. In six months their lease rights were revoked.

The story for Minnie and the black farmers had a better ending. Edgar B. Davis, devout and intuitive, had gained and lost fortunes in the rubber business. A vision and a voice directed him to Luling. He drilled for several years with limited success, losing more than he made. Davis persisted, guided by faith to various locations. In early autumn of 1922, he penetrated the dome of salt and the sea of oil flowed. Minnie and the black farmers of Luling shared in his fortune.

Edgar Cayce Petroleum was stuck in a holding pattern. The company could finance leasing, but not drilling. Edgar and Dave decided to establish an itinerary for travel; at each urban stop, Edgar would offer readings. Compensation for the readings would generate revenue immediately, while highlighting the potential of Cayce Petroleum for investment.

Their first stop was Birmingham, Alabama. Their contacts were good going in, and the eighteen days there were lucrative. Their next stop, however, was not on the itinerary. Edgar's eye had become inflamed from a bouncing cinder and needed medical attention. The closest stop was Nashville. In the phonebook, Dave found a physician named E. B. Cayce who was, they discovered, a cousin of Tom Cayce, Edgar's grandfather. An invitation to lunch after the treatment turned into a two week visit with steady stream of readings, many for doctors.

At the end of the second week in Nashville, Edgar was called to Washington D.C. for the third time. Woodrow Wilson had suffered a debilitating stroke while campaigning for ratification of the League of Nations treaty. Edgar likely gave a reading for the President concerning his health. Edgar's connections to Woodrow Wilson were multiple. The President's cousin Alf—brother of Cayce Petroleum partner Edwin Wilson—was in D.C. at this time, and would subsequently accompany Edgar to New York City to meet Dave Kahn and continue their fundraising. The other link was Will Starling, head of the Secret Service. Starling, a boyhood friend of Edgar's in Hopkinsville, not only protected the President but was his close friend and confidant.

In New York City, Edgar stayed at the McAlpin Hotel, on 34th Street and Broadway. During the five months he stayed in New York, he gave a series of trance sessions for Dr. William McDougal, Hereward Carrington, and Harry Houdini. McDougal was Dean of Psychology at Harvard, friend and successor to Hugo Munsterberg. Carrington was a noted investigator of psychic phenomena, who would co-author an early classic on astral projection. Houdini, of course, escaped and debunked his way to fame. The sessions were conducted by Gordon Nicodemus, a securities executive who Dave Kahn had engaged to raise capital for the Cayce Petroleum Company. Carrington and McDougal were impressed;

Houdini was quiet. While the master magician did not invest in Cayce Petroleum, he did invite Edgar, as his guest, to attend Jack Dempsey's heavyweight Championship fight. Nicodemus was a fine facilitator for the sessions and a better fundraiser for Cayce Petroleum. When Edgar returned to Texas in May of 1921, it was with $50,000 in cash and $100,000 in promissory notes at the disposal of the oil company.

The Edgar Cayce Petroleum Company had been reconfigured and reoriented. Dave Kahn's role first declined and then virtually disappeared as his management style did not suit the new group of investors and company officers. Gordon Nicodemus now conducted the sessions, and Fay Autry, daughter of a shareholder, was hired as a stenographer. The readings located a spot ninety miles northwest of Luling for the company's first well. The information from the readings on the well site, called Rocky Pasture #1, was extensive, detailed, and precise. The derrick was constructed in May, and drilling began soon afterward.

Once again, however, problems developed quickly and occurred with alarming regularity. The first issue was a discrepancy between the geological data given in the readings and the samples taken from the well hole. Either the competency or integrity of the driller was in question, or Edgar was inaccurate. Next, a set of tools vanished; a second set, bought to replace the first, vanished as well. As there were no other sites in the area, the thieves had to be among the Cayce Petroleum workers. A tombstone found in the well hole several weeks later bore this out.

Finances were again becoming an issue. Investors were holding back on their promissory notes as progress on Rocky Pasture #1 had stalled. In June, Edgar decided to revisit the fundraising strategy he and Dave Kahn adopted after their failure in Luling. Accompanied by Nicodemus, Edwin Wilson, Alf Butler, and Fay Autry, Edgar visited Fort Worth, Atlanta, Denver, Little Rock, and New York City. During this period more shares in the company were issued, and then sold at a reduced price to raise capital. Edgar and his entourage returned to Rocky Pasture in December. Soon after, their fortunes seemed to turn. A mixture of oil and water gushed from the well, indicating their proximity to the real strike. That night, however, a coupling was dislodged and another set of tools vanished, this time to the bottom of the well. Drilling was once again delayed. By summer's end, the Cayce Petroleum Company, finances decimated, lost the lease rights to Rocky Pasture #1.

Edgar's readings on oil wells were no less detailed, extensive, and accurate than his readings on health. The problem in regard to the health readings was the arrogance and stubbornness of doctors after the reading was given. The problem in regard to the oil readings was the greed, deviousness, and corruption that lay in wait before the readings were given. Edgar's profile in Texas was such that any site that he or his company worked was a target for sabotage. Land leases had timelines; they expired. The oil underground had no timeline or expiration date; it would wait for the next lease, and benefit whoever secured it.

From Denver to Birmingham to Dayton

Frank Mohr visited Edgar at Rocky Pasture toward the end of the summer of 1922. Edgar reflected on Mohr's well-intentioned efforts in 1911 to build a Cayce Hospital in Nortonville, Kentucky. The timing, of course, was wrong, as Mohr was undermined by the devious and self-serving agendas of Wesley Ketchum and Albert Noe. Edgar had predicted Mohr would lose his sight without specific adjustments after spinal surgery; Mohr's doctors did not concur. Ten years later, Mohr was blind. In the reading that preceded the surgery, Edgar told Mohr that, if necessary, hydrotherapy would restore his vision. Ten years after the reading, Mohr finally followed instructions. The therapy was costly but effective. He could see, but his assets had been depleted by the medical costs. Nevertheless, his enthusiasm for Edgar's trance work and the dream of a hospital remained. Edgar accompanied Mohr back to his home in Columbus, Ohio, as they continued their discussion of the Cayce hospital.

Dave Kahn was in Denver working for B. D. Townsend, a lawyer who represented oil interests. Townsend's prominence gave Kahn access to the city's economic elite, which included Frederich Bonfils, publisher of the *Denver Post*. Dave spoke to Bonfils about Edgar. The publisher wanted to experience a reading and offered to cover expenses for a trip to Denver. Edgar brought Frank Mohr along. Edgar gave Bonfils a detailed and extensive health reading. He then diagnosed a patient Bonfils selected in front of a contingent of doctors.

Bonfils was astonished. On the spot, he offered to contract Edgar's services at a wage of $1,000 a day. The contract, however, had a distinct set of stipulations: a white silk costume and a turban; a chauffeured limousine with curtains always drawn; bodyguards at all times; a veil hiding Edgar's face during readings; and two appointments every day, one of which was reserved for Bonfils. The turban was too much for Edgar, and he declined the offer. He did, however, remain in Denver to give readings for Bonfils' children.

Perhaps miffed that Edgar had not accepted his proposal, Bonfils did not pay for the readings or cover the cost of the return trip. Edgar and Mohr had not planned for this. They did not have the fare for the railroad trip east. In desperate straits, Edgar and Mohr were rescued by a women's club in Birmingham, Alabama. Edgar received communication from the secretary of the Birmingham Women's Club inquiring about his fee for a speaking engagement. Edgar tallied the cost of railroad tickets from Denver to Birmingham and telegraphed his sum to the secretary. The fee was wired back to Denver, and Edgar and Mohr arrived in Birmingham on September 13.

Two years earlier, Birmingham had been on the itinerary for Edgar and Dave's Fundraising adventures. Friendly then, it was even friendlier now that Edgar's reputation preceded him. The demand for readings was immediate and intense. Frank Mohr conducted the sessions; Fay Autry arrived in November to transcribe. In his 10th floor suite at the Tutweiler Hotel, Edgar gave 240 readings over a four month period, an unprecedented number. Edgar had grown to see the psychic work as his vocation and occupation.

Edgar's first reading in Birmingham was for William Darling, a two-year-old from Dayton, Ohio. In Denver, the doctors' diagnosis for the boy was terminal Lymphosarcoma. The distraught family had met Dave Kahn on the train east. Dave told them about Edgar. While William and his mother returned to Dayton, Alfred Darling went to Birmingham. In the reading, Edgar said that a drug had been given to dilate the uterus during labor. Residues of that drug were trapped in William's system; furthermore, the severance of the umbilical cord had not been clean. Edgar prescribed injections of atropine.

Edgar was becoming very comfortable in Birmingham. The acceptance and warmth of the people there touched him. A minor challenge came from the city authorities regarding medical licensing. A committee of doctors testified that Edgar was not practicing medicine, he was only advising. Clearly the physicians of Birmingham valued Edgar's advice. This appreciation—even adulation—in Birmingham translated into pledges of financial support for a hospital. This had become Edgar's overriding vision. In January of 1923, a session was held to determine a Birmingham site for the Cayce Hospital. Edgar was not prepared for what came through. Birmingham did not, over time, suit Edgar's trance work. Proximity to a large body of water was required. Virginia Beach, a small town on the coast of Virginia, was named as the appropriate site. This was not, in fact, a total surprise; thirteen years earlier, in a reading given in Anniston, Alabama, Virginia Beach had been named as the location which best complemented Edgar's service. Moreover, in that same reading, Dayton, Ohio was noted as the place the Work would truly begin.

Edgar revisited oil. Though his overriding vision was the Cayce Hospital, it needed financing. The return for health readings could support Edgar and his family, but the return for oil readings could build a hospital. Cayce Petroleum retained the lease rights to 25,000 Texas acres. Edgar went to Cleburne in March. By the end of the month he was in Meridian, Texas, talking to William Tex Rice, owner of the Penn-Tenn Company. The leases of Cayce Petroleum were transferred to Penn-Tenn. Tex Rice would recruit investors. Dave Kahn would administrate. Edgar would read. It was an unfortunate alliance. Tex Rice was opportunistic, persuasive, and corrupt. He would be indicted for land fraud within months. Tex Rice went down, and Penn-Tenn soon followed.

In June, Edgar traveled to Dayton. William Darling, now three, was recovering with the prescribed treatments. The symptoms of his cancer, numerous nodules on his body, were almost gone. While Edgar was in Dayton, William, playing by the swimming pool, fell. One of the remaining growths was struck in the fall and quickly expanded in size. Edgar immediately read for the boy, and prescribed as osteopathic procedure. The treatments were not carried out effectively. The boy had another fall. The osteopath was unfamiliar with the techniques Edgar proposed; within days, William was dead. Discord between the Darlings and Alfred Darling's alcoholism were the backdrop for the tragedy.

Edgar remained in Dayton through the middle of August. He stayed at the Phillips Hotel, giving readings in his hotel room. His stenographer, Fay Autry, joined him there. Edgar had befriended William Darling's godfather, Linden Schroyer. Schroyer had witnessed the trance sessions concerning his godchild. Following the boy's death, Edgar asked Schroyer to conduct the readings given during his stay in Dayton. Schroyer was an accountant. His employer was Arthur Lammers, owner of a large printing company. Schroyer told Lammers about Edgar. The wealthy printer asked for a reading, and Edgar agreed.

Lammers' initial questions pertained to business investments. Likely oil was discussed in and out of trance. Tex Rice had not yet been indicted; Penn-Tenn was still seeking investors. Lammers, however, was primarily interested in pursuing another line of inquiry. He and his wife Zelda had a deep interest in esoteric philosophy and metaphysics. They had studied the Theosophical literature and were well acquainted with the works of Helena Blavatsky. The library in their Victorian mansion was filled with books and manuscripts whose subject matter ranged from astrology and alchemy to yoga and eastern spirituality.

The first reading in the Lammers series was in June. In trance, Edgar spoke about body, mind, and spirit as the human trinity. Lammers asked about the soul. The response was that the soul left and returned to its maker, and the bond between soul and maker was not broken by death. Lammers asked about the accuracy of the information from the readings; the response was that the conductor and the person whose issues are addressed influence the process. Lammers asked if spirit communication was possible. An affirmative response included reference to the spirits proximity and eventual return to the physical plane.

Gladys Davis

By the third week of August, Edgar was back in Selma, reorganizing a storeroom in the Cayce Art Studio. He would store transcripts and give readings in the redecorated studio space. Fay Autry was in Houston and about to get married; Edgar needed a new stenographer. This was not a simple job—transcribing the sessions was challenging. The language of the readings ranged from sophisticated medical terminology to scientific geological data to the vocabulary of stock and commodities trading to metaphysical concepts. Furthermore, while in trance, Edgar spoke rapidly. The job interview was transcribing a reading for Virgil Graham, a three-year-old with a nervous disorder. On August 30, a dozen applicants sat in Edgar's converted studio space.

Virgil's aunt, Willie Graham, managed the chinaware department at Tissier's Hardware. Willie asked Gladys Davis, the stenographer at Tissier's, to transcribe a clairvoyant reading on her nephew's condition. Gladys, tall and blond, was the eldest of five siblings. Her father farmed peanuts. Her grandfather's cousin had been Jefferson Davis, president of the short-lived Confederacy. At 14, Gladys had enrolled in Business College to learn typewriting skills; at 15, she was working at a drugstore located on the floor beneath the Cayce Art Studio. During her time at the drugstore, she often noticed the Cayce family going up the stairs to their studio. Edgar was drilling for oil in Texas during this period. On a rare visit to Selma, however, he walked into the drugstore. Miss Gladys greeted him with a familiar, perhaps flirtatious, good morning. Gladys remembered the greeting.

As it turned out, Edgar remembered it as well. Though the room was cluttered with stenographers, Edgar recognized Gladys and smiled. His instructions stressed accuracy in transcription. Leslie conducted the session; Gladys focused. The medical terminology coming from Edgar was unfamiliar and unusual. Gladys stayed focused. There was really no competition—Gladys became Edgar's stenographer. It was a permanent position.

Metaphysics in Dayton

A week after Gladys was hired, Arthur Lammers visited Edgar in Selma. Lammers proposed a partnership and an enterprise: The Cayce Institute for Psychical Research. Under the mantle of the Institute, they could pursue oil ventures, the hospital, and a publishing company. He and other investors would provide initial funding. Shares of stock would be sold to increase the capital base. The Cayce Petroleum Company and Penn-Tenn would be reconfigured and repopulated on the management level. Lammers, after a few days in Selma, traveled to Meridian, Texas to meet with principals of Cayce Petroleum. Edgar, being Edgar, went with him. Gertrude and Gladys began to review and reorganize the archives of transcripts in the Cayce studio. Gertrude received a letter from Edgar several weeks later. He had commenced another fund-raising tour, giving readings and lectures in Chicago. Edgar asked if she and Gladys would meet him in Dayton, his next stop.

In Dayton, Edgar rented an apartment on East Fifth Street and a room at the Phillips Hotel for trance sessions. Before Gertrude and Gladys arrived, Edgar began the series of readings for Lammers that opened the metaphysical dimension in the trance work. In early October, Lammers asked for an astrological reading. He was not disappointed.

In trance, Edgar spoke fluently about the influences of the planets, emphasizing their angular positions and house placements. In Lammers' chart, Jupiter was emphasized, as was the placement of Venus in the eleventh house. More detail and character analysis followed. A few days after the reading, Lammers took Edgar to New York City to meet Evangeline Adams. Descendent of two Presidents, Evangeline had studied Astrology at Boston University. She had an international reputation and a client base that included movie stars, opera singers, championship prizefighters, British royalty, and the president of the New York Stock Exchange. Evangeline read Edgar's horoscope.

There was some unusual nuance to the astrological framework of Edgar's readings. He spoke of the soul residing on different planets in the Solar System. This accounted for that planet's influence on behavior and character. Moreover, the time at which the soul united with the physical body was astrologically important, but did not necessarily coincide with birth. In addition, he integrated a planet he called Septimus in the readings; this was likely a reference to Pluto, which would not be discovered by astronomers until 1930. As the Lammers readings continued through October into November, the exploration of astrology was followed by reincarnation and karma. The dramas of past lives and their relevance to the present one added a fascinating and compelling element to the life readings.

On November 14, Gertrude, Edgar Evan, and Gladys arrived in Dayton. Edgar took his family to the Phillips Hotel, where they settled until furniture arrived for the two-room apartment. Edgar was captivated by the elements of reincarnation that had entered his readings. As Gertrude and Gladys reviewed the transcripts of the sessions detailing Lammers astrological influences and past lives, they were intrigued. On November 19, Edgar gave a reading for his five-year-old son. In the session planetary influences and four incarnations were outlined for Edgar Evan. Readings for Gladys, Linden Schroyer and Gertrude followed in the next few weeks. In each case, the present life was viewed from the perspective of past life influences: skills, challenges and relationships had histories extending back centuries—indeed, millennia—into the past.

Gertrude and Gladys began to share Edgar's enthusiasm.

As December approached, however, Arthur Lammers grew strangely quiet. There were no further requests for readings. Communication was sparse and what little there was came through Linden Schroyer. By

January 1924, Lammers' silence spoke loudly. Under the influence of an expansive Jupiter, he had bought out smaller competitors through the past year, a business strategy which left Lammers overextended. Then he lost his largest account, the National Cash Register Company, in a dispute with the son of NCR's founder. The printing magnate was imploding financially. Bankruptcy for Lammers' Printing and Engraving was around the corner. Lammers would lose his company, his mansion, and his automobiles. Edgar would lose his financial lifeline. Without Lammers' support, Cayce Petroleum and Penn-Tenn went down as well.

Edgar was not in Birmingham, Selma, or Nashville; in Dayton, there was no church congregation, no extended family to aid him. He was completely isolated. Health readings, Edgar's sole source of income, covered rent on the two-room apartment, paid enough of the hotel bill to avoid arrest for non-payment of the balance, and fed the family meagerly once a day. When 16 year old Hugh Lynn arrived at the train station for Christmas, his school semester over, he was unaware of his of his family's plight. Embracing his father, he felt the bunched up newspaper under the Edgar's jacket. In the brutally cold Dayton winter, Hugh Lynn got the message. Yet the mood at the apartment was upbeat; the Christmas dinner table buzzed with talk of past lives and the expanding reach of the trance work. In fact, Hugh Lynn's Christmas present was the transcription of a reincarnation reading that Edgar had given for his eldest son two weeks earlier. At the time, Hugh Lynn was dumbfounded and distressed. Years later, however, in writings on reincarnation, he would call this aspect of his father's work one of the great gifts in his father's legacy.

The hardship continued into February of 1924. Linden Schroyer suggested Edgar read for himself. Despite some initial reticence, Edgar eventually lay down on February 9 on the couch in his room at the Phillips Hotel. Over the next seven days, Edgar spoke, in trance and at length, about himself. Gertrude did not attend the sessions. Early in the reading, an inclination toward secretive and intimate affairs was brought up. While Schroyer may have been surprised, Gertrude, if she had been in the room, would likely not have shared his reaction. She knew of Edgar's friendship with Margaret, the tobacco heiress from Louisville. Indeed the deterioration of Gertrude's health, during Edgar's time at the J.P. Morton Company, reflected the developing bond between her fiancé and Margaret.

Gertrude was also aware of Fay Autry. In 1921, Edgar had hired the young and vibrant Fay as a stenographer for the trance sessions at the

Rocky Pasture well site in San Saba County. She was in the entourage that accompanied Edgar on the fund-raising tour in the summer of that year. Fay traveled with Edgar to Ft. Worth, Atlanta, Denver, Little Rock, and New York City while Gertrude stayed home in Selma with the boys. In September of 1922, Edgar arrived in Birmingham; Fay joined him there as stenographer in November. When Edgar began to give readings in Dayton at the Phillips Hotel in 1923, Fay came there as well.

Edgar's relationships with Margaret and Fay supported the reading. His emotional intimacy with both women resonated with some sexual tension, but his Christian faith provided a counterbalance tempering the expression of the intimacy. Consummated or not, however, the affairs were undoubtedly real, expressed in the emotional bonding—and they would continue with Gladys, who had been hired to replace Fay.

Finally the reading spoke of Edgar's previous incarnations: a British soldier, trained in Canada, who died close to Dayton; a member of the French court during the time of Cardinal Richelieu; Xenon, a Greek sculptor and warrior who defended Troy; a prominent warrior and leader in Persia; and Ra Ta, an Egyptian high priest during the dynasty of Ramses. The incarnational dramas of Edgar's family, friends, and associates would be interwoven with his own narratives. Indeed, Edgar, Gladys, Gertrude, Hugh Lynn, and Edgar Evan would be mesmerized, challenged, and perhaps scandalized by the permutations of the bonds among them over the ages.

Better Days

Though it seemed the Cayces had hit rock bottom in Dayton, they survived. Fifty dollars from a friend in Chicago settled the bill at the Hotel Phillips, and one hundred dollars from an Oklahoma oilman with an interest in Rocky Pastures allowed Edgar and his family to relocate to a larger apartment on Grafton Avenue. Slowly, incrementally, their fortunes began to turn.

Early in 1924, an auto parts manufacturer named Tim Brown contacted Edgar. The two had met during Edgar's first stay in Dayton, and Brown was recently returned from California. He offered Edgar two avenues of interest: screenwriting, and technological innovation. A series of sessions produced two extended plot outlines for screenplays. The first roughly paralleled Edgar's life, though in this fictional retelling he was now Abe, a handyman whose psychic skills were discovered by New York socialites. The second was about archaeologists, Incas, and Peruvian gold. Neither story, however, ever made it to the screen.

The technological opportunities proved more viable. Brown was focused on creating a device that would eliminate static on radio broadcasts. Over months of readings, beginning in May, Edgar provided data on designing tubes for this "static eliminator". He also gave Brown information on companies which could properly produce the advanced technology. Brown followed instructions only up to the point of production—he chose not to heed Edgar's recommendations on choosing companies and laboratories. The project did not succeed, as had often been the case when Edgar's readings were disregarded. Nevertheless, Brown expressed his appreciation to Edgar by facilitating Hugh Lynn's acceptance with full scholarship to an elite school in Dayton.

By July, Linden Schroyer had moved to Florida, seeking employment and hoping to renew his association with Arthur Lammers. During a session he had been advised not to go, but chose to disregard the warning. With Schroyer gone, Gertrude began conducting the readings.

Edgar was upbeat. Through Lammers' initiative his readings had taken a spiritual turn, which Edgar felt had great potential for widening his field of service. The Cayce Institute for Psychic Research was on his mind. Like the hospital, however, creating the Institute would require capital and business expertise which Edgar lacked. He would find both in the person of Morton Blumenthal.

Morton Blumenthal

In June of 1924, Dave Kahn was at the Plaza Hotel in New York City pitching a furniture company alliance to 29-year-old stockbroker, Morton Blumenthal. At some point in the evening Blumenthal's interest in psychic phenomena came up in conversation, as did Kahn's connection to Edgar Cayce. Somewhat skeptical, Morton noted the trend in fraudulent mediums being exposed. Dave defended the legitimacy of Edgar's skills, offering to pay for a reading if Morton was not satisfied with the information he received. Morton agreed, but suggested that his girlfriend—a Broadway chorus girl named Miriam Miller—should receive the reading instead.

Two days later, Morton received the transcript in the mail. Edgar diagnosed Miriam with anemia, and suggested adding certain nuts and vegetables to the diet, and inhaling apple brandy fumes. The diagnosis proved accurate, and the remedy worked; impressed, Miriam requested several more readings, one of which involved past lives. Morton wrote to Edgar expressing his appreciation. In August, Edgar read for Morton twice, each reading increasing Morton's interest in Edgar and his abilities. Dave Kahn, now living in New York City, pleaded with Edgar to come east to meet Morton. The stockbroker offered to cover expenses for the trip, and in October Edgar boarded the train to New York City.

Edgar was impressed. Charismatic, visionary, and practical, Morton, who had been born in Altoona, Pennsylvania, had overcome the early death of his father, working during the day to support his mother and taking classes at The University of Pittsburgh and then at Columbia University in the evening. A degree in economics had won him a job at a brokerage house. Morton's younger brother Edwin followed him into the world of finance. A ghostly visitation had spurred Morton's interest in psychic phenomena, and led him to expand his research into the contemporary metaphysics of Ouspensky and Bergson.

Edgar spent ten days in New York City, reading for Morton and his brother, Edwin. Astrological readings were followed by reincarnation narratives. Morton's reading revealed that he had been a gatekeeper in Jerusalem, a sage in Egypt, and Achilles at Troy. Troy linked him through the readings to Edgar, Lammers, and Schroyer; in Egypt, he was again linked to Edgar, as well as to Gladys, Gertrude, and Hugh Lynn.

In November, Morton traveled to Dayton. Disturbed by the impoverished state of the Cayce household, he went to the market and splurged. The Cayces enjoyed an uncommonly large dinner that evening. Before leaving Dayton, Morton extended an invitation for the Cayce family and Gladys to visit him in New York City in January. Delighted, they gladly accepted.

Morton spared no expense for his guests. They stayed at an upscale hotel, dined in style, danced at the Silver Slipper nightclub, and saw a risqué Broadway show. During the visit, Morton asked Edgar for a reading about Adeline Levy, a young woman from New Orleans with whom he had become infatuated. A sophisticated world traveler, fluent in French, Adeline was skeptical in regard to psychic phenomena and disinterested in metaphysics. Morton was in love, but troubled. To Morton's relief, Edgar was positive about the relationship in the reading, even fitting Adeline into the Trojan narrative, identifying her as Helen of Troy. After some prodding by Morton, Adeline consented to a reading. After the third session she was converted, and Morton and Adeline married in June.

Morton had become a convert six months before Adeline. Now he assumed a different role: benefactor. He retained Edgar for fifty dollars a week with the expectation—but not the obligation—of readings for himself and his brother. Gladys would receive twenty-five dollars a week to transcribe the readings.

Virginia Beach

Edgar's readings had long been pointing him toward Virginia Beach; during a session in Anniston, Alabama, in 1910, Edgar had been asked about the optimal location for trance work, and Virginia Beach had been the unambiguous answer. In a Birmingham reading in 1923, focused on choosing a location to host the Cayce Hospital in that friendly and supportive Alabama city, he had again been directed to Virginia.

Morton Blumenthal paid attention to the recommendation, and in the fall of 1925, rented a two-story cottage a short distance from the Virginia shore. By the end of October, Edgar, Gertrude, Gladys, Hugh Lynn, and Edgar Evans had settled into their new home.

The Stock Market

In trance, Edgar reciprocated the generosity Morton Blumenthal continually showed toward his family. During the mid-to-late 1920s, Morton consistently requested readings analyzing the stock market and suggesting investment strategies. The sessions advised investing in about two dozen companies, including General Electric, Atlantic Gulf, Chrysler Motors, and IBM. Point fluctuations of specific stocks over determined time periods were accurately predicted, to within one or two points of the actual stock movement. Edgar's readings also supplied information on major shareholders' and CEOs' hidden motives, helping predict and explain their future investment strategies. Following Edgar's advice, the Blumenthal brothers were millionaires by the end of the decade.

In the stocks and commodities trance work, a new precedent emerged that would drastically alter the form of future readings. Four deceased individuals identified themselves as sources of the information conveyed during the sessions: Morton and Edwin's father, August Blumenthal; Marcus Loew, movie producer and owner of a chain of theaters; Elbert Gary, executive of U.S. Steel; and Felix Fuld, a founder of the Bamberger department store chain. The Blumenthals' father had died in 1919; the other three only had recently passed over.

In the tradition of Spiritualism, a channel for discarnate entities is known as a medium. Mediums tend to communicate messages from a variety of sources, much as Edgar Cayce did in this episode. As the extensive body of his trance work up to this point is considered—a range of topics that continued to broaden through the next phase of Edgar's life— it is clear that the multiplicity of his channeled sources was nothing new, though the identification of deceased individuals was unprecedented. Each type of reading—medical diagnostics and treatments, oil well locations, locating buried treasure, stock market analysis, astrological perspective, and reincarnation narratives—called for specialized expertise.

New Sources Speak

The Cayces' new home in Virginia Beach became the backdrop for increased variety in the subject matter of Edgar's trance work. Extensive sets of readings detailed the life of Jesus, and the rise and fall of the civilization of Atlantis. Dream analysis, particularly for the Blumenthal brothers, Gladys, and the Cayce family, were explored as well. Sophisticated technological data for the development of a perpetual motion motor was offered. Edgar also began to report a series of prophetic visions of the future: social, cultural, political, technological, and catastrophic predictions were made. The diversity of the sources underlying Edgar's trance work was confirmed, as more sources began to identify themselves. This included angelic beings; a forceful and belligerent Michael, as well as an authoritative Halaliel, identified themselves in group sessions.

The multiplicity of Edgar's sources, and the variety of topics on which they spoke, complicate the issue of credibility. While medical readings, analysis of drilling sites for oil, and stock market investment strategies could be evaluated empirically, these less concrete readings—reincarnation narratives, Atlantian history, prehistoric human origins, and hidden details in the life of Jesus—were another matter.

In and out of trance, Edgar Cayce's life was unmistakably modern. His interests were practical and progressive—tobacco, photography, oil, stocks and commodities, and bookselling—and his spiritual readings on astrology, reincarnation, and esoteric history reflected the growing public interest in these subjects.

Before his death in 1945, Edgar gave over 14,000 documented readings in full trance, filling fifty thousand transcribed pages. His results speak for the depth and accuracy of the knowledge he transmitted in his sessions. Between this unparalleled number and the wide range of topics upon which he spoke, it is easy to see why Edgar Cayce is the fourth major channel of New Age spirituality.

Jane Roberts and Seth

Beginning in 1966, Jane Roberts published a series of books integrating material from a discarnate entity calling himself Seth. Following a book on ESP with three volumes— *The Seth Material, Seth Speaks*, and *The Nature of Personal Reality*—Jane and Seth established themselves as a channel–source tandem by offering a compelling overview of the human psyche and a perspective on social dynamics and historical unfolding. The process began with a Ouija board, and evolved through clairaudient reception of a voice, to a trance state in which Seth would inhabit Jane's body and speak. Jane's husband, Robert Butts, would listen and record. Over time, Seth spoke volumes.

The quality of the material produced through the Jane–Robert–Seth collaboration legitimized the channeling process for the last quarter of the twentieth century. The majority of the Seth books were published in the 1970s, providing a timely precedent for the wave of channeling into the next decade. Furthermore, the popularity and commercial success of the Seth books—along with Carlos Castaneda's literary accounts of his apprenticeship with Yaqui shaman, Don Juan—spurred a general wave of interest in New Age subjects that continues into the twenty-first century.

Though her role in establishing the channeling paradigm was less foundational than the four previously named channels, it was no less formative. Jane died in 1984; the demand for the Seth books is still strong. For bringing the art of channeling forward into the modern age, Jane Roberts deserves recognition as the fifth major channel of the New Age.

CRYSTALS AND CHANNELING: PERSPECTIVE

These five channels—Emmanuel Swedenborg, Helena Blavatsky, Alice Bailey, Edgar Cayce, and Jane Roberts—share a degree of validity which sets them apart from many of their peers. The validation of their sources followed the quality and value of what came through the channels. Indeed, the quality and value of what came through these individuals was such that it transformed the topography of the modern New Age.

This transformed topography, however, invested a mystique in the channeling process itself. It also supported a tendency to elevate the source, thus also elevating the channel and endowing the channeled material with the authority of the source's status rather than the quality of its content. This tendency played through the ascendancy of the Besant–Leadbeater regime in the Theosophical Society, and reached dizzying depths in the banal and self-serving writings of Elizabeth Clare Prophet and others. It also underscored the proliferation of channels in the 1980s. Over time, quality tends to be sorted out. Much of the channeled material that played through the eighties has, at this time, no appeal and no audience.

Crystals and channels intersected in the 1980s. The chakra–color–crystal alignments were sorted out into seven lists of varying length. The astrological grouping of crystals generally worked through sun signs. In this case there are twelve lists, which may vary from book to book. In some books the lists are short; in others, they are quite long, with the same crystal associated with multiple signs. Beyond the chakra system and the astrological associations, channeled sources assign function and attributes to the hundreds of crystals and minerals available in the New Age marketplace.

Channeling finally is a process, and a source of information. Without an act of faith, this information may be fairly described as speculation. In regard to crystal sales in modern New Age retail, this speculation is literally on the money.

Crystal Availability in the New Age

In the modern New Age, the evolution of the crystal market began with quartz points. Plentiful yet uncommon, these crystals are white to transparent with a range of clarity, from milky and opaque to stunning translucence. Quartz points are distinctively formed, with six elongated rectangular sides, which incline and terminate through six triangular facets to one point. Though this is a standard shape, there is sufficient nuance and variation in this geometry to support expanding nomenclature and a number of distinctive narratives. Quartz crystals are marketed individually, or as clusters of points embedded in a matrix or material base. The primacy of clear quartz in the New Age market was reflected in the dozen books exclusively on clear quartz published in the '80s and '90s.

Amethyst followed quartz quite literally; it is a quartz-based mineral with traces of iron integrated in the silicon oxygen mix. The iron shifts the color to purple and violet hues, and tends to reconfigure the shape. Brazil, a rich source of clear quartz, has an abundance of amethyst as well. The Brazilian amethyst points favor six smooth facets leading to the tip. The sides are striated and uneven, narrow at the base and lacking the depth of color found around the facets and tip. Amethyst, like clear quartz, is marketed both in single points and in cluster form.

Rose Quartz, following clear quartz and amethyst in the New Age market, is comprised of silicon and oxygen as well, with traces of titanium, iron, and manganese shifting the color to pink. Unlike clear quartz and amethyst, rose quartz rarely forms in geometrical planes. It is mined in massive chunks and broken down, generally marketed in bigger and smaller pieces.

Crystals are defined by a regular and repetitive molecular structure; a *lattice*. The aggregate of latticed molecules may form a visibly geometrical shape, as in clear quartz and amethyst, or it may not, as in rose quartz.

For rougher crystalline material, the lapidary process of tumbling is often employed to create a more appealing specimen. Tumbling involves a lined barrel, abrasive grit, and liquid lubricant. The barrel rotates and, in a series of stages, the rough chunks are contoured and polished, enhancing the aesthetics and tactile quality of the rough mineral. The tumbled stones produced are small, inexpensive, and easy to display. The expansive range of minerals and crystals marketable as tumbled stones is significant.

In any case, the aesthetic appeal of crystals and mineral specimens is indisputable. The resonance of crystals, their therapeutic value, and ability to transform space may be questioned, but these ideas are clearly compelling for those who position crystals and minerals within their worlds, personal and social.

Bibliography and Suggestions for Further Reading

Windows of Light

Windows of Light, by Randall Baer and Vicki Vittitow Baer, was published in 1984 by Harper and Row. One of perhaps a dozen books focused exclusively on quartz crystals, *Windows of Light* combined metaphysics, sacred geometry, and usage techniques and exercises. This book is an accessible 160 pages, formatted into seven chapters with sixteen diagrams interspersed in the text and an extensive, sophisticated bibliography. *Windows of Light*, one of the few New Age crystal publications from a major publisher, was a commercial hit. The Baers were established as New Age aristocracy, just as interest in crystals was spiking in the mid-eighties. In 1986, a sequel titled *The Crystal Connection* was published. Longer and denser, it lacked the accessibility of its predecessor. This shortcoming was reflected in its sales. Moreover, the expanding variety of crystals and minerals entering the New Age market reduced the commercial appeal of literature limited to quartz.

Crystal Enlightenment

In 1985, *Crystal Enlightenment* by Katrina Raphaell was published by Aurora Press. Thirty pages detailing varieties of quartz crystals were followed by seventy-five pages divided among twenty-three different minerals. Raphaell's choices were astute in regard to availability and general familiarity. The book, 170 pages, with a glossy and vivid cover, was packaged well by Aurora, a fine mid-sized New Age publisher with a backlist including works by Elizabeth Haich, Mantak Chia, and astrologer Dane

Rudhyar. Raphaell followed *Crystal Enlightenment* with *Crystal Healing* in 1986. Seventy pages devoted to various formations in the quartz family were followed by narratives pertaining to eight other minerals. A third title, *Crystalline Illumination*, completed the trilogy. In this book, narratives for fifteen minerals precede and follow eighty pages describing nuances in formations of clear quartz crystals. In all of her books, Katrina explores the technique of laying-on-of-stones: that is, the placement of various crystals on the body in alignment with the chakra system.

Raphaell's attunement to the mineral kingdom was reflected in the commercial success of *Crystal Enlightenment* and its sequels. Demand tended to increase for the crystals and minerals discussed in the trilogy. In the case of a particular type of quartz formation—generally known as skeleton or alligator quartz and designated Elestials by Katrina—demand spiked with her Elestial narrative in *Crystal Healing*, with wholesale cost for these crystals quadrupling and retail prices rising astronomically.

Love is in the Earth

In 1995, Melody published *Love is in the Earth: A Kaleidoscope of Crystals*. In 700 pages of almost pure text, seven hundred crystals and minerals had narratives; in comparison, only fifty different minerals figured in Katrina Raphaell's trilogy. The initial *Kaleidoscope* was followed by several more books: two pictorial and supplemental volumes; a book on laying-on-of-stones; an anecdotal, biographical book; a Tarot Deck; and a masterwork with narratives for 1400 crystals and minerals in one thousand pages, retailing for $100.

The volume of Melody's channeled narratives had major ramifications through the mineral market. The limitations of brick-and-mortar retailers in accessing and capitalizing the variety of stones expanded the scope of internet trade. However, the range of minerals with metaphysical narratives—and thus value in the trade—increased exponentially.

The pure text and encyclopedic length of the initial *Kaleidoscope* served the reader well after acquiring the crystal. While it was something of an accomplishment to find a crystal not covered by Melody in her first book—and an even greater accomplishment with the *Love is in the Earth* masterwork—neither of these encompassing reference works were conducive to cover-to-cover reads as were *Windows of Light* and *Crystal Enlightenment*.

Crystal Bible

In 2003, Judy Hall's *Crystal Bible* was published in England by Godsfield Press. Hall had established her astrological credentials in the 1990s with works exploring Moon–Pluto dynamics and the nexus of astrology, as well as karma and reincarnation. Her hermetic mentor had been Christine Hartley, whose lineage in turn traced back to Dion Fortune.

Hall's first book on crystals, *The Illustrated Guide to Crystals*, published in 2000, was followed by *The Crystal User's Handbook* in 2002. Her third crystal book was *The Crystal Bible*. For Judy, the third time was indeed a charm. Brilliantly packaged and formatted, *The Crystal Bible* quickly became the resource of choice in a resurgent New Age crystal market. A compact 5.6 by 6.6 inches, one inch thick, the book was exceptionally user-friendly: easy to carry and easy to use as a reference tool. At 400 pages, the encyclopedic volume supplied perhaps 250 crystal narratives. At least half of the first page of each narrative was headed by a prominent photographic image of the crystal with a boxed and highlighted chart providing data on color, appearance, rarity, and source underneath the crystal image. Organized text, divided into sections on attributes, healing, and position followed.

The commercial success of *The Crystal Bible* spawned a series of Bible packages from Godsfield Press, covering a range of New Age subjects. Judy herself composed the astrology volume. Currently more than thirty Godsfield Bibles have been published, on topics ranging from angels to Reiki to secret societies to sacred sex. All the volumes have the same compact dimensions. Consistency for height, width, cover format, and price point for a series of books sharing some thematic link is a common strategy for publishers. Within the New Age arena, Thames and Hudson worked this technique effectively in their superb *Arts and Imagination* series; Element Books had an extensive *Elements of...* series; Llewellyn publishes a set of *Beginner's Guides*; and Weiser/Red Wheel currently offers a number of *Concise Guides*. What is unique about the Bible series from Godsfield is the consistent length of 400 pages for every volume. This consistent page length pattern may be unique in the history of series publishing, dating back to John, Mark, Luke, and Matthew.

The Crystal Bible 2 was published in 2009, with another 250 narratives. The five hundred narratives in Judy Hall's two-volume encyclopedia are only half of the number offered by Melody in her $100 Masterwork. Nonetheless, as reference sources, the *Bibles* and *Kaleidoscopes* coexist comfortably. Moreover, Hall's text seems to derive from Melody's narratives in a number of instances.

The *Crystal Bibles* are distributed in North America with the imprint of Walking Stick Press. Several other 400 page volumes in the Godsfield biblical canon are also available through Walking Stick and Sterling Publications. Judy Hall has at least a dozen crystal books published at this point, while Melody has only seven, and Katrina Raphaell (with the recent self-published *Crystalline Illumination*) has four books in print. Moreover, Judy Hall is one of the few authors of crystal literature whose résumé of published work extends beyond books on the mineral kingdom. To her credit, in *The Soulmate Myth*, she has offered an ambivalent and thus balanced assessment of a generally romanticized notion generally embedded in the fluffy periphery of the New Age.

Books about Quartz

Quartz is the prototype, paradigm, and prime image of the crystal. Translucent, geometrical, elongated, aesthetic: quartz formations are generally visually interesting, often compelling, and on occasion stunning. Quartz is comprised of silicon and oxygen—silicon dioxide. Formed ages ago, quartz crystals have a magical ambience, a vibratory quality. Quartz literature is primarily about tools, techniques, and grids.

Quartz Crystals for Healing and Meditation
Philip W. Burbutis
Universarium Foundation • 1983 • Out of Print

Cosmic Crystals
Crystal Consciousness and the New Age
Ra Bonewitzo
Turnstone Press • 1983 • Out of Print

Windows of Light
Quartz Crystals and Self-Transformation
Randall N. Baer & Vicki V. Baer
Harper & Row • 1984 • Out of Print

The Crystal Book
Dael Walker
Crystal Co. • 1985 • Out of Print

Crystal Power
Michael Smith
Llewellyn Publications • 1985 • Out of Print

The Crystal Connection
A Guidebook for Personal and Planetary Ascension
Randall N. Baer & Vicki V. Baer
Harper & Row • 1986 • Out of Print

Patterns of the Whole Vol. 1
Healing and Quartz Crystals
John D. Rea
Two Trees Publishing • 1986 • Out of Print

The Complete Crystal Guidebook
A Practical Path to Self Development, Empowerment, and Healing
Uma Silbey
U-read Publications/Bantam • 1986 • Out of Print

Healing with Crystals
(Originally *Newcastle Guide to Healing with Crystals*
Balancing the Human Energy Field for Physical and Spiritual Well-Being)
Jonathan Pawlick & Pamela Chase
New Page Publishing • 1988 • In Print

Crystal Personalities
A Quick Reference to Special Forms of Quartz
Patricia Troyer
Stone People Publishing • 1995 • In Print

Cookbooks

In Astrology, cookbooks provide a set of meanings and interpretations for 10 planets, their placements in 12 signs and 12 houses, and a range of aspects—that is, the geometrical relationships between the 10 planets. Similarly, crystal cookbooks give data, meanings, and interpretations for a range of crystals and minerals.

Healing Stoned
The Therapeutic Use of Gems and Minerals
Julia Lorusso & Joel Glick
Mineral Perspectives/Brotherhood of Life • 1976 • Out of Print

The Spiritual Value of Gemstones
Wally Richardson, Jennie Richardson & Lenore Huett
DeVorss & Company • 1980 • Out of Print

Magic of Precious Stones
Mellie Uyldert
Turnstone Press • 1981 • Out of Print

Gemstones, Crystals and Healing
Thelma Isaacs
Lorien House • 1982 • Out of Print

Crystal Enlightenment
The Transforming Properties of Crystal and Healing Stones
Katrina Raphael
Aurora Press • 1985 • In Print

Gem Elixirs and Vibrational Healing, Vol. 1
Gurudas
Cassandra Press • 1985 • Out of Print

Michael's Gemstone Dictionary
Metaphysical Properties of Gems and Minerals
Michael, Judithann H. David & J.P. Van Hulle
Michael Educational Foundation/Affinity Press • 1986 • Out of Print

Healing with Crystals and Gemstones
Balance Your Chakras and Your Life
Daya Sarai Chocran
Weiser Books • 1986 • In Print

The Crystal Handbook
The A-to-Z Guide to the Psychic Energies of More Than 100 Cosmic Crystals, Gems, Minerals & Healing Stones
Kevin Sullivan
Armadillo Press/Signet • 1987 • Out of Print

Crystal Healing
The Therapeutic Application of Crystals and Stones
Katrina Raphael
Aurora Press • 1987 • In Print

The Women's Book of Healing
Auras, Chakras, Laying on of Hands, Crystals, Gemstones and Colors
Diane Stein
Llewellyn Publications/ Crossing Press • 1987 • In Print

Cunningham's Encyclopedia of Crystal, Gem and Metal Magic
Scott Cunningham
Llewellyn Publications • 1988 • In Print

The Healing Power of Gemstones
In Tantra, Ayurveda, and Astrology
Harish Johari
Inner Traditions • 1988 • In Print

Healing with Gemstones
(Originally *Newcastle Guide to Healing with Gemstones*
How to use over Seventy Different Gemstone Energies)
Pamela Chase & Jonathan Pawlick
New Page Publishing • 1989 • In Print

Gemstones and Crystal Energies
Thelma Isaacs
Lorien House • 1989 • Out of Print

The Book of Sacred Stones
Fact and Fallacy in the Crystal World
Barbara G. Walker
Harper & Row • 1989 • Out of Print

Crystalline Transmission
A Synthesis of Light
Katrina Raphael
Aurora Press • 1990 • In Print

Love is in the Earth: A Kaleidoscope of Crystals
*The Reference Book Describing the Metaphysical Properties of the Mineral
Kingdom*
Melody
Earth-Love Publishing • 1995 • In Print

Crystal Power, Crystal Handbook
The Complete Handbook
Michael Gienger
Octopus Publishing Group • 1996 • In Print

The Crystal Bible
A Definitive Guide to Crystals
Judy Hall
Walking Stick Press • 2003 • In Print

The Book of Stones
Who They are & What They Teach
Robert Simmons & Naisha Ahsian
Heaven & Earth Publishing/North Atlantic Books • 2005 • In Print

The Crystal Bible 2
Judy Hall
Walking Stick Press • 2009 • In Print

Stones of the New Consciousness
Healing, Awakening & Co-creating with Crystals, Minerals & Gems
Robert Simmons
Heaven & Earth Publishing/North Atlantic Books • 2009 • In Print

Crystals
Jewels · Stones
Magic & Science

Isidore Kozminsky

This Book Is
Affectionately Dedicated
to my
Dear Wife

Acknowledgments

by Isidore Kozminsky

In these pages a sincere attempt is made to blend modern science with the ancient and occult philosophy of the precious, semiprecious and common stones of the earth. It will be shown that many of the seemingly absurd narratives of old authors are but cunningly concealed truths, the unraveling of which can be followed with interest and profit along the lines herein indicated. The ancient masters held that the influences exerted by the heavenly bodies entered into harmonious relations with various terrestrial substances. Hence we have the venerable philosophy of fortunate stones, planetary gems and "stones of power," which form a part of the vast department known as talismanic magic. It is the philosophy of sympathy and antipathy prevailing through nature—atom for atom, stone for stone, plant for plant, animal for animal, man for man.

This observation was subjected to an orderly scientific arrangement which for completeness of detail would compare, in some cases, more than favorably with the most careful synthesis of modern science. In order to make easily understood the matter treated and to secure pronunciations as nearly correct as possible, it has been considered advisable to render all foreign words, ancient and modern, in familiar letters.

I have to express my grateful thanks to the friends who have, in various ways, been helpful to me in regard to this work

To Mr. Kelsey I. Newman, for the use of his unique collection of opals and precious stones, including the wonderful opal, "The Flame Queen," and especially for his cooperation, without which this book could not have been published.

Likewise to The Right Honorable the Viscountess Astor, M.P.; Lieutenant Sir Edward Mackenzie-Mackenzie, Bart, for his original Heraldic drawings of the horoscopes of royal and notable persons from my charts; Professor Sir William Ridgeway, Sc.D., LL.D., Litt.D., F.B.A., of Cambridge University, England; Miss Kathleen Watkins, for her help in preparing the sheets for the press; Mrs. Beatrix Colquhoun, for her paintings of the Flame Queen and other gems from Mr. Kelsey I. Newman's collection; Mr. and Mrs. C. G. King; Mr. and Mrs. Henry T. Seymour; Mr. William Howat; Mrs. S. Kozminsky; Mrs. Alice Walker; Mr. G. S. Brown; Mr. G. A. Osboldstone,; Mr. James Mackenzie; Mr. M. Susman, Hobart; and to my wife to whom this book is dedicated.

Melbourne, Australia,
January, 1922

Part One

Crystal and Stones
in the Bible and World Mythology

CHAPTER I

STUDY OF PRECIOUS STONES IN EARLY TIMES

"A thing of beauty is a joy forever;
Its loveliness increases, it will never
Pass into nothingness."

— KEATS

The study of the precious and semiprecious stones of the earth has commanded the attention of man from the mists of ages when, according to Enoch, the angel Azazzel came to the earth plane to teach him the use of them. Hence man considered the actual benefit to himself of these stones until his natural curiosity led him to study more deeply the marvel of their existence.

There can be little doubt that the indicated use was talismanic, and that the pure wisdom of divine inspiration and a clear faith rendered man's intuition so keen that he was quite able to know the virtue of various stones without chemical analysis. Dr. Ennemoser has recorded the effects of precious stones on certain psychic subjects, giving the opinion that "it is not improbable that in the early ages the belief in the virtues of talismans was induced by similar observations." This, no doubt, is true and indicates to us that certain observed phenomena compelled a closer study.

We are then reminded of the experiments which have been attributed to the schools of Pythagoras and of the observed effects of certain stones in the hands of sensitives by Baron Reichenbach in the middle of the nineteenth century and of the still more recent experiments in the schools at Nancy. There are records of these experiments being carried out on magnetic somnambulists when diamonds, emeralds, rubies, lodestones, beryls, jaspers and other stones were found to produce varied and strange effects.

Gems in common with all manifestations of nature have the power of attracting certain colors to themselves: and so persistent are these colors that it has been observed that when they are changed by art they are

143

liable to revert slowly (for the action of the stone world is slow) to their original colors. This can be noticed especially with topaz which may on this account alone have been identified with the stubborn and indomitable Mars. The attraction of diverse colors by the various chemical compounds which are cohesive in the various stones must be a certain indication of vibratory power. Indeed, the ancients have indicated that the rates of vibration in the gems differ with the needs of the chemical entities composing them, and it may as well be emphasized here that life exists in a gem just as it does in another form in a plant or an animal. It need scarcely be repeated that color is vibration.

Color is crystallized in a gem and immense vibration defies the material senses of man. A violet amethyst vibrates at the enormous rate of 750 trillions per second whilst a red ruby vibrates at 460 trillions. Hence we can scientifically demonstrate distinct powers by the evidence of known vibratory action.

The people of antiquity classified gems in a manner different from that of the people of today, for they regarded color of primary importance and bracketed stones of similar shades thus establishing the first points of agreement in the department of vibratory power. It is inconceivable however, that the great masters were unacquainted with chemical components, for chemistry was one of the secret arts, and it is well known that the priests of Egypt experimented secretly in their temples and that the betrayal of scientific secrets was followed by the mysterious "punishment of the peach tree" (supposed to be death from prussic acid). Modern groupings are arranged with regard to chemical affinities so far as can be traced by close analytical investigations and experiments.

CHAPTER 2

THE MOST ANCIENT SCIENCE

"And God said, 'Let there be lights in the firmament of the Heaven to divide the day from the night; and let them be for signs:, and for seasons, and for days, and years.'"

—GENESIS 1:14

The old science of Astrology was known amongst the Hebrews as the Wisdom of Foreknowledge (HOK MAT HA NISSAYON), and with it was included Astronomy or Star Knowledge (HOK MAT HA HOZZAYON). It is spoken of as of heavenly origin, having been communicated to man by the angels after he had lost Eden. It was written that:

Kokabel communicated Astrology, Wisdom of the Stars.
Rakiel or **Barakel** communicated Astronomy, Star Gazing.
Shehakeel communicated The Wisdom of the Clouds.
Arkiel communicated The Symbols of the Earth.
Samsiel communicated The Symbols of the Sun.
Scuriel or **Sahriel** communicated The Symbols of the Moon.

From the observed influences of the Sun and Moon the old scholars were enabled to classify the influence of these orbs in the various parts of the heavens and to formulate special rules, which extended observation rendered more convincing and complete. The simple consideration of the lunar phases brought grains of knowledge, which included the calculation of tidal action, eclipses, etc. The unity of the forces of Nature was then demonstrated in the actions and influences of the planets and stars, and the blending of such influences with their zodiacal positions and aspects.

Universal unity was insisted on and the statements of the ancient scholars have not been discredited by the revelations of modern scientific discoveries. The Talmud calls the planets "moving stars," and sets

145

down that Alexander of Macedon was pictured with a ball in his hand to symbolize the spherical shape of the Earth. The planets were indicated as follows:

Mercury	the Planet of Mind	is The Star
Venus	the Planet of Beauty	is Splendor
Mars	the Planet of Contention	is Ruddiness
Jupiter	the Planet of Prosperity	is Benevolence
Saturn	the Planet of Restraint	is The Star of Sabbath

Comets are represented as arrows of flame bearing messages to mankind.

The various colors ascribed to the planets are:

Sun	Yellow, Golden, Orange
Moon	White, Silvery, pale opalescent Green
Mercury	Dove Grey
Venus	Delicate Color Tints, Shades of Green, pale Blue, etc.
Mars	Red
Jupiter	Purple
Saturn	Black
Uranus	Mixed Colors
Neptune	Doubtful

The colors ascribed to the 12 Signs of the Zodiac and the planets associated with them are:

Aries	White and Red Mixed	Mars
Taurus	White and Lemon Mixed	Venus
Gemini	White and Red Mixed	Mercury
Cancer	Green or Russet	Moon
Leo	Red and Green	Sun
Virgo	Black and Blue	Mercury
Libra	Dark Crimson	Venus
Scorpio	Dark Brown	Mars
Sagittarius	Sanguine Green	Jupiter
Capricorn	Black	Saturn
Aquarius	Sky Blue	Uranus
Pisces	Glistening White	Neptune

The approximate date of the Sun's entry into the various zodiacal signs enabled astrologers to select the Solar Talismanic Gem.

The Sun enters Aries	about March 21
The Sun enters Taurus	about April 21
The Sun enters Gemini	about May 22
The Sun enters Cancer	about June 22
The Sun enters Leo	about July 23
The Sun enters Virgo	about August 24
The Sun enters Libra	about September 21
The Sun enters Scorpio	about October 24
The Sun enters Sagittarius	about November 23
The Sun enters Capricorn	about December 20
The Sun enters Aquarius	about January 20
The Sun enters Pisces	about February 19

This brief statement of the most ancient science must suffice. It will enable the reader to understand the philosophy on which the wearing of talismanic jewels rests and may induce him to delve a little into the "wisdom of the fathers."

CHAPTER 3

The Ephod of the High Priest

"And yet, as angels in some brighter dreams
Call to the soul when men doth sleep,
So may some strange thoughts transcend our wonted themes
And into glory peep."

—Henry Vaughan

In the 28th chapter of Exodus we learn that those that are "wise hearted" and "filled with the spirit of wisdom" were selected to make for Aaron consecrated garments— a breastplate and an ephod, a broidered coat, a mitre and a girdle. On the shoulders of the Ephod (Hebrew, HEPOD) which was to be made "of gold, of blue, and of purple, of scarlet"— these being the colors of divinity— "and fine twined linen, with cunning work" were to be placed two stones, each to be engraved after the manner of a signet, with six names of the children of Israel.

Authorities generally agree with the translations in classifying these two stones as onyx, and there are very important reasons from an occult point of view why they should be so identified even though Josephus accounts them sardonyx which, he says, represents the sun and the moon. These onyx stones were to be worn "for stones of memorial unto the children of Israel." The ephod was similar to an upper body-garment of the Greeks (Josephus says it resembled the *Epomis*) and may be described as a kind of waistcoat held by straps which passed over the shoulders and were twined round the waist with the cunningly woven band. The two large onyx stones were set on the shoulder-straps, and on each stone were engraved the names of the children of Israel—"Six of their names on one stone, and the other six names of the rest on the other stone, according to their birth." In astrology, to which science perhaps on its more esoteric side we are impelled, we can quickly recognize the twelve signs of the Zodiac—six Northern and six Southern—in the twelve tribes of the children of Israel, more distinctly emphasized on the breastplate of the High Priest. The engraving on the two onyx stones, one of which would necessarily be somewhat lighter in color than the other, can never be explained in our prosaic terms for they were attuned to the whisperings of the Heavenly Hosts and typified the eternal wanderings of the Soul.

In my later remarks on the onyx I have noted the ancient philosophy regarding the descent of the Soul through the Gate of Cancer and its ascent through the Gate of Capricorn. Peter symbolically represented at the Gate of Heaven, is a veiled allusion to the stone (*Petros*) gateway through which the departing spirits of Earth pass on their everlasting pilgrimage in search of the pearl above price—the hidden knowledge of perfect truth—a stone so gloriously brilliant that mortal eyes can never gaze on it.

In earlier Egyptian symbolic lore it is assumed that the Heavens were of stone, the goddess Hathor being the Lady of the Turquoise Stones and other deities being represented by stones cut to forms and in their natural state. In rabbinical allegory the Creator, vibrating through the rays of sunrise, is reverenced as "The Opener of the Gates," and frequent allusions are made to the gates of tears, of prayer, of praise, and of repentance. There is an old Hebrew tradition that one Messiah will come through the Gate of Capricorn and another through the Gate of Cancer. Plato writes of the two gateways—one through which the Soul descends, the other through which the soul ascends— and Porphyry says that on this account the Egyptians did not begin the year like the Romans with Aquarius but with the Moon Sign Cancer.

The Qabalistic Books say that the soul of man passed through the four celestial worlds in its descent, receiving from *Aziluth*, the *Chaiah*, spiritual animation: from *Briah*, *Neshamah*, understanding: from *Jezirah*, *Ruach*, the passions: from *Nephesch*, material desires. He enters the world by the Gate of Generation (the Moon), the watery sign, the color of which is indicated as green, and he leaves the world of Matter for the land of the Immortals by the Gate of Material Death (Saturn), the Earth sign Capricorn, the color of which is black. The Sun's passage through the tribal signs expressed on the onyx stones of the Ephod symbolizes eternally the descent and ascent of immortal man.

CHAPTER 4

The Breastplate of Judgment

"The future things and those which are to happen, let them foretell unto thee."

—Isaiah 44:7

Attached to the Ephod was the famous HOSHEN-HA-MISHPAT or Breastplate of Judgment which was of "cunning work," fashioned like the Ephod "of gold, of blue, and of purple, and of scarlet, and of fine twined linen." It was a square pouch when doubled, a span in length and a span in breadth. Josephus writes that there were

> "twelve stones upon the Breastplate, extraordinary in largeness and beauty: and they were an ornament not to be purchased by men because of their immense value. The names of all those sons of Jacob were engraven in these stones, whom we esteem the heads of our tribes, each in the order according to which they were born."

We are told in the 28th chapter of the Book of Exodus that the Urim and Thummim were put into the Breastplate. Dummelow believes that these were two jewels or images engraved with distinctive characters employed in casting lots. Josephus and the Septuagint imply that the gems on the Breastplate constituted the Urim and Thummim. Gesenius says that the Urim and Thummim were two little images which were placed between the folds of the Breastplate. Dr. Chambers indicates the Urim and Thummim as a mysterious contrivance consisting either of the four rows of precious stones bearing the tribal signets, or of two images. It is pointed out that the images of Isis and Osiris, worked in precious stones, hung on the breast of the Egyptian High Priest to symbolize truth and justice. The Urim and Thummim may be identical with the Babylonian "Tablets of Destiny" which were the instruments by which the seers of Babylon conveyed the "urtu" or answer of the gods to the people. In Babylon the "Tablets of Destiny" were only effective when on the breast of the god, while amongst the children of Israel the Urim and Thummim were only potent when on the breast of the High Priest. Josephus says that the answer of the Urim and Thummim was revealed by rays of light, and the Talmudic account is in harmony with this statement.

It was necessary for accuracy that the oracle should only be approached by one on whom the Shekinah or Radiance rested: one filled with the splendor of inspiration, naturally gifted in the art of prophecy, and fitted by the beauty of his thoughts and his life to draw unto himself the divine Shekinah: he must be "covered with the robe of virtue as the bridegroom decketh himself with ornaments and as a bride adorneth herself with her jewels." The Rabbis identified Urim and Thummim as the "grand and sacred name of God," Urim indicating "Those whose words communicate light" and Thummim, "Those whose words are realized," while the Septuagint renders them as "Revelation" and "Truth." The generally accepted meaning of Urim and Thummim is "Lights and Perfections."

The connection of the twelve zodiacal signs with the twelve tribes of Israel and the twelve stones of the Breastplate is remarked by Josephus, and the Targum upon Canticles also links them together. Wilson in "Lights and Shadows of Northern Mythology" draws attention to the life-sized white marble figure of Aaron robed, wearing the Breastplate showing a sign of the Zodiac sculptured on each of the twelve precious stones, which figure is placed on the right side of the High Altar in St. Pietro, Piazza Bianchi, Genoa.

The *Matsebah* of Babylon are black pillar stones on which in three elemental divisions are sculptured the twelve zodiacal signs by which the twelve Assyrian gods are symbolized, and the twelve lions on either side of the steps leading to Solomon's throne represent the Sun in its progress through the signs of Heaven. Josephus mentions that he had seen the remains of an ancient pillar of stone on which Seth, foreseeing the great Flood, had engraved the elements of Astrology which "Adam had received from the Creator."

"Moses was willing," writes Josephus, "that the power of the Breastplate should be known not only to the Hebrews but to all the world.

"When God was present the stone on the right shoulder of the High Priest (the stone symbolizing the soul's descent) shone with a brilliancy not natural to it. This has appeared a wonderful thing to such as have not so far indulged themselves in philosophy as to despise Divine Revelation. Yet will I mention what is more wonderful than this: for God declared beforehand by those twelve stones which the High Priest bare on his breast and which were inserted into his Breastplate, when they should be victorious in battle: for so great a splendor shone forth from them before the army began to march that all the people were sensible of God's being present for their assistance.

"Whence it came to pass that those Greeks who had a veneration for our laws, because they could not possibly contradict this called the Breastplate 'the Oracle.' Now this Breastplate left off shining 200 years before I composed this book, God having been displeased at the transgression of the laws."

Father Kircher in *Oedipus Egyptianus* gives an engraving of the Tabernacle with the Sun, Moon, and Planets in the centre and Ephraim with a bull, Menasses with two infants, Benjamin with a Centaur, Dan with a scorpion, Gad with a ram, Asher with scales, Simeon with fishes, Reuben with a water-bearer, Zebulun with a fish-goat, Issachar with a lobster, and Judah with a lion.

The standards of the twelve tribes were given in the middle ages as follows:

Issachar	Sun or Full Moon
Reuben	Man's Head or Bust
Judah	A Lion
Gad	An Army of Men
Zebulun	A Ship
Simeon	A Citadel
Manassah	A Unicorn
Dan	An Eagle
Napthali	Deer
Benjamin	A Horse
Asher	A Tree

The Rabbinical writers generally favor the following tribal order: Reuben, Simeon, Levi, Judah, Dan, Napthali, Gad, Asher, Issachar, Zebulun, Joseph, Benjamin. Tobias ben Eliezer quotes an old Baraita which said that Zebulun was followed by Dan. Marbodus places them as follows:

1. Reuben   placed 3rd of the 3rd row in the Breastplate
2. Simeon   placed 3rd of the 2nd row in the Breastplate
3. Levi   placed 3rd of the 1st row in the Breastplate
4. Judah   placed 2nd of the 1st row in the Breastplate
5. Zebulun   placed 1st of the 1st row in the Breastplate
6. Issachar   placed 1st of the 2nd row in the Breastplate
7. Dan   placed 1st of the 3rd row in the Breastplate
8. Gad   placed 1st of the 4th row in the Breastplate
9. Asher   placed 2nd of the 2nd row in the Breastplate
10. Napthali   placed 2nd of the 3rd row in the Breastplate
11. Joseph   placed 2nd of the 4th row in the Breastplate
12. Benjamin   placed 3rd of the 4th row in the Breastplate

Another old list gives the order as follows:

Reuben, Dan, Judah, Levi, Issachar, Zebulun, Asher, Napthali, Gad, Simeon, Joseph, Benjamin.

Swedenborg groups the tribes thus:

Judah, Reuben and Gad; Asher, Napthali and Manasseh; Simeon, Levi and Issachar; Zebulun, Joseph and Benjamin.

It is unnecessary to quote further lists as I believe that the one I am now producing will be sufficient to redeem the confusion. It is in complete harmony with the order of Jacob's blessings (Genesis 49) and the signs of the Zodiac. It will be noted that Taurus with the tribe of Reuben leads the Zodiac, and it is related that under this sign the human race came to earth. On ancient zodiacs the Bull as a solar conception is shown wending his way through the stars.

1. Reuben   the Defiler   Taurus
2. Simeon and Levi   the Slayers   Gemini
3. Levi   "Held to" (i. e., to the altar) Cancer

4. Judah	the Lion's Whelp	Leo
5. Zebulun	the Haven	Virgo (Argo, the ship, is in the constellation Virgo).
6. Issachar	the Bender	Libra
7. Dan	the Adder	Scorpio
8. Gad	the Victor	Sagittarius
9. Asher	the Producer	Capricorn
10. Naphthali	the Comforter	Aquarius
11. Joseph	the Redeemer	Pisces
12. Benjamin	the Devourer	Aries

The sign Cancer is that of the tribe of Levi as servants and guardians of the Tabernacle, the name indicating "held to," i.e., held to the altar.

CHAPTER 5

INTERPRETATION OF THE BREASTPLATE
ACCORDING TO ANCIENT PHILOSOPHY

It is apparent that the identification of the stones in the Breastplate must present many difficulties. Lord Arthur C. Hervey in his Diction-ary of the Bible, says: "Whether the order followed the ages of the sons of Israel or, as seems most probable, the order of the encampment, may be doubted; but unless any appropriate distinct symbolism of the differ-ent tribes be found in the names of the precious stones, the question can scarcely be decided." Dr. C. Keil in "Biblical Archaeology" says: "The order of the rows of the precious stones is given in Exodus 28:17–20 and 39:10–13, but owing to the vacillating manner in which the early writers designate and describe the stones we are at a loss to know how it should be explained."

Dr. Deane is of the opinion that in many cases it is a difficult task to identify the Hebrew and Greek names used in these passages with the names of modern mineralogy. The Rev. J. R. Dummelow comments on the difficulties of identifying the stones, the meaning of the Hebrew words being doubtful. Josephus saw the Breastplate frequently in his day, and in his description the position of certain stones is changed. The Hebrew Bible translation also presents differences. Rosenmuller, the Ori-entalist, argues as to the position of the 6th and 12th stones, placing the 12th in the 6th and the 6th in the 12th. It may easily be assumed that in its wanderings stones were lost from the Breastplate and that the replac-ing of these stones was not always carried out by men with a knowledge of the qabalistic import of Urim and Thummim or even of the stones themselves.

To quote from Dr. Deane:

"The variation in the order of the stones prompts the enquiry whether the Breastplate which Josephus repeatedly saw and which Jerome might have seen in the Temple of Concord was identical with that of ancient times. If the whole of the original stones were preserved, the order must have been kept in consequence of the names engraved upon them. But it is not by any means unlikely that in the great vicissitudes of the Hebrew nation some of the original stones may have been lost and have been replaced by others."

More evidences of this kind would be superfluous.

The First Stone of the Breastplate

Now, ODEM, the first stone of the Breastplate is a Red stone. According to astrology the Red stone vibrates to the planet Mars and the zodiacal Aries; therefore its position as the first stone of the Breastplate is natural. In the mystic philosophy of the Hebrews the Ram "caught in a thicket by his horns," the blood of the lamb upon the lintel and side-posts, etc., and in mystic Christian philosophy the blood of the Lamb which redeems from worldly sin are expressed symbolically by the sign Aries, into which the Sun enters in the month of Nisan, approximately 21st March, the time of the Passover and of Easter. Not only then must the stone be a red one, it must be red of the color of blood.

But again, one must not lose sight of the fact that the first stone on the Plate was engraved not with the name of the tribe of Benjamin, the true Aries tribe, but with the name Reuben, a tribe under the lordship of the second sign of the Zodiac, Taurus. This may be explained by the fact that the earlier Breastplate of the two began with the sign Taurus. Agnes Mary Clerke, writing on the Old Zodiac, says:

> "So far as positive records go Aries was always the first sign. But the arrangement is, on the face of it, a comparatively modern one. None of the brighter stars of the constellation could be said even roughly to mark the Equinox much before 1800 B.C.; therefore during a long stretch of previous time the leading position belongs to the stars of Taurus. Numerous indications accordingly point to a corresponding primate zodiac.
>
> "Setting aside as doubtful, evidence derived from interpretation of cuneiform inscriptions we meet in connection with Mithraic and Mylittic legends reminiscences of a Zodiac and religious calendar in which the Bull led the way. Virgil's "*Candidus auratis aperit cum cornibus*

anum Taurus" perpetuates the tradition, and the Pleiades continued within historical memory to be the first asterism of the lunar zodiac."

The Egyptian worship of Serapis, who is frequently symbolized by the head of a bull surmounted by a uræus and disc, and whose color was of a blood red, may be noted. The worship of this god was introduced into Egypt by the Ptolemies, but his name is derived from Ausar-Hapi (Osiris-Apis) and he represents a blending of the older worship of Osiris with the Bull Apis which, says Herodotus, is a fair and sublime reflection of the soul of Osiris. In this connection Diodorus says that the soul of Osiris migrated into Apis and thus revealed himself to men through the ages. Attention is drawn to this worship to show that in Egypt a bull god was associated with the color red, and the "holding a red rag to a bull" may have its origin in the bullfights of old, in which case however it is clear that the Martial Red is the color of irritation.

We can see in the placing of Taurus, the Bull—or the tribal name Reuben—in the first section of the Breastplate a desire to harmonize it as far as possible with an older one, whilst the gem and its color represented the sign Aries—the sign of the Ram—symbolically the tribe of Benjamin, engraved as of old in the last division of the Plate.

The Hebrew word ODEM, signifying redness, is connected with the Hebrew word DOM, blood, and the stone to meet these requirements is the red hematite, the true bloodstone of antiquity, which is further described in the section of this book dealing more generally with the scientific and romantic aspects of precious stones.

The hematite is a true iron stone and in old astrology Iron is a metal placed directly under the rule of the planet Mars and the sign Aries. We have direct evidence of the use of this stone by the ancient Babylonians, who wore it as an engraved signet cut in cylinder form. We therefore identify the first stone of the Breastplate as the red hematite on which was engraved the name of the first tribe, Reuben.

The Second Stone of the Breastplate

The second stone of the Breastplate is given as PITDAH, variously interpreted as a topaz, peridot, yellowish-green serpentine, diamond and chrysolite. The Targums agree that a green stone is implied and some authorities seek to clear the mystery by advancing that the stone was of a yellowish-green.

The topaz of the ancients is not the topaz of today, but is identified with the stone known to us as the chrysolite or peridot. Traditionally the emerald is associated with the second sign of the zodiac, and Apion, who wrote much concerning ancient Egypt and whose story of Androclus and the Lion echoes through the ages, tells of a gigantic figure of Serapis seen at Alexandra. This figure, the height of which was about fifteen feet, was probably composed of glass resembling emerald. The emerald was sacred to Serapis who—as indicated in the previous chapter—was a Bull god associated naturally with the zodiacal Taurus. This sign and the color green blend truly for green is the symbol of life, of agriculture and of abundant nature, and amongst nations of antiquity holy festivals heralded the return of Spring whose praises are sung by the poets in the magical language of mythology. The many references to "green trees" in the Bible need only be noticed in passing.

The Veneralia of old was held once a year amidst budding plants and flowers, in gardens and on green lawns in honor of Venus to welcome Adonis returning in radiant beauty from the underworld. The ceremony took place towards the end of April, when the Sun had entered the Earth sign of Venus, Taurus, and it survives in the later May Day rejoicings.

The gem needed is therefore a green one, and this is traditionally the correct one for the sign SHOR or Taurus, in which NOGAH or Venus delights, and in which LAVANAH or the Moon exalts. The emerald was sacred to this period of the year. This gem was well-known amongst ancient nations, especially those of Egypt and Ethiopia where the chief emerald mines were. The children of Israel must certainly have known of the existence of the emerald which is mentioned in the Wisdom of Ptah-Hotep who lived ages before the time of Solomon and more than 1000 years before Hammurabi, the Wise, of Babylon. "Courtesy in Speech," says this sage, "is rarer than the emeralds which slave girls find in the stones."

It is recorded that the Egyptians employed many women at the emerald mines on account of the keenness of their vision, and it is highly probable that Israelite women were selected for this work with captives of other nations. Specimens of emeralds collected by Sir G. Wilkinson from Mount Zabarah in Upper Egypt now lie in the British Museum. Evidence is not wanting to prove that the ancients knew well how to engrave on an emerald, Pliny states that Ptolemy offered Lucullus at Alexandra an emerald with his portrait engraved on it.

The tribe Simeon corresponding to the zodiacal Gemini was engraved on the second gem of the Breastplate—although it has no connection with it—for the reason before noted.

It should be understood that by "emerald" is meant the precious emerald as we know it or its varieties beryl and aquamarine. It may be noted that the topaz, a gem most generally favored as the second stone on the Breastplate, is traditionally assigned to the opposite sign of the Zodiac, Scorpio.

The hero Gilgamesh in Babylonian story sees by the gates of the Ocean a wondrous magical tree which bore as fruit most precious emeralds. The emerald as a love stone was closely identified with Venus and was regarded as particularly fortunate for women, bringing happiness in love, comfort in domestic affairs, and safety in childbirth. The evil effects of the luminaries afflicted or of malefic planets in the sign Taurus, the latter degrees especially, have been shown to affect the sight; hence the employment of the emerald as an eye charm.

Hathor, the Egyptian Venus, who carries in her left hand the potent Crux Ansata was saluted as "The Lady of the Southern Sycamore," a tree which stood for the living body of Hathor on earth and which was called the Sycamore of the Emerald.

The Rosicrucian John Heydon of the 17th Century describes his meeting with the spirit Euterpe on the plains of Bulverton Hill one sweet summer evening. He describes her as "a most exquisite divine beauty of decent stature; attired, she was in thin loose silks, but so green that I never saw the like for the color was not earthly ... Her rings were pure entire emeralds for she valued no metal."

Similar legends of green fairies, green fields, and green lights are connected with the sign of Venus terrestrial, Taurus.

The emerald, then, is the second stone of the Breastplate, and on it was engraved the name of the tribe of Simeon.

The Third Stone of the Breastplate

The third stone of the Breastplate is simply expressed by the word BAREKETH which has been variously rendered as emerald, ruby, carbuncle, amethyst, rock crystal, green olivine, green feldspar. Its true meaning is "flashing," which the Targumic translators express as "brilliant." The Hebrew BARUK corresponds to an Arabic word meaning "to gleam, to flash;" the Assyrian word BARAKU and the Aramic BURUK have the same meaning, with which may be identified the Punic BARCAR, surname of the Carthaginian general Hamilcar; the Syriac BORKO and the Chaldean BARKAN can only be rendered "brilliant." There is a Sanskrit word MARKATA, meaning "flashing, sparkling," which corresponds to our word "marble," literally, "the sparkling stone," Latin MARMOR, cognate with the Greek MARMAROS from MARMAIRO to flash, shine, sparkle.

Hence the Flashing Stone may be identified as marble, and this traditionally answers the required conditions. In astro-philosophy marble is connected with the sign of the columns, Gemini—Simeon in association with Levi—and is known as the Day House of the planet Mercury. The *Midrash Bemidbah* gives the color of this sign as white, and Francis Barrett expresses it as "glittering."

The author remembers long ago taking some really glittering specimens of white marble, unstained by the hand of time, from an Egyptian mummy-case. Even at the present day pieces of white marble are buried with the dead body in some countries of the world, and the marble tombstone is universally used as a monument over the buried ashes which the ascending man has thrown aside as the serpent throws his old skin.

The shining marble is the emblem of spiritual resurrection which is symbolized in the sign of the Twins (Gemini). Mercury as the Egyptian Tehuti or Thoth, or the Greek Hermes, is ever connected with the spirits of the dead in the Hall of Judgment and, in harmony with the brilliant flashing white stone, the everlasting uplifting and spiritual progress. The sign Gemini but lightly veils the peculiar occult meaning associated with twins and connected names in hermetic philosophy. From Cain and Abel many may be enumerated including Simeon and Levi whom we find implicated in the massacre of the defenseless people of Shihem for which crime they drew upon themselves their father's curse. Greek legend gives Amphion, skilled in music and learning, and Zeuthus, who labors and follows the chase. The latter by hard labor rolled huge boulders together to build up the walls of Troy, whilst the former but struck the strings of the lyre given to him by Hermes and the great rocks followed him—a symbol of the triumph of mind which Hermes promises to his disciples. Simeon and Levi killed the Shechemites to avenge their sister Dinah; Amphion and Zeuthus drove Dirce, bound to a bull, to her death to avenge their mother Antiope. In the legend of the Roman twins, Romulus kills his brother Remus as Cain killed Abel.

The twin stories are well illustrated in the legend of Castor and Pollux, the "great twin brethren," sons of Jupiter and Leda. The former was mortal, the latter immortal, but so attached were they to each other that none ever saw them apart.

In these stories the mysterious union of the Soul and the Body is being continually forced forward, and sleep—which the old masters called a tenth part of death—is indicated in this legend of the Dioscuri when Pollux divides his immortality with his brother. Sanchoniatho or Sanchuniathon, who lived when Gideon judged Israel, says that Thoth of the Egyptians, Taaut of the Phoenicians, Thoyth of the Alexandrians, Hermes or Mercurius, was the inventor of letters, and took religion from the unskillful management of the vulgar forming it into a rational system; and "when Saturn came from the southern parts of the Earth he made Taaut, the son of Miser (identified as the Mizraim of the Bible), King of all Egypt," and the month Thoth began the Egyptian year and coincides with Tisri or Thishri which began the Jewish year and with Tisritu which began the Chaldean.

To continue further might lead outside the province of this book, and the plea for this digression is the endeavor to elucidate the hidden import of the various departments of the sacred Breastplate by the searchlight of the philosophical stories of our antique fathers.

Thoth or Hermes engraved all knowledge on two pillars or columns, and the Hermetic schools say that all knowledge is contained in the words, letters and continuations engraved on the two tables of stone. This writing of God graven upon the tables constituted the Commandments, five of which (and five is the number of Mercury,) were written on each stone, the complete ten indicating the Hidden Power of God—identified in the *Sepher Yetzirah* as the Path of Resplendent Intelligence and the Light which, too intense for the material eye of man, is around the Throne of the Supreme.

The association of marble with Hermes, the Guide of the Human Race, is traditional, and evidence favors it as the third stone of the Breastplate engraved with the name of the tribe of Levi.

The Fourth Stone of the Breastplate

NOFEK, the fourth stone of the Breastplate, has been identified with the emerald, carbuncle, jasper, red garnet, ruby carbuncle, almandine garnet and ruby. Two of the Targums classify it as emerald, possibly referring to a stone similar in color to the emerald. It is well known that all green stones were called emeralds by a large section of the ancient public, just as all red stones were called rubies, etc., hence much confusion followed. Dr. Emil Hirsch says that NOFEK (the correctness of which word has been doubted in some quarters) must have belonged to the green stones. In corresponding chrysoprase with "celestial love of truth" Emanuel Swedenborg draws attention to Exodus 28:18, indicating his identification of that gem as the fourth stone of the Plate. This gem which is of a soft green color resembles the tender hue of moonlight. The *Midrash Bemidbah* gives the color of NOFEK as sky blue, the Egyptians according to Müller as green, and the astrological, in considering Cancer the Mansion of the Moon, a moonlight green. The chrysoprase was anciently translated as "austerity directed against vice" which harmonizes agreeably with the traditional attitude of chaste Diana against evildoers.

The Boat of the Moon in ancient Egypt is pictured as a disc within a crescent, and the association of the moon (which was said to be in its Mansion in the watery Cancer) with the waters of the Earth was well known to the ancients and is referred to frequently in works on magic and astrology. In this connection may be mentioned the Egyptian story of a few thousands of years ago which is known as "The Legend of the Green Jewel" told to the Pharaoh Khufu by the Prince Khafra:

Pharaoh Sneferu, weary and sighing for amusement or relaxation from affairs of State, was advised by his scribe to go rowing with the loveliest women of his harem on the lake.

"I will go with thee, august One," said the scribe, "the green banks with the trees and flowers, the splash of the water under the oars will charm thine eyes and bring thee happiness."

For the excursion twenty beautiful young women were selected (twenty was a number of the negative or female side of the Moon, qabalistically expressed as "the Awakening"). They rowed the Pharaoh's boat with oars of ebony and gold, singing sweetly as they went, and his heart was glad. But with the turning of the boat the helmswoman's hair was touched by her steering oar and a green jewel she wore fell into the water.

She became, silent and raised her oar from the water, the other women doing likewise.

"Why cease?" asked the Pharaoh. "Let us continue."

They answered: "O Pharaoh, the steerer has stopped and her oar is raised from the water."

"Why is this so?" questioned the Pharaoh.

"O Majesty, my beautiful green jewel has sunk beneath the waters."

"What of that?" he replied. "Continue. I will present you with a new jewel."

"O Majesty," said the girl, "no jewel can replace my own green jewel."

So the Pharaoh turned to his scribe. "What can we do?" he asked. "This girl has lost her green jewel and will have no other."

The scribe uttered magical words over the lake and the waters divided as two walls. Between these walls the scribe descended and, having found the jewel, came up again into the boat, gave the green jewel to the helmswoman and spoke to the waters which closed up again. The Pharaoh was gratified, giving rich gifts to the scribe at whose power all marveled.

When the Pharaoh Khufu heard this legend from Prince Khafra he enjoined that offerings should grace the sepulchers of the Pharaoh Sneferu and his great scribe, the magician. This allegorical story, like many others of the kind, is full of hidden meaning and the connection of this boat with its twenty female rowers, its two (unit of the Moon) Illustrious Ones, the Pharaoh and the Scribe, the green vegetation on the banks of the lake, the lake itself, the division of the waters and the green jewel make the meaning especially clear to students of symbology.

In astrological enumeration from the earliest time the sign Cancer was said to rule the great oceans, the deep blue of which may have influenced the *Midrash Bemidbah* in its allotment of color, and in certain hermetic ceremonies connected with the soul's entry into matter through the Gate of Cancer from the blue ocean of the incorruptible Heavens.

The zodiacal Cancer, the Mansion of the Moon, is associated with the worship of Diana in her varied forms, and Diana—at one time a plebeian goddess only—was for a long period worshipped by the plebeian populations who used to hang her image to trees to increase their growth. Cancer is the sign of the people, and the Moon "which delights in this sign" represents their varying moods.

In the Acts of the Apostles it is related that Demetrius, a silversmith, and others made silver shrines of Diana (silver astrologically is the metal of the Moon) resenting the attempt of Paul to prejudice her worship, with the famous cry "Great is Diana of the Ephesians." Diana was worshipped as the goddess of Light by the Romans and whether as Artemis in her changing attributes, Selene, Luna, Leucophryne, Petamia, Munychia or Amarynthea, her influence as a moon deity remains. Her face resembles that of her twin brother Apollo to a very marked degree, and her hair like his is caught up in a knot above the forehead indicating the influence exerted by the Moon in its relation to the Sun, in the movements of the waters of the Earth.

That chrysoprase as we know it today was used in very early times is clearly proved by the Egyptian jewelry discovered in excavations. Hard as the stone is, the ancients knew how to cut it, various intaglios of ancient origin existing today to prove their skill. The apple-green hue of the chrysoprase is attractive, and it is probable that it was the stone of which fifty specimens were sent to Ashkalon as part of the tribute. Its inclusion in this department of the Breastplate is the result of much research, and it harmonizes with astrological tradition. This stone was inscribed with the name of the tribe of Judah.

The Fifth Stone of the Breastplate

In placing SHOHAM in the position of SAPIR in the fifth division of the Breastplate, traditional philosophy is harmonized. The fifth zodiacal sign, Leo, is not blue. It is the mansion of the Sun, and old almanacs symbolize it as a raging lion. The *Midrash Bemidbah* gives the color as black, but generally authorities agree that it is a shade of red, especially during sunrise and sunset, and a yellowish-red at noonday. The eleventh zodiacal sign Aquarius is given as sky blue by most authorities, and it is generally accepted. It has a mystic connection with the heavens, and without doubt its gem is the SAPIR. In the Zodiac the signs Leo and Aquarius are exactly opposite, and on the Breastplate the stone for the former is second of the second row, and for the latter second of the last row. Accepting this view no difficulty will be experienced. It might also be considered that the tribe of Judah is the tribe of the Lion, although for reasons previously stated, the name of this tribe is engraved on the fourth stone.

Accepting SHOHAM then as the fifth stone of the Breastplate we have yet to identify it. The Hebrew Bible, the Authorized Version, Josephus, the Vulgate, Marbodus, Dr. Deane all translate it as onyx, and Dr. Ginzberg half agrees with them. Dr. Emil A. Braun, the archaeologist, traced SHOHAM to the Arabic SACHMA, blackness. "Of such a color," he writes, "are the Arabian sardonyx which have a black ground color." However, this species can hardly be called true sardonyx defined by Pliny as "candor in sarda," graphically rendered by King as "a white opaque layer superimposed upon a red transparent stratum of the true red sard." The ancient and modern methods of imitating this gem are identical: A sard is put upon a red-hot iron block with the result that the part nearest the heated mass is transmuted into a white hazy layer upon which the cameo artist works.

It seems that the name onyx amongst ancient peoples was indifferently applied to both onyx and sardonyx, but in the case of the fifth stone of the Breastplate there seems to be no doubt that the sardonyx is the stone. The sign Leo astrologically rules the Heart in the human body, which in the Grand Man is symbolically the Sun, and the sard is of the color of the Heart. By ancient correspondence then the Heart, Leo, the Sun, the sard, the sardonyx, and the fifth department of the Breastplate are clearly connected.

The carnelian, sard, and sardonyx were most extensively used by the Egyptians, Greeks, Romans and other peoples of antiquity, and many specimens have been found engraved with various devices: finely worked Egyptian scarabei, antique intaglios and cameos. The sardonyx has been called a "royal stone," and the sign of the Lion is intimately connected with royalty. The winged, human-headed lions of Nineveh are emblematical of the Sun, and Daniel describing his vision (Daniel 8:4)connects the Winged Lion with the heart of Man.

In the Egyptian texts frequent allusion is made to the heart or HATI of Osiris. The HATI represented vitality, warmth, control, and silently within it were impressed the actions of its owner during his earthly life. It was to his HATI, lying on the Balance before the "Shining God," the attendant deities and the forty and two gods in the great Judgment Hall, that the shuddering soul cried out of the intense silence: "O heart of mine, testify not against me," words frequently impressed on scarabei and regarded as magically potent.

A symbolic image constructed by the Magi at the period of the Sun's passage through the sign of the Lion took the form of a crowned king enthroned, wearing a deep yellow robe, a globe at his feet and a raven by his heart. The crowned king, his yellow robe, the raven and the globe symbolize the Sun and its manifestations, and the Heart—the Sun of Man—symbolizes the Solar sign Leo. Another symbol of the Magi shows a crowned woman in a four-horsed chariot (four being the negative or female side of the Sun), a mirror in her right hand, a staff in her left, and a burning flame on her head. These emblems were directed to be engraved in the Hour of the Sun, the Sun being in Leo, on a carnelian stone. The famous seal of Solomon and David—the *Mogan Dovid*—was most potent when engraved on a sardonyx, a carnelian or a plate of gold (metal of the Sun).

All conditions necessary for this stone of the breastplate are fulfilled in the Sardonyx stone which, engraved with the tribe of Zebulun, filled the fifth place.

The Sixth Stone of the Breastplate

The sixth stone of the Breastplate is, without doubt, the JASHPEH accepted by the Vulgate, Marbodus, Dr. Emil Hirsch and Dr. G. Deane. Translated correctly enough as jasper, it is placed in the twelfth division in the Hebrew and Authorized Versions.

From an astrological point of view the YAHALOM has no claim on the sixth House whilst JASHPEH undoubtedly has. The latter is the third stone of the second row of the Breastplate and the former is the third stone of the fourth row. In astrological science they are opposite in the Zodiac, the JASHPEH belonging to the celestial Virgo and the YAHALOM to the celestial Pisces. The colors are given in the *Midrash Bemidbah* as "Mixed," and this is more correct than the "black speckled with blue," set down sometimes for the sign Virgo, but which scarcely expresses the aspect of Nature personified in the goddess Ceres. The jasper stone has not lost its identity in the march of time, and there is no reason to doubt that the ASPU of the Assyrians, the JASHPEH of the Hebrews, the JASPIS of the Greek, or the YASH of the Arabs is any other than the jasper, as we know it today.

The "panther stone" of the Targums of Onkelos and Jonathan is the well-known and very beautiful Egyptian mottled jasper so greatly esteemed in the ancient world. The jasper takes a very brilliant polish and is quite of the crystal brilliance indicated in the sacred books. It was the gem of the angel Raphael, emblematic of strength, courage, virtue and wisdom, and it is associated with a variety called the *Graminatias*, the markings of which resemble—to a very marked degree in some specimens—the letters of the Alphabet. Thus, it is the stone of Hermes or Thoth, the mercurial god who, possessed of illimitable knowledge, communicated it to the earth-bound spirit known as Man, by signs in the Heavens, in the air, in the sea, on the earth, in the flowers and stones of the earth, by omens, by hints and by incidents, but never—on account of his promise to Apollo—by spoken words.

Jerome calls the jasper "the stone of spiritual graces," and from Hermes to Christ called Son of the Virgin, this stone descends with all its spiritual attributes. It is associated with the Virgins of Egypt who provoked the words set down in the eighth chapter of Jeremiah: "The children gather wood and the fathers kindle the fire, and the women knead their dough to make cakes to the Queen of Heaven."

The jasper was a stone sacred to the Virgin Mary in Christian mysticism, and to the Son of the Virgin; and symbolically the Virgin of the Skies is ever immaculate, ever sublime and pure. The association of the sixth sign of the Zodiac with all virginity is further exemplified in the cult of the Virgins of Vesta. Corresponding with the sixth sign of the Zodiac these virgins were six in number, and the age of girls selected for the service could not be less than six years.

The poets tell the story of the beautiful Astræa, the holy Virgin, who in pity remained with men after the gods, provoked by man's wickedness, had departed in anger; remained with them until she was forbidden to gaze on a world defiled with crime and misery, and with bandaged eyes was led away to Heaven where her symbolic form stands eternally, scales in one hand, sword in the other. One gift she left with man—the gift of Hope, which has as its emblem the unpretentious jasper stone. The Virgin Astræa is familiar as the goddess of Justice, and her connection with Mercury—astrologically known as Lord of the Virgin—is apparent. Her special degree of the Zodiac is given as the twenty-third (*Zodiacal Symbology*, 96), which is a degree of sympathy, and for the correct administration of justice, deep and generous sympathy is surely necessary.

According to Swedenborg and other mystical writers the Virgin symbolizes all chaste love, "affection for good, charity towards others, lovers of truth, spirituality and sympathy, and the kindness of men to one another, as opposed to the cruel malice of war and destruction which is likened to false reasonings, lies and opposed to Divine Providence."

The Zebulun is the Haven into which they "who are weary and heavy laden" may enter, and it is significant that the Son of the Virgin dwelt in Capernaum which is upon the sea coast in the borders of Zebulun and Nephthalim (Matthew 4:13).

Having given birth to her sixth son, Leah thanks God for "a good dowry," and saying that now her husband will dwell with her because of her six sons, called his name Zebulun. In several ways a good dowry is associated with the sign Virgo, which is related to learning and commerce, will, patience, persistence and the reward of honest work. About the constellation of Virgo is the Argo or Ship of the Heavens, which star-lighted is ever gliding on the blue waters of the Celestial Harbor. A story of the loss of the jasper from the Breastplate is told in the Talmud, and after a long search for another to replace it one was found in the possession of Dama, son of Nethinah, and purchased from him for about £60 in our money.

It is quite conceivable that stones were lost from the breastplate, and it was no doubt the replacing of them that caused so much confusion. Jasper as the sixth stone of the Breastplate is easily identified and the tribe of Issachar was inscribed upon it.

The Seventh Stone of the Breastplate

The seventh stone of the Breastplate is given as LESHAM, variously rendered as ligure, agate, jacinth, hyacinth, amber, sapphire, turquoise, opal. The gem needed must, according to Dr. E. G. Hirsch, be "brilliant and of intense luster." The Midrash says that the stone was "white like the color of antimony." The color in the *Midrash Bemidbah* is given as sapphire blue, and by astrological authorities generally as dark crimson or tawny.

The sign is the airy home of the planet Venus: and its color can be more correctly gauged from the colors identified with the planet itself, which are given as follows: yellow, lemon yellow and pale blue, art tints in general, white and purple, white and shining, white in the morning, reddish in the evening, changeable, etc., Gesenius translates LESHAM as opal, and Dr. M. H. Breslau accepts his reading as correct. The opal is given for the seventh stone in translations from the Hebrew Bible, and this is most probably the correct one.

This beautiful gem was in great repute in ancient times, and Pliny in lauding its charms tells us that it was found in India, Egypt, Cyprus, Thasos and other places. It is found recorded on antique clay tablets whereon were impressed catalogues of treasures taken from conquered cities. Its softness and delicacy rendered it easy to cut and carve, and specimens of opal intaglios have been found. Mr. King mentions one in the Praun collection, of mediocre antique Roman work which was engraved with the heads of Jupiter, Apollo and Diana surrounded by nine stars. The same author mentions a big opal set in a qabalistically inscribed ring of gold with astrological symbols.

The midrashic "white like the color of antimony" may fairly describe a common variety of opal. Antimony is a brittle flaky metal of bluish-white color and crystalline texture. No gem can exhibit "the brilliant and intense luster" more than the precious opal which is not only brilliant and lustrous, but beautiful, tender and comprehensive of all the colors of the rainbow. What gem can answer so to the Talmudic identification of the qualities of Venus, viz., splendor? The Venus of Libra is more ethereal than the Venus of Taurus and is well presented in the charming statue of the Venus of Medici, that of Taurus being expressed in the figure known as the Venus of Milo. This ethereal Venus is the immaculate glorious woman whose absolute beauty the greatest poets, writers, painters, sculptors and musicians have striven to express in words, in form, in color and in sound.

Thus is Venus the noble cogency of divine pure love which has been striving through all the ages to make the world a paradise and to bring man back again to the Eden he has lost. No blood sacrifices stained the altars of this lovely goddess, and the ancients delighted in bringing to her temples sweet blossoms and fragrant spices for incense. So great was the charm and wonder of this Heavenly One that Momus, the god of Sarcasm, who spared neither god nor man, died of vexation because he could find in her nothing to ridicule, nothing to blame, nothing to jeer at, for before such pure beauty criticism and ridicule must be mute.

As Venus Urania she arises amidst the foam of the sea (the occult import serving but to intensify the beauty of the legend) with a blue sky above her head and peaceful sunlit waters at her feet, a symbol of that

eternal love which unites the elements and spreads the luster of true harmony wherever are to be found those wise enough to know it. Socrates
wrote that he was uncertain whether there was one Aphrodite or two,
and doubtless the philosopher recognized the various phases of the goddess when blended with, or corrupted by, anything less than the conception of pure idealism in all its expressions. The ancients called the opal
"Cupid"—a worthy tribute to the sublime beauty of his glorious mother.
One might compare the opal to the union of Thaumas (Wonder), the
Son of the Earth, with Electra (Brightness), a daughter of Oceanus, and
with their child Iris (Rainbow).

Issachar is the tribe of the Balance, "an ass bending between two
burdens." The ass in the East today, as it was in the days of the Bible, is
regarded as an emblem of constancy, patience, endurance and stolidity,
and frequent allusion is made to it in sacred writings: "Speak, ye that ride
on white asses, ye that sit in judgment, and walk by the way." (Judges 5:
10) Josephus replies with vigor to the assertion of Apion that the Jews
worshipped an ass's head. In the mythology of the Egyptians the good
and evil essences are symbolized by two wild asses, and mention is made
in *The Book of the Dead* of the duel between the ass and its "eater," the
night serpent.

The ass also, as a symbolic animal of Jupiter, represented Justice in
the ancient world, hence its association with the Balance becomes clear.
The tribe Issachar, this "servant of tribute," is symbolic of absolute truth
for "a false balance is abomination to the Lord: but a just weight is his
delight." (Proverbs 11:1), and "He that speaketh truth showeth forth
righteousness: but a false witness deceit." (Proverbs 1:17)

The entry of the Son of the Virgin into Jerusalem—the city of
Virgo—riding on an ass, as told in that chapter of parables, Matthew 21,
is not devoid of symbolic meaning. Hermes or Thoth is the recorder of
the scales in the Egyptian Hall of Judgment and he may also be said to
ride upon the scales for the sign Libra follows the sign of the Virgin. Libra
has been described as the most sensitive sign of the Zodiac, the opal is its
ideal gem and the opal is the gem for the seventh division of the Breastplate and on it was engraved the tribe of Dan.

The Eighth Stone of the Breastplate

The eighth stone of the Breastplate is SHEBO, rendered as agate by the Authorized Version, the Vulgate, Marbodus and others.

Gesenius gives the derivation of SHEBO from a root which means "to take prisoner," and his illustrious pupil, Julius Fürst, connects it with a root meaning "to glitter." Dr. Deane derives it from another meaning "to obscure, to dull," and expresses the opinion that the problem "cannot be solved by etymology alone." He believes SHEBO to be some variety of crystallized quartz. Dr. Breslau in translating SHEBO as agate has good supporters. The variety known as banded agate agreeably fits in with the demands of the planet Mars through the sign of its expression Scorpio, termed the sign of the Serpent. Its wavy lines typify the undulations of the serpent, the lines of a fortress or the restless waves of the sea. The opinion has been expressed that SHEBO may have some connection with the Indian Serpent of the Underworld—Sesha or Shesha—and the connection may be further extended to the huge serpent which slays and is slain by Thor as told in the Song of Vala.

The sign Scorpio is in astrology the sign of death, the dead and all connected therewith. It is expressed by the Serpent of Eden in that magical third chapter of Genesis, a chapter that has demanded the special study of mystical philosophers for ages. The sign Scorpio is also symbolized in the person of the goddess Serket, pictured as a human-headed scorpion or as a goddess with scorpion headdress. She protected the Canopic Jars which contained the embalmed viscera of the departed. Aesculapius, the god of medicine, was worshipped under the form of a serpent at Epidaurus, and in the Vatican statue he is represented leaning on a staff around which is coiled a serpent; statues of his daughter Hygieia show her with a serpent in different attitudes. In those and numerous other serpent stories all associated with the sign Scorpio to a greater or lesser degree, the majesty and the mystery of life and death are philosophically implied.

The traditional color of the sign Scorpio is given as brown, a shade of brown well describes the agate stone. The *Midrash Bemidbah* gives gray which, though not in agreement with other authorities, certainly does indicate a species of agate.

Dan is described in the Book of Genesis as "a serpent by the way, an adder in the path, that biteth the horses' heels" (the sign following Scorpio, Sagittarius—the sign of Gad) "so that his rider shall fall backward." The tribe was a mystical tribe possessing the knowledge of white magic and of black (Judges 18:30). The wisdom of the serpent is symbolized in it—"Dan shall judge his people."

The eighth stone of the Breastplate was the banded agate, and on it was engraved the tribe of Gad.

The Ninth Stone of the Breastplate

The ninth stone of the Breastplate is ACHLAMAH which, with few exceptions, is identified as the amethyst—beyond doubt the correct identification.

The *Midrash Bemidbah* gives the color as purple which is the dominant shade of this beautiful gem. Purple is also one of the chief colors associated with the planet Jupiter which in astrology is termed the Lord of Sagittarius, the ninth sign of the Zodiac. This sign is connected with rulers and people in authority from very early times; Josephus mentions that Joseph wore "purple and drove in his chariot through all the land of Egypt."

The amethyst was a royal stone and purple a royal color the right to wear which was bestowed by the King on inspired men who, like Joseph, were revealers of dreams. In the Book of Daniel also Belshazzar promises that the man who reads for him the "writing on the wall" shall be clothed with purple, shall have a chain of gold about his neck and shall rule as the third in the kingdom. This promise he fulfills when Daniel, "the prince of astrologers," told him what he would know. A similar promise is made by Darius, the son of Hystaspes, as a reward for the solving of his questions regarding the strength of Wine, Kings and Women. It is related in the Book of Esther that the same honor is bestowed on Mordecai by the King Artaxerxes.

In old Hebraic philosophy it was held that "whoso honoreth the prophet honoreth God." Purple is the color signifying royal dignity and imperial power: "to be born in the purple" is to be born essentially fortunate and, under the elevating influence of the planet Jupiter, ACHLAMAH—according to Dr. Hirsch—seems etymologically to imply the idea of being strong. Lord Arthur Hervey and several other writers hold that the Hebrew word is a verbal one from the root HALOM, to dream. In astrological deductions Sagittarius is the sign of dreams, prophecy and philosophy, and in its divine aspect it is referred to the wise centaur Chiron who tended the young hero Achilles. Sagittarius is the sign of the Horse and of Horsemen, and its connection with the tribe of Gad is not hard to understand.

Aben Ezra writes on Targum authority that Jupiter is best expressed by the name Gad, and Dr. Alfred Pearce remarks that in modern Hebrew TZEDEK, justice, was also translated as Jupiter "because of the just character of persons born under his influence." Gad, David's seer, is mentioned in 2 Samuel, as well as 1 and 2 Chronicles, and the prophetic nature of this son of Jupiter may well stand as a living symbol. Gad's birth is heralded by Leah thus: "A troop cometh," and "she called his name Gad."

The amethyst has ever been a gem symbolizing spirituality in its highest degree, and by the virtue of its power it opposed evils, drunkenness, and the sin of distorted appetites. Indeed, the amethyst was considered a sign of such holiness that evil was always courted by one wearing it whilst overindulging in eating and drinking. It was cut into sacred scarabei by the Egyptians and Etruscans and is frequently found engraved. Pliny writes of its fitness as a seal-stone, and Mr. King mentions a large pale amethyst, signed, in the Pulsky collection, on which is engraved the head of a Syrian king.

The amethyst has been frequently quoted as a stone of the celestial Aries, even ancient writers commenting on its sympathetic Aries vibration. The mistake arose from confounding the Babylonian Mars with the Mars of the Greeks and Romans. The Babylonian Mars of Centaur form is clearly identified with the sign Sagittarius.

The amethyst was the ninth stone of the Breastplate, and on it was engraved the name of the tribe of Asher.

The Tenth Stone of the Breastplate

Regarding the tenth stone of the Breastplate there is a general disagreement amongst authorities, some preferring simply to give its Hebraic name THARSHISH without attempting its meaning.

The tenth division of the Breastplate is the division of the zodiacal Capricorn, the color of which is generally regarded as black, the color of the planet Saturn, and which according to Dr. Simmonite, William Lilly, Madame Blavatsky and others, is, esoterically, green. The Targums describe the stone THARSHISH as of the color of the Great Sea, or sea color. This is found in the serpentine variety of a translucent deep green, oily color capable of receiving a high polish. The color of the Egyptian and Arabian serpentine (or hydrinus) is deep and a little heavy. Many intaglios and cameos of antique origin are found cut in serpentine; these specimens include Egyptian scarabei and Babylonian cylinders of about 5,000 years ago, clear evidence that the ancients knew the stone, appreciated it and worked it.

The sign Capricorn is a strange one, symbolizing the Gateway of Heaven through which men pass when life on earth is done. Hence it expresses the mystery of the deep seas which were compared with the seas of space in sacred philosophy. Amongst others, Manilius recognizes Capricorn as a sailor's sign:

> *But when receding Capricornus shows*
> *The star that in his tail's bright summit glows.*
> *Then shall the native dare the angry seas,*
> *A hardy sailor live, spurning inglorious ease.*

Rev. Mr. King writes of a cast from a gem engraved with a

"double-headed Capricorn with an owl's body standing upon and holding in his forefoot a rudder: in allusion to the doctrine laid down by Manilius that the star in the sign's tail is the proper horoscope of mariners and pilots. Or it may typify the usually fickle temper of one born under the sign. This sign likewise presided over all the space within tide mark, the alternate domain of sea and land; a dominion expressed by the half terrestrial, half marine composition of the figure. The region peculiarly under him was the West of Europe."

(This is speaking very generally of the region astrologically ruled by Capricorn.)

"The owl's body is given him perhaps as the attribute of Pallas, the designer of that prototype of navigation, the Argo."

Godfrey Higgins writes of the "whimsical sign called Capricorn which in the Indian Zodiac is an entire goat and an entire fish: in the Greek and the Egyptian the two are united and form one animal."

The place of dazzling brilliancy, called by the Greeks "The Milky Way" is the path of the souls, and is referred to by Macrobius, Cicero and other writers. The author of the *Anacalypsis* writes:

"The Milky Way is placed immediately under that degree of North Latitude which is called the Tropic of Cancer, and the two tropics of Cancer and Capricorn have been called by the astrologers "The Gates of Heaven or the Sun," at each of which the Sun arrives in his annual progress. The Southern Gate is called the Tropic of Capricorn, an amphibious animal, half goat, half fish in our present zodiacs, but in the most ancient zodiacs of India it is described as two entire beings—a goat and a fish."

Here, in this goat-fish sign Capricorn, are the mermen and mermaids, and the half-animal, half-fish beings of the sea. Of the tribe of Asher it is said: "Out of Asher his bread shall be fat, and he shall yield royal dainties," (Genesis 49:20), a statement very much in agreement with the sign Capricorn. Again in Deuteronomy 33:24 we have, according to the Authorized Version, "Let Asher be blessed with children: let him be acceptable to his brethren, and let him dip his foot in oil"; this passage, however, may be closer translated as follows: "More than all the children be Asher blessed: he shall be the most favored of his brethren and bathe his feet in oil."

The tenth Mansion of the Zodiac, the natural "Home" of Capricorn, is the House of fame, honor, reputation, credit, authority and dignity.

His mother called him Asher because she said, "the daughters will call me blessed," Asher being the Hebrew word for "blessed." A close translation of Judges 5:17, would read: "Asher remained on the seashore and abode near his bays."

In all these Biblical allusions to the tribe of Asher there is nothing out of harmony with the sign Capricorn; in fact, in every line the connection is clearly marked.

The tenth stone in the Breastplate is the serpentine and on it was engraved the tribe Naphtali.

The Eleventh Stone of the Breastplate

For reasons stated the SAPIR is placed in the eleventh division of the Breastplate instead of the SHOHAM, and we thus have complete harmony between the eleventh sign of the zodiac, Aquarius, the eleventh division of the Breastplate. The SAPIR stone is translated as sapphire in the Hebrew Bible, the Authorized Version, the Vulgate; as lapis lazuli or sapphire by Mr. Wodiska; and as lapis lazuli by Dr. Hirsch, Rev. J. R. Dummelow, and others. The Targums indicate a stone of blue color, and that this is the lapis lazuli there is no reason to doubt. In ancient times the lapis lazuli was termed SAPPHIRUS; Pliny describes it accurately as "opaque, sprinkled with specks of gold," and many antique intaglios in this stone have been found.

The lapis lazuli was a very highly esteemed stone amongst the old world peoples, who called it "The Stone of Heaven," "The Gem of the Stars," and the zemech stone, connected with all things heavenly. Traditionally it is the stone on which was engraved the law of Moses. In a qabalistic "Piut" is written:

"O, how dreadful is the place of the heavenly abode; for there the light dwelleth with him: and above the firmament is as a precious stone, as the appearance of the Sapphire stone which forms the glorious throne, and thereon He who is clothed with light is seated."

A close translation of Ezekiel 1:6 reads:

"And above, the vault that was over their head was like the appearance of a sapphire stone, the likeness of a throne: and upon the likeness of the throne was a likeness as the appearance of a man above it."

Ezekiel 10:1, similarly treated, reads:

"Then I saw and behold, on the vault that was above the head of the Cherubim, there appeared over them something like a sapphire stone, something similar in appearance to the likeness of a throne."

The connection of a blue stone with the blue heavens is consistent with ancient philosophy, and authorities agree in connecting this color with the sign of the mighty heavens—Aquarius. According to tradition Moses, the law-giver, was born under this sign. Akers in his *Introduction to Biblical Chronology* gives the date of this event as A. M. 3319, Adar third, year of the Julian period 2987, which answers to Thursday, February 13th, 1727 B. C. At that time the sun would be in the Celestial Aquarius.

Aquarius is the water-bearer, and the incident of the striking of the rock from which water gushed forth is mystically associated with it. In the Mythologies this water-bearer is Ganymedes, son of Tros, King of Troy, whom the gods, impressed by his beauty, carried away whilst he was tending the flocks on Mount Ida, in order that the Lord of Olympus might have a lovely cup-bearer.

In astrological deductions Aquarius is the sign of friendship—' 'Naphtali bringeth pleasant words." It is also the sign of hopes and desires: Of Naphtali he said, "O Naphtali, satisfied with favor, and full of the blessing of the Lord, take thou possession of the West and the South." (Deuteronomy 33:23). Then again, in the Septuagint Naphtali is referred to as "a spreading tree yielding leafy branches" and the tree raising branches heavenwards is an Aquarian symbol.

The law of Moses is spoken of as the "tree of Life" which contains the secret of actual and absolute immortality.

Now we are, according to periodic astrological deductions, at the Gate of the age of Aquarius, all the world is undergoing the process of change, and finally all the humanitarianism of Aquarius will replace the accumulation of evil thoughts that lay by the Gateway. Then will Naphtali prevail, his captivity will be over, and the slaves will hang up their chains amongst the sacred cypresses, for the Comforter will come.

The lapis lazuli then, is the stone of the eleventh division of the Breastplate and on it was engraved the name Joseph.

The Twelfth Stone of the Breastplate

Regarding the classification which places JASHPEH in the twelfth division of the Breastplate much controversy has arisen, and the consensus of opinion is against it.

Dr. Emil Hirsch holds the opinion that YAHALOM should replace JASHPEH, and in this surmise he is by no means alone. Astrologically JASHPEH has nothing in common with the last sign of the Zodiac—

Pisces—the color of which is given as "glistening white" by the *Midrash Bemidbah*. It has been more minutely described as "a white glistening color like a fish just taken out of the water" by William Lilly and Dr. Simmonite. There is little doubt that the stone was of a white glistening color.

YAHALOM is rendered as diamond by the translations of the Hebrew Bible, the Authorized Version, by Mr. Cattelle, Dr. Ginzberg and others; but although the diamond is mentioned by Pliny, it could not have found a place among the stones of the Breastplate as they were large stones all engraved with tribal names. To this treatment the diamond is not adapted. The YAHALOM is without doubt white crystal which is of a glistening color and traditionally associated with the twelfth sign of the Zodiac.

Diodorus writes that an artist named Satyreius cut on a small crystal a most exquisite and lifelike portrait of Queen Arsinoe, the beauty of the work amply excusing the miniature stone on which it was engraved. It is related that Nero, his star falling, in his rage against the world and mankind, smashed to pieces two costly crystal *cyphi*, or bowls, on which Homeric subjects were wonderfully engraved.

Articles in crystal still exist to demonstrate its extensive use by ancient nations. Fauno, in his 1553 edition of *Roman Antiquities*, mentions that during the building of a chapel of the King of France in St. Peter's, the marble coffin of Maria, wife of the Emperor Honorius, was discovered. Little remained of the body, but the jewels of the Empress were there, and amongst them were a talismanic plate of gold engraved with the names of the Archangels (Michael, Gabriel, Raphael, Uriel), in Greek letters, about thirty vases and other articles in crystal, and an exquisite Nautilus shell lamp of pure crystal mounted on gold—no doubt the special charm of the Empress.

The sign Pisces, the sign of "the fish with the glittering tails," is symbolically represented by two fishes, which ancient story tells us were Venus and Cupid thus metamorphosed to escape the giant Typhon in his fury. In Babylonian story it is told that the fish-god Oannes—the Dagon of the Book of Samuel—came out of the Erythraean Sea "which borders upon Babylonia" to teach men how to live, to make laws, to worship, to soften their manners and to humanize their lives. Thus, the fish-god was the teacher of the hidden mysteries, and the sign Pisces has always been associated with occult science and hidden things. Mummified fish have been found in the Egyptian tombs, and Clermont Ganneau describes a pair of fish-gods keeping watch over a mummy. Isis as the Great Mother is symbolized with a fish on her head. The old Egyptian town of Esna, nearly 500 miles from Cairo, was called by the Greeks Latopolis on account of the worship of the Latus fish by the inhabitants, and an interesting old Zodiac can still be seen there amongst the famous ruins.

The Babylonians accepted the fish as the symbol of the Resurrection, and the ninth chapter of the Book of Luke describes how 5000 people were fed by 5 loaves of bread (symbolic of Virgo) and two small fishes (symbolic of Pisces), a connection clear enough to the student of the mysteries. The fish was the symbol of the Messiah, and was adopted by the early Christians as the sign of Christ. The Roman Catholic church today has its fish days, and the Piscina is the basin that holds the Holy Water.

The tribe of Joseph is the tribe of the twelfth division of the Breastplate and the twelfth zodiacal sign, Pisces. Joseph in the Book of Genesis is the inspired prophet who reads the meaning of the famous symbolic dreams of the Butler, the Baker and the Pharaoh; who has his divining cup, and who was named by the Pharaoh, ZAPHENATH-PA'NEACH, which has been translated as "Savior of the World" by one writer, but more nearly as "God, the Living One has spoken" by Dr. Dummelow, and as "God spake and he came into Life," by Dr. E. A. Wallis Budge.

According to Talmudic story it was this Pharaoh who said that he saw the colors of rulership about Joseph. Joseph and his brethren are symbolical of the complete Zodiac. JOSHUA is the Son of the Fish (NUN, the Hebrew word for "fish," is probably connected with the Egyptian NAR), and Jesus has his fishermen, "fishers of men." The sign Pisces is the sign of hidden secrets and is mystically symbolized by a key. On the external plane it is the sign of increase, in which is concealed the mandate "Increase and multiply."

The connection of the sign Pisces with the twelfth division of the Breastplate is, as in the previous cases, beyond argument. The stone is the glistening crystal on which was engraved the name of the tribe of Benjamin.

CHAPTER 6

The Stones of the Breastplate
and the Zodiac

"Heaven's golden alphabet—
And he that runs may read."

— Young

The foregoing chapter dealing with the identification of the stones of the Breastplate has necessitated study and research, and the classification reproduced in the table following rests on a secure base. Many of the scholars of the past when endeavoring to render Hebrew stone names into our own language were hampered by a none-too-technical knowledge of the gems themselves, whilst many of the later writers were handicapped by lack of astrological knowledge so essential in a matter of this kind. This will be sufficient to explain the numerous contradictions regarding the identification and allotment of the famous stones by whose agency the psychic priests communicated with the angels of God.

It has already been explained in Chapter 5 why the tribal names do not agree with the signs of the Zodiac and the stones on which they were engraved. Some remarks of Philo Judaeus may with advantage be re-quoted here. In reference to the Breastplate he writes:

"Then on his chest there are twelve precious stones of different colors, arranged in four rows of three stones in each row, being fashioned so as an emblem of the Zodiac. For the Zodiac also consists of twelve animals and so divides the four seasons of the year, allotting three animals to each season.

"And the whole place is very correctly called the Logeum since everything in Heaven has been created and arranged in accordance with right reason and proportion: for there is absolutely nothing there which is devoid of reason. And on the Logeum he embroiders two woven pieces of cloth, calling the one Manifestation and the other Truth. And by the one which he calls Truth he expresses figuratively that it is absolutely impossible for falsehood to enter any part of Heaven but that it is entirely banished to the parts around the Earth dwelling amongst the souls of impious men."

THE CLASSIFICATION OF THE BREASTPLATE.

Hebrew Name of Stone	Modern Name of Stone	Equivalent Sign of Zodiac
1. Odem	Red hematite	Aries
2. Pitdah	Emerald	Taurus
3. Bareketh	Marble	Gemini
4. Nofek	Chrysoprase	Cancer
5. Shoham	Sardonyx	Leo
6. Jashpeh	Jasper	Virgo
7. Lesham	Opal	Libra
8. Shebo	Banded agate	Scorpio
9. Achlamah	Amethyst	Sagittarius
10. Tharshish	Serpentine	Capricorn
11. Sapir	Lapis lazuli	Aquarius
12. Yahalom	Crystal	Pisces

Name Engraved on Stone	Color	Approximate Date of Sun's Entry into the Zodiacal Signs
1. Reuben	Red	March 21st
2. Simeon	Green	April 21st
3. Levi	White	May 22nd
4. Judah	Green	June 22nd
5. Zebulun	Red	July 23rd
6. Issachar	Mixed	August 24th
7. Dan	White and Purple	September 24th
8. Gad	Brown	October 24th
9. Asher	Purple	November 23rd
10. Naphtali	Sea color	December 20th
11. Joseph	Blue	January 20th
12. Benjamin	Glistening White	February 19th

The *Baraita of Samuel* deals with astronomical and astrological philosophies, and in the 6th Chapter there is a detailed account of the instruction of scholars of Egypt on the original places of the planets and the zodiacal divisions. This Samuel was a physician and astrologer, and his remarks on the administration of medicines, the times for operations, etc., are much the same as those given in the best astrological treatises of today. He considers the last four days of the moon as an especially risky period for important operations. This *Baraita of Samuel* is a work of the 8th Century.

Talmudic writers say that besides the twelve tribal names, those of the patriarchs Abraham, Isaac and Jacob were at the top of the Breastplate, and at the end the words, "The tribes of Jeshurun." Others say that the final words were "The tribes of Israel;" Maimonides says, "The tribes of God." The reason given for these additions was that it was necessary for the entire alphabet to be employed so that the officiating High Priest could construct words from the letters, names and colors of the stones of the Breastplate, and reply in this way to all questions asked.

Some of the Rabbis say that six letters were on each stone, made up of the tribal names, the names Abraham, Isaac and Jacob, and the words "Tribes of Jeshurun." Thus the whole of the stones contained 72 letters—the number of SHEM HA MEFORASH. The number 72 is employed in the mysteries, and is given in *Numbers, their Magic and Meaning* as the number of the Angels and of Mercy. In verses 19–21 of 14th Chapter of Exodus the names of the 72 Angels of the name of God are concealed. It is a martial talismanic number, lightly cloaking the waxing and waning of the Moon.

CHAPTER 7

OLD LEGENDS

*"Within that awful volume lies
The mystery of mysteries."*
　　　—SCOTT

It was forbidden to use metal in the engraving of the stones of the Breastplate, neither was it permitted to mark them with pigments or paint. The work was done by the magical Shamir which had the power of eating into the hardest substances at the will of its holder. In the evening light of the first Friday this seventh of the ten marvels of Creation—followed closely by the Stylus, the knowledge of writing, and the two tablets of stone destined to bear the commandments of God—was given to mankind.

It was no larger than a barley grain, yet its power was intense: iron lying near it was shattered and stones were sliced like the leaves of a book. Moses, after tracing the tribal names with his forefinger on the Breastplate, simply held the Shamir over them and the letters were as by magic cut clearly into the stones without trace of fracture or flaw. The Shamir disappeared with the earth-death of Moses, and was not heard of again until the time of Solomon.

When the occasion came to build the temple, the priests reminded the King that it was not lawful to fashion the stones for the Holy Building with instruments of iron.

"What then shall I do?" enquired the King.

To this one of the priests answered: "O, great King, when the world was created the Shamir was created also, and with it Moses was enabled to fashion and engrave the stones of the HOSHEN-HA-MISHPAT."

"But how can I obtain this wonderful Shamir?" asked Solomon.

"What is there difficult for thee who knowest the secrets of Heaven and Earth?" replied the priest, at the same time asking Solomon to compel two demons, a male and a female, to come before him. The King, taking this advice, conjured the demons and bade them declare unto him the hiding-place of the Shamir. This they were unable to do, and they begged the Master-Magician to release them and obtain the secret from the Prince of the demons, Ashmadai. Further they told the King that amongst certain mountain ranges Ashmadai had sunk a deep hole which he filled with water and screened with a great stone sealed with his magical seal. In the dawn of each day he raised himself to Heaven where he learned heavenly wisdom, descending in the evening as the light faded to learn the wisdom of earth. Then he would break the seal, drink of the water, rebind the seal and go his way again.

Having dismissed the demons, Solomon sent his disciple Benaiah (the son of Jehoiada) with his own magical chain and ring on both of which was engraved the Divine Name, and some skins full of wine. Benaiah skillfully released the water from the pit of Ashmadai, leaving the wine in its place. As evening was falling the Prince of the Demons returned; the seal being intact, he raised the stone and to his surprise found wine where water had been. He murmured, "Is it not set down, 'Wine is a mocker, strong drink is noisy; and whosoever indulgeth therein will never be wise'?" Then he drank deeply and fell asleep.

Benaiah, stealing forth from his hiding place, bound him with King Solomon's chain. Ashmadai awoke and in rage attempted to break the chain; Benaiah called to him: "Desist, for the holy name of God binds you, and you are compelled to come with me to Solomon the King."

Brought before Solomon, Ashmadai asked: "Why have you brought me to you? Is not the whole world big enough for you that you would have me also?"

"Of thee I want nothing," answered the King, "but for the building of the Temple I must have the Shamir."

"Then ask the Prince of the Sea and his servant the Moorfowl," came the answer.

"And what does the Moorfowl with the Shamir?" asked the King.

"Splits the barren mountain rock-lands in order that the seeds of the trees and plants which he drops into the crevices may mature and render these places beautiful and agreeable to the wants of man; and then he brings it back to the Prince of the Sea who trusts his oath."

Armed with this information a search was made for the moor fowl's nest, and this when discovered was found to contain the bird's young. The searchers covered the young birds with glass so that the mother-bird might see but not reach them. The ruse succeeded. The bird flew away and shortly afterwards returned with the Shamir, placing it on the glass which split asunder. At that moment the emissary of King Solomon rushed from his hiding place and took the Shamir from the nest of the frightened bird, which thereupon killed itself because it had broken its oath to the Prince of the Sea.

There is another legend which states that the Shamir was brought from Paradise—where it had rested since the time of Moses—by an eagle, for Moses specially intended that the Shamir should be employed in the building of Solomon's temple. When the building of the temple was completed Solomon released Ashmadai, having proved his power over him. Solomon thus acquired authority over the world of Demons, and in the *Arabian Nights*, the Story of the Fisherman and the Genii tells of a demon who was bottled and bound for ages by this Magician King.

The Arabs say that King Solomon received instructions from the archangel Gabriel regarding the place where the Shamir was hidden. These and other legends connected with this wonderful Shamir have attracted the scientific philosopher. The traditional belief that it was a worm can be accepted if we connect the Greek SMIRIS, the emery of the ancient glyptic artists, with the Hebrew SHAMIR, for then the worm would be regarded as minute worms or grains so tough as to be capable of abrading and polishing hard substances. The word SHAMIR does not imply the common or garden variety of worm which is expressed in Hebrew by other words.

It is traditionally related that the four angels of Earth, Air, Fire and Water came to King Solomon, each giving him a jewel, with the instruction that the jewels be set in a magical ring which would symbolize and define his power over the elements. The Arabians say that the metals used in the construction of the magical ring were brass and iron—metals of Venus and Mars. Solomon summoned the good genii by tracing his command with the brass or Venus portion of the ring, and he compelled the evil genii to attend him with the Mars or iron portion. Astrologically Venus and Mars are the two planetary principles which control the emotions and passions of all the world.

It is further assumed that the four jewels of the ring were set on the famous double triangles called the Shield of David and of Solomon, which symbolically represented things of earth in relation to things of Heaven. When Solomon went to bathe, it was his custom to give the ring to Amina, one of his wives, for safe keeping, for it was not permitted to wear the talisman when washing the body.

One day Sakhr, a powerful evil spirit, appeared in the form of Solomon and thus obtained from Amina the magical ring. Thereupon Sakhr sat on the throne of Solomon and ruled for forty days and forty nights while the King wandered about, unknown and forlorn. However, the evil spirit could not maintain the form of King Solomon for longer than forty days and forty nights, so he threw the ring into the sea, thinking as he saw it sink that Solomon was deprived forever of his power over the elements. But he had forgotten that water was one of the elements, and the Angel of the Waters caused the ring to be swallowed by a fish, which was later caught by some fishermen who, surprised at its exceptional beauty, carried it to King Solomon. The King, acting on impulse, cut the fish open, and finding the ring, regained his power over the elements once more.

Passing on to the 16th Century of the Christian era we come to one of the great masters of the Qabalah—Rabbi Low Ben Bezalel of Prague. He is spoken of in the ancient capital of Bohemia as the greatest Bal Shem of his time. Many legends concerning him are extant in Bohemia. He made a Golem, an automaton figure to which he gave life by the simple act of placing under the tongue a charm or *Kemea* which was exactly like the SHEM HAMPHORASCH engraved on King Solomon's ring. It was the Rabbi's custom to take the *Khemeia* from under the tongue of the Golem every Friday at sunset. Once he neglected to do this, and the Golem becoming furious and swelling to a gigantic size, rushed to the old synagogue, spreading destruction all around.

The hymn welcoming the Bride of the Sabbath had not been sung. The Golem entered the Synagogue, stalked towards the Ark and was about to destroy it when Rabbi Low Ben Bezalel ran to the figure and tore the *Kemea* from beneath the tongue. The Golem trembled, quivered and fell in atoms to the ground. An automaton similar to that of the Rabbi was made by Albertus and destroyed in terror by his pupil, Thomas Aquinas.

It is related that the Roman Emperor, Diocletian, while on a hunting expedition, came upon a young ostrich. He had it put in a glass case and taken to his palace. For three days the mother-bird followed, trying in vain to break the glass and release her young. After many fruitless attempts she went away and returned with what is described as a THU-MARE (a name easily identified with SHAMIR) or magical worm. This she dropped on the glass cage which split into fragments in the same way as the glass which covered the nest holding the young of the moor fowl.

The belief that the gift of a precious stone brought great good to the receiver was, and still is, a popular Eastern conviction. It echoes from the Book of Proverbs to the great new age into which the world is now entering: "As a precious stone appeareth a prize in the eyes of him that obtaineth it: whithersoever it turneth it prospereth." (Proverbs 17:8) The blessedness of giving has always been lauded by the masters who constantly enlarge on the magical power gained by the act, for, say they, "God gives."

The gem given should always be carefully considered especially in accordance with the philosophy laid down in these pages, which is held to be a true presentation of ancient laws. The wish of the giver then, it is assumed, is translated into the gem which expresses the wish, translated in concrete form so that whenever the receiver gazes on it, realizes it, the wish of good fortune begins to bear fruit and "whithersoever it turneth it prospereth."

The Talmud relates that Abraham had a magical jewel which he wore suspended about his neck; some writers state that it was a pearl that would re-appear at the time of the Messiah; it was however his own natal stone which, when worn, enabled him by the touch of his hand to heal the sick—a practice which has endured, naturally with varied success, through the ages.

The gem in the ring of Aaron was said to shine out brilliantly when the Elohim favored the nation; and we are told that when the gem and the wearer were in harmony the brightness or otherwise of the stone would indicate faithfully the conditions surrounding him. In the writings of Bishop Epiphanius, a fourth century ecclesiastic of Jewish descent, there is a passage commenting on the Breastplate in which he repeats a still older belief that the stones all turned red when war and defeat faced the Children of Israel.

Some Qabalistic writers maintain that various colors indicating answers to the many questions asked were reflected from the stones over the whole plate; others say that the stone having reference to the tribe or to the direct question alone, gleamed out its special color; thus, for military triumph the symbol would be expressed by the beaming of the hematite; for bountiful production of the fruits of the earth the emerald would flash its message of comfort; for success in matters connected with education the marble would shine; for promise of a good water supply the sparkle of the chrysoprase would suffice; for the well-being of royalty the illumination of the sardonyx would promise well; for a good harvest the jasper would glisten; for success in negotiations with neighboring nations the gleaming of the opal would augur well; for protection from epidemics the glaring of the agate would be accepted as a favorable omen; for pro-phetic truth the radiation of the amethyst would stand; for the welfare of cattle the serpentine would vibrate; for the realization of hopes the lapis lazuli would electrify like the deep blue of the Heavens in serene weather; for success in secret negotiations the crystal would throw off its flashes of light.

According to the legends in the Targumin, Noah lit up the Ark with a stone of marvelous brilliancy; this is considered by some students to denote the Sun at noonday, by others it is called a carbuncle. The Manna of the wilderness, it is said, fell from Heaven accompanied by a rain of the most precious and beautiful stones: this is merely an alle-gorical expression of the "opening of the Heavens," although some more material writers indicate a fall of meteorites. Meteorites were held in especial reverence and were termed BETHEL or House of God by the old Jews, and BAETYLUS by the Greeks and Romans. They were assumed to carry all glorious influences from the Heavenly spheres and to bear the blessings of God.

Pliny mentions a curious stone which he terms "amianthus" and which is not affected by the action of fire. This substance, he says, effectually counteracts all noxious spells, especially those wrought by magicians.

It was considered a bad mistake to barter for a talismanic gem, that being in itself a crystallization of the sublime forces, and being holy does not admit of barter. Pliny tells of Ismenius the great flute player of his time, who loved to display numbers of gems: he set his heart on obtain-ing a beautiful emerald—his talismanic gem—on which was engraved a figure of Amymone (one of the Danaides), the gem being offered for sale in Cyprus for six golden denarii; he sent his messenger to purchase it for him, and this man on his return informed Ismenius that the jeweler had agreed to take two golden denarii less than was originally asked. On learning this the musician exclaimed: "By Hercules, he has done me a bad turn in this, for the merit of the stone has been greatly impaired by this reduction in price."

The seven precious minerals of the Buddhists are stated by Sir Moiner-Williams K. C. I. E. to be:

1. Gold.
2. Silver.
3. Pearls.
4. Sapphires or rubies.
5. Catseyes.
6. Diamonds.
7. Corals.

The list varies and lapis lazuli is given instead of pearls by some authors. There are also seven royal treasures amongst which is the jewel stone NORBU which throws its rays for several miles on the darkest nights.

Apollonius of Tyana, described by Barrett as one of the most extraordinary persons that ever appeared in the world, received during his travels in India from the sage Iarchus seven rings each of which contained a jewel symbolical of one of the planets. One of these he wore every day, according to the planetary order of the days of the week, and to the virtue of these gems—which Iarchus is stated to have received from Heaven—Philostratus, the biographer of Apollonius, attributes his long life, his strength and his attractions. The following were the gems inset in the rings which Apollonius wore, one on each day of the week:

Sunday	Day of the Sun	Diamond (In a ring of gold)
Monday	Day of the Moon	Cloudy crystal (? Moonstone) (In a ring of silver)
Tuesday	Day of Mars	Hematite (In a ring of iron)
Wednesday	Day of Mercury	Pink jasper (In a ring of silver)
Thursday	Day of Jupiter	Carbuncle (In a ring of tin)
Friday	Day of Venus	Coral (In a ring of bronze)
Saturday	Day of Saturn	Onyx (In a ring of lead)

Justin Martyr had a deep reverence for this great disciple of Pythagoras, and in his writings he expresses wonder at the potency of the talismans of Apollonius, which calm the fury of the sea, hold back the winds
of Heaven, cause wild animals to become tame;—"Our Lord's miracles
are held to us only by tradition, but the miracles of Apollonius are
uncountable almost, and truly were evident enough to charm all those
who saw them."

CHAPTER 8

STONES IN VARIOUS MYTHOLOGIES

Meru or the North Pole, the abode of the great Indra who, according to the Rigveda, "fixed firm the moving Earth, made tranquil the incensed mountains, who spread the wide firmament, who consolidated the Heavens," is symbolically presented as a shining mountain of jewels and precious metals.

The Lord of Patala (the infernal regions), Seshanaga, known as the King of the Serpents, is pictured in the Bhagavad-Gita (Revelations) as:

"Of appearance gorgeous and brilliant. He has a thousand heads and on each of them is set a crown of glittering gem stones. His neck is black, his body is black and black are his tongues.

"Like torches gleam his eyes: yellow-colored are the borders of his robe: from each ear hangs a sparkling gem stone: his extended arms are adorned with jeweled bracelets: his hands hold the holy shell, the radiant weapon, the war mace and the lotus."

Surya is the great Sun to whose chariot is harnessed seven green horses driven by the charioteer Arun, the Dawn. In his account of the Temple of Surya, Hort quotes the following from a very old traveler: "The walls were of red marble interspersed with streaks of gold. On the pavement was an image of the radiant Divinity, hardly inferior to himself in splendor: his rays being imitated by a boundless profusion of rubies, pearls and diamonds of inestimable value, arranged in a most judicious manner and diffusing a luster scarcely endurable by the sight." The Hindu work *Ayeen Akbery* is also quoted by the same author. In it the temple of Surya is thus described:

"Near to Jaggernaut is the Temple of the Sun in the erecting of which was expended the whole revenue of Orissa for twelve years. The wall which surrounds the edifice is one hundred and fifty cubits high and nineteen cubits thick: having three entrances. At the Eastern Gate are two very fine figures of elephants, each with a man upon his trunk. On the West are two surprising figures of horsemen completely armed, who having killed two elephants are seated upon them. In front of that gate is an octagonal pillar of black stone fifty cubits high. Nine flights of steps lead to an extensive enclosure, in which is a large dome constructed of stone, upon which are carved the Sun and the Stars: and around them is a border on which is represented a variety of human figures expressive of different passions: some kneeling, others prostrate: together with a number of imaginary strange animals."

Rama's monkey army is said to have built a bridge of rocks, called the Bridge of Adam, from the western point of India to Ceylon. Krishna, the eighth Avatara or incarnation of Vishnu, is represented in magnificent dress adorned with garlands of wild flowers and with strings of costly pearls around his ankles. His complexion is blue, as is also the large bee usually depicted flying above his head. The Avataras are all adorned with gems, flowers and loose gauze cloaks interwoven with gold and silver and colors, while they hold various symbols such as the Holy Shell, the axe, rings, etc.

The antique Temple Caves of Kanhari at Salsette contain remarkable stone carvings, some of the statues cut from the main rock being fifteen feet high. Of these sacred figures some are adorned with helmets, others have jeweled crowns, others great masses of hair. The famous necklace of the King of Maabar was composed of rubies, sapphires and emeralds, and the necklace taken from Jaipal, the Hindu King, by Mahmud (1001 A.D.) was made up of pearls, rubies and various precious stones, the whole being valued at over 500,000 dollars. These necklaces were regarded as religious objects. Buddha was worshipped symbolically as a black square stone, and the ancient Zodiac of the Buddhist has been known as the Twelve Heavenly Jewels. This is symbolized as:

An antelope or horse (in the place of Aries)
A bull
Twins
Crab
Lion
Virgin

Scales
Scorpion
Bow and arrow (in the place of Sagittarius)
Elephant (in the place of Capricorn)
Water-bearer
Swastika (in the place of Pisces)

The Zodiacal Treasures of the King are:

The Elephant	equaling Capricorn
The Horse	equaling Aries
The Beautiful Jewel	equaling Libra
The Wife	equaling Virgo
Holy Guide of the House	equaling Aquarius
The General	equaling Sagittarius
The Swastika	equaling Pisces

Mr. Samuel Beal, B.A.R.N., etc., gives the following account of the offering of the Alms Dish in his *Buddhist Records of the Western World*:

"The four Deva Sagas coming from the four quarters each brought a golden dish and offered it. The Lord sat silently and accepted not the offerings on the ground that such a costly dish became not the character of a hermit. The four Kings casting away the golden dishes offered silver ones. Afterwards they offered vessels of Po-Chi (crystal), Liu-Li (lapis lazuli), Ma-Nao (carnelian), Ku-Chi (amber), Chin-Chu (ruby), and so on.

"The Lord of the World would accept none of them. The four Kings then returned to their palaces and brought as an offering stone *patras* of a deep blue color and translucent. On their again presenting these the Lord to avoid accepting one and rejecting the others joined them all in one and thus accepted them. Putting them one within the other the Lord made one vessel of the four. Therefore four borders are to be seen on the outside of the rim of the dish."

Black stones have been repeatedly mentioned in the history of man. We have seen them in the transition of Aglauros, in the Buddhist devotion, and in the Biblical narratives. These *Matsebah* have been found engraved with the twelve signs of the Zodiac, sometimes symbolized as the twelve Gods of Assyria.

Gramaldi in *Zodiacs and Planispheres* mentions a black stone which exhibited ten out of the twelve zodiacal signs and ten decans out of the thirty-six. It was found near the Tigris in Bagdad, and is perhaps the oldest zodiacal monument extant, its date being set down at 1320 years before the Christian era. But the most famous of all black stones is the HAJER-ALASVAD which is now set into the southeast corner of the Ka'bah.

The story of this sacred relic is told very completely by Hadji Khan and Wilfred Sparrey in *With the Pilgrims to Mecca*: Having determined to form man in his own image, the Creator called the angels Gabriel, Michael and Israfil, each at a different time, requesting that they should bring for his purpose seven handfuls of earth from seven earth strata, and seven colors. But the Earth cried out that the anger of God would one day fall on her through the wickedness and folly of man, and so the angel departed without accomplishing the work. God then sent the Angel Azrail who, listening to no appeal, remorselessly carried out his divinely appointed task. God then made Azrail the Angel of Death, who ever after separated the souls of men from their useless bodies. The Earth was then set down between Mecca and Tayef where, having been pressed to a proper degree by the angels, it was shaped as a man by the Creator. The mass was then left for 40 years, being visited only by the Angels.

But the angel Edris who, "from being of those that are nearest to God, became the Devil," grew furious because he knew that man was designed to be his master. So with a vow that he would always oppose him, Edris kicked the image of earth which responded with an empty sound. Then the Creator breathed into the image His own Spirit and Man arose. He was given Paradise to inhabit, and out of his left side Eve was taken. When Man fell and was found no longer worthy of Eden, a peculiar stone fell too and, says the narrative, "this stone became the most cherished possession of the Muhammadan world."

The story continues:

> "It (the stone) was restored to Paradise at the Deluge, after which it was brought back to earth by Gabriel and given to Abraham who set it in the southeastern corner of the Ka'bah which he is said to have built. There it remained till the Karmatians overturned the fundamental

points of Islam, bearing it away in triumph to their capital. The citizens of Mecca sought to redeem the stone by offering no less than 5000 pieces of gold for it. The ransom was scornfully rejected by the impious sectaries.

"Some 22 years later, however, they sent back the stone voluntarily, covering their discomfiture by declaring it to be a counterfeit. The dismay of the Meccans was allayed when they discovered that the stone would swim on water, that being the peculiar quality of the stone they had lost; so they were satisfied that the true one had been returned to them."

At first the stone was whiter than milk, but it grew to be black by the sins of mankind. All believers, whatever may be the cause to which they attribute the change of color, agree that the defilement is purely superficial, the inside of the stone being still as white as the driven snow.

The silver box wherein it lies is about twenty inches square and is raised a little more than five feet from the ground. A round window having a diameter of some nine inches is kept open to enable the pilgrims to kiss or touch the treasure within, the treasure being known as "the right hand of God on Earth." In color it is a shining black; in shape hollow like a saucer, presumably the result of the pressure of devoted lips. If a pilgrim fails to touch the Stone he must make a reverential salaam before it and pass on. Special prayers are also said. The guide accompanying the authors recited the following lines from the *Fortuhul Haremeyn* before leaving:

"Think not that the KA'BAH was made from the earth: in the body of the world it took the place of the heart. And the stone you call the Black Stone was itself a ball of dazzling light. In ages past the Prophet said it shone like the crescent moon until at last the shadows falling from the sinful hearts of those that gazed on it turned its surface black. Now since the amber gem that came to the earth from Paradise with the Holy Ghost, has received such impressions on itself what should be the impressions which our hearts receive? Verily, whosoever shall touch it being pure of conscience, is like unto him that has shaken hands with God."

Other accounts state that the stone is about seven inches in diameter, oval and irregular, made up of a number of smaller and variously sized pieces, which inclines one to the opinion that it was at one time shattered by some hard blow and afterwards put together again. The most recent descriptions of the stone of Mecca agree that it is of a dark reddish-brown color with a brown border seemingly of pitch and small sand stones, the whole being set in a band of silver.

The most wonderful thing regarding the history of this relic of Islam is that one little stone, the Black Stone of Mecca, should have such powerful attraction for over 222,000,000 of the inhabitants of the world.

Included in Guerber's *Myths and Legends of the Middle Ages* is the following story of Roland and the Jewel:

"Charlemagne learning that the Robber Knight of the Ardennes had a precious jewel set in his shield called all his bravest noblemen together and bade them sally forth separately with only a page as escort in quest of the knight. Once found they were to challenge him in true knightly fashion, and at the point of the lance win the jewel he wore. A day was appointed when, successful or not, the courtiers were to return, and, beginning with the lowest in rank, were to give a truthful account of their adventures while on the quest.

"All the knights departed and scoured the Forest of the Ardennes, each hoping to meet the robber knight and win the jewel. Among them was Milon, accompanied by his son Roland, a lad of fifteen, whom he had taken as page and armor-bearer. Milon had spent many days in vain search for the knight when, exhausted by his long ride, he dismounted, removed his heavy armor and lay down under a tree to sleep, bidding Roland keep close watch during his slumbers.

"For a while Roland watched faithfully: then, fired by a desire to distinguish himself he donned his father's armor, sprang on his steed and rode off into the forest in search of adventures. He had not gone very far when he saw a gigantic horseman coming to meet him and by the dazzling glitter of a large stone set in his shield he recognized him to be the invincible Knight of the Ardennes. Afraid of nothing, however, the lad laid his lance in rest when challenged to fight, and charged so bravely that he unhorsed his opponent.

"A fearful battle on foot ensued, each striving hard to accomplish the death of the other. But at last the fresh young energy of Roland conquered and his terrible foe fell to the ground in agony. Hastily wrenching the coveted jewel from the shield of the dead warrior, the boy hid it in his breast. Then riding rapidly back to his sleeping father he laid aside the armor and removed all traces of a bloody encounter. Soon after Milon awoke and resumed the quest, when he came upon the body of the dead knight. He was disappointed indeed to find that another had won the jewel, and rode sadly back to court to be present on the appointed day.

"In much pomp, Charlemagne ascended his throne amid the deafening sound of trumpets. Then seating himself he bade the knights appear before him. Each in turn told of finding the knight slain and the jewel gone. Last of all came Milon. Gloomily he made his way to the throne to repeat the story that had already been told so often. But as he went there followed behind him with a radiant face young Roland, proudly bearing his father's shield in the center of which shone the precious jewel. At the sight of this all the nobles started and whispered that Milon had done the deed. Then when he dismally told how he too had found the knight dead, a shout of incredulity greeted him. Turning his head he saw to his amazement that his own shield bore the gem.

"At the sight of it he appeared so amazed that Charlemagne set himself to question Roland, and thus soon learned how it had been obtained. In reward for his bravery in this encounter Roland was knighted and allowed to take his place among the paladins of the Emperor. Nor was it long before he further distinguished himself, becoming to his father's delight the most renowned among all that famous company."

The Irish charm stones used to charm away vermin, are about one inch in thickness and about four inches long. The Australian natives carried magical stones which could never be seen by women.

Certain stones known as Dendrites exhibit markings which take the form of trees, grass, moss, etc. (see moss agate). The ancients considered them fortunate for prosperity in farming and in general affairs of life. Brigadier General Kenneth Mackay mentions in his book, Across Papua, various carved stones which were employed by the natives as garden charms.

CHAPTER 9

STONES AND THEIR STORIES

Abraxas Stones. These were stones used by the Gnostics or Knowers who existed in the early ages of Christianity. "Amongst this Christian philosophic sect," writes King, "the figure of Abraxas was held in high esteem. They used it as a teacher in obedience to whom they directed their own peculiar transcendental inquiries and mystic doctrines: as a token or password amongst the initiated to show that they belonged to the same sect: as an amulet and talisman: and lastly as a seal for their documents."

The figure of Abraxas was composed as follows: cock's head, human body, legs formed like serpents. In one hand he holds the whip of power, in the other the shield of wisdom. These are the five mystical emanations symbolically expressed—the Sun, the Inward Feelings, Awakened Understanding, *Dynamis* (Force), *Sophia* (Wisdom). Basilides, the Egyptian who is supposed to have founded the sect, is criticized in the writings of Augustine because he "pretended the number of the Heavens to be 365, the number of days in the year." Hence he glorified a "sacred name" as it were, namely the word ABRAXAS, the letters in which name, according to the Greek methods of enumeration, make up that number. The principal Abraxas stones were of jasper, plasma, sard, lodestone and chalcedony.

Alectorius. The alectorius, or as Camillus Leonardus has it, the alectoria, is said to be a stone never bigger than a large bean, which stone is taken from a cock. When this stone becomes perfect, says Leonardus, the bird will not drink.

The alectorus is said to be a stone like crystal, and very bright. It is related that Milo of Croton, the great wrestler and strong man of the ancients who lived in the year 520 B.C., carried a specimen with him always and only lost his strength when he lost the stone. Its virtues were many: it gave a wife favor in her husband's eyes; it banished thirst, bestowed eloquence and persuasive power, brought domestic peace, harmony, victory and honor. As the stone is attached to the zodiacal Scorpio it may have been a white topaz but identification is uncertain.

Bezoar Stones

"Everything that frees the body from any ailment is called the Bezoar of that ailment."

—LEONARDUS, *Mirror of Stones*

These stones, the name of which is derived from the Persian PAD-ZAHR, poison-expelling (*Zahr*, poison; *Pad*, to dislodge,) are concretions found in the stomach of the stag or goat, and are credited with great medicinal virtues. They are said to dislodge poisons and to remove poisonous diseases. In India and Persia the belief in the virtue of Bezoars is very widespread; it is said that those taken from the stomach of the wild goat of Persia (*Caprea Acyagros,*) especially if large specimens, are sold for their weight in gold. Dr. Anthony Todd Thomson, M.D., quotes Garner, an old writer, who gives the following curious origin of the Bezoar which he obtained from the Arabians:

"When the hart is sick and hath eaten many serpents for his recoverie, he is brought into so great a heate that he hasteth to the water and there covereth his body unto the very ears and eyes at which distilleth many tears from which the stone (the Bezoar) gendered."

These Calculi are composed chiefly of superphosphate of lime, but concretions of phosphate of ammonia or magnesia are also found. The Bezoar was highly esteemed as a remedy for diseases of the bladder and kidneys. Dr. Anthony Todd Thomson says that the belief in the curative power of these Bezoars "affords an addition to the many thousand proofs of the influence of mind over body, and how truly efficacious Imagination may prove in removing disease."

It was usual to bind the Bezoar to the part affected where that was possible. In China the MO-SOH or Bezoar was credited with the power of renewing youth and bestowing beauty, and similar beliefs prevail in parts of India. The Malays obtain this stone from monkeys and porcupines, and its magical virtues are held in great esteem. Known there as the *Guliga*, the Bezoar is exported in great quantities from Sarawak to Hindustan especially, where it is used as a remedy for asthma. It is said that the *Guliga* is procured from a red-colored monkey of the Semnopithecus species, and the *Guliga Landak* which is rarer and more highly valued from the porcupine. Jean Baptiste Tavernier (Baron d'Aubonne) during his travels in the East in the 17th century became acquainted with the Bezoar stone which he describes in his writings. "Genuine stones," it is stated, "if placed in the mouth spring up and attach themselves to the palate, or if placed in water will make the water boil."

Draconite. The draconite is described as a white, brilliant gem which must be cut from the head of a living dragon if its luster and virtue are to be retained. Philostrates writes that the seekers for the Draconite weave certain letters in gold into a robe of scarlet, and infuse opiates into the letters. The Dragon, when lured out of his cave by musical charm, succumbs to the power of the soporific robe. Immediately he does so the Indians rush on him and cutting off his head take from it gems of bright hues and indescribable virtues. But a dragon has often seized the man and his weapons and drawn him into his den. The draconite is associated with the zodiacal Scorpio and is partly, if not wholly, symbolic.

Enhydros or **Hydrolite.** This is a well-known water stone and within its crystal cover water can usually be seen clearly. Marbodus says that this stone "ceaseless tears distils." The enhydros is said to be a cure for gout and affections of the feet, and a charm for bestowing inspiration and clearness of thought. The water contained within the enhydros is said to be highly poisonous if taken internally. The stone is under the zodiacal Pisces.

Gnostic Stones. Besides the figure of the mystic Abraxas, the talismanic stones of the Gnostics were engraved with various devices. A large lodestone in the King collection is engraved with a figure of Venus dressing her long hair. Venus stands for the mystic Sophia or Achamoth, and as such represents Truth.

Iris. The "Iris resplendent with the crystal's sheen" which the "swarthy Arabs glean" is now known as rainbow quartz. The iridescence is produced by the reflection of light from the cracks in the stone. The same effect is produced if the crystal is first subjected to heat and then plunged quickly into cold water. The Iris obtained its name from the beautiful companion of Juno, who traveled on the rainbow with wings extended, clothed in glorious colors, radiant lights around her head. She was the guide and helper of the souls of women released from their bodies.

Lapis Armenus, or Armenian Stone, is a copper carbonate used as a medicine against infection. It is related in Arab books that a solution of this substance will retain its power for 10 years. In the East copper has been long used as a safeguard against cholera, and it has been observed that workers in copper mines have enjoyed immunity from the disease. Dr. Richard Hughes notes the value of copper in Asiatic cholera, adding: "There is now abundant evidence of its efficacy both among the workers in the metal and in those who have worn a plate of it next the body during the prevalence of the epidemic." The *lapis armenus*, like all copper compositions, is under the rule of the planet Venus.

Lapides Fulmonis. These "thunder stones," which are believed to be formed by the lightning in the clouds (see **OBSIDIAN**), are known by the peasants of Calabria as *cuogni di truoni*. The traditional belief is that they are plunged by a lightning strike six feet into the earth, and that every time it thunders they are drawn one foot nearer the surface. After the sixth or seventh thunder storm it is said that the stones are raised to the surface. The peasants test them by suspending them above a fire, attached to a blue thread; if the thread does not burn the stone is adjudged a true thunder stone and is carefully treasured as a potent talisman against the lightning strike.

Lapis Memphiticus. This stone of Memphis is described as a sparkling round body of about the size of a hazelnut. It is mentioned by Pliny as deadening the pain of surgical operations if taken in wine and water beforehand. If it be reduced to powder and applied, according to Dioscorides, as an ointment to that part of the body to which a surgeon was about to apply either fire or the knife, it produced insensibility to pain. This is an early instance of the recorded action of a local anesthetic.

Luz or **Luez.** This is said to be a stone or indestructible bone in the human backbone. Dr. John Lightfoot, a great Hebraic scholar of the 17th century, details the following legend:

> "How doth a man revive in the world to come?" was asked by the Emperor Hadrian of Rabbi Joshua Ben Hananiah. "From Luz in the backbone," he made reply and then went on to demonstrate this to the Emperor. He took the bone Luz and put it into water, but the water had no action on it. He put it in the fire but the fire consumed it not. He placed it in a mill, but could not grind it. He laid it on an anvil, but the hammer crushed it not."

Mandarin's Jewels. Each of the nine *Khioupings* or Mandarins of China proclaims his rank by a distinctive button of about an inch in diameter worn at the top of his cap, and distinguishing dress and insignia. The chief officers wear a ruby on the cap. They are divided into civilian and military sections.

The military wear a robe on which is embroidered a unicorn, the girdle being adorned with a jade clasp set in rubies. The civilian Mandarin is distinguished by a crane embroidered on both back and front of the robe.

Those of the second order wear a coral button in their caps. The military are distinguished by an embroidered lion and a gold girdle clasp inset with rubies, the civilian by a golden pheasant.

Those of the Third Order wear a sapphire in the cap. The military display a leopard and a clasp of wrought gold, the Civilian a peacock.

Those of the Fourth Order wear an opaque blue stone in the cap. The military display on their robes a tiger and silver button clasp, the civilian a wild goose.

Those of the Fifth Order have their caps adorned with a crystal, the military their robes with a bear and a plain gold clasp with silver button, the civilian a silver pheasant.

Those of the Sixth Order wear on their caps an opaque white shell. The military adorn their robes with a tiger-cat and clasp of mother-of-pearl, the civilian with an egret.

Those of the Seventh Order wear on their caps a wrought gold button. The military robe displays a bear and has a silver clasp, the civilian a Mandarin duck.

Those of the Eighth Order wear a plain gold button on their caps. The military have on their robes a seal and a horn clasp, the civilian a quail.

Those of the Ninth Order wear on their caps a silver button. The military are distinguished by a rhinoceros and a clasp of buffalo horn, the civilian by a long-tailed jay.

Median Stone. This is a mysterious gem, possibly symbolic, which is described as of black color. Marbodus says "'Tis white to heal us, black to slay our foes." It would then be symbolical of Black and White Magic.

Molochite. Mr. King is of the opinion that the Molochite is clear green jade, and so he agrees with Pliny's description of the stone, "opaque of hue with the vivid green of the emerald." Its virtue protected babies from harm, gave luck and beauty and opposed the spite of witchcraft.

Ophites. Ophites, or snake stones, are stones of black or grey color described by Orpheus as "black, hard, weighty, portentous balls surrounded by furrowed lines in many a mazy bend." They are variously described. There are in India snake charmers called *Sampoori* who assert that they can extract the snake stone from the head of a snake, but these assertions are unfavorably commented upon by some Indian authors. Still, it has been shown by Sir J. Tennent in his work on *Ceylon* and by Buckland in *Curiosities of Natural History* that some striking cures from snake bite have ostensibly been effected by the use of a so-termed snake stone which is said to absorb the poison if applied to the bite with a little blood before the poison has had time to invade the system.

Some authentic cures are quoted, notably that of a man bitten by a cobra; in this case the man was saved by "two small snake stones the size of a large pea." The snake stone, it is said, clings for a short time to the wound and then drops off. It is reported to be composed of some vegetable substance; the cobra stone, according to Farraday, the distinguished chemist, is but charred bone filled with blood a number of times and then again charred. In England and Scotland snake stones strung together used to be given to cattle to chew if bitten by vipers. The stone was considered to be a very potent charm against the evil blasts of occult forces. Albertus Magnus carried a stone which guarded against epidemics, evil magic and the bites of serpents, and by the aid of which he was able to attract serpents.

Orite. This stone is described as black and round. If mixed with the oil of roses it will cure fatal wounds, protect from wild animals and prevent childbirth.

Ovum Anguinum. The Ovum Anguinum is described by Pliny as a Druidic badge the size of an apple, surrounded by a gristly crust covered with protuberances like the suckers on the arms of a cuttlefish. The story goes that at a certain season of the year a crowd of snakes are found intertwined and bearing above them the magical Ovum, which the hunter had to catch in some soft material before it tumbled to earth, for if it did so it would lose its power. As soon as the hunter seized the magic stone the serpents rushed after him and his fate was sealed if they reached him before he crossed a flowing stream.

Pandarbes. Philostratus relates how Chariclea escaped unharmed from the funeral pyre on which she was condemned to perish by the jealous Arsace by secretly wearing the wonderful ring of King Hydrastes. In this ring was set a stone called Pandarbes, which was engraved as a talismanic charm against the fury of fire.

Pantheros. It is probable from the description, given by old writers, that it was a mottled brown Egyptian jasper opal. It was said to protect the wearer from enemies, wild animals and fear, which last, according to the healthy philosophy of the Rosicrucians, is the greatest of the vices and the gateway of weakness and failure.

Philosopher's Stone. The Philosopher's Stone is also known as *lapis philosophorum*, the Eye of the Philosophers, the Egg of the Philosophers. French writers call it *Pierre Philosophale*, and German writers *Der Stein der Weisen*. In the Rosicrucian mysteries it is known as "The Stone of the Wise," "The Sacred Stone," "The Stone of Wisdom," etc. In spite of the assertions made by overly sanguine critics as to the fallacy of the Philosopher's Stone on the material plane, scientists—mystic and material—have never ceased to search for a substance so precious. Phillips

(*Transmutation of Metals*, 1702) says that "this transmutation is what the Alchymists call the Grand Operation or Secret of finding the Philosopher's Stone which they give out to be so curious an Universal seed of all metals. If any metal be liquefied in a vessel, and this 'Power of Perfection' be thrown into the mass it will transform it into gold or silver."

Some of the philosophers call it "The Stone," *noster lapis*, "The Sublime Stone," "Our Stone." It is related that King Henry VI granted "4 successive Patents and Commissions" to several knights and Mass Priests to find the Philosopher's Stone. In his recent work on Alchemy, H. Stanley Redgrove, B.Sc., F.C.S., etc., writes:

> "We must not assume that because we know not the method now, real transmutations have never taken place. Modern research indicates that it may be possible to transmute other metals (more especially silver) into gold, and consequently we must admit the possibility that, amongst the many experiments carried out, a real transmutation was effected."

Timbs (*Alchemy and Chemistry*) emphasizes the fact that many of the opinions of the alchemists have been vindicated. He specially notes the condition of allotropism, or the quality which certain bodies possess of assuming two marked phases of chemical and physical existence. "This shatters the opinion," he writes, "on which our absolute repudiation of the doctrine of transmutation was based." Dr. Colange explains allotropy as that branch of chemical science which takes account of the different sets of properties possible to one and the same body.

Organic solids occur under one of the three conditions, viz., the crystalline, as the diamond; the vitreous, as glass; the amorphous or shapeless, as clay, chalk, etc. But there are many bodies any one of ,which without undergoing a change in chemical composition, may yet appear under one of the above three conditions with striking changes in physical and even chemical properties while still retaining, so to speak, its chemical identity. Thus, ordinary white phosphorus may by the application of heat be converted into a hard amorphous substance which is its allotropic form.

An excellent paper on *Allotrophy or Transmutation* was read before the British Association at Sheffield, England, a few years ago by Dr. Henry M. Howe. In it Dr. Howe dealt at greater length with what has been previously advanced on the subject. Since the discovery of radium and the extensive experiments of the late Sir William Ramsay, Mr. Cameron and others in the department of transmutation and disintegration, modern science has projected itself into the Halls of Alchemy and has joined hands with its parent science to search for that which the world of a few years back regarded with ignorant ridicule.

In the space at disposal it is impossible to enter into details of the numerous accounts of successful alchemy recorded. A number of these will be found in Dr. Franz Hartmann's works and in the excellent works on the subject by H. Stanley Redgrove and others. Perhaps the case noticed by Dr. Franz Hartmann is one of the most romantic. It came before the court at Leipsig on August 9th, 1715 and is reported in the acts of the judicial faculty of that town. A gentleman came late one night to the Castle of Tankerstein where the Countess of Erbach resided. He said that having accidentally killed a deer which belonged to the Palatine of Palatia he was being pursued, and therefore he asked protection. The Countess hesitated, but being impressed with the stranger's appearance she ordered that a room be given him.

He remained in the castle several days, and then being granted an interview with the Countess, he thanked her for her protection in return for which he offered to transmute all her silver into gold. The lady was incredulous but, her curiosity overcoming her, she gave the stranger a silver tankard which he melted and with a stone transmuted into gold. The Countess sent the gold to a goldsmith in the town, who having tested it pronounced it to be the purest gold. After this she asked the adept to transmute all her silver into gold. This he did and, receiving the lady's thanks as he tendered his own, departed. The Countess's husband, a great spendthrift who was serving as an officer abroad, hearing that his wife by some means had suddenly become wealthy returned home quickly. He demanded the gold for himself but the Countess would not surrender it.

Thereupon the Count brought his wife before the Court, claiming that as Lord of the territory (*Dominus Territorii*) on which the Castle belonging to his wife was built, all treasure found upon the land was his. He asked that the Court should order the gold to be sold and that after new silver had been purchased for his wife the balance of the money be paid to him. The defense urged that as the gold had been artificially produced it could not come under a law relating to buried treasure; again, that the silver had been transmuted into gold for the sole benefit of the

A Perfect Specimen of the English Gold Noble (1344) in the Kelsey I. Newman Collection. Traditionally stated to have been made from Alchemical Gold

Countess. The Court was asked to allow the lady to retain the gold thus obtained and judgment was given in her favor.

Some years ago a medal was exhibited in the Imperial Treasury in Vienna, which had been partly transmuted into gold by the stone used by the monk Wenzel Seiler who had been ennobled by Leopold I with the title Wenzeslaus Ritter von Reinburg. Recent tragic events make its present whereabouts doubtful. It is traditionally stated that the true Philosopher's Stone was hung in the Ark by Noah to give light to life and radiance to the world after the Flood-darkness. This legend is a parable expressing the highest truth, for the Philosopher's Stone that carries light into the darkness of materialism is the true Stone of the Wise. Among the discoveries made in the search for the Philosopher's Stone the following are given by Dr. Brewer: the invention of Dresden porcelain by Bötticher, that of gun powder by Roger Bacon, of the properties of acids and various substances by Prince Geber, of the nature of gases by Van Helmont, of salts by Dr. Glauber, etc.

Polish Stones, Poland Stones, Poles' Stones. It has frequently been stated that the Poles originated the wearing of birth stones, but this practice is a very remote one and was recommended by ancient philosophers long before the Polani came to Polska. The Poles are naturally gifted with fine imagination and psychic intuition; therefore they readily absorbed the spiritual philosophies of the Jewish wanderers who received asylum in Poland. The fondness of the Poles for beautiful gems is proverbial and the spread of the knowledge of the occult virtues found to exist in these beautiful crystallizations was more marked in Polska than in any other country.

It is also not to be wondered at that so many of the lists given are incorrect. In this book an endeavor is made to set right the many errors that have so naturally crept in. Usually the Poland Stones are doubtfully classified as follows:

THE MONTHS

January	Garnet, emblem of constancy.
February	Amethyst, emblem of sincerity.
March	Bloodstone, emblem of courage.
April	Diamond, emblem of innocence.
May	Emerald, emblem of love success.
June	Agate, emblem of health and longevity.
July	Carnelian, emblem of contentment.
August	Sardonyx, emblem of married happiness.
September	Chrysolite, emblem of protection from insanity.
October	Opal, emblem of hope.
November	Topaz, emblem of fidelity.
December	Turquoise, emblem of prosperity.

The emblems of the stones are fairly correct.

THE PLANETS

Saturn	Lead	Turquoise
Jupiter	Tin	Carnelian
Mars	Iron	Emerald
Sun	Gold	Diamond
Venus	Copper	Amethyst
Mercury	Quicksilver	Lodestone
Moon	Silver	Crystal

The metals of the planets are correctly given and do not appear ever to have been disputed. The turquoise of Saturn is correctly the odonto-lite or bone turquoise. The emerald is a stone of Venus, the amethyst a stone of Jupiter, the lodestone a stone of Mars. The crystal has often been admitted as influenced by the Moon although it is more acceptable for qabalistic considerations to identify it with Neptune.

THE ZODIAC

1. Aries	Ruby
2. Taurus	Topaz
3. Gemini	Carbuncle
4. Cancer	Emerald
5. Leo	Sapphire
6. Virgo	Diamond
7. Libra	Jacinth
8. Scorpio	Agate
9. Sagittarius	Amethyst
10. Capricorn	Beryl
11. Aquarius	Onyx
12. Pisces	Jasper

The confusion here is very marked, and the reader is referred to the chapters dealing with the High Priest's Breastplate.

Rings Bearing Stones of Invisibility. Perhaps the most famous of these rings is the ring of Gyges, the shepherd King of Lydia, described by Plato and Herodotus. When the stone was turned inwards the wearer was rendered invisible. By its aid Gyges assassinated King Candaules and seized his wife and children. It is related that Otnit, King of Lombardy, wore a ring given him by his mother, which had power similar to the ring of Gyges, as well as the special virtue of preventing the wearer from losing his way. Nizami, the poet of Persia in the early 13th century, tells the story of a shepherd, a story similar to that of King Gyges. Another ring of invisibility is the ring of Eluned or Sunet in the old romance of Ywaine and Gawaine.

Ring of Pope Innocent III. It is related by Matthew Paris that Pope Innocent III, well knowing the love that the English King John had for jewels, sent to him four gold rings set with precious stones. The Pope commented on the emblematical character of the gift, saying:

> "The rotundity of the rings signifies eternity, for we pass through time to eternity. The number four which is a square number indicates the firmness of mind which is neither depressed in adversity nor elated in prosperity. It signifies the four virtues which make up constancy of mind, viz., justice, fortitude, prudence, temperance. The material signifies wisdom from on high which is as gold purified in the fire. The greenness of the Emerald moreover denotes faith; the blueness of the Sapphire, hope; the redness of the Garnet, charity; the brightness of the Topaz, good works. In the Emerald, therefore, you have what to believe, in the Sapphire what to hope for, in the Garnet what to love, and in the Topaz what to practice. So that you ascend from one virtue to another until you see the Lord in Zion."

Ring of Reynard. In the story of Reynard the Fox, said to have been written by Hinreck van Alckmer though in reality it was written in the 15th century by Hermann Barkhusan of Rostock, Reynard believes himself possessed of a famous ring set with stones of red, white and green. The white stone cured all diseases, the red rendered night as bright as day, and the green made the wearer invincible. The story introduces Rabbi Abron of Trent who was wise above men, who spoke every language and knew the nature of every kind of herb, animal, and precious stone.

Ring of Solomon. Solomon, according to Rabbinical tradition, gazed on the stone of his ring and immediately knew everything concerning worldly affairs and much concerning heavenly. This ring is the subject of many legends.

Rock Crystallizations. Certain hair-like substances are found enclosed in crystals. They are also termed "penetrating minerals" and comprise rutile, asbestos, actinolite and tourmaline. These acicular crystals are called in France *Flèches d'Amour* (Love's Arrows). They are also known as Venus's Hair Stone, Thetis's Hair Stone, Pencils of Venus, Cupid's

Arrows, Cupid's Net, The Goddess's Tresses, etc. These specimens cut and polished are interesting and beautiful, and have always been esteemed as charm stones for ensuring a growth of beautiful hair, for beauty, for grace, for skill and fascination in dancing, etc. (See **RUTILE.**)

Sagda. A mysterious ocean stone which fixes itself to the keels of ships. A protection against shipwreck, it will cling to the ship so long as the timbers are not cut. It is said to be of dark green color, similar to prase.

Sakhrat. The Muhammadans say that the sakhrat is a marvelous stone of green color which reflects the deep blue tints on the crystal vapors of the heavens. The possession of the merest fragment of this holy stone bestows on the possessor the knowledge of all the secrets of the Universe.

Salamanders' Wool. Asbestos is so termed. It is also known as Mountain Flax, and is believed by the Tartars to be the root of a tree.

Sarcophagus. The word is derived from the Greek SARX, SARKOS, flesh, and PHAGO, to eat. A stone found at Assos in Troas. Used by the ancients, it was said to consume an entire dead human body with the exception of the teeth in 40 days. It was known as *lapis assius*, and is noted by Pliny. Sarcophagi were generally employed throughout the ancient world.

Saurite. The saurite is said to be a stone cut from a green lizard with a sharp reed knife.

Scorpion Stone. This may have been a stone of the agate class but its composition is obscure. It is mentioned by Orpheus who says that if the hunter Orion had known of its existence he would have given all the stars to gain this remedy for his fiery pain. It healed the wounds of arrows, the stings of insects and the bite of the scorpion.

Toad Stone. That the toad "wears a precious jewel in his head" was a profound belief in the Middle Ages, and a belief much commented upon in the works of writers of that period. Francis Barrett states that the stone of the toad was a cure for toothache. It was also given as an antidote for poison. In this latter connection it is said that, if set in an open setting and worn on the finger, it burnt the skin if poison were near. According to Fenton, a writer of the 16th century, "There is to be found in the heads of old and great toads a stone they call Borax or Stelon, which being used as rings gives forewarning against venom." The toad was believed to have a natural fear of man, throwing out poison at the sight of him. In some parts of the world the stone is said to be extracted from the head by numerous cunning means. It is generally described as a species of black pebble.

One of the special virtues of the Toadstone was to protect children from molestation by the fairies. It was also a cure for diseased kidneys and stomach disorders. According to Praetorius, the Prince of Alveschleben was given a ring of this land by a Kobold Brownie or Nixe as a house talisman to safeguard the fortunes of his family. A large toad is said to have dropped a black stone on to the bed of the wife of the Elector of Brandenburg after the birth of her son. Friedrich Wilhelm I ordered his jeweler to set the stone in a ring, which ring has always been worn by the head of the House of Hohenzollern as a symbol of prosperity, protection and good fortune. It was recently stated that the loss of this toadstone during the war was regarded as an evil omen for the ruling house.

World Stone. The World Stone, or Axial Lodestone of the Earth, is included in the philosophic mysteries of the old Rosicrucians.

CHAPTER 10

THE GREATEST CHARMS IN THE WORLD

"A deceased King is said to have entered the boat of the Sun in the form of the scarab."

—DR. WALLIS BUDGE

We will now turn to the ancient land of Egypt and dwell awhile on the sacred *scarabaeus* which was, without doubt, the most popular and venerated charm of antiquity. The scarab was a copy—in steatite, faience, obsidian, gold, beryl, crystal, hematite, cornelian, jasper, amethyst, turquoise, lapis lazuli, granite, serpentine and other stones—of the large black beetle, *Scarabaeus sacer*.

It was known in ancient Egypt as KHEPERA (he who turns), and besides symbolizing the eternal return of the Sun after the passing of the night reign, it represented the everlasting progress of life. As such it was not only inserted in the position of the heart in the bodies of the dead, but was placed in the tombs also. It was worn by those living on earth as a symbol of everlasting life and good luck, being specially prepared as a talisman by the priests of the various temples. The Greeks called it the *Cantharus* or *Heliocantharus*, the Latins the *Scarabaeus*. Throughout Egypt this sign of immortality was ever before the people. It was used in government offices bearing the Pharaoh's cartouche (an oval case in which his name was inscribed), was carried in battle by soldiers, was worn by the people generally throughout the land. It entered into their very lives, reminding them of the power of the deathless spirit, ever progressive, active and vital, molding dull matter to its will.

Hence the scarab was the ideal luck charm, the mere sight of which reminded man of his divine origin, and it was said that the soul of Ra impressed the seemingly inert matter which made up the scarab, giving it a life which ages could not destroy.

Generally strange stories connected with scarabs are explained in every way but the correct one. The ancient Egyptians were until the time of their decline essentially a religious people, and their knowledge of the continuity of life may be one reason for their existence as a nation for so many thousands of years—an existence only terminated by excess of luxury and the dominance of materialism by which so many great nations have been destroyed.

At least four diverse species of the scarabaeus or *Ateuchus sacer* have been identified in the hieroglyphic inscriptions, viz., 1. *Ateuchus semipunctatus*; 2. *Ateuchus laticollis*; 3. *Ateuchus morbillosus*; 4. *Ateuchus puncticollis*. Professor Flinders Petrie recognizes other varieties of beetles. Misses Brodrick and Norton, in their useful and concise *Dictionary of Egyptian Archaeology*, observe:

> "The Scarabaeus is remarkable for the peculiar position and shape of its hind legs which are placed very far apart and at the extreme end of the body. This is to enable the insect to roll the ball of refuse containing its eggs into some place of safety. At first these balls are soft and shapeless, but as they are pushed along by the scarab's hind legs they become firm and round, and increase in size until they are sometimes an inch and a half in diameter. This insect is looked upon by the Arabs as an emblem of fertility."

The Egyptians saw in the number of its toes (thirty) the days of the month; and the time it took to deposit its ball was compared to a lunar month. The passage of the ball was compared to the sun and its operation on the earth. Being regarded as of the male sex only, the scarabaeus symbolized, according to Horapollo, the self-begotten, the self-created. The god Khepera is the father of all the gods, the self-created one identified with the god NEB-ER-TCHER. A hieratic papyrus in the British Museum is thus translated by Dr. Wallis Budge:

> "I developed myself from the primeval matter which I made. My name is Osiris, the germ of primeval matter. I have worked my will to its full extent in this earth, I have spread abroad and filled it . . . . I uttered my name as a word of power from my own mouth and I straightway developed myself by evolutions. I evolved myself under the form of the evolutions of the god Khepera and I developed myself out of the primeval matter which has evolved multitudes of evolutions from the

beginning of time. Nothing existed in this earth (before me). I made all things. There was none other who worked with me at that time. I made all evolutions by means of that soul which I raised up there from inertness out of the watery matter."

Large numbers of funereal scarabs have been discovered in different substances, the best being formed from hard green basalt or serpentine. These were suspended on a gold wire from the neck of the mummy, or attached to a heart on which were the symbols for life, immovability, preservation.

Ornamental scarabs were very largely worn. Dr. Wallis Budge says of these: "By an easy transition the custom of placing scarabs on the bodies of the dead passed to the living, and men and women wore the scarab probably as a silent act of homage to the Creator of the world who was not only the god of the dead but of the living also."

It has been suggested that scarabs were used for exchange or barter, but Mr. Percy E. Newbury (*Scarabs*) points out that such contention "is not supported by the inscriptions or by any of the scenes depicted in the monuments." He continues:

"But we do find that during the Hyksos period (circa 1700 B.C.) and later under Amenhetep III (circa 1400 B.C.), the *Khetem* or 'seal' is given as a measure of value, although here it is probable that it was not the seal itself that is meant but the *impression* of it upon another substance. Polyaemus relates that the Athenian general Timotheus, being in want of money to pay his troops, issued his own 'seal' for coin, this substitute being accepted by the traders and market people, trusting in his honor.

"This can only mean that *impressions* of his signet on clay or some other substance were put into circulation as representatives of value and were so received by the sellers. It is in the impression of a seal or stamp upon a piece of gold or other metal that we have the origin of coined money."

The inscriptions, mottoes and symbols on the Egyptian scarabs are diverse and numerous. A large number have the names of the Kings, Queens, members of the Royal Household, Public Officers, etc. One rare specimen in the British Museum is adorned with the name of the very ancient King NEB-KA-RA; another has the name KHUFU. M. de Morgan describes one of lapis lazuli bearing the name NE-MAAT-RA (Amanemhat III) found at Dahshur. The Cairo Museum has a beautiful Queen's scarab, found also at Dahshur, on which is "The Royal Wife who is joined to the Beauty of the White Crown."

Many bear the seal of the famous Thothmes III (MEN-KHEPER-RA), the Rameses, Shashanq, and all the kings of Egypt. The Queen of Amenhetep is called on the scarabs "The Royal Wife Thyi," and "The Great Divine Wife Thyi beloved of Isis." Amenhetep IV is inscribed "Lord of the Sweet Wind." The Queen of Rameses II is immortalized as "The Royal Wife UR-MAAT-NEFERU-RA, daughter of the Great Chief of the Kheta." The horse of Amenhetep II is shown in a scarab of yellow jasper with his name "Firm of Heart"; this scarab is now in the British Museum.

Many have inscriptions denoting office, such as "The Royal Sealer and General, SA-NAB," "The Superintendent of the Meat Department, HOR-ANKH," "The Scribe of the Army, NEFER-IU," "The Director of Stores, SEHETEP-AB-RA," "The Chief Secretary of the Great Prison, SA-SEBEK," "The Superintendent of the Labor Bureau, ANTEF," "The Superintendent of the Royal Temple, AAHMES," "The Mayor of Heliopolis, BEN son of MA," "The Superintendent of the Gold Workers, HAAIU," "The Superintendent of the Granary of Amen, AAHMES," "The Hereditary Mayor and Priest," "The Governor of the Royal City," "The Vezir Paser."

On some motto and charm scarabs are ANKH NEFER, Life and Beauty; NEFER MAA, Beauty and Truth; An Eye; Two Fish; A Fish and a Scorpion (perhaps astrological); The Lotus; Flowers; Monkeys; Uraei, etc. Besides these there are the famous Heart Scarabs, Mystic Scarabs, and those known as Hunting and Historical Scarabs. But whatever the Scarab has stood for, it was primarily a symbol of good fortune, long life and divine protection. Its universal popularity has made it the greatest charm in the world. So great was its fame that it traveled beyond the Egyptian borders to other lands.

Next to Egyptian, the most famous scarabs were those of Phoenicia (especially in green jasper), those of Greece, and those of the Etruscans who carved them out of hard stones such as the sard, agate and carnelian.

These were engraved with exquisite figures, in fine intaglio style, usually of the gods and goddesses of ancient Greece, sometimes accompanied by Etruscan inscriptions or words and encircled with an engrailed or guilloche margin. When we consider the Egyptian Priests' practice of speaking "words of power" into these scarabs, we have cause for additional wonder at the recorded act of the great Law-Giver in striking the rock instead of speaking to it, as he had been commanded.

Part Two

Precious and Semi-Precious Gems
Arranged in Alphabetical Order

CHAPTER II

AGATE — AMAZONITE

AGATE

"By the rushing fringed bank
Where grows the willow and the osier dank
My sliding chariot stays,
Thick set with agate."

— MILTON

The name occurs as agath, agget, agot, agat, agett, agott, aggat, aggot, achate, etc. The great Greek philosopher and scientist, Theophrastus, in his writings *Of Stones*, says that the agate obtained its name from the river Achates—now known as the Drillo—in Sicily, because near its banks the first specimens were found. Dr. Bochart derived the name from the Hebrew word NAKAD, meaning "spotted." Most authorities agree that this stone was the eighth stone in the Breastplate of the High Priest and that it was known in Hebrew as SHEBO.

In Rabbinical writings there is an allegorical story of the discussion in Heaven of the import of the lines in Isaiah (54:12) "And I will make thy windows of agates," but it is a matter of considerable doubt if the Hebrew word KADKOD can correctly be rendered agate. In the controversy between Judah and Ezekiel, Sons of Rabbi Hayya, in the same writings the former calls it a beryl, the latter a jasper, and the voice of God said "Kadkod will include both of these," in allusion to the unity of all things.

The agate is a variegated chalcedonic variety of quartz, formed of successively attracted colored layers, and is remarkable for the beauty and peculiarity of the patterns. Lines or bands run through the stone: when these are straight or ribbony the agate is called the "ribbon agate"; when they are zigzag it is known as the "fortification agate" because of its

221

resemblance to a fortification; when the lines follow the form of an eye the term "eye agate" is often employed.

In this last form it was considered an excellent instrument for the seer or prophet to hold, as it symbolized the third eye now known as the Pineal Body. Clearly the gray tint of the eye of stone approaches in color the matter of the human eye. The importance of this peculiar organ, which lies upon the corpora quadrigemina of the brain in front of the cerebellum, was held in great respect by ancient scholars who regarded it as the organ of occult sight, of inner perception and intuition. This hidden eye is bigger in a child than in an adult, and in the woman it is bigger than in the man. There is little doubt that the ancients regarded these markings on the agate stone as symbolic of the faculties of the high spirit of man, of prosperity in peace, and protection in war.

The ring of Pyrrhus is recorded by Pliny as representing in its natural colors Apollo with his lyre standing amongst the nine Muses, each with her correct attribute. The Muses and their attributes as indicated in their statues are as follows:

1. Calliope, the muse of epic poetry. A tablet and stylus, or a roll of paper.
2. Clio, the muse of history. An open scroll.
3. Euterpe, the muse of lyric poetry. A flute.
4. Melpomene, the muse of tragedy. A tragic mask, the club of Hercules or a sword.
5. Terpsichore, the muse of choral dance and song. A lyre and the plectrum.
6. Erato, the muse of erotic poetry. The lyre.
7. Polyhymnia, the muse of sublime hymn. Pensive and meditative, carries no attribute.
8. Urania, the muse of astronomy. Staff and globe.
9. Thalia, the muse of comedy or idyllic poetry. A comic mask, a shepherd's staff or a wreath of ivy.

The Rev. C. W. King mentions that agates are still found "adorned with designs which one feels the greatest difficulty in admitting to be the mere fortuitous result of the arrangement of their shaded strata, so exactly does that result imitate the finished production of art." He instances the "Egyptian Pebble" in the British Museum which shows the head of the poet Chaucer covered with the hood, a faithful portrait even more remarkable when it is considered that the specimen was just broken in two pieces and not even polished. A specimen in the Galleria of Florence shows in the markings of yellow and red a running Cupid. Such curious markings are continually exhibiting the silent, magical symbols of Nature by the aid of which the great but humble philosophers of ancient days read the messages of the Divine.

Many and various are the virtues ascribed to the agate by the ancient masters, and when considering these it is well to remember their passion for making meanings obscure in order that the hidden secrets might be successfully guarded. The "pleasant scent of the agate"—obtainable most truly by rubbing together two polished specimens—is lauded by Pliny, and Orpheus recommends that the "changeful agate" be steeped in wine to improve the flavor. Powdered and bound on wounds, it healed them, and Rabbi Benoni of 14th century fame advised that an agate be held in the mouth to quench thirst and soothe fever. It was regarded as a charm against poisons, which no doubt accounts for its being used to form vases, bowls, cups, and vessels for holding foodstuffs, specimens of which are still found in more or less perfect state in the excavations.

Mr. King mentions the Carchesium or two-handled agate cup of Charles the Bold (presented by that King to the Abbey of St. Denis) which was used to hold the wine at the ceremony associated with the coronations of the kings of France. It was stolen in 1804, the year Napoleon Bonaparte was crowned Emperor at Paris, and was not used, therefore, at his coronation—a significant circumstance in the career of this man of Destiny who, with his innate love for the occult must have known long before this event that the agate was his birthstone. Shortly after the vase was recovered uninjured, but its jeweled setting had been removed from it, never to be seen again.

The agate, especially the eye agate, was reputed as a cure for tired eyes, also bestowing on the wearer strength and health, and inclining him to grace and eloquence. As one of the seven sea gems, a banded agate was credited with the power of taking away the terrors of the ocean, while to dream of one was held to denote a sea journey. Being astrologically connected with the death sign Scorpio, it was potent in seeking divine aid in this life and in the life to come. It rendered the wearer agreeable, gave him the favor of God, if he employed it as a holy instrument it turned the words of his enemies against themselves, rendered him—symbolically speaking—invisible, gave him victory and induced happy dreams. It was a charm against lightning, thunder, tempests, and all wars of the elements.

Albertus Magnus gives it efficacy against eruptive skin diseases; the Muhammadans engraved on it the symbols of Hassan and Hussein, the grandsons of the Prophet of Islam, and placed it round the necks of children to protect them from falls and accident. They also mixed it, in powdered form, with certain fruit juices and administered it as a cure for insanity. It was also prescribed for hemorrhage, the spitting of blood, boils, ulcers, gravel and affections of the spleen and kidneys. Used as a powder it hardened tender gums and arrested bleedings. Some Arabian writers advise against the use of powdered agate as an internal medicine unless carefully blended with other substances. An agate worn about the neck banished fear, indigestion and lung troubles. It was recommended by Dioscorides as a charm against epidemics and pestilential diseases. It protected from the bites of serpents and insects, and was bound to the horns of oxen to induce a good harvest. It was said to have been the "fortune stone" of the Trojan hero Aeneas, protecting him in war, voyages and storms.

The agate is always adorned with a system of bands which exhibit variety in hue, shade and tint. The Chalcedony (See Chalcedony) is more compact and regular in color, the two stones therefore being easily distinguishable. Swedenborg sets the agate down as the symbol of the spiritual love of good. It is astrologically attached to the martial sign Scorpio.

ALABASTER

> *"Why should a man whose blood is warm within,*
> *Sit like his grandsire, cut in alabaster?"*
>   —SHAKESPEARE

The Greek ALABASTROS was derived from Alabastron, a town in Upper Egypt where this beautiful white massive variety of gypsum was found. It was used by the ancients for fashioning perfume bottles, the vials to hold oil for anointing kings, priests, initiates into the mysteries, etc. These articles were commonly called *alabastra*, and the name continued in use long after other materials had replaced alabaster in their manufacture. The quarries of Hat Nub and those near Minieh supplied ancient Egypt with the material which was compared by ancient masters to the purity of the soul. No doubt this accounts for its use in holy works, and in the making of sarcophagi, statues, etc.

In the Book of Matthew we read of the woman having an alabaster box of very precious ointment. In Mark "she brake the box and poured it (the ointment) on his head." In Luke we are told that "a woman in the city brought an alabaster box of ointment," etc. "Box" is a mistranslation; the "box" holding the oil was an alabastrum, and this "oil of holy ointment compound after the art of the apothecary," as set down in the Book of Exodus, was put in the alabaster vases which were sealed in such a way that the tops had to be broken in order to release the liquid. This was seemingly done to prevent evaporation. Many of these vases have been found amongst the ruins, together with other Egyptian vases called Canopic jars in which were placed the embalmed viscera of the departed. On the covers of these canopi were drawings of the heads of the genii of the dead known as the four children of Horus—Kesta, Hapi, Tuamutef, and Qebhsennuf. A vessel surrounded by receptacles for holding a number of alabastra was called an ALABASTROTHECA.

Pure specimens of alabaster were also employed as milk-stone talismans. Oriental alabaster, known as the Algerian onyx, is a solid crystalline carbonate of lime, precipitated from water in stalagmitic form. This Oriental alabaster is considerably harder than true alabaster, which is easily scratched. Pliny writes of columns of alabaster over thirty feet in height. In ancient times it was regarded as a species of onyx, and was made into cups, vases and other utensils. Pliny says that it was "of the color of honey, opaque and spirally spotted." There are also specimens in color brown mixed with lemon, and others of the color of the finger-nail.

Leonardus regards alabaster as the right substance for preserving unguents, and Dioscorides employed it in medicine. It was used as a charm against accidents, especially whilst traveling, for securing public favor, for success in legal affairs, etc.

It may be mentioned that the beautiful sarcophagus of alabaster which was found by Giovanni Belzoni in 1817 in the tomb of Seti I (circa 1400 B.C.) and purchased by Sir John Soane for £2,000 sterling, now rests in the Soane Museum in Lincoln's Inn Fields, London. It is adorned with texts and scenes from the Book of the Gates. In this old Book the names of the Twelve Gates of the Tuat, or underworld, and of the Guardians of the Gates are given. The denizens of each section are identified, as well as their petition to Ra and his responses. The Book of the Gates, rich in magical formulae, is one of the oldest books in the world.

Alabaster proper and Oriental alabaster are under the zodiacal sign of Cancer.

ALEXANDRITE. The alexandrite is a variety of the chrysoberyl. This remarkable gem was discovered about 60 miles from Ekaterinburg, on the birthday of Czar Alexander II of Russia, from whom it obtains its name—the horoscope of that Emperor indicates the stone as a symbol of misfortune to him.

The alexandrite presents the curious phenomenon of changing its color according to the different rays of light to which it is exposed. By daylight the gem is of a charming olive or emerald green tint, which changes in artificial light to a columbine or raspberry red. The stone is favored by Russians on account of its blend of national colors, red and green. These mixed colors are distinctly Aquarian. No mention seems to have been made of this peculiar variety of chrysoberyl in ancient writings, and it stands as a herald of the new Aquarian Age into which we are now moving. The Alexandrite has been described as an emblem of loyal regard, and to dream of it is a symbol of struggle and progress. It is under the zodiacal Aquarius.

AMAZONITE or **AMAZON STONE.** The Amazon Stone is a green variety of Feldspar. The name is said to have been derived from the Amazon River, but no specimens have been found there. The meager evidence available about this stone certainly does not favor its connection with the Amazon River in any way.

This river was named the Amazon in the 16th century by the Spanish explorer Orellana in consequence, it is said, of an encounter he had with a band of women warriors on its banks. He called the mighty stream the Amazon after the women described by Herodotus, Diodorus, etc., and the Amazon stone also was named after them. In a letter to the author (1905) the late Comte de Glenstrae wrote:

> "It is to the Amazons led by Myrina (Diodorus Siculus) that we owe the establishment of the Samothracian mysteries which their Queen

founded after aiding Isis and Horus in the war against Typhon, as the Amazons of an earlier date had aided Neith (Athene) and Amoun against the usurpation of Chronos. I have always had a great admiration for the Amazons, and few again have noticed that the coins of the seven cities of Asia (Apocalypse) bore generally the figure of an Amazon as each of those cities was said to have been founded by one of their Queens. There is much in their symbolism. That story of their breasts being amputated is nonsense, being refuted by every monument. As Sanchoniathon says, "the Greeks confused nearly every legend."

It was said that the Amazons had their right breasts singed off, the better to enable them to draw their bows; however, the word Amazon does not mean "without breast," nor does it appear to have any connection with the word *mazos* meaning "a breast." There does not seem to be any reason to doubt that the Circassian word *Maza*, the moon, explains its origin. The Amazons of Thermodoon in Asia Minor are termed "worshippers of the moon." The Amazons were votaries of the "chaste Diana" in one of her attributes, and no male was allowed to live among them. No matter by what name she is called, Diana is a moon goddess and a woman's goddess, and no male was allowed to offend her modesty. Actaeon who saw her bathing was charmed into a stag, and fell a victim to his own hunting dogs, while the hunter Orion, ardent in his passion for Eos, the Morning, was slain by the "sweet arrows" of Diana.

Thus, the Amazon stone received its name from the romantic Amazons or worshippers of *Maza*, the moon. It is under the Zodiacal Cancer.

Chapter 12

Amber — Azurite

AMBER

"Pretty, in amber to observe the forms
Of hairs, or straws, or dirt, or grubs, or worms!
The things, we know, are neither rich nor rare,
But wonder how the devil they got there."

—Pope

Amber is a fossil vegetable resin which has undergone change owing to chemical action. The name is derived from the Arabic word AMBAR. Amber is also known as succinum (a word derived from the Greek SUCCUM, juice) on account of its vegetable origin. At one time it was also known by the Oriental word *Karabe*, straw-attractor. HASH-MAL was its name in Hebrew and by the Greeks it was known as ELE-KTRON, from which our word electricity has been derived. That painstaking scholar of the 17th century, Dr. Philemon Holland, thus translates from the 37th Book of Pliny:

> "To come into the properties that amber hath; if it bee well rubbed and chaufed between the fingers, the potentiall faculty that hath within is set on work and brought into actuall operation whereby you shall see it to draw chaffe, strawes, drie leaves, yea and thin rinds of the Linden or Tillet tree after the same sort as the loadstone draweth yron."

According to Callistratus it is good as a preventative of delirium, and as a cure for strangury if taken in drink or attached as an amulet to the body. This last author gives the name chryselectrum to an amber of golden color which presents most beautiful tints in the morning, and attracts flame with the greatest rapidity. igniting the moment it approaches fire. Worn upon the neck, he says, it is a cure for fever and other diseases, "and the powder of it either taken by itself or with gum mastick in water is remedial for disease of the stomach."

The writer has had strong evidence of the efficacy of amber in the cure of asthma, hay fever, croup and various diseases of the throat, and knows a number of medical practitioners who are convinced of its beneficial action. A well-known chemist also assured him that his wife had suffered from asthma all her life until five years ago, when she expressed a desire to wear a string of amber; since wearing this she has not experienced the slightest symptom of her former trouble. The writer has an amber necklet, the beads of which are mud-colored and cracked after having been worn for a few months by a lady suffering from hay fever. There is no doubt of its curative influence, no doubt that ancient observation was correct, and the statement in some modern medical text books that amber has "absolutely no curative value" is difficult indeed to follow.

It is remarkable that distilled amber yielding a pungent, acrid but not unpleasant oil, known as Oil of Amber or Oil of Succinite, is recognized as a potent ingredient in various embrocations. It is, therefore, hard to reconcile the statements that while amber has "absolutely no curative value," Oil of Amber has. Mr. C. W. King says: "Repeated experiments have proved beyond doubt that the wearing of an amber necklace has been known to prevent attacks of erysipelas in a person subject to them." He also writes of its efficacy "as a defender of the throat against chills."

Ancient writers said that amber eased stomach pains, cured jaundice and goiter, and acted against certain poisons, Camillus Leonardus recommending it as a cure for toothache and affections of the teeth. In the Middle Ages it was used as a charm against fits, dysentery, jaundice, scrofula and nervous affections. Thomas Nicols, a 17th century writer, says:

"Amber is esteemed the best for physic use, and is thought to be of great power and force against many diseases, as against the vertigo and asthmatic paroxysms, against catarrhs and anthreticall pains, against diseases of the stomach and to free it from sufferings and putrefactions and against diseases of the heart, against plagues, venoms and contagions. It is used either in powder or in troches, either in distempers of men or of women, married or unmarried, or in the distempers of children."

The dose formerly administered for coughs, hysteria, etc., was from ten to sixty grains.

Amber cut in various magical forms was extensively used as a charm against the evil eye, witchcraft and sorcery. It was and still is used as a mouthpiece for cigar and cigarette holders and smoking pipes, etc. Its employment in this capacity was originally talismanic, for it was implicitly believed that amber would not only prevent infection, but would act as a charm against it. Francis Barrett, in his work on Natural Magic, says that amber attracts all things to it but garden basil or substances smeared with oil. In China today amber is greatly esteemed, being used in the making of certain medicines, perfumes, and as an incense, which use dates back to the Bible times.

In such esteem is amber held in the East that the Shah of Persia is said to wear a block of amber on his neck to protect him against assassination. Perhaps no legend has been more ridiculed than the one which relates that amber was the solidified urine of the lynx; but the old writers Sudines and Metrodorus show that the lynx was not an animal but a tree from which amber is exuded, and which was known in Etruria as a Lynx.

Pliny repeats from Ovid's Metamorphoses the tradition among the Greeks that amber was the tears of the Heliades (Phaethusa, Ægle, Lampetia), the Sun Maidens, who harnessed the steeds of the Sun to the chariot when their rash brother Phaethon set forth on his fatal journey. The horses of the Sun were wild and strong; fire flew from their nostrils, and the youthful charioteer was not strong enough to keep them to their rightful course. The chariot, as its speed grew faster, became luminous, electric and fiery; the hair of the driver caught fire, the earth began to smoke and burn. Libya was parched into a waste of sand, Africa was afire, rivers were dried up, vegetation was destroyed, and the heat was so intense that the inhabitants of the stricken countries changed from white to black.

Gaea, in fear for the earth, called on Jupiter for protection, who, with a lightning-bolt, struck the chariot, hurling the "stricken wagoner," as Shakespeare calls him, lifeless into the River Eridanus—the Padus or Po—at the mouth of which river were found the *Electrides Insulae* (Amber Islands). The three sad sisters were transformed into poplars, and their tears of amber never ceased to flow. "To these tears," says Pliny, "was given the name of Electrum, from the circumstance that the Sun was usually called Elector." It requires but little thought to unveil this beautiful allegory which told the exact truth even while the nature of amber was disturbing the minds of scholars, its vegetable origin being doubted.

The old story that amber was a concretion formed by the tears of the birds is a variation of the Phaethon legend which Thomas Moore has so gracefully rendered in *The Fire Worshippers*.

"Around thee shall glisten the loveliest amber
That ever the sorrowing sea-bird hath wept."

That amber is found containing the material remains of extinct insects, etc., is alluded to by Pope in his lines quoted at the head of this chapter. That it was especially well known and esteemed in the ancient world can be accepted without the slightest doubt. Amber beads have been found in the tombs of Egypt as far back as the 6th dynasty (B.C. 3200), of the ancient Empire, a dynasty which ruled in old Chem long before the time of Joseph.

HASHMAL as the Hebrew for amber has been doubted by some scholars who take it to signify the metal electrum, a substance combination of 4 parts of silver and one of gold, used by the Greeks, and from which some of their coins were struck; but other authorities accept it as indicating amber which was known long before electrum was compounded. Delitzsch believes the Hebrew HASHMAL to be derived from the old Assyrian word ESHMARU, and the connection is a very probable one.

The Rabbis employ other words to express amber, as for example, KEPOS HAYARUDIN, amber of the Jordan. This occurs in a curious passage in which Rabbi Nathan states that if honey were mixed with the amber of the Jordan it became "profane." Honey, according to Porphyry, is a symbol of death, and hence could not be mixed with amber which is a symbol of life. This would be as repulsive to the Rabbinical mind as the violation of the command: "Thou shalt not seethe a kid in its mother's milk" would be. Libations of honey could only, according to Porphyry, be offered to the terrestrial gods. Philo Judaeus in Book III explains the matter as follows:

"Moreover it also ordains that every sacrifice shall be offered up without any leaven or honey, not thinking it fit that either of these things should be brought to altar. The honey perhaps because the bee which collects it is not a clean animal, inasmuch as it derives its birth, as the story goes, from the putrefaction and corruption of dead oxen, or else this may be forbidden as a figurative declaration that all superfluous pleasure is unholy, making indeed the things which are eaten sweet to the taste but inflicting bitter pains difficult to be cured at a subsequent period, by which the soul must of necessity, be agitated and thrown in confusion not being able to settle on any resting-place."

In addition, the lines of Virgil, *Georgics IV*, may be considered:

"His mother's precepts he performs with care:
The temple visits, and adores with prayer:
Four altars, raises: from his herd he culls
For slaughter, four the fairest of his bulls:
Four heifers from his female store he took,
All fair and all unknowing of the yoke.
Nine mornings thence, with sacrifice and prayers,
The powers atoned, he to the grave repairs.
Behold a prodigy! for, from within
The broken bowels and the bloated skin,
A buzzing noise of bees his ears alarms:
Straight issue through the sides assembling swarms.
Dark as a cloud, they make a wheeling flight,
Then on a neighboring tree, descending, light:
Like a large cluster of black grapes they show,
And make a large dependence from the bough."

      —DRYDEN'S TRANSLATION

We must again look to symbology if we desire to understand the meaning. Of old the Bee was a symbol of the Soul, and by the laws of Muhammad bees were admitted to the joys of Heaven. The votaries of Ceres adored the Moon under the symbol of a bee—a symbol appearing on some of the Greek coins, notably on those of Ephesus where Diana, goddess of the Moon, was worshipped and whence the cry, "Great is Diana of the Ephesians," reached the ears of Paul (Acts 19). Porphyry writes: "The Moon presiding over generation was called a bee and also a bull, and Taurus is the exaltation of the Moon." He adds symbolically: "But bees are ox-begotten, and this appellation is also given to soul proceeding to generation." (*Cave of the Nymphs.*)

The explanation of the veiled mystery is that the Moon at the full is the symbol of the soul, the emblem of which is a bee. It comes from the body of a bull or Taurus, the second sign of the zodiac, in which as Porphyry observes she is in her exaltation and powerful; Taurus is the earth sign of the planet Venus in the guise of the goddess of Generation, and as the soul enters the world, new born, the waters of the Jordan are needed to purify it as, when it leaves the body, water was left for it to wash off the emanations of its deserted covering. Further into the mysteries it is unnecessary to go. The veil of Isis hides the truth, and only he who will strive to understand heavenly wisdom can hope to pierce that veil.

Amber has been placed under the sign Leo, the sign of the Sun, by some of the old masters, while others have allotted it to the sign of Venus (Taurus), to which it more probably belongs. It is very soft, is easily cut with a knife, and burns freely. Large quantities are found on the coast of the Baltic, which the Greeks called in consequence the Amber Sea. In Oriental stories, Amberabad (Amber City) was a city of Jinnistan (Fairy Land).

To dream of amber was said to denote a voyage, and according to the philosophy of the Qabalah the indication was of some kind of movement or change.

Amber has been imitated in preparations of mellite, copal and anine, also by a blending of sulfur and gutta percha at high temperature, etc., but mellite is infusible by heat, burning white. Copal catches fire and falls from the instrument on which it is heated in flat drops, while the general attracting power of most substitutes falls far short of the true substance.

AMETHYST

"The purple streaming amethyst is thine."

— TENNYSON

The amethyst is a species of transparent, violet-colored quartz, the name of which is derived from the Greek AMETHYSTOS, from the traditional belief that this stone possessed the power to oppose the effect of the fumes of intoxicants, an opinion not entirely shared by Plutarch. Amongst the Greeks and Persians an amethyst bound on the navel was said to counteract the evil effects of wine. The amethyst is described by Trevisa in the 15th century as "purple red in colour medelyd wyth colour of uyolette," and in Sir Philip Sidney's *Arcadia*, we read:

> "The bloodie shafts of Cupid's war
> With amatists they headed are."

The stone is found under the names ametist, ametiste, amatites, amaethist, and it was not until about the middle of the 17th century that its present form began to be adopted. To enjoy the full vibrations of the amethyst an old custom recommended that it be worn on the third finger of the left hand—a practice at one time followed by medical practitioners—and some form of ancient belief demanded that the amethyst must come in contact with the left hand before its action could be appreciated and understood.

It is well known that the magic of the ancient Egyptian temples included the art of magnetism, and the action of various mineral substances on the magnetized patient has also been noted by the more modern investigators including Dr. Babbitt, Baron Reichenbach, Dr. Ennemoser, Dr. Edmonson and Dr. de Lignieres. Stones of the earth have been especially employed by these scholars with results of such marked importance that the contention of the ancients regarding the amethyst as a charm against drunkenness, deserves respect. To be effective in the induced magnetic sleep, stones had to be placed in the left hand. Connected with the ancient belief in the sobering power of the amethyst is the beautiful allegorical legend telling that Dionysius, enamored of a graceful nymph, pressed his love upon her, but Diana intervened, transforming her into a purple amethyst. In respect for the transformed nymph Dionysius vowed that whosoever wore the amethyst would be protected from the evils of intoxicating wines.

The amethyst was worn in ancient Egypt, and a scarab cut from a specimen was held in great esteem by soldiers who carried it on the field of battle as a charm against death by the shafts and swords of war. This practice was carried far into the Middle Ages, and many amethysts were worn for the same purpose in this last terrible war of nations. When worn by a Bishop of the Church, the amethyst is a glyptic symbol of heavenly understanding. Swedenborg likens it to a "spiritual love of good," and Dr. Brewer writes of purple shades, indicating "love of truth even unto martyrdom."

It is stated by Patrick in *Devotions of the Roman Church*, that the wedding ring of the Virgin Mary and Joseph was of amethyst or onyx. Mr. King writes that this ring, exhibited in the Abbey St. Germain des Prés, is engraved "with two nobodies—probably liberti—whose votive legend: 'Alpheus with Aretho' is but too plainly legible in our Greek-reading times." The ring, having been saved at the burning of the Abbey in 1795, was secured by General Hydrow and given to the Imperial Russian Cabinet.

In what is described by Camillus Leonardus of the 16th century as one of the magical books of King Solomon, a charm for gaining influence over princes and nobles is a rider on horseback holding a scepter, engraved on an amethyst and set in double its own weight in gold or silver.

The amethyst has always been regarded as symbolical of the pioneer in thought and action on the philosophical, religious, spiritual and material planes. The virtues ascribed to this stone are many. It was regarded as a charm against witchcraft, poison and evil thoughts; it was an aid to chastity, a power against all forms of overindulgence and a strengthener of the mind; it was a charm for securing the favor of princes, rulers, churchmen, people of wealth, influence and power, people with prophetic ability, poets, travelers, publishers, etc. It would strengthen the wisdom, faith and religion of the wearer and aid in prayer and in dreaming. If bound to the left wrist the amethyst enabled the wearer to see the future in dreams; to dream of the stone itself indicated success to a traveler, clergyman, sailor, philosopher, teacher or mystic, also protection, faith and fruitful thoughts. For pains in the head (headache, toothache, etc.), it was recommended that an amethyst be immersed in hot water for a few minutes, taken out, dried carefully and gently rubbed over the parts affected and the back of the neck.

Almost all authorities agree in translating the Hebrew ACHLA-MAH as amethyst and in identifying it as the ninth stone of the High Priest's Breastplate. It was the seventh precious stone which the sage Iarchus gave to Apollonius of Tyana as an emblem of piety and dignity.

Many writers on the subject of planetary influences have placed this gem under the celestial Pisces, the fishes, because anciently Pisces was one of the mansions of Jupiter; but the sign of the Fishes is transparent and glistening in hue, whilst in the nature of kinship a fiery gem belongs to a fiery zodiacal sign. In this direction, the fiery Mars, as ruler of the sign Aries, has been confused with the Babylonian and Assyrian MARDUK or MERODACH. Marduk or Merodach represented the planet Jupiter, and to him Nebuchadnezzar addresses his songs of praise: "Merodach, the great lord, the senior of the gods, the most ancient has given all nations and people to my care." "I supplicate the king of gods, the lord of lords in Borsippa, the city of his loftiness." "O, god Merodach, great lord, lord of the house of the gods, light of the gods, father, even for thy high honor, which changes not, a temple have I built," etc.

The "house of the gods" is the ninth celestial house, naturally the sign Sagittarius, and in the Qabalah the ninth heavenly sphere is the Primum Mobile, the star-decked Heaven. (See *Numbers, their Meaning and Magic*.) The name Merodach or Marduk is a corruption of Mardugga (the sacred son), and because they saw the life-giving orb rising from the sea, the ancient Chaldean masters accounted Jupiter his first offshoot, hailing him as "Marduk:"—"Marduk, first born of the mighty deep, make us pure and prosperous." The giving of prosperity is ever an attribute of Jupiter, and the measure and the source of the gift are shown in the nativity or map of the heavens at a person's birth.

An effective talisman for the protection of horses and their riders was a winged horse cut on an amethyst. The ancients connected the amethyst with the ninth celestial mansion—the mansion of Sagittarius—and there is no reason for allotting it to any other.

ANATASE. The name is derived from the Latin ANATASES, elevation. It was so named from the length of its chief axis. This mineral is composed of Titanic acid which crystallizes in fine, transparent stones of brown, dark blue or black, of adamantine luster. The anatase, which equals the opal in hardness, cannot be traced in ancient writings. It is rarely used in jewelry. In harmony with the philosophy of gem influence it is connected with the sign Sagittarius.

ANDALUSITE. This stone, first discovered in Andalusia, derives its name from that rich mineral province of Spain—the Tarshish of the Bible, the Tartessus of ancient geography, the Bætica of the Romans. Its colors are light bottle-green, pearl grey, flesh and pink. It is extremely dichroic, showing the twin colors red and leaf-green—the red gleaming from the stone in antithesis to its common hue. The andalusite is as hard as the garnet or zircon. Professor Dana moistened specimens with nitrate of cobalt, after which they assumed a blue color. This mineral may have been known to the ancients, but identification is difficult. Ancient philosophy would connect it with the zodiacal Aquarius.

APATITE. Apatite is a mineral which obtained its name from the Greek word APATAO, to deceive, because it deceived old students who confounded it with aquamarine, chrysolite, tourmaline, etc. Abraham Werner (the author of the Neptunian theory that all mineral substances were once contained in watery solution,) first demonstrated in the 18th century the true nature of apatite which is a phosphate of lime with fluorite and chloride of calcium. The luster varies from transparent to opaque, and is vitreous to sub-resinous. It is much softer than tourmaline, its degree of hardness being but 5; for this reason it is but little used in the manufacture of jewelry. Its colors are pale sea-green, blue-green (in which coloring it is sometimes called Moroxite), yellowish-green (in which coloring it is often called Asparagus stone), yellow, violet, white, grey, brown, red, colorless, and transparent. Professor Judd, F.R.S., found a concretion specimen of apatite when cutting a mass of teak wood—a particularly rare find. In agreement with the ancient system the apatite is astrologically under the zodiacal Pisces.

APOPHYLLITE. Apophyllite is a hydrous silicate of potassium and calcium which obtains its name from the Greek word APOPHULLIZO, to exfoliate, because it falls in leaves before the blowpipe. It is extremely soft, being from between 4 and 5 in Mohs' scale. The stone is found in a variety of colors—milk-white, greyish, green, yellow, red, pink. It is seldom used by jewelers. The apophyllite is under the sign Taurus.

AQUAMARINE. (See **BERYL.**)

ASBESTOS. The word is derived from the Greek ASBESTOS, incon-sumable, and is identified with the amianthus (impollutible) of the ancients. It is a variety of hornblende, of a fine and fibrous texture, of which Marbodus wrote:

> *"Kindled once it no extinction knows*
> *But with eternal flame increasing glows.*
> *Hence with good cause the Greeks Asbestos name,*
> *Because once kindled naught can quench its flame."*

The incombustibility and weak heat conducting qualities of asbestos render it extremely useful as a protection against fire. The ancients used it for the wicks of their temple lamps, and in order to preserve the ashes of the departed their dead bodies were laid on asbestos before being placed on the funeral pyre. Cloths of asbestos were thrown in the flames for the purpose of cleaning them. So fine and flaxy is the mineral that gloves have been made of it. Asbestos is under the zodiacal Gemini.

AVENTURINE. Aventurine or goldstone is a quartz of a brownish, semi-transparent character, spangled with spots of golden-yellow mica. This stone is identified with the stone called by Pliny the "Sandaresus"— "of stars of gold gleaming from within." The name aventurine (*per adventura*, by accident), arose, it is said, from an accident in a Venetian glass factory, where a workman found that eight parts of ground glass, one part protoxide of copper and two parts of oxide of iron well heated and allowed to cool slowly, produced the peculiar appearance admired in the real gem to even better effect. The aventurine variety of quartz is under the zodiacal Leo.

AXINITE. The name axinite is derived from the Greek AXINE, an axe, on account of the sharp and axe-like form of the crystals. The axinite is about the same degree of hardness as the spodumene or the demantoid garnet (6.5 to 7). It is pyro-electric and highly vitreous. The colors vary between pearly-grey, clove, brown, honey-yellow, violet, plum-blue. The axinite is under the zodiacal Sagittarius.

AZURITE. Azurite is a blue copper carbonate obtaining its name from its color. It is kindred with malachite, from which it differs but slightly. Some mineralogists call it blue malachite. It is under the zodiacal Libra.

CHAPTER 13

THE BERYL FAMILY

BERYL

> "What rings of Eastern price his fingers hold,
> Gold decks the fingers, beryl decks the gold."
>
> —PARNELL

The name beryl is derived from the Greek and Latin BERYLLUS; some say also from the Persian BELUR. Some of the old fashions of writing the name are included in the following: beril, beryll, berall, birrall, byral, byrrall, byralle, berial, beryall, bureall, beryl stone.

Dr. Holland's rendering of Pliny's remarks on the beryl (Chapter 36) is interesting:

> "Many are of the opinion that beryls are of the same nature that the emeraud, or leastwise verie like: from India they came as from their native place, for seldom are they to be found elsewhere."

Beryls are pale green stones colored by iron. Some very large crystals have been found. Professor Rutley mentions one specimen found at Royalston in Massachusetts, which weighed nearly 2½ tons.

EMERALD

> "As when an emerald green enchas'd
> In flaming gold, from the bright mass acquires
> A nobler hue, more delicate to sight."
>
> —J. PHILIPS

The name in days of old was variously written: emeraud, emeraude, emraud, emeroyde, emmorant, emerant, ameraud, emerode, emrade,

The Flame Queen Opal was discovered in 1914 in New South Wales, Australia. In Kozminsky's lifetime, it was in the Kelsey I. Newman Collection. It is now in the Jack Plane Collection. (Photo by David Plane)

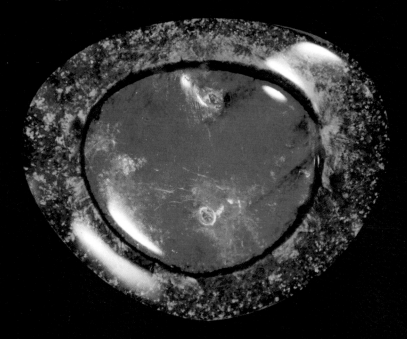

Above: Labradorite crystal
Below: Carnelian
Opposite above: Malachite
Opposite below: Crystal display
   at Seven Stars
(Photos by Stuart Weinberg)

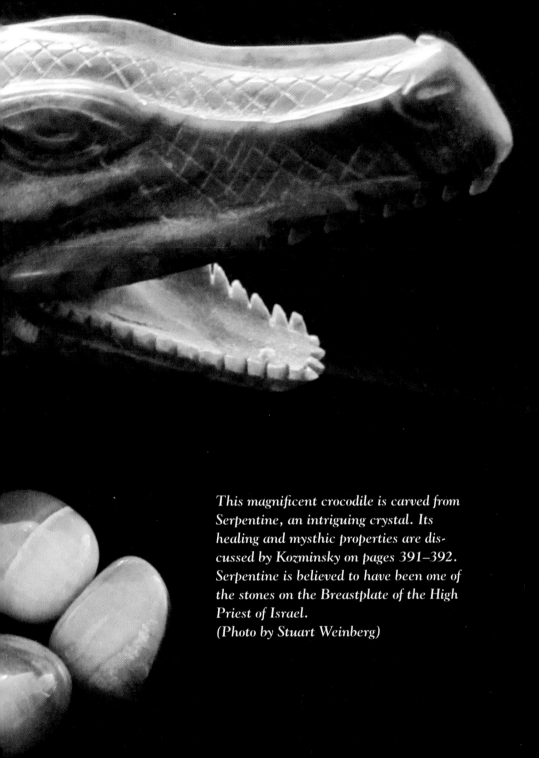

This magnificent crocodile is carved from Serpentine, an intriguing crystal. Its healing and mysthic properties are discussed by Kozminsky on pages 391–392. Serpentine is believed to have been one of the stones on the Breastplate of the High Priest of Israel.
(Photo by Stuart Weinberg)

Above is an Azurite Crystal
Below is an Amethyst Crystal. (Photos by Stuart Weinberg)

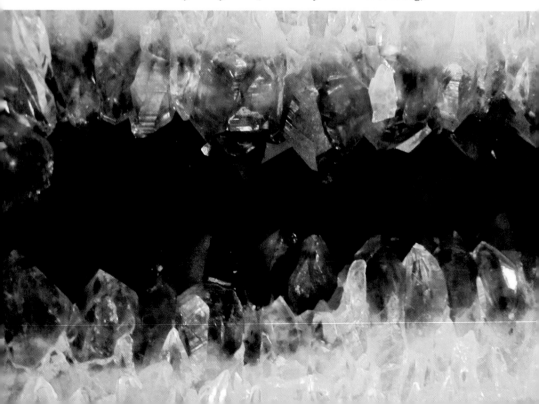

Here is a beautiful Amber necklace. (Photo by Stuart Weinberg)

Seven Stars Bookstore in Cambridge Massachusetts is one of the foremost New Age bookstores and crystal emporiums serving the spiritual community. Stuart Weinberg, proprietor and author of Crystals and the New Age, searches the world's finest sources for his inventory. At right is the detail of one of the store's many displays. Below is a wider view of the many books, statues, and crystals featured in this unique shop. (Photos by Yvonne Paglia)

hemerauld, smaragdus. The derivation is from the old French word *Esmeralda*, through the modern French *Emeraude*; Greek SMARAG-DOS, Latin SMARAGDUS.

Amongst some large sized emeralds Professor Dana notes one in the cabinet of the Duke of Devonshire, which specimen is 2¼ inches long by about 2 inches in diameter; a finer specimen weighing six ounces, once in the possession of Mr. Harry Thomas Hope; one formerly in the Royal Russian collection, 4½ in. in length, 12 in. in breadth, 16¾ pounds troy in weight; another weighing six pounds, which is 7 in. long and 4 in. broad.

Dr. Holland's translation of Pliny (Book 37) is as follows:

"True it is that we take great delight to behold green hearbes and leaves of trees but this *is* nothing to the pleasure we have in looking upon the emeraud, for compare it with other things, be they never so green, it surpasseth them all in pleasant verdure."

The Emerald is the beautiful green variety of the beryl family, colored by chromium.

AQUAMARINE

"One entire stone of a sea-water green known by the name of agmarine."

—STOW. CHRON. 1598

The word is derived from the Latin AQUA, water, and MARE, the sea. It was known under various forms: aigue marine, ague marine, aque marine, agmarine, etc. In color the aquamarine is pale blue, bluish green and light sea-green.

Here may be mentioned the golden emerald—an emerald of charming golden color, and the rose beryl named Morganite after the late J. Pierpont Morgan.

The whole beryl family is classified under the sign Taurus. Their crystalline form is hexagonal (six-sided), and six is the traditional number of Venus, whose earth house or mansion in astrology is the heavenly Taurus. Beryllium enters largely into their composition, and because of the sweetness of its salts this element is also termed glucinum (Greek GLYKYS, sweet).

Glycina was first discovered by the great chemist Vauquelin while experimenting with emeralds in 1797. Much confusion has arisen amongst authors on the subject of gems and the Heavens, from confounding the beryl with the tourmaline—a distinctly Mercurial gem. The beryl, aquamarine and emerald present only color shade differences. It is more difficult, however, to find really fine emeralds than it is to find other varieties of the same family. The emeralds found in the workings of the old Cleopatra mines, whose very existence was at one time doubted, are of the lighter or beryl variety. These gems were much sought after in ancient times, the Egyptian women being esteemed the best searchers "because of their superior eyesight." There is no doubt, as before noted, that the sex was considered as well as the sight, and the selection of women "daughters of Venus" for this work was not without design.

The splendor of the canopy of purple and gold under which Holofernes, the Assyrian general, rested was enriched according to the Apocrypha with emeralds and precious stones (Judith 10:21). This symbol of Assyrian luxury—considering the accredited virtue of the emerald amongst the ancients—was of evil import to the leader of the army of Nebuchadnezzar, the "King of all the earth."

Astrology notes that a person born in the sign Taurus, especially from the 20° to the 30° amongst the nebulous stars of the Pleiades, or with violent stars in that sign at birth, has his sight always affected to a greater or lesser extent, hence the accredited virtues of the emerald as an eye stone, and no pharmacy of the Middle Ages would have thought of omitting it from its dispensary. As eye stones the stones of the beryl family have always been held in high esteem, Pope John XXI affirming that a diseased eye treated with an emerald became sound again. It was not claimed that the emerald would restore lost sight, but it was regarded as extremely potent in eye disease, injury or trouble of any kind. Sometimes it was sufficient, especially in the case of inflamed eyes, to bathe the eye in water in which emeralds had been steeped for six hours; at other times the stone was reduced to the finest powder, an extremely small quantity of which was placed in the eye at stated intervals. Tom Moore sings in *Lalla Rookh*:

"Blinded like serpents when they gaze
Upon the emerald's virgin blaze."

The tradition that when a serpent fixes its eyes on an emerald it becomes blind is echoed from Hebrew philosophy, and Ahmed Ben Abdalaziz in his *Treatise on Jewels* has it that the luster of emeralds makes serpents blind. As this ancient statement has occasioned some mirth and ridicule amongst those swayed by surface considerations, it may be as well to consider the matter from another point of understanding. The symbolist will at once perceive the hidden parable: in astrology, serpents have been classed under the Scorpion of the zodiac, and the Venusian Taurus in the zodiac is opposite to the Scorpion.

In the story of the Garden of Eden it is the Scorpion (snake) who tempts Eve, and her fall is held by occult students as a symbol to compel Man to exert his highest strength to enable his triumph over the lowest to be complete. The zodiacal Scorpio is accursed on its lower expression, and is symbolical then of the corruption which can menace virgin purity. Man, on the lowest borderlands to which overindulgence will ever draw him, has been faced by serpents and reptiles whose immaterial lives exist only in those dark realms.

The story of Circe and the Swine finds its parallel in the power of the pure and beautiful Venus to expel even by her symbolic emerald lust, envy, malice and grossness, to destroy the serpent's gaze and to call the blind and suffering Man back to his peaceful Heaven again. So, as the Moon in astrological philosophy is exalted in Taurus, Diana the goddess of the Moon is the friend of chaste women. In Cutwode's *Caltha Poetarium, or the Humble Bee*, written in 1599, Diana adorns the heroine with an emerald ring.

It can easily be seen why the emerald is the emblem of true happiness and the preserver of chastity, and why it was said to fracture if chastity were violated: to one taking vows of chastity and breaking them, the emerald could never appear the same again—before his spiritual vision it would be broken and shattered. Leonardus said that the emerald protected women in childbirth, and most old writers are impressive in warning men to wear one as a charm against spiritual and mental weakness.

The Peruvian goddess Esmeralda was said to reside in an emerald as big as an ostrich egg, and it was the custom of this little Venus in her

symbolic emerald egg to receive emeralds as offerings from her devotees
who also, it was said, sacrificed their daughters to her.

Stevenson (*Residence in South America*), writing of the emerald mine
of Las Emeraldas, says:

> "I never visited it owing to the superstitious dread of the natives who
> assured me that it was enchanted and guarded by an enormous dragon
> who poured forth thunder and lightning on those who dared to ascend
> the river."

It is peculiar how the symbols of mankind coincide: the dragon is
another of the zodiacal Scorpio varieties ever opposite Taurus, and was
of old regarded as the agitator of thunders, lightning, and earth commo-
tions. Prescott, in his *History of Peru*, tells us how the Spaniards after
murdering the trusting Indians raided their dwellings and seized their
ornaments and precious stones, for this was the region of the *esmeraldas*
or emeralds. One of the jewels that fell into the hands of Pizarro was as
large as a pigeon's egg.

Fra Reginaldo di Pedraza, one of the Dominican missionaries, told
the Spaniards that the method of proving the genuineness or otherwise
of emeralds was to try if they could be broken with a hammer. Prescott
adds: "The good Father did not subject his own jewels to this wise experiment, but as the stones in consequence of it fell in value, being merely
regarded as colored glass, he carried back a considerable store of them to
Panama." The Indians held that the emerald protected against poisons
and cleansed man from sin.

As an emblem of Eternal Spring, Iarchus included the emerald in
the mystic necklace of Apollonius of Tyana. In Rosicrucian philosophy
it is advised that if an emerald set in a ring of gold be placed on the solar
finger of the left hand when the Sun entered Taurus, the wearer would
attain his cherished aim and be enabled by the sweating of the stone to
detect poisons. Experiment has shown that heat causes the emerald to
lose water but does not affect its color; hence the reports of the "sweating" emerald cannot be set aside as mythical. Specimens of the beryl family have been found in tombs and in old excavations, and there is little
doubt that the stones "of the color of transparent sea-water" found by the
old Romans at Cyprus belonged to it.

The Romans greatly esteemed the emerald as an eye stone and a natural specific for ophthalmia, holding that what healed and calmed the spiritual eye would heal and calm the natural eye. The Persians applied ashes of burnt emeralds to ulcers with curative effect. They said that the emerald brought mental tranquility, cured unnatural thirst, stomach troubles, jaundice, liver troubles, obstructions, gravel, stricture, bodily pains and epilepsy. Albertus Magnus also recommends it as a cure for epileptic attacks. Mystics have always regarded the emerald as of the highest worth. It is spoken of by Cardanus as an ideal gem for divinatory purposes—no doubt because of its pure spiritual import. Aristotle writes that an emerald hung from the neck or worn on the finger protects from the "falling sickness."

The ancient writers held that all kinds of divination were helped by the emerald, and when worn during the transaction of honest business it gave favor to the wearer. In Brazil, medical students on becoming doctors of medicine wore on their fingers rings of emeralds as an indication that they had received their diploma. The lighter emerald, or beryl, bound man and wife together in mutual love, and raised the wearer to success and honor.

Among the Hindu philosophers the emerald held its place as a gem of the zodiacal Taurus, and in the First Heaven of the Muslims the tents of the faithful are represented as studded with emeralds, pearls and jacinths.

Mr. E. W. Lane (*Modern Egyptians*) writes that the inhabitants of Paradise are said to be clothed "in the richest silk, chiefly of green, and all superfluities from their bodies will be carried off by perspiration which will diffuse an odor like that of musk"—a plant recognized by old astrologers as belonging to the sign Taurus. Paracelsus wrote that the emerald was in sympathy with the metal copper—also recognized as the chief metal of Venus. Mr. King notes a fine emerald, a quarter inch square, belonging to the earliest Christian periods, on which is cut a fish, which besides being an early Christian emblem is symbolical of Venus and later of the Virgin. Venus is exalted in the Zodiacal sign of the Fishes which enters largely into the Christian mysteries.

The beryl was used in magical rites as an instrument for foretelling future happenings. For special magical purposes the stone was held in the mouth when—says Freeman, writing in the early part of the 18th century—a person may call an elemental and receive satisfaction for any question he might ask. In this connection one is tempted to think of the delightful Venusian spirit Ariel in Shakespeare's *Tempest*. Again the beryl is recommended by Leonardus as a charm against diseases of the throat and jaws. In the "water divination" of the Middle Ages a beryl stone was suspended just to touch the surface of the water in the bowl, and it answered questions by automatically striking the edges of the vessel. It was also thrown into a shallow dish of water, information being gathered from the reflections seen in sunlight in the water.

Herodotus tells the story of the Thalassokrat (Sea-king) Polycrates of Samos whose never-failing fortune so alarmed his friend and ally, the Pharaoh Amasis of Egypt, that he wrote to him begging him to sacrifice something he valued most highly to propitiate the fateful Nemesis, goddess of retribution. In obedience to this request Polycrates, with many regrets, threw from a boat his precious emerald ring into the sea far from the shore. Some few days afterwards a fisherman caught a fish so large and shapely that, thinking it a prize for the King, he took it to the palace of Polycrates. When the cook was preparing the fish for the King's table he found within it his master's emerald ring.

Amasis, when informed of the incident by Polycrates, was greatly concerned as it foretold to him a fatal end for the Thalassokrat, with whom he broke off negotiations and alliances. Polycrates, being induced by his crafty enemy the Persian satrap Oroetes to visit him, was seized and crucified. The story is discredited by some historians—notably Grote—but this is not the only story of a fish swallowing a ring or some other article of value. The legend of Solomon's ring has been already alluded to.

Mr. King collecting evidence from Herodotus, Pausanius, and other old writers finds that the ring of Polycrates was a "signet of emerald set in gold, the work of Theodorus of Samos." That famous father of the church, Titus Flavius Clemens, better known as Clemens Alexandrinus, says that on the emerald ring of Polycrates was engraved "a musical lyre." A fine quality emerald bearing a similar device was found about fifty years ago in a vineyard at Aricia, and that this may have been the famous ring is not impossible.

In the reign of Philip II, of Spanish Armada repute, there appeared in Spain a strange ring of gold, in the center of which was an emerald cut so as to contain a ruby surrounded by diamonds. This curious ring is said to have been the symbol of misfortune wherever it came. The church which received it as a gift from the King was destroyed by fire; the fatal ring, rescued from the fire, was placed in a museum that was badly damaged by lightning; whilst again in the possession of the King of Spain, Spain was defeated in the war with the United States of America. Finally this ring of ill omen was buried in an iron coffin in a secret place.

Its evil influence can readily be accounted for in the light of occult philosophy—the ruby is a stone under the Celestial Leo, while the emerald is under Taurus. These signs form the evil square, being counted in astrological science 90° apart. A square aspect is always accounted an evil one. The admixture of the beautiful crystal symbols was unfortunate. Spain again is under the celestial Sagittarius, and would not hold gems of Taurus. Philip II himself had an evil influence on Spain. Astrologically neither the emerald nor the ruby would be in harmony with his nativity, and the diamond would be fatal.

John of Salisbury states that Pope Adrian VIII confirmed the right to hold and govern Ireland on Henry II of England with the gift of a rare emerald set in a ring of gold, and the Papal bull or seal. The right to bestow all islands was claimed by the Pope by virtue of the laws of Constantine. It is curious in connection with this historical transaction that Ireland and the emerald come under Taurus, and that the right of Henry II as sovereign of Ireland is confirmed by the Papal Bull!

Tennyson in *Elaine* says that Arthur, "the glorious King"

"Had on his cuirass worn our Lady's Head,
Carved of one emerald centered in a sun
Of silver rays, that lighten'd as he breathed."

The beryl was the symbol of undying youth, the emerald of incorruptibility and triumph over sin, the aquamarine of social uplifting. One of the four rings sent by Pope Innocent III in the year 1205 to King John of England was an emerald which, wrote the donor, is the emblem of faith.

To dream of beryls is said to denote happy news to come; to dream of aquamarines is interpreted as symbolical of loving friendships; to dream of emeralds is set down as a sign of worldly benefit and goodness. The Angel of the beryl family is the inexpressibly beautiful and tender Anael. Emanuel Swedenborg says that the beryl signifies "the good of charity and faith or the spiritual love of truth; the emerald the appearance of the divine sphere of the Lord in the lowest heavens; the emerald family as indicating the sphere of divine love and wisdom."

The wonderful aquamarine which adorned the crown of James II of England has been recently found to be merely a piece of colored glass. This fact was recently communicated by Sir George Younghusband, so well known as the keeper of the Jewel House in the Tower of London. It is presumed that the real stone was replaced by this imitation, but how and when is a matter of speculation. All members of the emerald family were regarded as stones of fortune for King James II.

Before closing this account of the beryl family it may be interesting to recall the fatal emerald of Russia. This large and beautiful gem was given to Peter of Holstein-Gottorp (afterwards Peter III), by Empress Elizabeth Petrovna. Peter was assassinated. Emperor Paul wore it next and was strangled. Alexander II then had the stone newly set and it fell from his finger after his assassination. Alexander III would not wear it, but Nicholas II, allured by its beauty, did. Who now has the fatal emerald?

CHAPTER 14

BALAS — CRYSOCOLLA

BALAS. (*See* **SPINEL.**)

BLOODSTONE. (*See* **HEMATITE** and **JASPER.**)

BONE TURQUOISE or **ODONTOLITE.** Bone turquoise is often mistaken for true turquoise. It is really fossil teeth or bones colored blue by the action of phosphate of iron. Its organic difference can easily be seen under a good glass. Odontolite is under the influence of the zodiacal Capricorn; it is a degree less in hardness than the true turquoise, being in this respect equal to apatite and lapis lazuli.

BORT. (See **DIAMOND.**)

CAIRNGORM or **SCOTCH TOPAZ.**

"O Caledonia, stern and wild."
          —SCOTT

The mountain Cairn Gorm, the name of which comes from the Gaelic *Carngorm*, meaning Blue Hill, is between the shires of Aberdeen, Banff and Inverness, and it is there that the cairngorm stones are mostly found. The stone is a variety of quartz of a fine smoky yellow or brown color. It is found in other places than the Cairngorm Mountains, and has usurped many of the attributes of the true topaz. It is remarkable for its brilliance and beauty, and was known to the ancients.

According to Pliny, this stone was used by old physicians for cauterizing affected parts of the body by directing the sun's rays through it after the manner of a "burning glass." It was carried in times of epidemics as a protective charm, and it was held to bestow a degree of craft and subtlety on the wearer. As a martial stone in harmony with Scotland, it was set in the head of dirks and other knives, and adorned the Highland dress.

The cairngorm was considered a talisman against venereal diseases, sore throats, etc.

It is under the zodiacal Scorpio.

CARBUNCLE

"The Carbuncle
Which from it such a flaming light
And radiancy ejecteth
That in the very darkest night
The eye's to it directed."

—DRAYTON

The name Carbuncle is derived from the Latin CARBUNCULUS, diminutive of CARBO, a coal. During the past centuries it has been written as charbucle, charbokel, charbokll, cherbukkill, carbokyl, charboncle, carbunculum, karboncle, carbunacle, carbuncle stone. Of it Dr. Wilkins writes: "It is believed that a carbuncle does shine in the dark like a burning coal, from whence it has its name."

The carbuncle is the iron alumina garnet known as almandine or almandite, which varies in color shades from red, ruby red, columbine red to brownish red. The name is said to be derived from the town of Alabanda in Asia Minor where, according to Pliny, the *Carbunculi Amethystozontes* were cut. Dr. Holland's translation of the passage relating to the carbuncle in Pliny, Book 37, is as follows:

"Amongst these red gems the rubies otherwise called carbuncles challenge the principall place and are esteemed richest; they have their name in Greek of the likenesse unto fire, and yet fire hath no power of them which is the reason that some call them apyroti."

The apyroti is our pyrope, which indicates "fiery" in Greek. It is a magnesia alumina garnet and was, as it now is, cut en cabochon. Specimens chosen for this purpose are from deep to black red.

Almandines form the pathways of the Fourth Heaven (Dar as-Salam) of the Muhammadans; and the traditional symbol of the Ark illuminated by a large carbuncle stone occurs in the Rabbinical writings. To students of the mysteries this must ever appeal as a forceful and subtle symbol of man's immortality and sublime power. Leonardus writes of the carbuncle "brandishing its fiery rays on every side and in the dark appearing like a fiery coal… It is regarded," he says, "as the first among 'burning gems.'" That the carbuncle gave out a glowing light without reflection is frequently repeated by ancient authors, and the Palace of the Magician in the Russian story of King Kajata was hewn out of a single carbuncle which lit up the whole surrounding district. Sir E. Tennant quotes from a Chinese work a narrative which tells that

> "Early in the 14th century the Emperor sent an officer to Ceylon to purchase a carbuncle of unusual luster which was fitted as a ball to the cap of the Emperor of that country. It was upwards of an ounce in weight and cost 100,000 strings of cash. Each time a grand levee was held at night the red luster filled the palace, and hence it was designated the Red Palace Illuminator."

Nathaniel Hawthorne's beautiful story of "The Great Carbuncle" in his *Twice-told Tales* is based on the Indian tradition which is, he says, "too wild and too beautiful to be adequately wrought up in prose." Nevertheless the author does so with old-world charm:

> "Some few believe that this inestimable stone is blazing as of old, and say that they have caught its radiance like a flash of summer lightning, far down the valley of the Saco. And be it owned that many a mile from the Crystal Hills I saw a wondrous light around their summits and was lured by the faith of poesy to be the last pilgrim of the Great Carbuncle."

In the Middle Ages the carbuncle was worn as a charm to protect the wearer against the plague, and it was said to protect travelers on long voyages by sea from drowning, and by land from accidents. It was also credited with the power of resisting poisons, of averting evil thoughts and dreams. It was an uplifter of the soul and a preserver of the health of the body. When its luster changed, the death of the wearer was indicated.

In addition to being the stone of undying hope and the dispeller of sadness, the Indians and Arabs credit it with protecting from wounds and harm in the midst of battle. A story was told to the author by the mother of an Australian Captain born, according to astrology, with the Sun rising in the sign of the Archer. This officer wore at the author's suggestion a ring of carbuncle. At Gallipoli he, with a few men, was cut off by incessant gunfire which, although directed their way, did not injure them and from which they were eventually rescued. During this ordeal the Captain looked often at his calm, flame-burning ring, the unearthly brightness of which seemed to him an emblem of salvation.

Emanuel Swedenborg compared the carbuncle with the good of celestial love, and it was regarded as a heart stimulant by some old medical writers. It represents the red arterial blood and is connected with the fiery sign of the zodiac Sagittarius. A great part of Australia is much influenced by this sign according to astrology and large quantities of extremely beautiful almandines—which were at one time mistaken for rubies and termed "Australian rubies"— have been already found.

To dream of the carbuncle was said to indicate acquirement of wisdom.

The carbuncle is under the zodiacal Sagittarius.

CARNELIAN

"Let not the Muse the dull Carnelian slight,
Although it shine with but a feeble light."

— MARBODUS

The Carnelian obtains its name from the Latin word CARNIS, flesh, which describes its color. The sard (Greek, SARX, flesh) called by Swedenborg and the ancients the "sardine stone," of a deeper brownish red is said by Pliny to have been named from Sardis in Asia Minor. Carnelian is also written cornelian, cornelien, and carnelion. Woodward in his *Natural History* (1695) alludes to the ancient Roman tradition that the pale red carnelians were called females and the deeper colors males. The yellow carnelian was anciently regarded as the female loved by the Sun.

These gems are extremely sensitive, being affected by oils and acids. It has been demonstrated from olden times that carnelians exposed to the rays of the sun were brightened and heightened in color, a result which could not be obtained by ordinary heat. The carnelian and sard were greatly used in all ages, and many beads, charms and ornaments have been found in the old lands. The writer had in his possession two beautiful Etruscan scarabs of sard—one bearing a portrait of Aesculapius and the snake, the other portraying Venus disrobing—neither of which had suffered much from the attacks of time.

Mr. King describes a sard intaglio showing an ibis stepping out of a nautilus shell, seizing a snake—a symbol of the eternal war between the Sun, represented by the ibis on the stone of the Sun, and the earth moistures, represented by the snake. Another from the Rhodes collection represents Venus showing Cupid how to use the bow, appropriately cut on a sard or heart stone; another, also cut on sard, shows Cupid riding on a lion—symbol of the Sun and the heart (organ of the Sun in astrophilosophy).

Alaric the Goth entered the city of Rome with his victorious army August 27th in the year 410 A.D. His birthday cannot be ascertained with any degree of certainty, but it may have been somewhere near that time for he wore on his finger a large carnelian talismanic ring on which was engraved: "Alaricus Rex Gothorum."

Madame Blavatsky relates stories of the Shamans of Tartary who carried carnelians under their left arms, and by employing these stones in certain ways they were enabled to separate the astral from the physical body. The carnelian was used by them in certain magical work and was reputed to be a stone of wonderful power. It is significant that these Shamans carried the carnelians on their left sides, near the great Sun of the human body—the heart. Madame Blavatsky herself possessed a carnelian to which special virtue was attached. She was born when the Sun was in the sign of the Lion, and the carnelian was therefore one of her chief talismanic gems.

The carnelian was sometimes called the Stone of the Martyrs. It is said to bestow the power to see into the astral plane if, when placed before a light for about four minutes, it is steadily gazed upon. Considering the powerful effect the Sun has on the carnelian, it were best that, if phenomena of this order are to be obtained through the agency of such an instrument, the stone be first exposed to the rays of the sun. It is inadvisable, however, to look directly at the sun with the naked eye.

The carnelian is said to bring content to the wearer, and Albertus Magnus said that it made the soul happy, drove away the evil effects of sorcery, witchcraft, enchantment and fear. It was the stone of the victor and of victory, and was used as a charm against bad temper—for bad temper, according to the masters, is a form of black magic. Black magic was evilly directed in the light of a waning moon, and it was detected by the varying sheen of the protective carnelian or sard. Also in dreams the stone was a symbol that evil thoughts were being directed against the dreamer.

It represented the magical force of Faith and the weakening folly of skepticism in the Rosicrucian mysteries. Medicinally the stone was used to stop bleedings, and in the Middle Ages it was administered in powdered form. At this period it was stated that the yellow variety was the gem for *Dies Solis* or Sunday. Both the carnelian and sard are attached to the zodiacal Leo, the Mansion of the Sun, and the connection apart from tradition is proven scientifically by the effect of the solar rays on the stone itself. It is said to promote coolness in argument and dignity in dispute, and the Muhammadan tradition tells that Muhammad held that to procure contentment and blessings, it was necessary with right mind to Allah, to wear a carnelian.

CATSEYE

> *"The Catseye is one of the jewels of which the Singhalese are especially proud."*
>
> — TENNENT's *Ceylon*

The catseye is a chalcedonic quartz, translucent, of various colors—yellow-green, yellow-brown, hyacinth-red, grey, green-grey, etc. It is of a peculiar opalescence, resembling the eye of a cat, when cut en cabochon, an effect produced by amianthoid asbestos filaments which run parallel through the stone. The virtues ascribed to the catseye are many. It was said to put color into pale faces, to give pleasure to the mind, to relieve the soul of melancholy, to cure chronic disorders and wasting diseases, and to keep the wearer from financial distress and ruin. It is said to have been successfully employed in relieving croup and asthma.

Pressed on to the forehead between the eyes it aided thought and helped foresight. Carried by those with Capricorn rising in the horoscope, or with the Sun, Jupiter or Venus in Capricorn, it is credited with especial value as a charm for success in speculative ventures. Enwrapped in women's hair, it was employed as a birth charm, and if calcined and applied to wounds, said Rabbi Ben Adoulah, it healed them. Further, it cured inflammations of the eyes, if lightly rubbed on the closed lids. To dream of a catseye was said to warn of treachery. It was the Eye of Belus in old Assyria, and a talisman which made the wearer invisible to his enemies. Old Indian masters advise that the specimen worn be as perfect as possible, saying that bad stones should not be worn at all.

The catseye is attached to the sign Capricorn.

CEYLONITE. (See **SPINEL**.)

CHALCEDONY

"With luster fair is the Calcedon graced."

—MARBODUS

The chalcedony obtains its name from Chalkedon in Asia Minor, and appears written as calcedony, calsydoyne, calcidoine, chalcedun, calcideny, chalcidonye, calcedon, calchedonie.

This stone includes a number of varieties such as carnelian, sard, agate, catseye, prase, plasma, heliotrope, chrysoprase, moss agate, onyx, sardonyx, hornstone or chert, and flint. Chalcedony is classed under the great Silica family. It is translucent, waxy, white, pale grey, light brown or bluish.

The blue chalcedony is identified with the ancient sapphirine—a stone confused with our sapphire. Mr. King says that the "finest Persian cylinder known, engraved with the usual type of the King fighting with the lion, was formed out of this variety: the signet doubtless that once graced the wrist of some Darius or Artaxerxes of the latter days of the Persian monarchy."

It is said that Albertus Magnus first identified the chalcedony of today in the 13th century, although according to many authorities this was not done until the 15th century at the very earliest. The ancient chalcedony is classed amongst such stones as the leucachates and cerachates. Pliny describes the ancient chalcedony as of "green mixed with blue as the feathers of the peacock's tail or of the pigeon's neck," and Holme quoting from Pliny in *The Armory*, 1688, says: "The chalcedon or calchedoine, being well chafed and warmed, will draw a straw or a rush to it." The calcedon described by Pliny was not found in his time, but our chalcedony was greatly used in fine art work in all ages. A chalcedony showing tiny red and brown spots has been termed the stone of St. Stephen, in allusion to the martyrdom of that Saint as described in Chapter 7 of the Acts.

The chalcedony is a symbol of enthusiasm, and is the emblem of Victory Divine amongst the jewels of the Rosicrucians. It has also been termed the Mother Stone, and under the name of leucachate was sacred to Diana. It protected the voyager on the ocean tracts from tempests and terrors, drove away evil spirits, banished sadness and melancholy, secured public favor and protected the wearer in times of political revolutions.

The chalcedony is under the zodiacal Cancer.

CHALCEDONYX. The chalcedonyx is really a chalcedony adorned with lines of white and grey. It is included in the zodiacal Cancer.

CHIASTOLITE

"On her white breast a sparkling cross she wore."

—POPE

The chiastolite obtains its name from the Greek word CHIASTOS, crossed. It is also known as macle, from the Latin *Macula*, a spot. It is a form of andalusite found in certain metamorphic rock. During the process of crystallization, certain impurities of a carbonaceous nature are dispersed across the stone which displays from this cause different forms of cross, tessellated or lozenge-shaped markings, which show out curiously when the stone is cut or broken. The hardness of the stone is not great—specimens sometimes being as low as 3 in Mohs' scale. The color varies from grey to yellow, pink, red, white, and deep brown.

The chiastolite is reported to have been first found in Andalusia in Spain, at which place legend says St. James suffered martyrdom. A further amplification of this legend tells that the origin of the chiastolite dates back to that time when it sprang into being just where the Apostle laid his hands on the rocks. At the time of Pedro the Cruel of Spain (14th Century,) a peasant, by name Miguel Perez, found a rare specimen of this stone over an inch in diameter. It exhibited two crosses, the most marked being of a rich dark red hue. Wishing to obtain this remarkable gem as a present for his ally Edward the Black Prince (whose title, be it said, was not bestowed from the color of his armor but as Froissart says, "from the terror his arms inspired,") Pedro ordered the peasant to bring it to him.

When Perez was ushered into his presence the King demanded the gem under pain of death. The terrified peasant, after faltering for a few moments in nervous fear, at length held out the gem for the King to take. As Pedro was about to seize it, the blood-red cross met his gaze and he fell in a swoon on the palace floor. The stone seems to have disappeared for a long period, and it is believed to have been discovered in the possession of Philip V of Spain who carried it as a jewel charm till his death when it was hung about the neck of the statue of St. James in the St. Jago di Compostella. Marshal Soult, having plundered the Cathedral during the Peninsular War, gave the stolen stone to Napoleon Bonaparte, who presented it to Murat. Astrologically, the chiastolite would not be a fortunate stone for Pedro, Soult, Napoleon, Murat or the Black Prince— notwithstanding the latter's name. It would be a fortunate stone for Philip V.

It is quoted as a fact that when Columbus sailed on his voyage of discovery to America he wore a charm of chiastolite. The historical Chiastolite of Spain is said to be at the present time in the possession of the French family De Bodts.

The chiastolite is a symbol of prudence, faith, caution and sincerity. To dream of one is a sign of struggle, delay or limitation. It is a stone of the zodiacal Capricorn. Chiastolite is also written as chiastolith and chiastolithe. The name was bestowed on it in the year 1800. Some very fine specimens have recently been found in South Australia.

CHRYSOBERYL

"Time will run back and fetch the Age of Gold."

—MILTON

The name is derived from CHRYSOS, golden, and BERYLLOS, beryl. Suitable stones are cut into catseyes of opalescent gleam. The chrysoberyl is harder than the topaz, and is composed of alumina and glucina. The colors of the stone are asparagus green, grass green, greenish white. The alexandrite variety changes its colors in real and artificial light.

The chrysoberyl was credited as a charm against evil spirits and a disordered imagination, against deceit, craft and conspiracy. To dream of a chrysoberyl was a warning against waste. It is under the zodiacal Pisces.

CHRYSOCOLLA. This hydros copper silicate derives its name from the Greek CHRYSOS, gold, and KOLLA, cement. It obtained its name from its resemblance to a gold solder known and used by the ancient Greeks. It is a very soft, light substance, varying in color from a blue-green to a sky or turquoise blue. The texture is enamel-like, and the occurrence is earthy and massive. Chrysocolla is a musical charm, to dream of which was favorable for musicians, florists and singers. It is under the zodiacal Taurus.

CHAPTER 15

Chrysolite — Crystal

CHRYSOLITE

"When morning rose, to land
We haul'd our bark, and moored it on the strand,
Where in a beauteous grotto's cool recess
Dance the green Nereids of the neighboring seas."

—Homer (Pope's Translation)

The Chrysolite obtains its name from the Greek CHRYSOS, gold, and LITHOS, a stone. This gem is of a light green-yellow; when deep olive green it is known as a **PERIDOT**, when yellowish-green as true **OLIVINE**. Among the ancients the chrysolite was our topaz. Its name, literally "Golden Stone," indicates the beautiful golden topaz so highly esteemed by gem-lovers, which, we are told, derives its name from that mysterious Island of the Mists which Pliny calls Topazion. Dr. G. F. Herbert Smith writes of the variety peridot as bearing the pretty name of "the evening emerald," and the most charming specimens resemble the light green of the sea waters near the shore, illuminated by the setting sun.

This gem appears to be the amianthus of post-Biblical writers, known as "the gem of miracles," which drove away the spirits and influences of evil, protected against obsession, dissolved enchantments, and the phantoms of the night, gladdened the heart with hope, strengthened the soul, inspired thought, banished illusion, despair, madness, aided the faculties of inspiration and prophecy.

In *The History of Monsieur Oufle*—quoted by Brand—it is advised: "To expel phantoms and rid people of folly, take the precious stone chrysolite, set it in gold, and let them wear it about 'em." Francis Barrett says that it is good for the lungs and cures asthmatic complaints; also that when held under the tongue it cures fevers, aids prophecy, bestows eloquence and inspiration. The peridot was known as *"the"* precious stone, and was often valued more than the diamond.

The hardness of the chrysolite is from 6 to 7 on Mohs' scale. It is under the zodiacal Pisces.

CHRYSOPRASE. The chrysoprase derives its name from the Greek CHRYSOS, golden, and PRASON, a leek. It is an apple-green chalcedony, the color being caused by oxide of nickel. The chrysoprase was esteemed the perfect stone of dreams in ancient Egypt, Greece and Rome. It was believed that if one condemned for any offense held a chrysoprase in his mouth, he would escape punishment. It was a stone for the voyager on deep seas, a kindler of the imaginative faculties, a banisher of greed, selfishness and carelessness. It was the stone of happiness and enterprise, awakening slumbering faculties. It calmed irritability, the pains of gout, and, bound to the left arm, it prevented or cured the stone. It was the stone of prudence, adaptability and versatility, rousing to action, progress and adventure.

To gaze into the chrysoprase was said to strengthen the eyes, especially when the Moon was passing through Taurus and Cancer. In many ways the chrysoprase was a religious symbol. In its Hebrew name of NOFEK it was the fourth stone of the Breastplate, and as the tenth jewel of the Rosicrucians it was the symbol of strength, moral and physical, and of invisible power. Swedenborg sees in it "the supreme heavenly love of truth," and the Fathers see "triumph over sin." Its symbology is reflected to the gateway through which the soul passed when entering the sphere of earth, and its dream influence was like an angel's smile. Light in excess has an unfavorable effect on this stone, robbing it of its color. Introduced into England in the reign of Ann, it was much loved by the Queen. It enjoyed great popularity during the times of the 3 Georges, and was a favorite gem of Queen Victoria.

The chrysoprase is under the zodiacal Cancer.

CINNAMON STONE. (See ESSONITE.)

CITRINE. Citrine is a clear light yellow quartz crystal, obtaining its name from its citron tint. It is correctly called false topaz, and incorrectly Brazilian topaz. It presents no cleavage like the topaz. It is also known as Spanish topaz and Occidental topaz. The citrine was carried as a protective talisman against miasmatic exhalations, plague epidemics, eruptive diseases, evil thought forms, alcoholic and other forms of indulgence. It was also employed as a charm against the bites of snakes, venomous reptiles and insects, and against scandal, libel and treachery.

The Citrine is under the zodiacal Scorpio.

COAL

> *"A live coal from the altar (Isaiah 6:6) signifies divine love from which all purification is derived."*
>
> —SWEDENBORG

Coal derives its name from the Anglo-Saxon word KOL, to kindle. It is a well-known solid black combustible substance, the remains of old forests and earth vegetation which chemical action has changed chiefly by the elimination of oxygen and hydrogen. Many dyes, acids, gases, flavorings, etc., are obtained from this important product. Amongst these are tar, coke, creosote, carbolic acid, naphtha, sal ammoniac, ammonia, various explosives, drugs, mineral vanilla, etc.

Dr. Brewer explains that to "haul over the coals" is historically and literally true: "At one time," he says, "the Jews were 'bled' whenever the Kings or barons wanted money, and one very common torture, if they resisted, was to haul them over the coals of a slow fire to give them a roasting." Sir Walter Scott alludes to this practice in *Ivanhoe*. Professor John Henry Pepper, writing on *Coal and Coal Mines*, introduces the following interesting details:

> "In olden time, before a cargo of coals could be discharged from a collier, it was necessary to obtain the permission of the Lord Mayor who, for a certain consideration, granted the required permission. This much honored magistrate and his worthy coadjutors, the aldermen, with the common councilmen and livery called the Corporation were permitted to lay a tax upon the "black diamonds" that amounted to something like £50,000 per annum. In 1830 the heaviest of the coal duties were abolished: and since that time the trade has assumed gigantic proportions which have made it the marvel of the civilized world.
>
> "The first licenses to dig coals were granted to the burgesses of Newcastle by Henry III and in 1281 a very good trade existed in that fuel. A proclamation in the reign of King Edward I shows the introduction of coal as a substitute for wood, and a charter of Edward II

indicates that Derbyshire coal was used in London. In the same reign coals were first sent from Newcastle for the benefit of those trades which required fuel: and in 1316 a petition was made from Parliament to the King praying His Majesty to forbid all use of the new and pestilent fuel called "coals," which was acceded to, and a proclamation made, commanding all use of coals to cease and determine, and threatening all who burnt coals to be mulcted, and on a second offense to have their furnaces demolished. In the reign of Queen Elizabeth the burning of stone coal was again prohibited during the sitting of Parliament. At a subsequent period, about 1648, coals were once more placed under a ban . . . In 1520 Newcastle coal was first exported into Paris."

A piece of coal was carried by thieves in the belief that it would protect them from detection, and help them to escape when pursued. To dream of coals is indicated as a symbol of disappointment, trouble, affliction and losses, except if the coals be burning brightly. Then, the symbol gives promises of uplifting and advancement, for the fire symbol of Mars is rousing to action the coal symbol of Saturn. Coal is under the celestial Capricorn.

CORAL

"In the pleased infant see its power expand
When first the coral fills his little hand."
  —SPRAGUE

Coral is a carbonate of lime effected by gelatinous marine mollusks known as "polypi."

For long ages coral was supposed to be a marine plant of which Trevisa wrote in 1495: "Corall is gendred in the Red See, and is a tree as long as it is coveryd with water, but as it is drawn out it torneth into stone," and Jordan in 1699 tells us that "coral also being a plant and nourished with this juice, turns to a stone." The name is derived from the Greek word KORALLION, and is found written as corale, corral, correil, curalle, curroll, quyral, etc.

The various species have been set down as follows:

Pink Coral
Red Coral
White Coral
Black Coral
Blue Coral
Yellow Coral, etc.

In more modern times species have obtained names from their appearance. Thus:

Brain Coral
Cup Coral
Mushroom Coral
Organ-pipe Coral
Star Coral

The appeal of coral to the poet finds expression in some charming legends:

Ovid (*Metamorphoses*) wrote that Perseus, after he had cut the head from the body of the dreadful Medusa, laid it on the branches of the trees which grew by the sea shore; but the power never departing, turned these branches, as it had turned every other living thing, into stone. The sea nymphs drew these fossils beneath the waves and they became the coral seeds. A variation of this legend tells that the blood which fell from the bleeding head on to the shrubs, flowers and trees turned them into seeds of coral which the sea nymphs drew beneath the waves. It arose again in flower-like beauty with Venus when she emerged in all her glory from the sea, symbolical of the exaltation of Venus in the zodiacal Pisces, and in this connection also concealed a deeper meaning.

No gem has been more employed as a charm for averting the fell spell of the evil eye than the innocent coral which was credited with the power of destroying the first stroke of the glance, after which it—like the drawn fang of the serpent—was rendered incapable of injury. Scot writes in *Discovery of Witchcraft*: "The coral preserveth such as bear it from fascination or bewitching and in this respect corals are hanged about children's necks." Pliny mentions that the Romans hung on babies' cradles and around their necks pieces of red coral as an aid in teething and an influence against the falling sickness and infantile diseases.

Plato says: "Coral is good to be hanged about children's necks, as well to rub their gums as to preserve them from the falling sickness. It hath also some special sympathy with Nature, for the best coral, being worn about the neck, will turn pale and wan if the party that wears it be sick, and comes to its former color again as they recover health." Brand mentions a similar idea in the *Three Ladies of London*, 1584: "Coral will look pale when you be sick." Little bells were also attached in the Middle Ages to children's coral charms in order to ward off evil spirits, storms and pestilence, and scare away the Furies; this same belief exists in Japan, China and other countries. It is a fact that coral is affected by the health of the wearer; some writers say that it becomes spotted or stained when the illness is of a serious nature. It was regarded as a very potent charm for women.

In Italy the coral was also called the Witch Stone, because it was said to protect women from the wizards and men from the witches. In connection with these Paracelsus writes: "They are the outgrowths of an intense and sensual imagination of men and women, and which Rabbinical traditions relate in an allegorical manner, are connected with Adam (the animal Man), and Lilith, his first wife. They are afraid of red corals as dogs are afraid of a whip: but the brown corals attract them. Red corals are disagreeable to monsters, Incubi, Succubi, Phantasmata and all evil spirits, but brown corals are not, and they delight in them."

In commenting on this Dr. Franz Hartmann, a physician of note and distinguished writer, says that he knew of cases of melancholy, depression of mind, hypochondria, etc., that had been successfully treated by the wearing of red corals, while other articles employed for the same purpose had no effect, the cure therefore not being merely attributable to the belief of the patient. He concludes: "The ignorant will find it easier to ridicule such things than to explain them."

A curious passage in Bartholomeus (*De Proprietatibus Rerum*, 1536) is of interest:

"Wytches tell that this stone withstondeth lyghtnyng, whirlewynde, tempeste and stormes fro shyppes and houses that it is in. The Red Corall helpeth ayenst the feudes, gyle and scorne, and ayenst divers wonderous doyng and multiplieth frute, and spedeth begynnyng and ending of causes and of nedes."

Oriental mystics warn against the wearing of dull, dirty or discolored specimens. The pure coral was deemed a protection from plague, poison, storm and tempest. In a house it charmed away disharmony, envy and evil influences. It banished evil dreams and the "terrors of the night," wild animals, the lightning strike, witchcraft, epilepsy, stomach complaints, night sweats, etc. It was a cure for sores, diseased gums, whooping cough, disorders of the spleen, teething troubles, troubles of the feet and toes, madness, etc.

It is interesting to note that natural corals in the form of vegetable growths were, and in some places still are, tied to fruit trees to ensure their fertility, and that women of ancient times wore such specimens as charms against sterility. Thus, "she who hath risen from the sea foam," Venus, was regarded as employing the moistures so needed in perfecting the material dresses of the animal, mineral and vegetable worlds when entering earth conditions. The ancient masters held that such examples of the doctrine of Sympathies, Similitudes, Signatures and Correspondences guide man to a correct knowledge and understanding of the mysteries of Nature.

The ancient Greeks attached coral to the prows of their ships to protect them from the onslaughts of sea and storm. Lemnius says: "Bind coral to the neck, it takes off turbulent dreams and allays the nightly fears of children." The gem of the Arabian Garden of the Everlasting Life—Jannat al Khuld—is the yellow coral.

To dream of red, pink and coral of beautiful luster is said to denote recovery to the sick and good health to anyone, but ill-conditioned specimens symbolize the opposite. As a cardiac stimulant, for stopping hemorrhages, warding off contagion, etc., the old physician Rulandus (*Medicina Practica*, 1564) prescribed half a dram of powdered coral.

The 17th century prescription shown on page 266 was administered as a cure for colic, purging and vomiting, and is given here as of especial interest:

Amongst the Spaniards it was usual at one time for conjurers and jugglers especially to wear tight-fitting coral-colored costumes. Good specimens of coral are greatly esteemed by dancers. It is especially a luck

Tabellæ Corallatæ:

R̟   Corallorum rubeorum præparatorum

℥ij   margaritar præparator

℥i   boli armeni

℥ß   ligni aloes

Ði   sacch. albissimi Dissoluti in aquâ rosaru cinnamoni tenuioris

quantum sufficit: fiat confectis in tabellis.

A 17th century prescription for colic, purging and vomiting

gem of the ballet, the sign Pisces of the Zodiac—under which all corals are placed—ruling the feet.

CORUNDUM. Also written at earlier periods as coriundum, corundon, corindon. (See under **RUBY, SAPPHIRE.**)

CORDIERITE. (See **IOLITE.**)

CROCIDOLITE. Also written krokydolite, krocidolite. This stone was named in the year 1831, from the Greek KROKIS, a variation of KROKUS, the nap of woolen cloth, and LITHOS, a stone. It is well described as an asbestiform variety of hornblende of indigo-blue, leek-green or golden-brown color—the latter variety being also known as tiger's eye. When cut en cabochon this stone has a fine chatoyant effect.

There is little doubt that the ancients knew of this stone of the asbestos family under the zodiacal Gemini. It was regarded as a fortunate stone for people of literary or mercurial tendencies, and as a nerve and lung soother. Held against the temple when the Moon is passing through the sign Gemini, in good aspect to Mercury, it would assist thought and mental speculation.

CRYSTAL. The crystal obtains its name from the Greek word KRUST-ALLOS, ice. It is a pure and transparent variety of Quartz, so called because of its resemblance to clear ice. In literature it appears as cristalla, cristal, crestal, kristall, cristalle, christall, chrystal. Webster writes that the English spelling was gradually changed to *crystal* between the 15th and 17th centuries. We have evidence of its early use by man; Egyptian scarabei and Babylonian cylinders having been found, dating back as far as 1500 B.C.

In the trial of Psyche—that beautifully symbolic legend—Venus gives this graceful lover of Eros the magical vase of pure crystal with the request that it be filled with the waters from the Fountain of Forgetfulness. The Fountain waters flowed through a narrow channel at the summit of a steep mountain, and they murmured: "To attempt is to perish. Be warned. Be warned. To attempt is to perish; fly from us." Psyche saw two caves, one on each side of these icy waters, and in these caves were two terrible dragons. With the precious vase in her trembling hands, the faithful lover prayed for help in her perilous task. Jupiter heard her prayer in pity, for love had been kind to him, and he sent his eagle to her. The eagle drew the vase from Psyche and, filling it with the waters, brought it to her. Then she ran to Venus, thinking that pitying love would exact no more. "Thy witchery has gained thee these waters," said the Goddess, "I have another test for thee."

The King of the Ethiopians showed the messengers of Cambyses amongst other wonders the tombs of pure crystal in which could be seen the bodies of the departed, perfect in form and feature. In the imperial vault of the Hapsburgs in the Church of the Capuchins, Vienna, there are 150 crystal vases, gold mounted, with a crown on the top of each, which contain the hearts of the Royal members of the Family. This practice dates from Duke Francis who, dying in Switzerland, directed that his heart should be preserved and sent to Vienna.

In China and Japan the crystal is called SINSHO. The Japanese know it also as TAMA or Jewel of Perfection, and it is used by them for making crystal balls and beautiful objects of art. It is cut in the shape of a ball, esteemed in Japan as the Stone of Concentration, and several in a family will sit round gazing at a specimen in which they see guidance and help in the path of life. In China it is also known as CHING, and symbolized as an upright triangle of three suns, it has always been highly esteemed. It is cut with great patience into figures of deities and sacred objects. The Chinese regard it as a talisman of concentration and per-severance; it recalls to them the magnificence and immensity of what man calls space, this "jewel of perfection" which the Japanese also term "Breath of the White Dragon."

The Medicine Indians of South America say that a holy spirit is in the crystal, and for this reason the sacred stones must not be seen except by initiates. The aboriginals of Australia and Tasmania regarded the crystal in a mystic way. It was known by the Murray tribes as *Katto* and *Maako*. The South Australians generally termed large crystals *Kanwen-muka*, and smaller specimens *Kanyappa*. It is the *Teyl* of the West Austra-lian, the *Leeka* and *Heka* of the Tasmanian and it is called *Tendeagh* by the East tribe and *Mughramallee* by the South.

The late Mr. James Bonwick says that the natives usually wore the crystal in its bag, suspended from the neck; he gives their song of magic as follows:

Kano Kano wimmari	(lizard)
Kano Kano Kanwemuka	(crystal)
Kano Kano Makkitya	(flint)
Kano yeruka Makkitya	
Makkitya mulyeria	

Mr. Bonwick also gives instances of the prevalence of crystallomancy amongst the aboriginals, the use of the Rain Stone, the Coradgee Stone which was wrapped in hair and was not to be seen by a female, "not always a simple white' stone, it was more commonly a quartz crystal." He says further "Some men, by proper use of this magical agency (the crystal) could work wonders."

Thus, the crystal has been employed by savage and civilized man in all ages. It was said to enclose within its bright form all the knowl-edge and secrets that have ever been; if worn during sleep it banishes evil dreams and spells, and guards the wearer against sorcery, witchcraft, secret enemies and evil thoughts. It was said to indicate the presence of poison by clouding or by breaking—hence its employment in the manu-facture of precious goblets by the ancients. It was employed as a pre-ventive of watery, wasting and infectious diseases, tumorous complaints, blood impurities, heart, bowel and feet troubles, renal affections, etc.

Gazing Crystal on Dragon Stand. Presented to the Author by the Late Judge Casey of Victoria, Australia

Pliny recommends it as an external medicine for women when in the form of fine powder mixed with honey. With regard to the employment of crystal balls and lenses for medical purposes, this venerable author says: "I find it asserted by physicians that when any part of the body requires to be cauterized it cannot be better done than by means of a crystal ball held against the sun's rays"; it is interesting to compare this statement with a more recent one made by the late Dr. E. D. Babbitt, M.D.:

> "Sunlight can lubricate and even vesicate the skin without causing much pain or without leaving any permanent scars like those formed by sinapisms, moxas, lancings, etc. Many a tumor which under the old system is cut out without even reaching the cause, is destroyed by concentrating the light upon it through a convex lens."

Many beautiful crystals bearing intaglios of a large size have been discovered. Mr. King mentions two choice specimens of Valerio il Vicentino and his rival Geo. del Castel Bolognese. Some crystals have been found encasing drops of water very much like the spirit in the spirit-level. These are known as hydrolites or, as Pliny writes them, enhydros. They are mentioned by the poet Claudian as—

> "A stream unfettered pent in crystal round,
> A truant fount by hardened waters bound."

Mr. King received information that miners in California have died from drinking the water from a hydrolite, and this circumstance exhibits the subtle action of some of the stones attached to the sign of the Fishes. The crystal, wrongly but frequently termed "beryl" stone, is highly esteemed as an instrument for heightening the imagination and bringing out the gazing power of the third eye previously mentioned. Mr. William Jones gives an illustration of the seal of a divination ring from Licini's *Antiqua Schemata.* It shows a half nude woman holding a serpent in her left hand, the head of which is bending towards a crystal ball held by a nude man, his right leg resting on a wooden stand, his left stretching towards an altar on which the sacred fire is burning. The female bends over the male who gazes intently into the crystal ball. The work is full of expression and force.

In the Highlands of Scotland large pieces of crystal were used for charms, and cattle were given to drink water which had been poured over crystals. Similar crystals were employed for the protection of cattle in Ireland, a fine specimen being still kept by the Tyrone family.

The sign Pisces is the natural 12th celestial House, ruling large cattle. It is also the sign of occult and mysterious things and of the elevation of Venus. Thus, all the legends, stories and philosophies connected with this bright stone of the sign Pisces are easily understood. Professor Sir William Ridgeway, of Cambridge, England, in his work, *The Drama and Dramatic Dances of Non-European Races*, draws attention to the fact that

> "crystals have always been and are still regarded as the most amuletic of precious stones, and comedians also are frequently cut into faceted shapes by the Arabs and others. The diamond and spinel are both octahedral. The Japanese are especially fond of rock crystal, one of their favorite amulets being a double gourd cut out of such a crystal."

Swedenborg recognized in the crystal "Divine Truth in all its brightness" and truth certainly has its correspondence in the clear glistening magnetic crystal.

CHAPTER 16

The Diamond

DIAMOND

"The lively diamond drinks thy purest rays."
— Thomson

The diamond derives its name from the Greek ADAMAS, ADA-
MANTOS, adamant. It has been written at various times as dya-
mawnte, dyamamaunt, dyamant, diamant, diamownde, dyamonde, dya-
mount, diamonde, diamont, dimond, dymauntz, and adamant stone. It
is but pure crystallized carbon, and Arnott (*Physics*, 1830), writes: "The
diamond has nearly the greatest light-bending power of any known substances, and hence comes in part its brilliancy as a jewel." It is remarkable also for its extreme hardness and for its variety of colors—steel,
white, blue, yellow, orange, red, green, pink and black. This "prince of
gems" in days of old was considered the royal stone which only a prince
was privileged to wear.

The highly electrical properties ascribed by the ancients to the diamond were proved in the 17th and 18th centuries by the chemists Boyle
and Du Fay, and Dr. Kunz has demonstrated today that all diamonds
"phosphoresce when exposed to the rays of radium, polonium, or acti-
num, even when glass is interposed." In a paper read to the Royal Society, London, November 5th, 1914, the late Sir William Crooks said:

"Many substances become colored by direct exposure to radium, the
color depending on the substance. Diamond takes a full sage-green,
the depth of tint depending on the time of exposure to the radium. In
addition to the change of color the diamond also becomes radioactive,
continuously giving off α, β, Υ rays. The acquired color and activity withstand the action of powerful chemical agents and continue for
years with apparently undiminished activity. Removing the surface by

272

mechanical means removes both color and radio-activity. The appearance of an autoradiograph made by placing an active diamond crystal on sensitive photographic plate and the visual examination of its scintillating luminosity suggest that there is a special discharge of energy from the corners and points of the crystal."

The several experiments for the production of diamonds by artificial means have since 1880 been conducted by some eminent scientists, notably Professor Marden, Professor Henri Moissan and Sir William Crooks. For many years Sir Charles Parsons has been working closely at the problem, and the main conclusions arrived at by this scholar were communicated to the Royal Society, London, in 1918. They were as follows:

That graphite cannot be converted into diamond by heat and pressure alone within the limits reached in the experiments;

That there is no distinct evidence that any of the chemical reactions under pressure have yielded diamond;

That the only undoubted source of diamond is from iron previously heated to high temperature and then cooled.

That diamond is not produced by bulk pressure as previously supposed, but by the action of gases occluded in the metal and condensed into the center on quick cooling.

In connection with these experiments it will be found interesting to read Balzac's Search for the Absolute, in which it is told how after many ruinous attempts to produce a diamond by artificial means one, self-formed, is found in the old chemist's laboratory after his death.

The worth and romance of the old mines of Brazil and India are dwelt on by many of the writers of the past, and although diamonds were discovered in South Africa in the 18th Century, yet no important discoveries were made until 1867, when a large stone was found by children of a Dutch farmer, Mr. Jacobs, not far from their farm near Hopetown on the Orange River. Not knowing what the stone really was and attaching no value to it, Mrs. Jacobs gave it to Mr. Schalk van Niekerk, a neighbor, who entrusted it to Mr. O'Reilly, a hunter and trader, asking him to submit it to some mineralogist for an opinion.

Mr. O'Reilly took the stone to Colesberg and showed it to Mr. Boyes, the acting commissioner for that district, at whose suggestion it was submitted to Dr. W. G. Atherstone of Graham's Town. Thanks to his mineralogical knowledge, Dr. Atherstone proved the stone to be a diamond. It was exhibited in Paris in March, 1867, as "The First African Diamond Discovered," and was purchased by the Cape Governor, Sir Philip Wodehouse, for £500. Sir Philip sold it to Garrards and it has changed hands several times since then. The weight of this stone was 21 carats. The famous Du Toit's Pan was found through a Boer farmer actually discovering diamonds in the mud bricks of which his house was built.

As early as 1866, Mr. C. W. King expected that quantities of diamonds from Australia would reach the world's markets, and there is no doubt that this expectation will be realized when those parts of the vast Commonwealth from which many diamonds have already come, have been thoroughly tested and proved. In 1885 several companies were working at Bingera, a township in New South Wales, 350 miles from Sydney, and many small but pure hard stones were found. The writer has handled some few specimens of fine blue white from Bingera, ranging from a quarter to half a carat after cutting. The hardness of the Australian gem—which may well add another point to Mohs' scale—has counted against it, but modern cutters will not consider this a bar especially if sufficient quantities be submitted for treatment.

Gold has also been found at Bingera and, as Mr. King writes: "The observation made of old by Pliny that the diamond always accompanies gold has been fully borne out by the experience of succeeding ages." The first Australian diamonds were found in New South Wales, at Reedy Creek, near Bathurst, in 1851. In 1869 during a gold rush near Mudgee some fair diamonds were found by the miners. Professor Liversidge of Sydney describes the occurrence of diamonds at Bingera

"as being situated in a sort of basin about four miles long and four miles wide, hemmed in by hills on all sides, save on the North. An old river-drift, probably an ancient bed of the river Horton, rests upon rocks of Devonian or Carboniferous age, and is associated with basalt by which it appears to be overlain. In some places the materials of the drift are compacted together into a conglomerate, so that the mode of occurrence of the diamond at Bingera strikingly resembles that at Mudgee.

"The minerals composing the gravels are also generally similar in the two cases, though points of difference are not wanting. Some of the diamonds are clear and colorless, others have a pale straw tint. Thousands have been found in this district, as well as in many other localities of New South Wales."

The gravels enclosed agate, sapphire, ruby, zircon, jasper, rock crystal, garnets, grey corundum, ilmenite, tourmaline, gold and tin. Mr. A. R. Pike who, with his partner, Mr. John O'Donnell, has had much experience with Australian diamonds at Inverell, New South Wales, writes interestingly concerning them.

"With slates and diorites from the bedrock, gold is found in the wash, in addition to its diamond output. Rich yields of alluvial gold have been won from the Gulgong district. The wash deposit of this field also carries diamonds and a special class of semiprecious gems. They embrace sapphires in large numbers and various tints; cornflower, blue, green, dark blue, straw, yellow, and blood-red are plentiful. The red sapphires in many cases are true rubies of the desired pigeon-blood color. Unfortunately all the sapphires represent small flat fragments and are too small for cutting purposes."

A few months ago the writer picked out about a dozen fair but small diamonds for a "fossicker," or prospector, from a little bag of different stones that he had found in Spring Creek, Beechworth, Victoria.

It is recorded that diamonds were first brought to Europe from the first known of the mines of Golconda, the mine of Sumbulpour, in 1584. The mines of Brazil were discovered in 1728. Boetius de Boodt asserted in the year 1609 his belief in the inflammability of the diamond, and in 1694 the Florentine academicians demonstrated the truth of Boetius' belief and Newton's deductions—Sir Isaac Newton having based his similar conclusions on the refracting power of the diamond in 1675. Boyle discovered in 1673 that when the diamond was submitted to high temperature it ejected a pungent vapor in which a part of it was consumed. In 1695 Averani experimenting with the concentrated rays of the sun on the diamond demonstrated that "it was exhaled in vapor and entirely disappeared while other precious stones only grew softer." That the diamond can be burned is easy of proof, as is also the fact that acids have no effect upon it.

The gnomes figure in the elemental system of Rosicrucian philosophy, being described as small people who guard the mines and treasures of the earth, the precious stones and the metals. They are robust little fellows of a brown color, and their sympathy extends to philosophic minds amongst both miners and scholars. They hate frivolity, for they are serious little fairies. Comte de Gabalis details an argument with their Prince who came to the upper earth in respect to the will of the Irish sage Macnamara. Macnamara has sympathy for the gnomes whom he calls "the unhappy guardians of treasures," in the mystical chapters on "The Irreconcilable."

There are numerous legends of the Gnomes, the meanings of which are not difficult to interpret if the mind of the student is filled with the desire to know. It is said that these little fairies suffer much, and that when they grieve for those they have loved and lost their tears change into diamonds, which remain as the jewel emblems of pure and unselfish grief. That great old English traveler of the 14th Century, Sir John Mandeville—a copy of whose manuscript, said to date from the time of the author, is in the Cottonian Library—wrote that the diamond should always be worn on the left or heart side of the body, and that it is possible for a diamond to lose its occult virtue after being handled by evil people: for in the human body there is more potency for good or ill than is generally understood.

There are many stories of misfortune and discord following the possessors of stolen diamonds. Ample evidence exists that substances handled by diseased persons are quite capable of conveying their symptoms to others. The Diamond, ever a symbol of purity, was regarded as a charm against all evil, but—said the philosophers—it must not be touched by evil, by lemures, incubi, succubi or by the formed or formless devils of the material and super-material spheres. In this philosophy it is advised that a woman about to give birth to a child should refrain from wearing diamonds. Rabbi Benoni wrote in the 14th Century that the diamond was capable of producing somnambulism and spiritual ecstasy, a suggestion which was acted on in the last century by experimenters at Nancy. According to Boetius de Boodt, diamonds were of different sexes, and some Hindu writers classified them as masculine, feminine or neuter.

In the Mani Mali it is stated that:

an ill-shaped	diamond carries danger
a dirty	diamond carries grief
a rough	diamond carries unhappiness
a black	diamond carries trouble
a 3-cornered	diamond carries quarrels
a 4-cornered	diamond carries fear
a 5-cornered	diamond carries death
a 6-cornered	diamond carries fortune

However, the three, four and five cornered diamond would not be reckoned evil in a flawless stone of good color. It is asserted by some of the Hindu masters that diamonds, according to their colors and qualities, appealed to the taste as sweet, sour and salty. Marbodus calls the diamond a potent magical charm for protecting the sleeper from evil dreams and the child from the dreaded goblin. The fifth Arabian Heaven, the Garden of Delights, Jannat al-Naim, is said to be composed of the purest diamonds.

In the second voyage of Es-Sindibad of the Sea (commonly known as Sinbad the Sailor) in the *Thousand and One Nights*, E. W. Lane's translation, the hero finds himself in the Valley of the Serpents:

"Then I arose and emboldened myself and walked in that valley: and I beheld its ground to be composed of diamonds, with which they perforate minerals and jewels, and with which also they perforate porcelain and the onyx: and it is a stone so hard that neither iron nor rock have any effect upon it, nor can anyone cut off aught from it or break it, unless by means of the lead stone…

"I then walked along the Valley, and while I was thus occupied, lo, a great slaughtered animal fell before me, and I found no one. So I wondered thereat extremely: and I remembered a story that I had heard long before . . . that in the mountains of the diamonds are experienced great terrors, and that no one can gain access to the diamonds, but that the merchants who import them know a stratagem by means of which to obtain them: that they take a sheep and slaughter it, and skin it, and cut up its flesh which they throw down from the mountain to the bottom of the Valley: so descending, fresh and moist, some of these stones stick to it.

"Then the merchants leave it until midday, and birds of the large kind of vulture and the aquiline vulture descend to that meat, and, taking it in their talons, fly up to the top of the mountain: whereupon the merchants come to them and cry out at them and they fly away from the meat. The merchants then advance to that meat, and take from it the stones sticking to it: after which they leave the meat for the birds and the wild beasts and carry the stones to their countries. And no one can procure the stones but by means of this stratagem."

In his notes and comments on this passage, Mr. Lane says:

"Though I believe that there is no known substance with which the diamond can be cut or ground except its own substance, I think it not improbable that the Eastern lapidaries may be acquainted with some ore, really—or supposed by them to be—an ore of lead, by which it may be broken, and that this is what is here called 'the lead stone' or 'the stone of lead.' It is well known that those diamonds unfit for any other purpose than that of cutting or grinding others, are broken in a steel "mortar.'"

In further notes on The Valley of Diamonds, Mr. Lane added the following:

"El-Kazweenee after describing the diamond, saying 'It breaketh all other stones except that of lead (el-usrub, a bad kind of lead): for if it be struck with this the diamond breaketh,'—relates as follows:

"'To the place in which the diamond is found no one can gain access. It is a valley in the land of India, the bottom of which the sight reacheth not: and in it are venomous serpents which no one seeth but he dieth: and they have a summer abode for six months, and a winter abode (where they hide themselves) for the like period.'

"El-Iskender (either Alexander the Great or the first Zu-l-Karneyn) commanded his men to take some mirrors and to throw them into the Valley that the serpents might see in them their forms and die in consequence. It is said also that he watched for the time of their absenting themselves (or retiring into their winter quarters) and threw down pieces of meat, and diamonds stuck to these: then the birds came from the sky and took pieces of that meat, and brought them up out of the valley whereupon El-Iskender ordered his companions to follow the birds and to pick up what they easily could of the meat.

"The valley or valleys of diamonds we also find described by other writers, among them Marco Polo, in his account of the Kingdom of Murphili or Monsul. Mr. Marsden observes: 'This is no other than Muchli-patan or, as it is more commonly named, Masuli-patam: the name of a principal town by a mistake not unusual, being substituted for that of the country. . . It belongs to what was at one period termed the Kingdom of Golconda, more anciently named Teligana. Golconda, of which Masulipatam is the principal seaport, is celebrated for the production of diamonds.'

"In the astronomical observations of Mr. Topping, printed in Dalrymple's *Oriental Repertory*, mention is made of the famous diamond mines of Golconda at a place named Malvellee, not far from Ellore. Caesar Fredericke who was at Bijanagar in 1567 mentions that the diamond mines were six days' journey from that city. Es-Sindibad's adventure in the Valley of Diamonds has been amply illustrated by the learned writer from whom the above remarks are borrowed, and by Hole.

The following is an extract from Marco Polo's *Travels*:

"In the mountains of this Kingdom (Murphila) it is that diamonds are found. During the rainy season the water descends in violent torrents amongst the rocks and caverns, and when these have subsided the people go to search for diamonds in the beds of the rivers, where they find many. In the summer, when the heat is excessive and there is no rain, they ascend the mountains with great fatigue as well as with considerable danger from the number of snakes with which they are infested.

"Near the summit, it is said, there are deep valleys full of caverns and surrounded by precipices amongst which the diamonds are found, and here many eagles and white storks, attracted by the snakes on which they feed, are accustomed to make their nests. The persons who are in quest of the diamonds take their stand near the mouths of the caverns and from thence cast down several pieces of flesh which the eagles and storks pursue into the valleys and carry off with them to the tops of the rocks. Thither the men immediately ascend, drive the birds away, and recovering the pieces of meat frequently find diamonds sticking to them."

Mr. Marsden transcribes from Hole's ingenious work part of a quotation from Epiphanius, upon which he remarks:

"Thus it appears incontrovertibly that, so early as the fourth century of our era, the tale of the valley of diamonds and the mode of procuring the precious stones from it was current, divested, it is true, of the extraordinary incident of the adventurous sailor's escape, but in conformity with what was related to Marco Polo—with the exception of the scene being laid in Scythia or Western Tartary where, in fact, diamonds are not found.

"The question of locality is however determined by another Oriental navigator Nicoli di Conti, who visited the coast of the peninsula in the 15th Century. . ."

Hole observes that a story somewhat resembling this of the Valley of Diamonds is recorded in the travels of Benjamin of Tudela and that the translator supposes it to have been borrowed from *The Thousand and One Nights*. "However," he adds with better judgment, "I rather suspect that the account of Benjamin of Tudela and of Es-Sindibad were derived from some common origin."

Perhaps the smallest diamond ring mentioned was placed by Cardinal Wolsey on the tiny finger of the little Princess Mary, aged just two years, daughter of Henry VIII, on October 5th, 1518, on the occasion of her marriage with the baby Dauphin of France, son of Francis I. The baby bride's dress was of cloth of gold and her black velvet cap sparkled with jewels. Another historical diamond ring was that sent to the imprisoned Lord Lisle, giving freedom and forgiveness—an act so unexpected that it caused the unfortunate man to die of joy.

The ring sent by Mary, Queen of Scots, to Queen Elizabeth, is described by Mr. William Jones, quoting from Aubrey, as

"a delicate piece of mechanism consisting of several joints which, when united, formed the quaint device of two right hands supporting a heart between them. This heart was composed of two separate diamonds

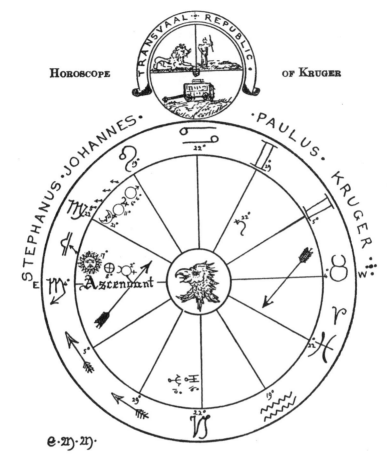

HOROSCOPE OF KRUGER

Kruger's Diamond was once in the possession of Chaka, the Zulu chief, killed by his brother who was in turn murdered. It is stated that this stone changed owners 15 times, tragedy following each possessor.

held together by a central spring which, when opened, would allow either of the hearts to be detached. Queen Elizabeth kept one moietie and sent the other as a token of her constant friendship to Mary, Queen of Scots, but she cut off her head for all that."

Another story of Elizabeth, quoted by Fairholt, is that Sir Walter Raleigh wrote on a window with his pointed diamond ring: "Fain would I rise, but that I fear to fall," the Queen writing beneath with her ring: "If thy heart fail thee, do not rise at all." Very different was the experience

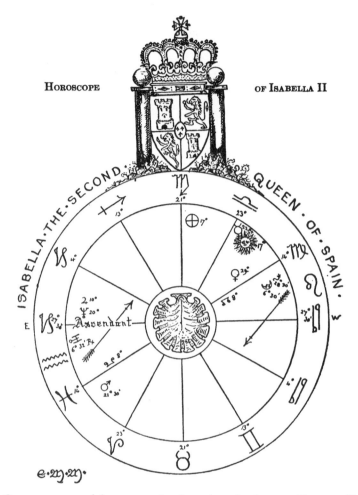

This Queen was saved from assassination when the dagger of her would-be murderer glanced off the diamond she wore.

of Queen Isabella who was saved from death by a diamond. Ex-President Kruger's diamond had a bad history that did not change with its different holders.

In allusion to the Diamond Jousts instituted by King Arthur, Dr. Brewer says:

"He named them by that name since a diamond was the prize. Ere he was King he came by accident to a glen in Lyonnesse, where two broth- ers had met in combat. Each was slain, but one had worn a crown of diamonds which Arthur picked up, and when he became King offered the nine diamonds as the prize of nine several jousts—'one every year, a joust for one.' Lancelot had won eight and intended to present them all to the Queen when all were won. When the knight laid them before the Queen, Guinevere in a fit of jealousy flung them out of the palace window into the river which ran below."

The affair of the Diamond Necklace is familiar to readers of history and romance. It attracted the perceptive mind of Dumas who molded it into an interesting story, but of its reality no doubt has ever been entertained. To forward her own nefarious designs the Countess de Lamotte persuaded the Prince Cardinal de Rohan, who entertained a secret affection for Queen Marie Antoinette, that the Queen reciprocated his passion. By thus working on the Cardinal's feelings, Madame de Lamotte managed to relieve him of some sums of money, and succeeding so well in this way, she and her husband resolved on a more imposing venture.

Louis XV had had made a wonderful diamond necklace which he intended as a present for his favorite Madame Du Barry. Before it was finished Louis had passed away, and his favorite had been driven from court. The necklace, which was made by Boehmer, consisted of 500 magnificent diamonds, the whole when completed being valued at 1,800,000 livres. Madame de Lamotte represented to the Cardinal the Queen's desire for this handsome necklace, asking him—as Her Majesty was at the time unable to pay the amount of the purchase money, which she said amounted to £700,000 sterling—to become security for her for this amount. This he gladly consented to do, and added his name to the forged signature of the Queen.

On February 1st, 1785, the Cardinal carried the precious jewel to Versailles, whence by arrangement a messenger from the Queen was to take it. The next day, as arranged by Madame de Lamotte's husband, an accomplice dressed in the uniform of a court official entered the Cardinal's apartments at Versailles and muttering several times "De par la Reine" (in the Queen's name) relieved the trusting Cardinal of the necklace. It was afterwards broken up and disposed of by these three conspirators, in England it is believed.

Some time afterwards Boehmer, not receiving his payment, applied to Marie Antoinette for his money. She denied all knowledge of the affair. Boehmer thereupon brought the case before the Parlement de

Paris in 1785, and in May, 1786, after a trial of 9 months, the Cardinal, Monsieur de Lamotte and his accomplice were acquitted, but Madame de Lamotte was sent to prison for life, each shoulder being branded with the letter V (*Voleuse*, thief).

The Indians were the first to polish a diamond with its own dust, but their cutting only consisted in burnishing the original facets or concealing defects by a number of new and smaller ones. Louis van Berghem is credited with being the first to cut and polish diamonds with their own dust in 1456, but both Emanuel and King refer to four large diamonds which adorned the clasp of the Emperor Charlemagne 1373, and to numerous cut specimens of older date set in church monuments. Emanuel mentions in particular the skillful Herman who worked in the year 1407.

Towards the end of the 16th Century, Peruzzi invented the double cutting known as *"Brillants recoupes,"* and of late years the modern cutters have reached a high degree of artistic excellence, producing the most beautifully cut specimens the world has seen. Clement Birago and Jacopo da Trezzo were the first to engrave upon the diamond, and both "enriched in the service of Philip II."

In giving the Papal Sacred Banner and Blessing to William of Normandy when about to invade England after the excommunication of Harold, Pope Hildebrand sent a diamond ring, said to enclose a hair from the head of Peter the Apostle. In the Comtesse d'Anois' pretty fairy story, *The Yellow Dwarf*, the mermaid gives the captive King an all-conquering sword made from a single diamond, which rendered invincible anyone who carried it.

The diamond is astrologically under the sign of the Sun Leo, and has power especially in Aries and Libra. To dream of diamonds was considered symbolical of success, wealth, happiness and victory, and its reputed power of binding man and woman together in happy wedlock has made it a favorite stone for engagement rings, and in some countries for wedding rings.

BORT or **BOART** is the name applied to imperfect greyish or blackish specimens, which are powdered and used for cutting and polishing diamonds and hard gems, among other purposes.

CHAPTER 17

Some Famous and Wonderful Diamonds and their Stories

"Jewels
Of rich and exquisite form: their value great."

—Shakespeare

THE KOH-I-NOOR. This famous stone is said by Dr. Brewer to have been found in the Golconda mine in the year 1550, but Dr. G. F. Herbert Smith states that it was known as far back as 1304, "when it fell into the hands of the Mogul emperors, and legend traces it back some four thousand years previously." Mr. Emanuel says that the Hindu accounts "deduce it from the time of the God Krishna," while Mr. King states that it was turned up by a peasant when plowing in a field 40 miles distant from Golconda, "and was in its rough state fully as large as a hen's egg."

The traveler Tavernier saw it amongst the jewels of the great Mogul King Aurungzebe. This was after it had been badly cut and unskillfully reduced by Hortensio Borgio from 793 carats to 186$\frac{1}{16}$ carats. According to Tavernier its original weight was 787½ carats. Borgio's work so angered Aurungzebe that he deprived the unfortunate cutter of all his possessions, grudgingly allowing him to escape with his life.

The Koh-i-Noor had an evil reputation amongst the Hindus who held that it "produced inordinate greed, viciousness and various misfortunes on the King who possessed it." In 1739 Nadir Shah sacked Delhi and took the gem from Muhammad Shah, naming it the "Koh-i-Noor," or "Mountain of Light." Returning victorious to Persia, Nadir Shah was murdered by his officers. One of these, Ahmed Shah Doorannee, founded the Afghan kingdom, and the last of his dynasty Shah Sujah was starved into surrendering the stone to Runjeet Singh. The latter when dying sent it to the Temple of Juggernaut. His successors, however, would not let it remain there, and when the British annexed the Punjab in 1849 it was presented by Lord Dalhousie on behalf of the East India Company to Queen Victoria and, writes Mr. King,

> "within ten years the usual consequences of its possession were manifested in the Sepoy revolt and the all but total loss of India to the British Crown in which beams its malignant luster, lighting up a very inauspicious future for that region, fated ever apparently to be disturbed by the measures of ignorant zealots at home and the plots of discontented and over-powerful allies in the country itself."

The Koh-i-Noor was re-cut in 1862 by Mr. Coster of Amsterdam, losing 80 carats in the cutting. The weight of the stone is now given as 106¹⁄₁₆ carats, and its value is estimated at £100,000 sterling, by Dr. G. F. Herbert Smith, and at £120,664 sterling by Dr. Brewer.

It was believed that all diseases could be cured by the water in which the Koh-i-Noor had been placed. The stone could never be fortunate for India according to astro-philosophy because India is a Saturnine country ruled by the celestial Capricorn. It is more fortunate for England because England is a martial country ruled by the celestial Aries.

PITT or **REGENT DIAMOND.** This famous gem, bought in Golconda from an Indian merchant by William Pitt, grandfather of the Earl of Chatham, and said to have been originally stolen, was found at Gani-Puteal, 150 miles from Golconda in 1701. Mr. Pitt gave £20,400 sterling for the gem which weighed 410 carats, and returning to England he had it re-cut at a cost of £5,000 and two years' work. In this process the weight of the stone was reduced to 163⅞ carats, the fragments when sold returning £2,000 over the cost of cutting. Possession of this gem worried Mr. Pitt who sold it to the Due d'Orleans, regent of France, whence it obtained the name "Regent," for £135,000 sterling.

It was stolen from the Garde-Meuble when the Sun was in the Diamond sign Leo, August 17th, 1792, and was mysteriously returned. Napoleon Bonaparte, who had the Sun in the sign Leo—the sign of France—at his birth, had the Regent set in the pommel of his sword. It was exhibited at the French Exhibition in 1855, and is now shown in the Apollo Gallery of the Louvre, Paris. During the attempted advance on Paris in the late war, it is stated that one of the French ministers took the Regent with him to Bordeaux whence the danger being passed, it was afterwards returned to its honored place in the capital city of France. Its value is stated at £480,000 sterling.

THE ORLOFF DIAMOND. This gem was stolen by a French soldier from a temple near Trichinopoli in Mysore, where it was set as an eye stone in the statue of Brahma. The weight of the stone, which is rose cut, is 194¾ carats. The soldier sold it to an English ship's captain for £2,000—Mr. Emanuel says £2,800—and the captain sold it to a London dealer for £12,000 sterling. It was afterwards sold to Prince Orloff, whence it obtained its name, for £90,000 sterling, and an annual pension of £4,000. The Prince presented it to Empress Katherine who had it set as an ornament at the top of the imperial scepter.

This large diamond was a stone of ill omen for Russia, a country ruled by the celestial Aquarius and opposed to the diamond sign Leo. When we reflect, in harmony with celestial philosophy, that the late Czar Nicholas II, the last of the Romanoffs, had the sign Leo in the 12th heavenly mansion at birth we can only see in the Orloff diamond the symbol of sorrow and restraint.

THE SANCY DIAMOND. Few historical objects surpass the beautiful Sancy Diamond in romance and importance. Its origin is involved in uncertainty prior to the early 15th Century. The first definite account concerning the famous gem states that after the battle of Nancy, January 5th, 1477, it was taken from the dead body of Charles the Bold by a Swiss soldier. Charles adorned his dress with many diamonds, the Sancy holding the place of honor. The soldier, not knowing the value of the gem he had stolen, sold it to a minister of religion for a gulden. The minister sold it some years later to a dealer in Lucerne for 5,000 ducats. King Manoel, known as the Fortunate, of Portugal, purchased it in 1495, two years before he dispatched the navigator Vasco da Gama, on his voyage of discovery.

Don Antonio, known as Prince of Crato and King of Portugal in partibus, sold the gem to Nicolas de Harlai Sieur de Sancy, whence it obtained its name. As the friend and treasurer of Henry IV of France, the Sieur, in order to aid the King to protect his crown, raised a loan for him on the security of the stone, from the bankers of Metz. The servant entrusted with the safe delivery of the diamond being waylaid by robbers, swallowed his master's precious gem to protect it; the thieves in fury at

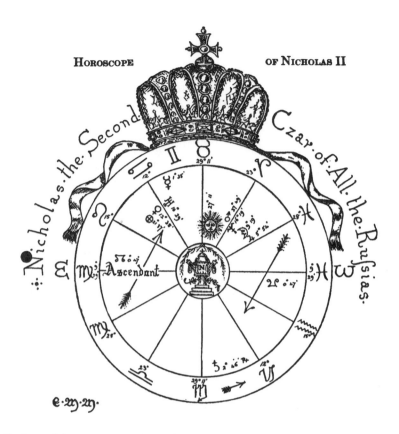

The last of the Czars, to whom the ancients would consider the diamond a symbol of ill omen.

being unable to discover the stone, on the person or in the baggage, of the loyal servant, murdered him. The Sieur evidently knew what his messenger would do in an extremity, and he afterwards recovered the gem from the body of the murdered man.

It was next sold to the English Crown when it was worn by Queen Elizabeth. It remained in possession of the Crown, and is mentioned in the Tower inventory of March 22nd, 1605, until the reign of James II, who took it when he fled to France to seek asylum at the court of the Grand Monarque. James then sold the Sancy to his sympathetic friend Louis, for £25,000 sterling. Another account states that the Sancy came into the possession of Cardinal Mazarin who had it re-cut and included amongst the twelve famous diamonds in the Crown of France, known as the Mazarins. Robert de Berquem says that Queen Henrietta Maria proudly wore it (*Merveilles des Indes*, 1669). Louis XV, it is recorded, wore the Sancy at his coronation in 1715, and his Queen, Maria Lesczynska, daughter of the dethroned Polish King Stanislas, afterwards wore it as a necklace pendant.

When Marie Antoinette became Queen of France she had this royal pendant taken from the necklace and mounted in brooch form. With the tragic end of the unhappy Queen some uncertainty follows the wanderings of the Sancy. It is stated that the widow of Charles IV of Spain gave it to the "Prince of Peace," Manuel de Godoi, Duke of Alcudia. One account states that Godoi sold it to Napoleon, another that Godoi's son after vainly endeavoring to induce Louis XVIII to purchase it in 1822, sold it to Prince Demidoff. The Prince sold it to Monsieur Levrat, Director of the Society of Mines and Forges of Grisons, Switzerland, for £24,000. A dispute over the price led to an action at law and a verdict in favor of the Prince on June 1st, 1832.

The stone was afterwards purchased by Sir Jamisetjee Jeejeebhoy in 1865, from the family of Prince Demidoff. It was sent from Bombay to London by Messrs. Forbes & Co., the agents for Sir Jamisetjee Jeejeebhoy, and was exhibited by M. M. Bapst at the Paris Exposition of 1867. During the tour of King George (when Prince of Wales) in India, the Sancy is said to have been worn at the Great Durba by the Marajah of Puttiali.

In 1892 the beautiful gem passed into the possession of the Astor family, having been purchased by the Hon. William Waldorf Astor for his wife, Mary, daughter of James W. Paul, Esq., of Philadelphia, U. S. A. It now passes into the hands of the Right Hon. Viscountess Astor who wore it on taking her seat as the first lady elected as a member of the House of Commons. The writer is indebted to Lady Astor for her kindly interest in this book, and for a presentation of a handsome volume on the Sancy Diamond by William Waldorf Astor, published in 1892. The Sancy Diamond is described by Dr. Smith as of an almond shape, covered all over with tiny facets by Indian lapidaries. The weight is given as 53½ to 53¾ carats.

Considered astrologically, a diamond would be unfortunate for Charles the Bold who was born at Dijon 10th November, 1435. It would be considered fortunate for Henry IV of France in whose horoscope the planet Jupiter was ascending in the sign Libra. Jupiter being in the 12th

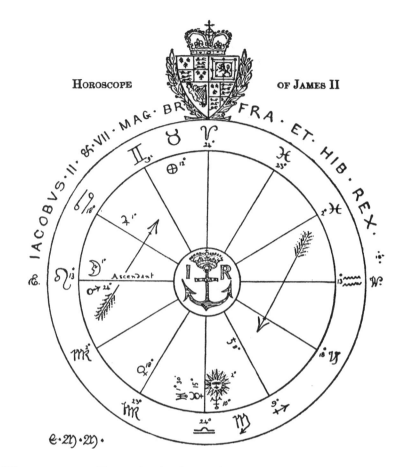

The ancients would consider the diamond a symbol of fortune and adventure for this King.

Heavenly Mansion would be considered fortunate for secret negotiations and diplomacy, and it is worthy of notice that the Sancy Diamond should be employed as a powerful helper in these very matters. The sign of the Lion, the sign of France, is also on the Mid Heaven of the King's nativity, and Leo is distinctly a diamond and Royal sign. It was a truly fortunate gem for King James II of England whose horoscope is here shown with the Royal Lion ascending.

THE HOPE DIAMOND. Dr. G. F. Herbert Smith says of this gem that it is of "a steely or greenish blue, not the royal blue color of the glass models supposed to represent it." If the accepted history of the stone be true, it must be regarded as a strange specimen.

It was stated to have been discovered at the Kollur mines, and to have been purchased by Tavernier in 1642. In 1668, Tavernier interested Louis XIV in the gem so much that he purchased it. After this the fortunes of the great traveler began to change. His son defrauded him of a large sum of money, and he was later, being a Protestant, compelled by the Edict of Nantes (1685) to fly from France and seek protection in Switzerland. Thence he went to Berlin, where the Elector of Brandenburg offered him the Directorship in a projected East India Company. In the endeavor to find a road through Russia to India, Tavernier left Berlin, but he succumbed to fatigue and financial worry soon after, dying, it is said, in want, in his 84th year at Moscow.

After wearing this diamond at a Court Ball, Madame de Montespan lost the favor of her Royal lover. It was a stone of ill fortune for Marie Antoinette, to whom, however, all diamonds were unfortunate. After the tragic death of Louis XVI and his Queen, the stone was stolen with the French regalia. Afterwards it is stated to have been stolen from Fals, the Dutch gem cutter, by his son. Fals died a broken-hearted man, and his son, after selling the gem to Francois Beaulieu, went insane and killed himself. Beaulieu, after selling the stone to Daniel Eliason, a London dealer, died suddenly the following day. Mr. Eliason sold it to Mr. Thomas Philip Hope, the banker, in 1830 for £18,000 sterling.

Mr. Hope's grandson, Lord Henry Francis Hope, married the Australian actress, Miss May Yohe, in 1894. This lady wore the diamond and misfortune followed her. In 1901 Lord Hope was glad to sell the stone to Mr. Weil, a London diamond merchant, who, without waiting for its influence to affect him, sold it immediately to Mr. Simon Frankel, jeweler, of New York, who suffered financial hardships consequent on the difficulty of finding a purchaser. At last he sold it to Mr. Jacques Colot, a French dealer in gems, and with it went his troubles also. Monsieur Colot quickly sold the gem to the Russian Prince, Kanitovski, and, it is stated, became insane and died mysteriously a few weeks afterwards.

The Prince lent it to Mademoiselle Lorens Laduc of the Folies Bergeres, with whom he was in love. As she wore it one night on the stage the Prince in a mad fit shot her. A few days later he was himself stabbed to death by some members of a secret political club. The Blue Terror next came into the possession of the Greek jeweler, Simon Montharides, who, after having sold it to the Sultan, Abdul Hamid, was killed by accident with his wife and two children whilst driving. Abu Sabir, the Sultan's lapidary, was entrusted with the polishing of the jewel, and whilst he had it he accidentally destroyed a large pearl belonging to Abdul Hamid, who ordered him to be severely flogged and cast into prison. A little later the keeper of the Sultan's jewels was found murdered, and his successor was hanged by a mob in a street of Constantinople. The Sultan's favorite, Salama Zubayba, incurred his anger by wearing the blue gem and the infuriated ruler shot her as Prince Kanitovski had shot Lorens Laduc. All diamonds, however, would be unfortunate for Abdul Hamid.

The diamond then fell into the hands of the Turkish revolutionary party and was sold by them to Senor Habib, a rich Spaniard, who was drowned in the wreck of the French mail steamer, Seyne, off Singapore. The gem was not lost with its owner, and was later sold to Messrs. Cartier Bros. of Paris and New York by Monsieur Rosenau, a well-known diamond merchant. In 1911 it was bought by Mr. Edward McLean, proprietor of the *Washington Post*, for £5,000 sterling, from Cartier Bros. It is said that both Mr. and Mrs. McLean were doubtful about the wisdom of purchasing this stone of ill omen which, according to report, had been previously refused by the Court of England on account of its evil reputation.

Misfortunes quickly followed the new owners, culminating with the tragic death of little Vinson Walsh McLean, their only son, who was knocked down and killed by a motor car close to his father's estate. After leaving the possession of the McLean family, the stone found a purchaser in Monsieur de Hautville. Within three months the same peculiar misfortune which had befallen its previous owners befell them. Madame de Hautville, sharing the same fate as little Vinson McLean, was killed by a motor car whilst crossing a street in Paris. Following on this the eldest son, having taken poison by mistake, died in terrible agony. Mademoiselle de Hautville was accidentally drowned and the younger son whilst out shooting was blinded by the explosion of his gun. Quickly the de Hautvilles parted with this peculiar gem of ill omen.

Where will it next find a home? The weight of the Hope diamond when sold by Tavernier to Louis XIV was 67 carats; its present weight is 44½ carats. It presents a curious psychical study and an undeniable evidence of fatal influence which it would indeed be difficult to explain away.

THE PAUL THE FIRST. This diamond is described as a brilliant red, weighing 10 carats. It was one of the Russian Crown jewels, being purchased by Emperor Paul the First for 100,000 rubles. It was a stone of ill omen for both Paul and Russia. He was murdered in 1801, and in his nativity the planet Neptune was, as in that of Marie Antoinette, in the sign Leo, accompanied by unfortunate planetary afflictions.

THE DRESDEN. The Dresden diamond which is in the Green Vaults at Dresden is described as of the purest apple-green color. Authorities differ as to its weight, which is variously given at 40 and 48½ carats. It is stated that the gem was purchased by Augustus the Strong in 1743 for 60,000 thalers, but this Augustus died of an old wound in 1733. It was probably his son Frederick Augustus III who died at Dresden in 1763.

THE NIZAM. This gem which belonged to the Nizam of Hyderabad was, to judge by its particular native cutting, probably employed in certain sex mysteries. Its weight is 340 carats, and strangely enough, it fractured just before the Indian Mutiny. The diamond is not a stone of harmony for India.

THE CUMBERLAND. After the battle of Culloden (1746) the city of London presented this diamond, which weighed 32 carats and cost £10,000, to the Duke of Cumberland. During Queen Victoria's reign the stone was claimed by the City of Hanover, to which place it was sent by the Queen's command.

THE NAPOLEON. This diamond which was bought by Napoleon Bonaparte for £8,000 sterling was worn by him when he married Josephine in 1796.

EUGENIE. This gem was purchased by Katherine II of Russia, who gave it to Potemkin. It is a very pure gem of 51 carats. Napoleon III gave it to Eugenie as a wedding gift. Afterwards it came into the possession of the Gaekwar of Baroda.

THE POLAR STAR. This brilliant jewel formed one of the chief ornaments in the Russian regalia. The weight is given as 40 carats.

THE SHAH. The Shah diamond was given to the Czar of Russia by the Persian prince Chosroes in 1843. It is a flawless, pure gem which originally weighed 95 carats and was engraved with the names of three distinguished Shahs of Persia. In the re-cutting this engraving was eliminated and the stone reduced to 86 carats.

MOON OF THE MOUNTAINS. After the assassination of Nadir Shah, who stole this gem from Delhi, it was taken by a soldier who sold it to Shaffras, an Armenian. It was included in the Russian Crown jewels. Many diamonds adorned the regalia of Russia, but they are no more fortunate to Russia than they are to India.

AKBAR SHAH, SHEPHERD'S STONE. This gem belonged to Akbar, the Great Mogul, and was formerly engraved with Arabic writing. After having been lost for some years it was identified as the Turkish Shepherd's Stone. It originally weighed 116 carats, and was reduced by cutting in the elimination of the engraving to 71 carats. It was purchased by the Gaekwar of Baroda for £23,330 sterling.

RIVER OF LIGHT. This beautiful rose diamond of 186 carats was seized by Nadir Shah at Delhi. It adorns the Persian regalia and is known as the Darya-i-Nor, or River of Light.

GRAND MOGUL. This remarkable diamond was seen by Tavernier amongst the jewels of the Emperor Aurungzebe in 1665, five years after its recorded discovery in the Golconda mines. Its original weight is given as 787 carats by some records and as 787½ by others. This was greatly reduced in cutting to a rose shape by Hortensio Borgio when, it is said on account of numerous flaws, it lost 547 carats. Tavernier describes it as "rounded rose cut, taller on one side." The present whereabouts of the "Grand Mogul" are unknown.

THE GRAND TABLE. This gem is also recorded by Tavernier who saw it at Golconda in 1642. Its weight is given at somewhat over 242 carats. Where it now is, is not known.

THE NASSAK. This gem which came from the Deccan loot was sold in London in 1837. Mr. Emanuel, into whose possession it came, sold it later to the Duke of Westminster for £7,200 sterling. Its original pear-shaped form was altered to triangular, an operation which left the weight at 78⅝ carats.

THE PIGOTT. Lord Pigott obtained this stone in India in 1775, and disposed of it for £30,000 sterling. The weight is given as 47½ carats. Ali Pacha, the last owner of the gem, left instructions to destroy it at his death, and his wishes are said to have been respected.

THE PACHA. This brilliant of 40 carats is mentioned as having been acquired by Ibrahim Pacha for £28,000 sterling. Very little seems to be known about it.

THE TUSCANY. This yellow-tinged stone, of double rose cut and 133¾ carats, was formerly in the possession of the Dukes of Tuscany. Mr. King states that, being mistaken for a piece of yellow quartz, it was purchased for a trifle at a bric-a-brac stall in Florence.

STAR OF ESTE. This diamond which weighs 25½ carats is mentioned by Dr. Smith "for its perfection of form and quality." It belonged to the ill-starred Archduke Franz Ferdinand.

WHITE SAXON. The White Saxon is a square gem, 48¾ carats in weight, for which Augustus the Strong is said to have given a million thalers.

THE GREAT WHITE. This large, clear diamond is also known as the Imperial or Victoria. Its weight before cutting is given as 457 carats, and after cutting at 180 carats. The Nizam of Hyderabad purchased it for £20,000 sterling in 1884.

THE MATTAM. The Mattam is a pear-shaped diamond of the purest water, recently—and probably still—in the possession of the Rajah of Mattam. Found in 1760—Dr. Smith says 1787—at Landak, Borneo, it is held responsible for much worldly trouble. Its weight is stated as 367 carats. Mr. Emanuel says: "The Dutch Governor of Batavia offered two gun-boats with stores and ammunition complete and £50,000 sterling for it: but the offer was refused, the Rajah replying that on its possession depended the fortunes of his family." Its genuineness is doubted by Dr. Smith.

THE STAR OF THE SOUTH. This most perfect brilliant was discovered at Bagagem in July, 1853. It is said to be the largest Brazilian diamond yet found. It weighed 254½ carats in the rough, and 125½ carats when cut by Mr. Coster of Amsterdam. Although not perfectly white, it is regarded as one of the finest large diamonds of the day. £40,000 sterling was paid for it before cutting.

THE ENGLISH DRESDEN. This brilliant was also found at Bagagem in Brazil four years after the "Star of the South." Its weight before cutting was 119½ carats, which was reduced in cutting to 76½ carats. Its present form is an egg-like oval drop.

THE DE BEERS DIAMONDS. These were discovered in the famous De Beers mine; the first, a pale yellow, 428½ carats in the rough, 228½ when cut, in 1888; the next 503¼ carats, of similar hue, in 1896. Some others weigh 302, 409 carats, etc.

THE STAR OF SOUTH AFRICA. This gem was found in the Vaal River diggings in 1869. Weight before cutting was 83½ carats, after cutting 46½ carats. It is triangular in shape, and was bought by the Countess of Dudley for £25,000 sterling.

THE JUBILEE. This faultless brilliant was found in the Jagersfontein mine in 1895. Before cutting, its weight was 634 carats; after cutting, 239 carats. The Jubilee was exhibited at the Paris Exhibition of 1900.

THE STAR OF AFRICA. This remarkable stone was discovered in the Premier mine near Pretoria, January 25th, 1905. It was named the "Cullinan," after the chairman of the Premier Company, Sir T. M. Cullinan. It was renamed the "Star of Africa," at the desire of King George V.

Dr. Smith writes as follows with regard to it:

"The rough stone weighed 3,025¾ carats (about 1⅓ lbs.): it displayed three natural faces and one large cleavage face, and its shape suggested that it was a portion of an enormous stone more than double its size: it is transparent, colorless, and has only one small flaw near the surface.

"This magnificent diamond was purchased by the Transvaal Government for £150,000 sterling and presented to King Edward VII on his birthday, November 9th, 1907. Messrs. I. J. Asscher & Co. of Amsterdam, cut from this a drop brilliant 516½ carats, a square-shaped brilliant 309³⁄₁₆ carats, another drop brilliant 92 carats, a square-shaped brilliant 62 carats, a heart-shaped stone 18⅜ carats, two marquises 8⁹⁄₁₆ and 11¼ carats, an oblong stone 6⅝ carats, a drop brilliant 4⁹⁄₃₂ carats, and 96 small brilliants weighing together 7⅜ carats: the total weight of the cut stones amounts to 1036⁵⁄₃₂ carats."

The large drop brilliant adorns the scepter, the large square brilliant the crown. The "Star of Africa" comes from the mine to adorn the regalia of the British sovereigns. It has no record of evil, no doubtful past, nor is it tainted with evil desires, violence or sorrow.

THE BRAGANZA. This stone, the weight of which is given as 1680 carats, is in the Portuguese regalia. It is believed, on good grounds, to be a large white topaz.

THE TIFFANY. This orange-tinted brilliant which was found at Kimberley, South Africa, in 1878, is in the possession of Messrs. Tiffany. Its weight is given as 125⅜ carats.

STAR OF MINAS. This stone was discovered at Bagagem in Brazil, in 1911. Its weight in the rough is given as 174¾ carats.

THE ARABIAN DEATH. The first Earl Lytton became possessed of a fine diamond on which were engraved certain Arabic words, and his death, which took place soon after he had obtained possession of it, has been attributed to its malignant influence. The gem was bequeathed by Earl Lytton to Madame la Comtesse Greffuhle, who showed it to a learned Indian Prince who was in Paris at the time. After reading the mysterious Arab words the Prince told the Comtesse that it was a stone of death, and advised her not to keep it. The lady, desiring to end the power of the stone for mischief, threw it into the river Seine from the Pont Neuf.

THE MOONSTONE. The famous novel by Mr. Wilkie Collins entitled *The Moonstone* is based on the histories of "the magnificent stone which adorns the top of the Russian imperial scepter, once the eye of an Indian Idol," and the Koh-i-Noor. Some writers confuse this Moonstone with the well-known orthoclase feldspar. The following extract from the Prologue of Mr. Collins's book states:

> "The earliest known traditions describe the stone as having been set in the forehead of the four-handed Indian God who typifies the Moon. Partly from its peculiar color, partly from a superstition which represents it as feeling the influence of the Deity whom it adorned, and growing and lessening in luster with the waxing and waning of the Moon, it first gained the name by which it continues to be known in India to this day—the name of the Moonstone. A similar superstition was once prevalent, as I have heard, in ancient Greece and Rome: not applying, however, as in India to a diamond devoted to the service of a god, but to a semi-transparent stone of the inferior order of gems supposed to be affected by the lunar influences—the Moon, in this latter case also, giving the name by which the stone is still known.
>
> "The adventures of the Yellow Diamond began with the 11th century of the Christian era. At that date the Muhammadan conqueror Mahmoud of Ghizni crossed India: seized on the holy city of Somnauth and stripped of its treasures the famous temple . . . the Moon God alone escaped the rapacity of the conquering Muhammadans . . . . An age followed another until the first years of the 8th Christian century saw the reign of Aurungzebe, Emperor of the Moguls. At his command havoc and rapine were let loose . . . . The shrine of the four-handed God was polluted . . . and the Moonstone was seized by an officer of rank in the army of Aurungzebe . . . The warrior who had committed the sacrilege perished miserably.
>
> "The Diamond fell into the possession of Tippo, Sultan of Seringapatam, who caused it to be placed as an ornament in the handle of his dagger—and after, General Baird himself found the dead body of Tippo under a heap of slain."

(See KOH-I-NOOR, REGENT, ORLOFF)

CHAPTER 18

DICHROITE — IOLITE

DICHROITE. (See **IOLITE**.)

DIOPTASE. The name is derived from the Greek DIA, through, and OPTOMAI, to see. This pretty emerald-green copper silicate was named in 1801 by Hauy, who found on looking through it cleavage directions. As the crystals are usually so small dioptase, which is of about the same degree of hardness as lapis lazuli, is seldom used in jewelry. According to ancient philosophy, dioptase would strengthen the sight of those who gazed upon it, and benefit if worn on the neck in throat troubles. Astrologically, dioptase is under the celestial Taurus.

DISTHENE. (See **KYANITE**.)

EMERALD. (See **BERYL**.)

ENSTATITE. Named from the Greek ENSTATES, an opponent, because of its infusibility before the blow-pipe and its resisting power against acids. It occurs in various colors—grey, brown, yellow, colorless, and chiefly green; hence it has been erroneously called the Green Garnet. The enstatite is a silicate of magnesium, and is scarcely as hard as the opal, yet it is found with the diamond, hardest of stones. It is esteemed as a talisman in examinations, arguments, debates and all contests in which the mind is employed. The enstatite is under the celestial Gemini.

EPIDOTE. This stone is named from the Greek EPIDOSIS, increase. It was first used by Hauy (*Mineralogie*, 1801), as *"lit qui a recu un accroissement,"* but—writes Dr. Smith—"not on very precise crystallographical grounds." There are several varieties, chief among which is the pistacite, or true epidote, of a yellow-green color like the nut of the Pistachio. The epidote is nearly as hard as the garnet. According to ancient philosophy it may be used as a charm for fruit and cereal growers. The epidote is under the celestial Taurus.

ESSONITE. From the Greek ESSON; also, known as hessonite and more familiarly amongst jewelers as **CINNAMON STONE.** It is a garnet of the lime alumina order, of a reddish brown or cinnamon color, and granular structure. This stone is often confounded with the hyacinth and other varieties of the zircon with which it is found. It is regarded amongst ancient philosophers as a protective talisman for virgins born between August 24th and September 23rd. The essonite is a gem under the celestial Virgo.

EUCLASE. The name is derived from the Greek EU KLASIS, easily fractured. It is a silicate of aluminum and beryllium and is related to the emerald. Westropp says: "The euclase is of the same chemical composition as the emerald." (*Manual of Precious Stones*) It is a very rare and expensive mineral, glassy and extremely brittle. The euclase closely resembles the aquamarine in its varying shades of pale blue and pale green. Sometimes it is found quite colorless. It is frequently found with topaz, and is of the hardness of the beryl. As a love talisman it is advised that it be worn in the rough. The euclase is under the celestial Taurus.

FLINT

> "So stubborn flints their inward heart conceal
> Till art and force th' unwilling sparks reveal."
> —CONGREVE TO DRYDEN

Flint derives its name from the Greek PUNTHOS, a brick. It has been written at various times as vlint, vlynt, flent, flend, flynd, flynt, flynte. Flint is described as an "intermediate between quartz and opal, consisting almost entirely of silica with a little lime, oxide of iron, water, carbon and sometimes traces of organic matter." Mr. G. R. Porter says that flint is silica "in a state nearly approaching to purity." (*Porcelain and Glass*, 1832.) Today it is classed amongst the varieties of chalcedony and is found in various colors—greyish white, grey, black, light brown, red and yellow. It is semi-translucent, breaking with a well-defined shell-like fracture.

This mineral was extensively used by aboriginal man in the making of implements, weapons, magical instruments, etc., and many fine worked specimens are still found in all parts of the world. Mystery and magic are associated with the flint which was used in ancient Egypt for fashioning scarabs and making the first incision in a dead body, prior to embalming. The Ethiopian Arrows noted by Herodotus were, as discovery has proved, arrow heads of flint. The Elf Arrowhead or Elf Dart with a hole drilled through it was regarded especially in Scotland and Ireland as an effective talisman against poison, witchcraft, and the evil wishes of enemies. Sir Edward Mackenzie, Bart. built his charming little story *The Romance of the Elf Arrow* on these beliefs. Robert Gordon, of Straloch, who wrote in the year 1654, relates that a friend of his while out riding on horseback was struck on the top of his riding boot by one of these fairy stones. In this case there is no doubt that the horse's hoof caused the incident, but chance was not admitted by the old masters who would regard the hoof of the horse as the instrument made use of by the mischievous fairies.

Pliny relates that Chias, being the first to demonstrate the fire flashing of struck flint, was given the name of Pyrodes. Aubrey states that it was an old custom to hang on a string a flint with a hole in it "to hinder the nightmare." "It is best of all, they say, hung about their necks, and a flint will do it that hath a hole in it. It is to prevent the night mare, viz., the Hag, from riding their horses which will sometimes sweat at night. The flint thus hung does hinder it." Another writer, Grose, quoted in Brand's *Antiquities*, says: "A stone with a hole in it hung at the bed's head will prevent the nightmare. It is therefore called a Hag Stone from that disorder which is occasioned by a Hag or Witch sitting on the stomach of the party afflicted. It also prevents witches riding horses: for which purpose it is often tied to a stable key."

> "Hang up Hooks and Sheers to scare
> Hence the Hag that rides the mare."
>
> —HERRICK

These flints were called Holy or Holey Stones in the North of England, also Ephialtes stones, Night Mare or Witch Riding Stones, and Butler mentions the chasing away of evil spirits by hollow flint. The "Mare" of Night Mare is derived from the *Saxon Mara,* an incubus, which attacked during sleep, depriving the victim of movement and speech. The Mara or Mare is an order of vampires. Similar, perhaps, is the Hebrew MARIA, an evil spirit against which the flint is a charm.

As a correspondent of flint, Emanuel Swedenborg gives Truth. Its connection with the ninth heavenly mansion is well defined. Flint is under the celestial Sagittarius.

GARNET

"Without the aid of yonder golden globe
Lost were the garnet's luster."

—SMART

The garnet derives its name from the Latin GRANATUS, grain-like. Mr. King gives *Granatici,* from its resemblance to the scarlet pomegranate blossom. It is found written as garnet, gernet, garnette, garnat, garnet or garnat stone.

The mineral group passing under the general name of garnet exhibits some distinct peculiarities which, adopting the classification given by Professor James Dana, can be considered under three heads, as follows:

Alumina Garnet   *Iron Garnet*   *Chrome Garnet*

ALUMINA GARNET. The sesquioxide base is chiefly aluminum.

(a) Iron Alumina Garnet. Shades of color: Red, ruby red, hyacinth red, columbine red, brownish red. Precious garnet is translucent, common is not.

Example: Almandine or carbuncle. Astrologically classed under the celestial Sagittarius.

(b) Lime Alumina Garnet. Shades of color: Pale green, cinnamon, amber.

Example: Essonite or cinnamon stone is cinnamon colored; grossularite (Latin **GROSSULARIA,** a gooseberry), is pale green; succinite

(Latin **SUCCINUM,** amber), is of the color of amber. The grossularite is a health talisman, the succinite a charm for securing harmony and success in dealing with employees. They are both under the Celestial Virgo.

(c) **Magnesia Alumina Garnet.** Shades of color: Deep red changing to black and green.

Example: PYROPE. Under the celestial Aquarius.

The pyrope or Bohemian garnet derives its name from the Greek word PUROPOS, fiery, and is known to Pliny as *Apyroti*. It is a stone of the same hardness as the beryl and is commonly called the "Cape ruby," or the "Arizona ruby." In the regalia of Saxony, set in the Order of the Golden Fleece, is a large pyrope, 468½ carats in weight, and that strange Emperor Rudolph II under whose patronage Tycho and Kepler worked at the Rudolphine (Astronomical) Tables, is said by De Boodt to have possessed a specimen worth 45,000 thalers. One as big as the egg of a pigeon lies in the Green Vaults at Dresden. Large pyropes are, however, rare.

Swedenborg corresponds pyrope to "good," and it is regarded as a talisman of faithfulness and stability, of hope, of happiness and true friendship. Its influence is said to aid psychic development and occult understanding. It is a health stone, and in the East is regarded as a banisher of plagues and poison, changing color, it is said, when danger or mishap of any kind threaten the wearer.

(d) **Manganese Alumina Garnet.** Shades of color: Red, brownish red, hyacinth red.

Example: Spessartite or spessatine. Under the celestial Virgo.

The Spessartite obtains its name from Spessart in Germany. It is sometimes called the brown garnet, but is little used in jewelry. The spessartite is a prayer charm for the uplifted soul.

IRON GARNET. The sesquioxide base is chiefly iron.

LIME IRON GARNET. Shades of color: Various.

Example: Andradite, named after the Portuguese mineralogist D'Andrada. In the variety called topazolite (so named after the topaz), the color is wine yellow, in jelletite it is green, and in **MELANITE** and pyreneite it is black or grey-black. The aplome (named by Hauy after the Greek word APLOOS, simple), is red. The **KOLOPHONITE,** named after Kolophon in Ionia, is coarse, granular, resinous and frequently iridescent. Green andradite has been termed the Uralian emerald and the ohvine (wrongly so-called under this head). Brilliant specimens have been named by jewelers demantoid.

A dark, almost black, andradite showing a gleam of red was much used in mourning jewelry. This is the stone which Leonardus said drove away pestilential airs and banished unworthy thoughts. It was a binding charm for friends. It protected from epidemics and the lightning strike, and lent favor to the desires of the native. Specimens have been found engraved with the names of angels in Chaldaic, Hebrew, Greek and other ancient languages. It is under the celestial Aquarius.

CHROME GARNET. The sesquioxide base is chiefly Chromium.

Shades of color: Emerald green.

Example: Ouvarovite, uvarovite or uwarowite, after the Professor of that name of the late Russian Imperial Academy at Petrograd. This variety will not, like other varieties, yield to the blow-pipe. It is a hard stone and few specimens large enough for cutting have been discovered. It is under the celestial Aquarius.

Many specimens of ancient engraved garnets have been found. Friction produces in the stone a positive order of electricity which has a perceptible effect on the magnetic needle.

GREENSTONE. (See JADE.)

GROSSULARITE. (See GARNET.)

HEMATITE

> *The Hematite, named by the Greeks from blood,*
> *Benignant Nature formed for mortals' good."*
>   —MARBODUS

The Hematite obtains its name from the Greek HAIMATITES, blood-like. It is a specular iron ore of reddish, brown, steely gray, and iron black colors. Commercially it is spelt Hematite, though it is also written as Ematite, Emathites, Emathitis.

Sotacus, described by Pliny as one of the most ancient writers, classified five varieties of hematite, as follows:

1. *Ethiopic,* which he said was a remedy for burns and inflamed eyes. It is probable that this is the Ethiopian stone, a hard species of flint. (See under **FLINT.**)
2. *Androdamus,* or Conquerer of Man, which is given as a remedy for bilious attacks. This stone is described by Sotacus as "very black and heavy," and by Marbodus as "silvery white with the hardness of a diamond." It would seem that each writer is describing a different stone. Sotacus' description would imply a species of iron stone, that of Marbodus may stand for a corundum or even a diamond, and man may be subdued by either the iron stone or the diamond.
3. *Arabian,* recommended for stomach troubles and burns.
4. *Elatite,* or when burned melitite.
5. Mixed stone for eye troubles.

The varieties given by Professor James D. Dana are:

1. Specular iron. Luster perfectly metallic.
2. Micaceous iron. Structure foliated.
3. Red hematite. Submetallic or unmetallic brownish red.
4. Red ochre. Soft and earthy and often containing clay.
5. Red chalk. Firmer and more compact than red ochre and of fine texture.
6. Jaspery clay iron. A hard, impure, siliceous, clayey ore, having a brownish-red jasper-like look and compactness.
7. Clay iron stone. The same as the last, the color and appearance less like jasper.
8. Lenticular argillaceous ore. An oolitic red ore consisting of small flattened grains.
9. Martite. Martite is hematite in octahedrons, derived, it is supposed, from the oxidation of magnetite.

Pliny says that hematites are found in mines and when burned have the color of minium. (Minium of today is our red lead of commerce, red oxide of lead). He recommends it for affections of the bladder and for the healing of dangerous wounds, bites of serpents and as a check to female disorders. It seems probable in these enumerations that he refers to Lode-stone (q. v.), for he says "the sanguine Loadstone called Haematite."

The hematite and the lodestone were used in Babylon, Assyria and other ancient lands as far back as 2000 B.C. Amongst the specimens handled by the author was one notable hematite intaglio cylinder of very fine workmanship—an old magistrate's seal of great antiquity. The ancient Egyptians generally selected hematite as a fitting pillow (URS) for the head of the Mummy to rest upon. On it were often cut verses from Chapter 166 of the *Book of the Dead*—the PER EM HRU, or *Coming Forth by Day.*

An old 17th century writer, Andreas Balvacensis, advances the curious idea that the hematite was made of "dragon's bluod," and Holme in his *Armory* says that it is called a stench stone, for its accredited virtue of stopping the flow of blood. Generally the old writers of the Middle and later ages followed Galen in prescribing hematite for inflamed eyes and headaches, and he was undoubtedly learned in the wisdom of the Egyptians and the old medical philosophies mentioned by Sotacus. Several modes of use are mentioned; one was to mix the powdered stone with honey and apply it to the eyelids, another was to rub the smoothed stone lightly over the lids.

The kidney ore hematite, which has a strong metallic silky luster and is formed somewhat like a kidney, was recommended for external application over the region of that organ when ill conditions prevailed. This application of a Mars substance for the cure of a Venus affection is technically dealt with in works devoted to medical astrology, ancient and modern. The hematite is under the celestial Aries.

HIDDENITE. (See SPODUMENE.)

HORNSTONE. Hornstone obtains its name from the Anglo-Saxon STAN. It is a fragile variety of flint, and is known in its more impure state as chert. It had some reputation as an eye stone in certain parts, and is regarded as under the celestial Taurus.

HYACINTH

"The island of Sandareeb . . . containeth varieties of jacinths and different kinds of minerals."
—*The 6th Voyage of Es-Sindabad of the Sea*

The name of this stone is derived from the youth Hyakinthos. It has been written at various times as hiacinth, hiacinthe, hyacint, hiacynth, hyacinthe, hiacint, etc. The true hyacinth, which is not to be confounded with the sapphire, the hyacinthus of the ancients, is a brilliant zircon (q.v.) of a transparent red or ruddy cinnamon color. It is found with a garnet of similar hue which is also called hyacinth but which shows structural differences and is classified under the name essonite (q.v.). The peculiar granular nature of this hyacinth can be seen, even when cut, under an ordinary lens.

It is said in ancient story that Apollo caused the death of the lovely and beloved youth Hyakinthos when throwing his disc, and that from the blood which fell to the ground a lovely flower sprang. The myth symbolizes the fertility of Nature and was celebrated by the festival Hyakinthia, which expresses the grief of Apollo over the precious life he had taken and the subsequent joy when the flower gave promise of the return of the slain one in harmony with Nature's immortal moods.

The gem hyacinth was considered a charm against bowel disorders, as a mental tonic and a strengthener of the mind against all kinds of temptation. It promised bountiful harvests to the farmer and filled the *Cornu Copia* of the Virgin Goddess. The name **JACINTH**, usually applied to the yellow variety of the gem, is a contraction of hyacinth, and appears as iacincte, iacynkte, iassink, jacounce, jagounce, jacincte, jacynct, jacynth, etc. Like all the Zircon family these stones are electric and attract fluff and exhibit phosphorescence. Thomas de Cantempre describes the jacinth as a stone of yellow color which protected the wearer from melancholy and poison, drawing to him the love of God and man.

Leonardus said that it brought sleep to the tired brain and gave wisdom and protection in times of pestilence. De Boodt also recommends the gem as a cure for insomnia, advising that it be worn enclosed in a small bag of brown material suspended just over the solar plexus. Francis

Barrett in the section of his book devoted to Natural Magic says: "The jacinth also possesses virtue from the sun against poisons, pestilences and pestiferous vapors: likewise it renders the wearer pleasant and acceptable: conduces also to gain money: being simply held in the mouth it wonderfully cheers the heart and strengthens the mind."

So in ancient astrology these stones which are under the celestial Virgo have these powers: Wisdom and Prudence, Worldly Gain, Wealth. It is said that so powerful were these gems of the zircon family that one wearing them could pass unharmed through places infected with fever and pestilence. Mystic authors wrote that the jacinth grew dull when stormy weather was approaching, and bright with the promise of fine weather; similarly it indicated the degrees of health of the wearer (Virgo is a sign of health and sickness). Cardanus says that in tempestuous weather the hyacinth assumes "the ruddy tint of a glowing coal."

As an amulet against plague it was said to change color when touched by affected persons. Avicenna (Ibn Sina,) the famous Arabian philosopher of the 10th century, compared the action of the jacinth with that of the magnet. Paracelsus says that it is distinctly under the government of the planet Mercury. In old Polish pharmacies a jacinth was kept set in a mount of silver, ready to be used to avert mortification in cases of accident. Held against the forehead it was reputed to give clearness of thought and calmness of mind.

Swedenborg corresponds it to "intelligence from spiritual love and in an opposite sense, intelligence from infernal love which is self-derived intelligence." To dream of the hyacinth is interpreted as protection in approaching worries; to dream of the jacinth indicates triumph. Jacinths are placed with almandines in the Dar as-Salam, the Arabian Garden of Peace, and amongst the Rosicrucian jewels the hyacinth represents the true knowledge of absolute love and the triumph over the crude elements of earthly understanding. These two zircon varieties are under the celestial Virgo.

HYDROPHANE. (See OPAL.)

HYPERSTHENE. The name is derived from the Greek HYPER, over, and STHENOS, strength. It is also written as hyperstene. It is a stone of the Pyroxene group, a silicate of magnesium and iron. Its colors are brown-green, grey or green-black, pinchbeck brown. Its hardness is about the hardness of lapis lazuli. The hypersthene is under the celestial Scorpio.

IOLITE. The iolite derives its name from the Greek ION, violet and LITHOS, a stone. Hauy named it the **DICHROITE** (DIO, twice, CHROA, color). It was known also as the **CORDIERITE,** and more familiarly as the water sapphire. It is a silicate of alumina magnesia and protoxide of iron. It possesses extraordinary dichroism, the smoky blue and yellowish-grey being easily seen with the naked eye. it was this circumstance which induced Hauy to name it dichroite. Viewed in two directions it presented different colors. These colors are shown to advantage in stones cut for ornament. In 1758, Sir James Hill wrote a *History of the Iolithos or Violet Stone*, a work now most difficult to obtain. The iolite is a stone of friendship and friendly help. It benefits the eyesight and is an aid to high thoughts. It was also written as yolite, iolithe. It is of about the hardness of quartz. The iolite is under the celestial Aquarius.

CHAPTER 19

JACINTH—LODESTONE

JACINTH. (See HYACINTH.)

JADE. (*See* NEPHRITE.)

JARGOON. The Jargoon or Jargon, by which name it is known in France, is derived from the Italian *Giacone*. It is a greyish or smoky variety of the zircon (q.v.), which so closely resembles the diamond that it is often sold by unscrupulous dealers for the more precious gem. In allusion to this, Sir A. H. Church in his work *Precious Stones* says: "The diamond and the jargoon do not improve or bring out each other's qualities for they have too many points in common."

The jargoon, however, is nearly three degrees softer than the diamond and more easily injured. It is usually brilliant and rose-cut. At Matura in Ceylon where it is found in fair quantities it is frequently termed the "Maturan diamond." The jargoon is frequently used set as a talismanic charm against plagues and disease, for which purpose it was esteemed greatly in the Middle Ages in the East and in Europe. Worn on the little finger, set in a ring of silver, it was reputed to help the physician to correct diagnoses—especially if, when in doubt, he held the stone against his forehead, at a point between the eyes. The jargoon is under the celestial Virgo.

JASPER.

> "Jasper stone signifies the divine truth of the Word in its literal sense, translucent from the divine truth in its spiritual sense."
>
> —SWEDENBORG

Jasper derives its name from the Hebrew JASHPEH, Greek JASPIS, Arabic YASH. It is found written as jasp, jaspre, iaspere, iaspar. It is a hard siliceous mineral of dark, dull colors, chiefly red, green, yellow and black. In the variety termed riband, the mixed and striped colors form in concentric irregular zones. Ruin jasper occurs in darker shades of browns and yellows, giving the appearance of venerable ruins.

The lapis lydius or Lydian Stone of the ancients—our basanite, commonly known as touchstone—is a velvety black flinty jasper, used as much today as ever it was, for ascertaining the fineness and quality of gold and precious metals, and says Bacon, "Gold is tried by the touchstone and men by gold." Its connection with Mercury is shown in the Greek story of the transformation of the betrayer Battus into touchstone by the god. The heliotrope or so-called **BLOODSTONE** variety is green with spots of red.

Pliny enumerates ten varieties, giving preference to the purple and rose-colored. Marbodus in the *Lapidarium* writes of seventeen species all differing in color, the best of all being the bright translucent green. The jasper was held in high favor by the ancients, and Babylonian seals as old as 1,000 years before the Christian era have been found. The THET or Buckle of Isis was made chiefly of jasper. In those times the stone was found in quantities in the vicinity of the historic town of On or Heliopolis. Thomas Nicols, writing in the 17th century, protests that the Egyptians knew how to infuse artificial colors into this gem: "It is ascribed by way of glory to the King of Egypt that the first adulteration of jasper by tincture was from him, but the glory of this praise, if I be not mistaken, doth even become his shame."

St. Isidore of Seville (16th century) writes of the green jasper as "shining with the greenness of glory," and this variety—commonly known as bloodstone because it is spotted with red specks resembling drops of blood—is regarded as an essentially religious substance, and is associated with the old Easter ceremonies. There is an old legend, frequently retold, that the green jasper lying at the foot of the Cross at the Crucifixion received the blood drops from the five wounds of the dying Christ, which drops were forever impregnated in the stone. Five is the number which in mystic writings is identified with the planet Mercury, and the significance of the blood of the Son of the Virgin in the stone of the Virgin will be understood by those who search for truth beneath the mantle of parable.

Mr. William Jones in *Finger Ring Lore* gives an illustration of a Christian octagonal-shaped ring of the 3rd or 4th century, set with a red jasper in which is cut in intaglio a shepherd and his flocks: the import of this is clear enough. A jasper bust of Christ in which the red spots are so manipulated by the skillful artist as to represent drops of blood is mentioned by Professor James Dana as being in the royal collection at Paris.

"Some indeed assert," writes Claudius Galenus, the famous physician of the second Christian century,

> "that a virtue such as is possessed by the green jasper which benefits the chest and mouth of the stomach if tied upon it, is inherent in precious stones. . . I have had ample experience having made a necklace out of such gems (jaspers), and hung it round the neck, descending so low that the stones might touch the mouth of the stomach, and they appeared to be of no less service than if they had been engraved in the way laid down by King Nechepsos."

This is the famous anodyne necklace so valued, especially in England, and the source of which the distinguished physician Dr. William Cullen ascribes to Galenus. Several books are credited to King Nechepsos (circa 600 B. C.). Galenus alludes to this King's jasper amulet which took the form of a rayed dragon. This dragon form symbolizes the mystery of the three zodiacal signs—Virgo, Libra and Scorpio—known to students of Rosicrucian philosophy as the Wheel of Ezekiel, and personified in Pallas Athene or Minerva, the embodiment of wisdom, sympathy and strength.

Galenus carried as his talismanic gem a jasper engraved with a man carrying a bundle of herbs, as an aid to his judgment in indicating various diseases—a power long ascribed to stones under the celestial Virgo. A similar sigil is given by the ancient Israelite Rabbi Chael:

> "A man with broad shoulders and thick loins, standing and holding in his right hand a bundle of herbs engraved on a green jasper is good against fevers and if a physician carries it about with him it will give him skill in distinguishing diseases and knowing the proper remedies. It is also good for hemorrhoids and quickly stops the flow of blood."

The same authority recommends for good luck in buying and selling "Aquarius cut on a green jasper," which is also termed "a stone of good counsel for traders," as all trade is under Mercury, the ruler in astrology of the signs Gemini and Virgo. A man's head facing and a bird holding a leaf in its beak, cut in jasper, was held to give riches and favor; a hare cut in jasper protected from evil spiritual forces.

The green jasper, as before stated, was also known as the heliotropion (heliotrope), a word derived from Greek HELIOS, the sun, and TROPOS, a turn—probably in allusion to the planet Mercury which turns nearest the Sun. It is stated that if this stone were placed in water it would reflect the blood-red disc of the sun, and if held before the eyes it would assist in the observation of the solar and lunar eclipses.

Mottled jasper was worn to protect from death by drowning, or from death whilst on or near the water, and this presents one of the many instances of what astrologers term "sign reflection," for the water sign of the Fishes (Pisces) is opposite to the earthy sign Virgo and serves as an apt illustration of antipathetic action. Another virtue ascribed to jasper was the calming of uneasy minds and the securing of victory in battle. In this latter connection Cardanus, physician, philosopher and astrologer of the 16th century, says that it has action on the feelings, causing something akin to timidity which induces caution and the evading of needless risks—a distinctly Mercurial attribute.

Trallianus, a 6th century philosopher, recommends the jasper for pains of an acute nature in the stomach or bowels—a use for which it was especially esteemed by all ancient scholars. De Boodt likewise advises the wearing of jasper to check hemorrhage and relieve stomach pains. The stomach was regarded as the seat of the soul by the remarkable Baptista van Helmont. Deleuze credits him with "creating epochs in the histories of medicine and physiology, and of first giving the name of 'gas' to aerial fluids," adding that without him, "it is probable that steel would have given no new impulse to science."

Van Helmont writes: "In the pit of the stomach there is a more powerful sensation than even in the eye or in the fingers. The stomach often will not tolerate a hand to be laid upon it because there is there the most acute and positive feeling which at other times is only perceived in the fingers."

For purposes of experiment Van Helmont touched a root of aconite with the tip of his tongue—a risky action—taking care, however, not to swallow any of it. "Immediately," he says,

"my head seemed tied tightly with a string and soon after there happened to me a singular circumstance such as I had never before experienced. I observed with astonishment that I no longer felt and thought with the head but with the *region of the stomach*, as if consciousness had now taken up its seat there. Terrified by this unusual phenomenon, I asked myself and enquired unto myself carefully, but I only became the more convinced that my power of perception had become greater and more comprehensive.

"This intellectual clearness was associated with great pleasure. I did not sleep, nor did I dream . . . I had occasionally had ecstasies but these had nothing in common with this condition of the stomach in which it thought and felt and almost excluded all cooperation of the head. This state continued for two hours after which I had some dizziness."

Van Helmont writes of the "Sun tissue" in the region of the stomach which from the earliest recorded times has been identified with the zodiacal Virgo around which so many myths, parables and legends cluster. Jasper is associated with this part of the body of man, and to dream of it is said to symbolize love's faithfulness known to the mind before the heart:

"*Love looks not with the eyes but with the mind.
And therefore is Dan Cupid painted blind.*"

Amongst the symbolic jewels of the Rosicrucians this stone was regarded as the center stone of the vibrations of light and of its penetrating diffusions. All varieties of jasper are under the celestial Virgo.

JET

"*Your luster too'll draw courtship to you as a iet (jet) doth straws.*"
—BEN JONSON

The name jet is derived from the Greek GAGATES, from Gagas, a river in Syria. It is also written as jesstone, and jeetstone. Dr. Murray gives the following forms: gete, geet, get, geete, geyte, geitt, gett, gette, geytt, gate, giette, geate, ieet, iete, ieit, ieate, iet, jeat, jett, jette. It is a variety of coal resembling cannel coal, but harder, of deeper color and with a higher degree of luster.

Pliny writes that "Gagates is a stone so-called from Gages, the name of a town and river in Lycia." When burnt it gives out a sulfurous smell which, according to the Venerable Bede (7th century), drove away serpents. Its virtue was esteemed in cases of hysteria, in detecting epileptic tendencies and in loss of virginity. A decoction of jet in wine was esteemed as a cure for toothache, and in combination with wax it was used in cases of scrofula. Magicians, it is said, make use of gagates in the practice of what is known as "Axinomancy"—a form of magic in which a piece of jet is placed on a red-hot axe— prophesying events according to the burning of the substance.

Jet is highly electrical and will attract fluff in the same way as amber does, hence it was known as black amber, especially in the 16th century, by the people of the Baltic coast. It was much used in magical ceremonies, especially those in connection with the dead, as a charm against evil magic, spells and envy, and as a cure for dropsy, colds, chills and loss of hair. The fumes from burning jet are no doubt very relieving in what is commonly known as cold in the head. The action is homeopathic in this case, as such discomforts are Saturnine and the employment of jet is the employment of a saturnine substance for the removing of a saturnine affliction.

The use of jet for rosaries is noted by Cardan: it cooled the passions and protected the wearer against evil influences. Its fumes were considered potent in female disorders. Boetius says that it protected the wearer against nightmares and night terrors. Mr. King mentions the discovery of a number of jet ornaments at Cologne in 1846 which were believed to have belonged to the ancient priestesses of Cybele or Rhea, the goddess of the mountain-forests and caves of the earth. Her worship was wild and weird, her votaries with torches ablaze rushing through the trees in the darkness of the night, fighting and wounding each other to the accompaniment of the screeching of the pipes, the clashing of cymbals and the mad uproar of drunken song. Cybele was associated as a mountain goddess with the forest-god Pan, the goat-god, who is identified with the Zodiacal Capricornus, and jet was used in her worship. It was regarded as a banisher of melancholia and a protective badge for travelers. To dream of it was said to signify sadness.

In the form of a shield against the bites of serpents it was advised that powdered jet be taken and mixed with the marrow of a stag. To many writers this has seemed ridiculous but beneath the surface the true meaning may be detected. Astrologically jet is under the zodiacal Capricorn and the planet Saturn, the stag is under Gemini and the planet Mercury, the marrow of the stag is ruled by Venus and in this case signifies the essence supreme, the serpent is under the planet Mars. Interpreted, this symbolic passage would read: Use wisdom and caution (jet) knowledge (stag) and love (marrow) then wilt thou overcome, subdue and defeat the lower self (serpent) and the sting of sin. Crypts of this kind were very frequently employed by Hermetic brotherhoods for conveying their teachings to each other. The use of parables, secret signs, tokens and symbols was the real method of conveying truths employed by the ancient masters. By this means concentration was impelled and the soul prepared to receive great truths.

KAURI GUM

"As some tall Kauri soars in lonely pride."
       —RENWICK

Kauri obtains its name from the Maoris and appears in various forms: kowrie, cowry, courie, coudie. It is gum of a light amber color which has exuded from the Kauri pine (*Dammara australis,*) a species of Dammar growing in New Zealand. The gum is obtained by digging over spots where the trees once grew, and it is found sometimes in lumps the size of a football. Kauri gum is electric and much softer and less durable than amber. It has been suggested as a useful substitute for amber in throat troubles, asthma, hay fever and glandular swellings. It is under the celestial Taurus.

KOLOPHONITE. (See GARNET.)

KUNZITE. (See SPODUMENE.)

KYANITE. Kyanite derives its name from the Greek KUANOS, blue. It is also written as cyanite and, because of its unequal hardness, **DISTHENE** (twice strong). White specimens are termed rhoetizite. Chemically kyanite harmonizes with andalusite (q. v.) for both are silicates of aluminum, but as Dr. Smith writes, "points of difference show how large a share the molecular grouping has in determining the aspect of crystallized substances."

Usually kyanite is found in long, thin blade-like crystals and more rarely in short, full crystals. Its colors are light blue, blue and white, white, grey-green and, more rarely, black. Its hardness varies from 5 to a little over 7 in Mohs' scale. When cut the blue variety resembles the light sapphire although it cannot display the same brilliancy. The stone is, however, very little employed in jewelry. The peculiarities of kyanite place it under the celestial Aquarius.

LABRADORITE

"The beautiful opalised kind of felspar called Labrador stone."

—PINKERTON

Also written labrador, is an opalescent grey-blue feldspar of extraordinary gleam, often reflecting green, yellow and red. It obtains its name from the place of its origin, as it was first found by Moravian missionaries in 1770 at St. Paul Island off the coast of Labrador. Specimens have also been found in stones of meteoric origin. The stone is effective and might with advantage be more extensively used in jewelry. Its hardness is the same as the opal. Labradorite is under the celestial Aquarius.

LAPIS LAZULI

"The appearance of the Lord's divine sphere in the spiritual Heavens."

—SWEDENBORG

Lapis lazuli derives its name from the Latin word LAPIS, a stone, and the Arabic AZUL, blue. It has been variously written as zumemo lazuli, zemech lazarilli, stellatus, lapis lazary, lapis coelestus, the azure gem, the Armenian stone, lapis lazari. Its composition includes for the greater part silica and alumina, with soda, lime, iron, sulfuric acid, sulfur, chlorine and water. It is assumed to be a product of contact metamorphism, and is described by Pliny as "opaque and sprinkled with specks of gold" (yellow pyrites).

It is found in Persia, Tartary, China, Tibet and Siberia. Badakhshan or Budukhshan in Central Asia is famous for its lapis lazuli mines in which, it is recorded, the rock is split with the help of fire. The stone is often found in tints of green, red, violet, or colorless, but these may be termed varieties. The miners of Budukhshan call the blue lapis "*Nil*," the sky-blue "*Asmani*," and the blue-green tints "*Sabzi*." Some of the finest lajward (lapis lazuli) is sent from the Persian markets whence formerly specimens of rare beauty were exposed for sale at the fairs of Nijni-Novgorod. From very remote times Persia supplied the ancient world with the greatest quantities of lajward.

The "sapphirus" of old is the lapis lazuli of today, and it is recommended that the 26th chapter of *The Book of the Dead* should be recited before a deific figure cut from this stone. As early as 1500 years before Christ we have a record that the lapis lazuli placed on the neck of a sick child reduced fever. Many of the Egyptian priests wore images formed from the stone which was regarded as an emblem of the heavens. Epiphanius, Bishop of Constantia in Cyprus, at the latter part of the 4th century, quotes from older sources the tradition that the tables of the Law of Moses were written on two blocks of lapis lazuli, which is identified as the eleventh stone of the magic Breastplate.

In the ceremonies of the Temple of Heaven in China, ornaments of LIU-LI (lapis lazuli) were used, and the Chinese sacred writings record how at one time the priest-kings bore it as an offering to the Lord of the Universe. In accordance with the desire of Catherine II of Russia her favorite room in the Zarskoe Selo palace was adorned with lapis lazuli, symbolic of the country she governed, and amber, as a symbol of herself. The ancient Greeks and Romans considered a piece of lapis lazuli—the stone of Heaven—as the most fitting distinction to bestow for personal bravery. It was regarded as a true stone of friendship and of the affection arising from friendship.

Ancient physicians regarded this gem as of potent value in eye troubles, one old prescription advising that a specimen be placed in a bowl of water, warm but not hot, for the space of some few minutes, and then that the eye affected be bathed in the water which must be as pure as can be obtained. The stone was also valued if placed, just warm, on swellings or seats of pain. It was also regarded as a cure for ague, melancholia, disorders of the blood, neuralgic affections and spasmodic action. As a talisman it was worn to protect against injuries, especially to the ankles, to attract friends, gain favors and realize hopes.

Lapis lazuli was used by many of the old alchemists in special work of an esoteric nature and is frequently alluded to as the Stone of Heaven in which the stars are held. It is under the zodiacal Aquarius.

LIMONITE. This stone was named limonite by Professor Hausmann in 1813 from the Greek word LEIMON, a meadow. It is a species of brown hematite (scarcely as hard as the opal) which according to Professor Dana appears to have been the result in all cases of the decomposition of other iron-bearing rocks or minerals. It is under the celestial Aries.

LODESTONE

"The magnet weds the steel, the secret rites
Nature attends and th' heavenly pair unites."
—Claudianus of Alexandra

The lodestone—which is also written, though not so correctly, load-stone—obtains its name from the Anglo-Saxon LAD, a course, LITHAN, to lead, and STAN. Another form is lodysshestone, the stone that shows the way. It is also known as magnetite or the ancient magnet, from the Greek MAGNES. The lodestone or magnetite is a black iron ore of high magnetic quality, and this peculiar attracting force is said to have first indicated what we now term magnetism.

According to Pliny a Greek shepherd—Magnes, by name—whilst tending his sheep on Mount Ida, found pieces of lodestone clinging to the ferrule of his shepherd's staff. Titus Carus Lucretius, in his great philosophical work *De Rerum Natura* (about 55 B. C.), calls the magnetite the magnesium stone, which he said obtained its name from Magnesia, a town in Thessaly. Another name applied to this stone is siderit, but its best-known appellation in the ancient world was heraclion, or stone of Hercules. It is interesting to recall the legend of the old Phoenician mariners, which tells that Hercules, admiring their daring and skill, desired to help them in the science of navigation. For this purpose he obtained from Helios a cup of heraclion which always turned to the North.

This seems to indicate that the mariners' compass is of older date than the 11th century; indeed the Chinese assert that in the year 2634 B.C. the Emperor Houangti first constructed a magnetic compass. The Greek traveler and historian Pausanias in his *Helbados Periegesis* published in the second century, writes of the rough stone image of Hercules in the Temple at Hyettos, which the sick came but to touch in order to be healed of their disorders. As a stone of healing the lodestone was highly esteemed as a cure for gout, rheumatism, cramp, disorders which frequently yield to treatment wherein iron is employed. It was used during childbirth and in diseases of the generative organs. Finely powdered and mixed with oil or grease it was regarded by ancient writers as a preventive of or cure for baldness.

In the Orphic *Lythica* it is stated that holding this stone to the head, the voices of the gods could be heard, heavenly knowledge gained and divine things seen. It is here advised that one should sit alone in earnest meditation asking the celestial powers for guidance or help in some particular trouble, when the reply flowing through the stone would be quickly sensed and understood by the sincere petitioner. A woman's moral character was said to be betrayed by the lodestone, which endowed strength, will and the ability to look into the future. It was also carried as a charm to protect against shipwreck.

It is related that after the death of his sister-wife Arsinoe, Ptolemy II (Philadelphus) planned with his architect Dinochares a temple to be built of lodestone in order that her iron statue would be held for ever in suspension, seemingly in space, but death defeated the plan. In referring to the power of lodestones Professor Noad (*Electricity*) states: "The smallest stones have greater attractive force in proportion to their size than larger ones."

Francis Barrett under the heading of "Antipathies" writes that a diamond disagrees with a lodestone and being present suffers no iron to be drawn to it. However, it is as a lovers' token that the lodestone is most extolled; it is often found set in lovers' rings of the Middle Ages. Claudianus in his *Idyl* published in the latter part of the 4th century gives a record of a temple wherein was a statue of Venus in lodestone, and another of Mars in iron—symbols of the attraction of the wife for the husband and of the husband for the wife.

There is an old belief that the magnet was affected by the onion, and in this connection the following extract from *Notes and Queries*, December, 1917, is interesting:

"The notorious Count de Benyowsky at the end of Chapter III of his *Memoirs and Travels* mentions the stratagem which he tried at sea to falsify the compass by the use of iron and garlic. I now find that in the 17th century the belief actually prevailed in England that an onion would destroy the power of the magnet. Thus Sir John Pettus of Suffolk, Kt., after describing his visit as a youth to the lead mines of Derbyshire in company with Sir Thomas Bendish says that having magnetized the blade of his knife and hearing that contact with an onion would utterly destroy that power, he preferred to believe rather than risk losing his magnet. The passage occurs in a rambling note on 'Mineralls' in the second part of his *Fleta Minor*."

It might be considered in connection with such stories that the onion as well as the lodestone is of the zodiacal Scorpio. To dream of the lodestone warns of subtle dealings and contentions. It is under the celestial Scorpion.

CHAPTER 20

Malachite—Nephrite

MALACHITE

*"Melochites is a grene stone lyke to Smaragdus and hath that name
of the colour of Malawes."*

—Trevisa

The Malachite derives its name from the Greek MALACHE, marsh
mallow, from its resemblance to the soft green leaves of this plant. It
is variously written as melochite, malachquite, etc. It is a green carbonate of copper which comes to us through the ages as a symbol of children
and of the child of the year—eternal Spring.

It has been confused with the molochite of Pliny, but it is more likely
the *smaragdus medicus*, as identified by Mr. King, and the chrysocolla of
Theophrastus. In Rosicrucian philosophy it was the symbol of the ver-
nal equinox and the arising of the spiritual man. Malachite and azurite
(q.v.) have been found together in single specimens. Malachite is much
employed for decorative purposes by the Russians, who have produced
some excellent works of art in this material. It was greatly favored by the
Egyptians and antique cameos and intaglios have been frequently found
patinated by the hard hand of age.

The virtues ascribed to this stone are many. It strengthened the
stomach, head and kidneys, prevented vertigo and rupture and saved
the wearer from evil magic, seduction, falls and accidents. The Egyptians held it to be efficacious in cholera and rheumatism. It was said
to bestow strength on children, to aid them during dentition, to ward
off convulsions, all harm, witchcraft and the evil eye. Some old writers
give directions for swallowing powdered malachite, especially for cardiac
affections—a practice dangerous and undesirable. The action of stones
and gems is subtle and the intense vibratory action is so gentle as to be
usually quite unfelt by the material senses. Powdering a specimen dis-

turbs the cohesive molecules and deprives them of their insidious action. A stone multiplies from without and by the laws of correspondence its action on man is always from external to internal.

The Malachite was also called the Sleep Stone from its reputation of charming the wearer to sleep. It was also regarded as a protection from lightning. Massive malachite bears a close resemblance to the kidneys in the human body. It is under the zodiacal Libra.

MARBLE

"And the cold marble leapt to life, a god."
    —MILMAN

Marble derives its name from the Latin MARMOR, cognate with the Greek MARMOROS, from MARMAIRO, to sparkle. It has been variously written in England as marbre, marbyr, marbel, marbal, marboll, marbelle, merbyl, marbill, marbyll, marbull, marbell, etc. It is carbonate of lime, pure when the color is white and of various shades of color when combined with oxide of iron and other substances.

The marble favored by the ancients was the Parian which is finely granular, waxy when polished, and lasting. The beautiful Venus de Medici and other exquisite Greek statues were formed of Parian. Another favorite variety was the more finely grained and whiter marble of Pentelicus from which the Parthenon was built. The Pyramid of Cheops and other famous structures of the kind were built of a variety known as nummilitic limestone, which is composed of numerous disk-shaped fossils known as nummilites. Portor is a deep black Genoese marble with yellow veining. The deep black marble of antiquity is known as Nero-antico; Rosso antico is a deep blood-red besprinkled with white minute marks; Verde antico is a misty green; Giallo antico a deep yellow with yellow or black rings. Carrara marble is greatly used by modern sculptors and was well-known to the ancients; it is a fine-grained pure white marble traversed by grey veins.

Pure white marble was an emblem of purity and as such has always been regarded as fitting for tombstones and other sepulchral monuments. As an emblem of immortality it is expressed by the triform symbol of the planet Mercury (the cross, the circle and the crescent), with which is associated the Christ resurrection in Christian mysticism. Amongst

Rosicrucian students the cross is symbolical of the pain of matter, for on it matter is fixed;—the circle the ascent of the soul which is above matter and never ending; the semi-circle which surmounts the whole, the spirit which is over all everlastingly.

Evidence of the old custom—still followed in many countries—of placing pieces of white marble in the grave with dead bodies was some few years ago brought to light in Ireland. Dr. Holland's translations from Pliny record "a strange thing of the quarries of the island Paros, namely, that in one quarter thereof there was a vein of marble found which when it was cloven in twaine with wedges shewed naturally within the true image and perfect portraiture of Silenus imprinted on it."

All marble is under the celestial Gemini.

MARCASITE. (See PYRITE.)

MEERSCHAUM

> "A meerschaum pipe nearly black with smoking is considered a treasure."
>
> —J. Nott. Dekker's *Gull's Horn Book*

Meerschaum obtains its name from the German *Meer*, sea, and *Schaum*, foam, which is, according to Dr. Murray, a literal translation of the Persian KEF-I-DARYA (foam of the sea). It is also called keffekill and kiffekiefe, which has been credited with meaning the "earth of the town of Keffe or Kaffe," the Crimean town whence it is exported. Its technical name is sepiolite, and its various forms are given as myrsen, meershaum, meerchum, mereschaum, merschaum, meerschaum. It is a hydrous silicate of magnesia, extremely soft and light, smooth to the touch and in color of white, grey-white, yellow and sometimes pinkish.

Kirwan, the mineralogist, writing in the latter part of the 18th century says, "Kefferkill or Myrsen is said, when recently dug, to be of a yellow color and as tenacious as cheese or wax." It is well-known that the Tartars use newly dug meerschaum as we use soap, on account of its excellent lather. The peasantry at one time really believed it to be the petrified foam of the sea. The meerschaum is included amongst the galactites or milk stones. On account of its lightness it was first fashioned into a smoking pipe by a Hungarian shoemaker, Kavol Kowates, skilled in

"Inspiration" — *Marble Group in Central Hall, Art Institute Chicago.*
Signed—Kathleen Beverly Robinson. Memorial to Florence Jane Adams.
Presented by Friends and Pupils of Mrs. Adams, 1915.

wood carving and metal work, in the old town of Pesth, in the museum of which town it now rests. The piece of meerschaum from which Kowates made his pipe was brought to Hungary by his patron Count Andrassy on his return from a diplomatic mission to Turkey. The meerschaum is under the celestial Gemini.

MELANITE. (See GARNET.)

MOONSTONE

"Soon as the evening shades prevail,
The Moon takes up the wondrous tale.
And nightly to the listening earth
Repeats the story of her birth."

— ADDISON

The moonstone is an orthoclase feldspar of the opalescent variety of Adularia, of a pearly moonlike luster—hence the name Stone of the Moon. It appears under the forms of moona, mone, mon, mowne, moone, moyne, mione, mune and muni; it is known in France as *Pierre de la Lune.*

Its abundance in Ceylon has earned for it the name of "Ceylon opal." The Indians call it *Chandra Kanta,* and according to them it grows under the rays of the moon and absorbs in the process of formation an atmospheric ether which impregnates it with peculiar occult and magical properties. These properties once infused into the stone never leave it. They are said to have a remarkable effect on the psychic nature of man, enabling him to prophesy—according to Leonardus—in the waning of the moon and to love in the waxing. The natives of Ceylon have a story that every third seventh year moonstones of opalescent blue are, by the influence of the moon, hurled on the island shore by the waves. Pliny says that in the stone an image of the moon is impressed, which waxes and wanes in harmony with the luminary.

It is related that Pope Leo X possessed a wonderful specimen which, obscure and dull when the moon was old, increased in brilliance as that orb grew from new to full. It is recommended that in order to know the future and to obtain spiritual guidance a moonstone be held in the mouth, under a waning moon. It is also necessary to be quite alone and to send out a mental prayer to the angel Gabriel (angel of the Moon) asking help by God's grace.

The moonstone was considered as a charm against cancer, dropsy and affections of a watery nature. In fever, if applied to the temples it reduced the temperature and protected the patient. It also cooled heated imaginations and protected against moon-strokes and lunacy. The moonstone is said to protect the wearer from danger on the ocean and to give good fortune whilst traveling. As a symbol it signifies Hope, and as a dream symbol it indicates traveling and health—good when the stone is bright and clear, and bad when it is dark and lusterless. It is under the celestial Cancer.

MOSS AGATE or MOCHA STONE

"Whilst on that agate which dark Indians praise
The woods arise, the sylvan monster strays."

—MARBODUS

The mocha stone is said to have obtained its name from the Arabian city of Mocha whence it was exported. It has been written in various ways: mocus, mocoe, mocoa, mochoe, mochoa, mocha, mocho. It is called *Piedra de Moca* in Spain, *Pierre de Mocka* in France, and *Mokkastein* in Germany. The mocha stone is called dendritic because of the plant and moss-like infiltrations exhibited. These are like frost crystals often formed by the magic hand of Nature, and often also by plants held in hollows wherein the siliceous mineral was composed. The mocha stone besides being called moss agate is also called tree agate in common with silicified trees in which the original structural details are accurately preserved.

Remarkable pictures formed by Nature in the agate have already been noticed. Pliny hints at the employment of artifice in the production of many of these stones, and the secret was long a cherished knowledge of the Italian workers in gems. Early in the 19th century, however, some German scientists obtained possession of the secret and within the past few years artificial productions from Oberstein have reached the gem markets.

The mocha stone was accounted a most fortunate stone. It is associated with the influences of the planet Venus and was always noted as a sign of fertility. For this reason farmers tied specimens to their fruit trees, to the harness of their horses and to the horns of their cattle. In the early 19th century it was highly esteemed in Europe, and in England especially it was used for luck rings, oftentimes surrounded with rubies (stones of the sun). It was also used for mourning jewelry as an emblem of the resurrection and of the eternal life which alone is permanently manifest throughout Nature. Orpheus advises that to secure the smiles of the gods a piece of the stone should be worn, also that the ploughman carrying it would receive heavenly bounty. It was greatly esteemed by physicians and apothecaries as a base on which to prepare their medicines. As a symbol it stood for good health and long life and to dream of it, heralded increase of possessions. It is under the celestial Taurus.

MOTHER OF EMERALD. (See PRASE.)

MOTHER OF PEARL. (See NACRE.)

NACRE

"Tis a valley paved with golden sands,
With pearls and nacre shells."

—SYLVESTER (1605) TRANS. DU BARTAS

Nacre, or **MOTHER OF PEARL,** is the inner layer of various mollusks and is more particularly applied to the *Meleagrina margaritifera*, or large oyster shell, in which the precious pearl is formed. The French call it *Mere Perle*, and it is found written as moder perl, mother perle, mother pearle. Nacre is said to have derived its name from the Persian word NIGAR, painting, because of the iridescent colors displayed, but Dr. Murray, although remarking on its probable Oriental origin, regards its derivation as uncertain. Various forms are noted, as: nackre, nacker, nakre, naker, and there is no doubt of its antique application. Hoole in 1658 wrote that "the oyster affordeth sweet meat—the nacre pearls."

Mythologically the mother of pearl shell is symbolical of Latona or Leto, "goddess of the dark night," mother of the Sun god Apollo and the Moon goddess Artemis or Diana. She, as ancient story tells, whilst fleeing from the fury of Hera, Queen of Heaven, reached an island rock, driven about by the restless waves, which when solidly fixed by Neptune became the famous island of the Aegean Sea—Delos. Here were born the radiant twins Apollo and Artemis in a flood of golden light whilst the sacred swans encircled the island seven times. The golden light, so powerful at this event, is the light which at conjunction (new moon) blends with the silvery light of the night orb.

The pearl shell like its child, the pearl, is always associated with female life which in astro-philosophy is moon-ruled. The natives of Western Australia, hidden in the bushes, charmed women by the aid of the reflected light from the shell of the mother of pearl. These big shells are thick, flat and roundish, in size often as much as a foot in diameter. The two varieties are known as black-lipped and silver-lipped, and within them rests the protected pearl. The pearl shell is greatly in demand for the manufacture of many and varied articles of commerce. It is under the celestial Cancer—the mansion of the moon and the sign of the deep ocean.

NEPHRITE

"Many of the Indians wore pieces of Greenstone round their necks which were transparent and resembled an emerald. These being examined, appeared to be a species of nephrite stone."

—COOK'S VOYAGES, 1790

In ancient times the minerals comprising or included in this important group were commonly known by the name lapis nephriticus or kidney stone, and from this name in the 18th century Dr. A. G. Werner suggested the term nephrite. To the nephrite varieties the general term **JADE** is universally applied. The name occurs in old writings as jad and jadde, and is derived from the Spanish *Hijada*, kidney. Sir Walter Raleigh in 1595 wrote of this "kinde of stones which the Spaniards call *Piedras Hijadas* and we use for spleene stones."

Chemically the species included under the name "jade" are not the same, the nephrite jade being a silicate of lime and magnesia and the jadeite a silicate of sodium and alumina, but the modern scientist in common with the ancient scientist binds them together under the one denomination—kidney stone. In the 19th century Professor A. Damour demonstrated the chemical difference between jade and jadeite.

The well-known camphor jade of China is a white jadeite, some specimens containing certain percentages of chromium exhibiting those apple-green patches so highly praised by gem collectors. Burmese jade, known as *Chauk-Sen*, (which since the 13th century has been principally exported to China) is chiefly jadeite, and the imperial jade of charming pale or apple-green color, known as FEI-TSUI and set down by some writers as chrysoprase, is more properly prehnite.

The nephrite charms—*Piedras Hijadas*—known in Mexico as Chalchihuith when the Spanish invaded that country were probably jadeites. The Chinese have held the jade family in the highest esteem and reverence for many centuries, and it poetically expresses to them all the virtues of many precious stones blended together. It is said that most of the nephrite used by them came from the Kuen-lun Mountains in Turkestan, but the discovery of the mineral at no great distance from Peking in 1891 helped to make that city a great working center. The Chinese word for jade is YU, expressed in their hieroglyph as a cross over a kind of semicircle. Jade stone they know as YU-CHI, and precious objects of jade as OUAN YU. The words KHITCHINJOU-YU indicate a gem rare as jade, and the Imperial Academy was known as Jade Hall. The Turkestan name for jade closely resembles the Chinese YU in its form YASHM, YUSHM or YESHM.

Ages before the Christian era the jade was said to indicate the nine accomplishments, Charity, Goodness, Virtue, Knowledge, Skill, Morality, Divination, Rectitude, Harmony. YU may also be rendered "courage," and in its connection with the jade stone or YU-CHI it included the five cardinal virtues—YU, bravery, JIU charity, JI modesty, KETSU equity, CHI, discrimination. In her *Wanderings in China* Mrs. C. F. Gordon Cummings says:

"The Chinese name for jade is YU-SHEK—(it may also be written YU-CHI) and that by which we call it is said to be a corruption of a Spanish word referring to a superstition of the Mexican Indians who deemed that to wear a bracelet of this stone was the surest protection against all diseases of the loins: hence the Spanish named the mineral *Piedra di Hijada* (stone of the loins) by which name it became known in Europe."

Jade is the concentrated element of love which protected the infant and the adult and preserved the bodies of the dead from decay. Dr. Kunz quotes the Chinese mystical writer Ko Kei who asserted that the body of a man who had consumed 5 pounds weight of jade powdered did not change color when he died, and that when several years later it was exhumed no evidences of change or decay were visible.

When vibrated this stone produces musical notes, and it was regarded as expressive of music and harmony, poets singing its praises. It was the emblem of love, beauty, protection and charm, and it graced the holy altars. For the altar of earth the symbolic jade stone was of yellowish hue, whilst during lunar festivals white jade was employed. Black—mentioned, but doubtful indeed—was the North Jade, and red the South. White was the West and green the East. It was said that in sickness the heat of the body drew out virtues from the jade, healing virtues soothing and life protecting. In *Buddhist Records of the Western World* Mr. Samuel Beal writes that

"in the kingdom of Kuichi or Kuche in the Eastern Convent known as the Buddha Pavilion, there is a large yellowish-white jade stone shaped like a sea shell which bears on its surface what is said to be Buddha's footmark. This footmark is one foot 8 inches long and 8 inches in breadth. It is said that the relic emits a bright sparkling light at the conclusion of each fast day."

Professor E. H. Parkes, M.A. in *Ancient China Simplified* mentions a custom of burying a jade symbol of rulership in the ancestral temple to protect the fortunes of the family, and jade symbols adorned private family insignia. Strangely enough the world's people have always reverenced the nephrite as the kidney stone—the use of it goes further back than the knowledge of man. It was used in old Egypt as in old China, and Pliny mentions the Adadu-nephros or kidney of Adonis. This is an early identification of jade with the Venusian Adonis and the parts of the body over which Venus astrologically presides.

The Indians call it the Divine Stone which is credited with being a cure for epilepsy and as a charm against the bites of animals and poisonous reptiles. It was also said to remove thirst and hunger, to cure heartburn and asthma and to affect favorably the voice, organs of the throat,

Old Maori Charm of Greenstone known as "Hei Tiki"

the liver and the blood. Its greasy surface led to its employment as a hair improver, but its chief excellence was in nephritic disorders and specimens worn over the region of the kidneys or on the arm are said to have acted in a wonderful and unexpected manner in the banishing of these troubles. It is claimed also as a power for the removal of gravel.

The Maoris of New Zealand according to the best authorities noted six varieties of jade. *Punamu* is their name for the whole species termed by authors of the last decade "green talc of the Maoris." The well-known greenstone variety is termed *Kawakawa* by the Maoris, the paler and more precious *Kahurangi*, the greyish *Inanga*. The *Tangiwai* stone is a pellucid serpentine or variety of bowenite. The nephrite is a sacred stone to these sturdy New Zealanders who use it in the construction of their offensive and defensive weapons and sacred objects. These greenstone weapons are amongst the finest of known stone tools.

The sacred and curiously formed charm, the Hei Tiki, is an esoteric symbol which is worn as a precious emblem and never parted with except for very weighty reasons. For example, a Hei Tiki recently handled by the author was given by an old chief on his deathbed to an English officer who had saved his life in the Maori war. The Tahunga stone—the stone of the magicians by the aid of which the flashes of light were directed by the Medicine Man to bewildered eyes, was usually formed from a *Kahurangi* type of greenstone, and the Mere or Pattoo Pattoo, a club of dark *Punamu*, was said to send its victims to the world of Spirits.

A variety of jade of dark green color, discovered in the Swiss Lake dwellings and the dolmens of France usually in the form of Celts was termed chioromelanite by Professor Damour. This nephrite has also been discovered in New Guinea where it was fashioned by the natives into clubs and other implements. Other Nephrites have been termed fibrolite or sillimanite. The Pâté de Riz is merely a fine white glass, and Pink Jade is usually a piece of quartz. Some beautiful specimens of translucent green jade are collected by children on the Island of Iona and many specimens have been unearthed in various parts of Europe. Professor Max Muller discovered in old Egypt a remarkable green stone used as a charm against hysteria; this interesting specimen is now in the Museum of Natural History, New York.

The nephrite family is under the celestial Libra.

CHAPTER 21

Obsidian — Onyx

OBSIDIAN

"There may be ranged among the kinds of glasses those which they call obsidiana for that they carry some resemblance of that stone which one Obsidius found in Æthyopia."

— Holland's Pliny

This natural volcanic glass obtains its name, according to Pliny, from Obsidius or, as he is sometimes called, Obsius, who discovered it in Ethiopia. It is very hard, brittle and remarkably vitreous, and is variously colored black, pink, green, grey, striped and spotted. It was early discovered to be a useful material from which to fashion knives, mirrors and other objects of ornament and use. An ancient Egyptian custom of cutting the dead bodies of their kings and priests with knives of obsidian was followed by the Guanchos of the Canary Islands. The ancient Mexicans used ITZTLI as they called it very generally in the manufacture of various implements. They quarried it from the *Cerro de les Navajas* or Hill of the Knives not far from Timapau.

Pliny, noting that genuine gem stones could not be cut or scratched with obsidian, recommended the use of splinters of the substance for testing purposes. The same author, attesting the report that statues were made of obsidian, says: "I myself have seen solid statues in the material of the late Emperor Augustus of very considerable thickness." The Greeks and Romans found it an easy material for fashioning into cameos and intaglios which later were copied in glass. In the 18th century connoisseurs applied the term "obsidians" to all antique pastes.

The so-called "Obsidian Bomb" has been much discussed and written about. Professor F. W. Rudley says: "It was believed for a long time to be a variety of obsidian but its different fusibility and its chemical composition are rather against its volcanic origin." It is known as moldavite, so called by Mr. A. Dufrenoy from Moldanthein in Bohemia, where quantities have been found. On account of its olive-like or bottle-green color it is also called bottle stone or *Bouteillenstein*. Dr. F. G. Suess suggested tectite from the Greek TEKTOS, melted. Mr. R. H. Walcott called them obsidianites. They have also been termed australites, billitonites (from Billiton Island) etc. They were highly regarded by the Australian aboriginal as charm stones in sickness and trouble.

Mr. W. F. Chapman, A. L. S., of the Melbourne Museum agrees with Professor Rutley as to the non-volcanic origin of the obsidianite, and indicates the action of lightning in their formation. In this he would have the support of the ancient student who connects the obsidian with the heavenly Aquarius, the "sign of air."

OLIVINE. So-called by Werner in 1790. (*See* **CHRYSOLITE.**)

ONYX

> "*Called by the onyx round the sleeper stand*
> *Black dreams; and phantoms rise, a grisly band.*"
>   —MARBODUS

The onyx derives its name from the Greek ONYX, ONYCHOS a finger-nail, and is as previously stated a variety of chalcedony. It has been variously written as onyx stone, onyx, onix, oniche, onice, onyse. The name of the stone is said to have sprung from the legend which tells that Cupid, finding Venus asleep on the river bank, cut her nails with the sharp point of his arrow. In this story is enwrapped the mystery of earth birth which through love enters the gate of Cancer and with the aid of the moistures, materializes. The same parallel is expressed in the Book of Genesis where it is written that previous to the birth of the world the "Spirit of God moved upon the face of the waters."

This occult philosophy is stressed by the Platonist Macrobius who writes that the soul, descending to the sphere of its spiritual death, the Earth, passes through Cancer, the Gate of Man, and enters under the planetary conditions that influence earth matters, receiving on the way the souls of the planets to whose influence it is exposed whilst manifesting in an earth body. As the soul descends it gathers sensation and earthy feelings from the celestial Leo, and long before its absolutely material birth obtains its first breath of matter.

Herein is the mystery of the "two onyx stones enclosed in mountings of gold graven with the names of the twelve tribes of Israel which he put on the shoulders of the ephod that they should be stones for a memorial to the children of Israel, as the Lord commanded Moses." As previously noted, on one onyx the names of six tribes were engraved, on the other the names of the remaining six, and each tribe was symbolized by a sign of the zodiac. The two onyx stones are the material emblems of the two Gates—the Gate of Cancer and the Gate of Capricorn—through which the self or soul enters and leaves the earth sphere, gathering first, and throwing off afterwards, the earth elements from ethereal to gross, from gross to ethereal, as described by Macrobius.

Many of the writers of the Middle Ages place the onyx under the signs Cancer and Capricorn and there is no reason to oppose them. The onyx of Cancer is white and light-colored whilst that of Capricorn is black; the birth of the child is white and bright, and with black and somber colors those on earth mourn for the earth loss of the departed. So the "coming in" and the "going out" symbolized by the two stones of onyx set in gold, the metal of the Sun, in true talismanic style was the memorial to the children of Israel, as it is to the world's children forever.

Phillips, an author of the middle 17th century, notes an old belief that the onyx is the congealed juice of a tree called Onycha, which is commanded to be used in a sacred way in the 34th verse of the 30th chapter of Exodus, and which Emanuel Swedenborg corresponds to "interior natural truth." The statement, then, that the onyx is the congealed juice of the onycha is but a cryptic way of expressing the congealing of the waters of generation—a method followed by the occult masters through the ages. Old Rabbi Benoni sees in the onyx a bound spirit which, wakeful by night only, disturbs the wearer in sleep, and the master Ragiel in his *Book of Wings* recommends that a camel's head or the heads of two goats among myrtles be cut on an onyx to control and constrain demons and to make the wearer see the terrors of the night during sleeping hours. This refers to the dark or Saturnine onyx which is also recommended to be enclosed in a setting of lead (metal of Saturn) and engraved with the figure of a king crowned or a witch seated on a dragon especially in the practice of dark or doubtful occult things.

Certain varieties of onyx presenting the appearance of an eye were largely employed as eye stones and it was recommended that such specimens be lightly rubbed over the closed eyelids after work wherein the eyes have been employed. Leonardus of the 16th century says that this onyx enters the eye of its own accord and, if it finds anything within that is noxious, it drives it out and tempers the hurtful and contrary humors. As a higher Saturnine stone the onyx aids spiritual inspirations and helps the wearer to restrain excessive passion.

In the writer's book on *Zodiacal Symbology and its Planetary Power* the first degree of the sign Cancer is symbolized as "a curious ring set with a large heart of white onyx." The 1st, 2nd, 10th, 11th, 12th, 28th, 29th degrees of Cancer are much influenced by the planet Venus and to these degrees especially applied the white onyx engraved with a figure of Venus, a charm recommended by old masters as a talisman of beauty and strength. It was considered ideal for a baby girl born under those degrees of Cancer according to astro-philosophy. Mr. King mentions a beautifully executed onyx intaglio showing Castor naked, in his hand a large broadsword, weeping over the tomb of Aphareus. The onyx in this case would be of a more somber hue and would be classed amongst the Saturnine or mourning varieties.

The famous Nicolo—known as Ægyptilla by the ancient Romans— was obtained by cutting a blue section surrounded by black out of the stone which then presented a fine turquoise blue with a deep black base. On this stone some of the finest ancient work is found. It is supposed to have obtained its name from the Greek word NIKOLAUS: "Its strange derivation," wrote Mr. King, "from the Greek was to suit the virtue ascribed to it, as if it meant Victor of Nations." Its modern derivation is from *Onicolo*, an Italian word signifying a little onyx.

A variety of onyx marble with bands of brown found in the cavern limestone of Gibraltar is known as Gibraltar stone. Professor Dana mentions the famous Mantuan vase at Brunswick which, cut from a single stone 7 inches high by 2½ broad, takes the form of a cream pot. The color is brown on which are raised figures of white and yellow, illustrating Ceres and Triptolemus searching for the lost Proserpine. The Saturn side of the onyx is taken by the Arabs who call it EL JAZA or sadness, but the color was always considered and the varieties were thus identified:—

1. Those resembling the human finger nail, under Cancer.
2. White striped with red, under Cancer.
3. White striped with black, under Capricorn.
4. Black, unstriped, under Capricorn (probably the true EL JAZA).
5. Black with white stripes, under Capricorn.

One of the most remarkable pieces of modern work in onyx is said to be the staircase of a New York millionaire. The cost of this is set down as 300,000 dollars.

The **SARDONYX** or Sardian onyx as it is sometimes called was written at various periods as sardonyse, sardony, sardonix, sardonice, sardonyches, sarderyk, sardonique, sardonick. Swedenborg corresponds it to "Love of Good and Light". It exhibits sard and white chalcedony in layers, but some ancient authors account as fine only those specimens which exhibit three layers at least, a black base, a white zone and a layer of red or brown—the black symbolizing humility, the white virtue, and the red fearlessness. The sardonyx is under the heavenly Leo, the sign of sensation, feeling, "the first aspect of its (the soul's) future condition here below." In the Rosicrucian jewels the sardonyx appears as the gem of victorious ecstasy and rapture which flow from the eternal font of delight, banishing grief and woe. It was said to give self-control, conjugal happiness and good fortune, and it is said that if the woman whose talismanic stone it is neglects to wear it she will never marry. It was frequently engraved with an eagle or a hawk as a talisman of fortune and it is under the celestial Leo.

The "Sainte Chapelle," the second largest cameo known, is stated by Sir William Smith and others to measure 12 x 10½ inches. Mr. C. W. King gives the measurements as about 13 x 11 inches and states that it is a sardonyx of five layers. The central carving of this "Grand Camahieu," as it was called, represents the return of Germanicus from Germany in the year 17 A.D., Tiberius and Livia enthroned receiving him. In exergue, the grief-stricken captives are shown. Above is the apotheosis of Augustus by which the whole work is now known. This remarkable cameo was for a long time believed to typify "the triumph of Joseph in Egypt," and was regarded as a sacred relic. The learned Nicholas Claude Fabri de Peiresc, the great antiquary of France, proved in 1619 the falsity of this inconceivable belief, and was the first to classify correctly the subject of this massive gem. By pawning this sardonyx to Louis X of France

Large and rare cameo. The Argonauts Consulting Hygieia.
Kelsey I. Newman Collection

for 10,000 silver marks the unfortunate Baldwin II, Emperor of Constantinople, was able to save his throne a little longer. This cameo is in the
Bibliotheque Nationale, Paris.

Another five strata sardonyx cameo—the largest known—is the
Carpegna cameo, formerly in the possession of Cardinal Carpegna and
now in the Vatican. This large specimen is 16 inches long by 12 inches.
"The subject," writes Mr. King, "is the *Pompa di Bacco*, or Bacchus and
Ceres," Virgil's *"duo clarissima mundi lumina*," as symbolizing the Sun and
Moon, standing upon a magnificent car: the god holding a vase and a
thyrsus, the goddess her bunch of wheat ears. On his right stands winged
Comus. The car is drawn by 4 centaurs, two male and two female: the
first bears a rhyton and a thyrsus, the second a torch whilst he snaps the
fingers of his right hand: one female centaur plays the double flute, the
other a tambourine. On the ground lie the mystic basket and two huge
vases.

The large cameo, 9 x 8 inches, known as the "Coronation of Augustus" shows that Emperor enthroned, holding a scepter in his right hand
with Livia by his side as Roma, etc. Between Augustus and Livia is
the zodiacal sign Capricorn, under the third degree of which Augustus
was born according to Firmicus. Beneath the various figures (Neptune,

Cybele, Drusus, Tiberius, Victory, Antonia, wife of Drusus as Abundantia, and her children Germanicus and Claudius), are Roman soldiers erecting trophies, their unhappy captives in the foreground.

The word "cameo" is said to be of unknown derivation. Dr. Brewer says it means "onyx" and there seems evidence enough to indicate that on account of the great use of onyx and sardonyx for cutting symbolic figures in relief, the term onyx was usually accepted as indicating the completed work. The derivation from the Arabic CHEMEIA, a charm, is noted by Mr. King who draws attention to the light in which such relics were universally considered in those ages by Orientals and Europeans alike. The Arabic word has affinity with the Talmudic Hebrew word KHEMEIA, an amulet, and there seems little reason to doubt that *Chemeia* or *Khemeia* is the parent of our word "cameo," known in the ancient world as an onyx, meaning a charm, an amulet or a talisman.

CHAPTER 22

THE OPAL

OPAL

"Everyone knows how capriciously the colors of a fine opal vary from day to day and how rare the lights are which fully bring them out."

—RUSKIN

The word "opal" is derived from the Latin OPALUS, and is identified with the Sanskrit UPALA, a precious stone. It appears under the forms opale, opall, opalle, opalis, ophal.

This beautiful inimitable gem is a hydrous silica, and is allied to the non-metallic minerals of the agate family from which, however, it differs in brilliancy, luster and degree of hardness. It is sensitive to the action of strong chemicals and does not present, like other minerals, crystalline form. As a gem of the Sun it exhibits flows of fire like the sun at midsummer—as a gem of Venus its delicate beauty radiates her colorful charms, and as a gem of Uranus its refusal to submit to the all-embracing law of mineral structure harmonizes with the iconoclastic character of that planet according to astro-philosophy.

"Grey years ago a man lived in the east,
Who did possess a ring of worth immense,
From a beloved hand. Opal the stone,
Which flashed a hundred bright and beauteous hues,
And had the secret power to make beloved
Of God and man the blessed and fortunate
Who wore it in this faith and confidence."

—"NATHAN THE WISE," LESSING

There are a number of varieties of opal:

CACHOLONG. An opaque white or bluish-white variety of opal which obtains its name from the river Cach in Bokhara, according to some authorities, and from the Tartars according to others. The Easterns set a high value on the stone which glistens with the opalescent gleam of Mother of Pearl. It is associated with chalcedony and being of a porous nature sticks to the tongue when touched by it. The cacholong is a stone of pure friendship, sincerity and truth.

FLOAT STONE. A porous opal of a fibrous type which floats on water. It occurs in concretionary masses and is esteemed as a stone over which the most sacred promises may be made. Lovers join hands over a float stone floating on a vessel of water and pledge their troth with the utmost solemnity, misfortune being bound to dog the footsteps of the faithless one.

GIRASOL. The girasol is the Mexican fire opal which reflects hyacinth and yellow colors. Good specimens are attractive and fairly popular. This is the opal indicated in Scott's *Anne of Geierstein*.

HYALITE. The name is derived from the Greek word for glass, and the stone—a transparent glass-like opal—has been called Muller's glass by Dr. A. G. Werner who is said to have discovered it. It is very like clear gum arabic and is probably one of the esteemed eye stones of the old writers.

HYDROPHANE. This variety of opal is very porous and beautifully translucent and opalescent after being left for a little time in water. It is otherwise of an opaque white or yellow and not very attractive. In the United States it has been termed Magic Stone.

MENILITE. This variety is found in slate not far from the French capital. It is termed also liver opal, and is said to have talismanic action on that organ. It is a concretionary opal, brown or liver-colored.

OPAL JASPER. Opal jasper is a jasper-like resinous, dark red, ferruginous variety of opal, identified as the opal of beautiful wisdom.

ROSE OPAL. A beautiful rose-colored opal found at Quincy in France. This is the opal of the baby Cupid and is termed the opal of Childhood.

SEMI-OPAL. A silicified wood-opal of waxy luster, transparent to opaque. It is found in various colors—white, brown, grey, red, blue, green. It has the appearance of petrified wood. It is a tree-growing charm and is no doubt the forest opal.

TABASHEER. Corrupted from *Tabixir*, is a siliceous aggregation found in the joints of certain bamboo known in the Malay as the Mali Mali, Rotan jer' nauf (blood of the dragon Rattan) and Buluh Kasap (rough bamboo). In appearance it is generally like clear gum arabic, although sometimes opaque, and is the sap transformed by evaporation. Under reflective light it is a kind of blue, and under transmitted light it is either light yellow or amber-red. It is extremely absorptive.

In Marco Polo's account of the expedition of the Great Kaan against Chipangu, we are told that

> "when the people of the Kaan had landed on the great Island they stormed a tower belonging to some of the islanders who refused to surrender. Resistance being overcome, the Kaan's soldiers cut off the heads of all the garrison except eight. On these eight they found it impossible to inflict any wound. Now this was by virtue of certain stones which they had in their arms inserted between the skin and flesh with such skill as not to show at all externally. And the charm and virtue of the stones were such that those who wore them would never perish by steel. So when the Kaan's generals heard this they ordered that the prisoners be beaten to death with clubs. After their death the stones were extracted from their bodies and were greatly prized."

Friar Odoric says that these Stones of Invulnerability were tabashir specimens which were used by the natives of the Indian Islands where their virtue was esteemed. According to Avicenna, the tabashir was a powerful eye stone and remover of past fears, present dreads and future anxieties.

PSEUDOMORPHIC OPAL. The word PSEUDOMORPH is derived from the Greek PSEUDO and MORPHES, disguising one's form.

Opalized shells, bones, etc., are found in quantities in opal country. These specimens are unique and of much curious interest. A number of shells from the new fields 150 miles North West of Tarcoola (on the East-West Railway, over 250 miles from Port Augusta) were submitted to the author. In these the silica slowly and progressively took the place of the primary substance until it was completely opalized, the old form of the material being only retained.

It is remarkable to contemplate the change of conditions which placed the former substance so completely at the mercy of the consuming opal. Such transformation is continual in Nature, manifesting variously in the mineral world, proving that eternal progress is eternal change. It was the observation of similar material phenomena that led ancient scientists to the conclusion that transformations could be accomplished by the skill, knowledge and wisdom of sincere and gifted men who undaunted by superficial criticism persevered, and the triumphs of the chemist served to indicate how much more could be done by those brave enough to prove the immortality of man by reducing the unknown to terms of the known.

The Opal in Myth and History

Ancient and modern poets unite in singing the praises of the opal. Onomacritus, known as the religious poet of the ancient Greeks, over 2,400 years ago wrote that "the delicate color and tenderness of the opal reminded him of a loving and beautiful child." Joshua Sylvester (16th century) writes of "the opal-colored morn," and the poet Campbell of a time when "the opal morn just flushed the sky," thus echoing William Drummond of Hawthornden's:

"*Aurora … with her opal light*
Night's horrors checketh, putting stars to flight."

Emerson writes of the "opal-colored days," and Poe with true poetic fancy sees even the air opal tinted:

"*A wreath that twined each starry form around*
And all the opal'd air in color bound."

Shakespeare in *Twelfth Night* links the mind of the Duke with the opal (written "opall" in early editions.) Boetius, Cardanus and a host of writers pay their tributes to the "orphan" of the Greeks, and Petrus Arlensis writes:

"The various colors in the opal tend greatly to the delectation of the sight; nay, more, they have the greatest efficacy in cheering the heart, and the inward parts especially rejoice the eyes of the beholders. One in particular came into my hands in which such beauty, loveliness and grace shone forth that it could truly boast that it forcibly drew all other gems to itself, while it surprised, astonished and held captive without escape or intermission the hearts of all who beheld it. It was of the size of a filbert and clasped in the claws of a golden eagle wrought with wonderful art; and had such vivid and various colors that all the beauties of the heavens might be viewed within it. Grace went out from it, majesty shot forth from its almost divine splendor. It sent forth such bright and piercing rays that it struck terror into all beholders.

"In a word it bestowed upon the wearer the qualities granted by Nature to itself, for by an invisible dart it penetrated the souls and dazzled the eyes of all who saw it: appalled all hearts, however bold and courageous: in fine, it filled with trembling the bodies of the bystanders and forced them by a fatal impulse to love, honor and worship it. I have seen, I have felt, I call God to witness: of a truth such a stone is to be valued at an inestimable amount."

Turning back again, we read Pliny's poetical opinion that

"the opal is made up of the glories of the most precious gems which make description so difficult. For amongst them is the gentler fire of the ruby, the rich purple of the amethyst, the sea-green of the emerald, glittering together in union indescribable. Others by the intensity of their hues equal all the painter's colors, others the flame of burning brimstone or of fire quickened by oil."

In admiration the Romans called the gem *Cupid-Paederos*, child beautiful as love, and it was also known as *Orphanus*, the orphan, because of its isolated glory. Leonardus wrote that it partook of all the virtues of those stones whose colors it showed, and Porta said that it not only drove away despondency but malignant affections also. So highly valued was the stone in the ancient world that the Roman Senator Nonius, who wore an opal ring worth 20,000 sesterces, preferred to be exiled by Marcus Antonius, who wished to purchase it to present to the Egyptian Queen Cleopatra, to giving it up. This famous ring was some few years back discovered in the tomb of the firm-willed senator of old Rome.

Opal was called *Opthalmios* or Eye Stone in the Middle Ages, and in the time of Queen Elizabeth it was written ophal and opall. Our "Rare" Ben Jonson writes of an opal "wrapped in a bay leaf in my left fist to charm their eyes with." The opal—ophthalmis lapis—was famous as an eyestone, taking precedence over the emerald and all gems credited with such virtue. It was advised by medieval writers that it be wrapped in a bay leaf to sharpen the sight of the owner and to blunt that of others with whom he came in contact: hence also its reputed virtue of bestowing the gift of invisibility which earned it the name "*Patronus furum*," the patron of thieves.

The Bay tree is identified in astro-philosophy as a tree of the Sun and the zodiacal Leo (House of the Sun), and is an ancient recognized charm against evil forces, thunder, lightning and the afflictions of Saturn which is the heavenly symbol of darkness, as the Sun is the heavenly symbol of light. Albertus Magnus, regarding the opal as a symbol of the loveliness of light, says that "at one time, but not in our age, it sparkled in the dark." The zodiacal Leo or Lion is the ancient recognized sign of royalty and old writers say that kingly government was established on the earth in the Leonine age. Alluding to the great translucent opal in the Crown of the Holy Roman Empire, Albertus said that it safeguarded the honor of the kings.

The stone was always considered to protect the wearer from cholera, kidney troubles, and similar diseases, to soothe the heart, the eyes and the nerves, and to protect from the lightning strike. The belief in its power to ward off lightning was universal in the ancient world when amongst the people it was believed to have fallen from the heavens during thunder storms—hence its old name, KERAUNIOS, thunder stone, amongst the Greeks, and CERAUNIUM amongst the Romans.

The opal was essentially the stone of beauty, which coveted gift it bestowed upon the wearer who, however, must have entered earth life with the Sun in Leo (approximately between July 24th and August

24th), Libra (September 24th to October 24th) or Aquarius (January 21st to February 19th). It favored children, the theatre, amusements, friendships, and the feelings. Held between the eyes it gave proper direction to the thoughts. Held in the left hand and gazed upon it favored the desires. It is the stone of hope and achievement and has been truly described as the "gem of the gods." Above all, it is a stone of love, but if the lover be false its influence is reversed, and the opal proves a sorry gem for faithless lovers.

Mr. Emanuel comments on the two fine opals which were amongst the imperial jewels of France, one of which was set in the clasp of the royal cloak. The opal, astrologically considered, is one of the fortunate gems for France. A beautiful uncut opal discovered at Czernovitza in Hungary has been valued at over £50,000 sterling; this specimen, in length 5 inches by 2½ and weighing 3,000 carats, was placed in the Museum of Natural History at Vienna. The mines at Czernovitza are known to have been worked over 500 years ago, and at a more remote period they no doubt supplied the ancient world.

There is little doubt, however, that the wonderful opals from Australia's fields have eclipsed anything yet found. The White Cliffs, the Lightning Ridge, and the newer field out North West are responsible for some of the most beautiful gems that have ever been unearthed. A kangaroo hunter accidentally discovered the White Cliffs field in New South Wales over 40 years ago whilst following the trail of a kangaroo. Rich "blacks" were discovered later in the iron sandstone of Lightning Ridge (New South Wales) and the new fields North West of Tarcoola are yielding white and light varieties. Opal country is dry and dreary and the diggers deserve all they find.

Sir David Brewster's theory of the color blends which flash from an opal is that "the stone is internally traversed with undulating fissures of microscopic minuteness upon which refraction and decomposition of light takes place. The variations in the nature of these minute cavities cause the appearance of the opal to vary considerably, and the different effects of color thus produced are technically known as the pattern of the gem." Hauy held that color in the opal is caused by thin films of air which fill the interior cavities.

Dr. G. F. Herbert Smith writes

"that the coloration is not due to ordinary absorption but to the action of cracks in the stone. This is shown by the fact that the transmitted light is complementary to the reflected light; the blue opal, for instance, is a yellow when held up so that light has passed through it . . . . Opal differs from the rest of the principal gem stones in being not a crystalline body but a solidified jelly, and it depends for its attractiveness upon the characteristic play of color known, in consequence, as opalescence which arises from a peculiarity in the structure.

"Opal is mainly silica (SiO_2) in composition, but it contains in addition an amount of water, thereby differing slightly in refractivity from the original substance. The structure not being quite homogeneous, each crack has the same action upon light as a soap-film and gives rise to precisely similar phenomena: the thinner and more uniform the cracks, the greater the splendor of the chromatic display, the particular tint depending upon the direction in which the stone is viewed. The cracks in certain opals are not filled up, and therefore contain air."

The opal is a very sensitive gem and should not be put near strong acids nor greasy substances. The heat of the body improves its luster for the opal is essentially a stone to be worn, but it is unsafe to put these gems near liquids or to submit them to fire.

"Truth is as impossible to be soiled by any outward touch as the sunbeam."

—MILTON

Perhaps against no other gem has the bigotry of superstitious ignorance so prevailed as against the wonderful opal. The reason for it dates no further back apparently than the 14th century. It was at this time that the dreaded "Black Death" was carrying off thousands of people in Europe. The year 1348, an astrological Martial sub-cycle, saw Venice assailed by destructive earthquakes, tidal waves and the Plague. The epidemic in a few months carried off two-fifths of the population of the city, sparing neither rich nor poor, young nor old.

It is said that at this time the opal was a favorite gem with Italian jewelers, being much used in their work. It is further said that opals worn by those stricken became suddenly brilliant and that the luster entirely departed with the death of the wearer. Story further tells that the opal then became an object of dread and was associated with the death of the victim. On the astrological side it might be considered that the city of Venice comes under the watery Cancer, and cannot, therefore, claim the opal as its jewel. But, admitting that under special and rare conditions certain diseases can influence the opal if worn on the body, the truth of the Venice story can be reasonably doubted.

Another theory of the origin of the superstition is traced to the rigorous order of Jerome Savonarola for the destruction of the vanities in the year 1497. This remarkable ascetic caused great bonfires to be lighted in various parts of the city of Florence, the largest in the Piazza Signoria. Into these bonfires were thrown works of art and beauty, pictures, statues, jewels and beautiful raiment. The fanatical spirit so gained ground owing to the impassioned preaching of Savonarola that women threw into the flames their costliest jewels, authors their books, students their manuscripts and poets their love songs.

It is assumed that the opal, the gem and symbol of the beauties of Venus came under the ban, and history relates that the most direct onslaughts were made on the pictures and statues of the goddess. Astrologers show that the year 1497 was dominated by the planet of war and destruction, Mars, and it is deplorable that so many wonderful works were sacrificed during that unhappy period. The artist F. W. W. Topham, R. I., has illustrated this event in his well-known painting "Renouncing the Vanities by Order of Savonarola," which picture now hangs in the Art Gallery of New South Wales.

There is also a story which tells that during the Crimean War the gem was popular with the English army and navy and that it was found in quantities on the bodies of the slain. Sir Walter Scott's romantic story *Anne of Geierstein*, was a powerful influence in advancing the superstition against the opal, although Sir Walter alluded to the Mexican opal known as girasol, and not to the better known precious opal. Even whilst these superstitions were growing, to dream of an opal was regarded as an indication of great possessions, of the favor of ladies and people of influence, and—if the stone be dark—of sudden happenings of a beneficial nature.

Another modern superstition says that it is not fortunate to set opals and diamonds together in jewels. Qabalistically, opals and diamonds are set down as particularly harmonious stones which, in combination, have a fortunate and positive-negative influence. Astrologically the diamond is attached to the zodiacal signs Aries, Leo and Libra, and the opal to Leo, Libra and Aquarius, and astrology is absolutely the special guide to talismanic construction.

The fine fiery opal known as the "Burning of Troy" given by Napoleon to Josephine, is sometimes quoted as evidence of the evil power of opals. It rather provides peculiar testimony in favor of old talismanic lore. This opal was lost and has never since been found—opals would be regarded as unfavorable for Josephine. Passing over trivial superstitions containing neither truth nor interest, we may conclude this section with the story of the Grand Opal of Spain which is said to have brought disaster to the Royal House:

When Alfonzo XII of Spain was a wanderer he was deeply attracted by, and fell in love with the Comtesse de Castiglione, then a reigning beauty. Immediately Alfonzo became King the Comtesse hastened to greet him with the fond desire to become his queen. However, when she found that he had set her aside and married the Princess Mercedes her anger knew no bounds. Resolving on revenge, she sent Alfonzo "in memory of the old friendship" a wedding present of a magnificent opal set in a filigree ring of gold—a style of mounting in great favor with the jewelers of Spain.

The delicacy of the jewel so attracted Queen Mercedes that she asked the King to grace her finger with it. A few months afterwards she died of a mysterious illness and Alfonzo gave the ring so admired by her to Queen Christina, his grandmother, whose death shortly followed. The King then presented the ring to his sister the Infanta Maria del Pilar, who was in turn carried off by the same mysterious illness. A few weeks afterwards the King's sister-in-law, the youngest daughter of the Duc and Duchesse de Montpensier, who had asked the King for the ring also died. The King then placed it on his own finger and in a little time the same illness which had affected his wife and kindred ended his troubled earth-life.

After these calamities Queen Christina attached the ring to a chain of gold and set it about the neck of the patron saint of Madrid, the Virgin

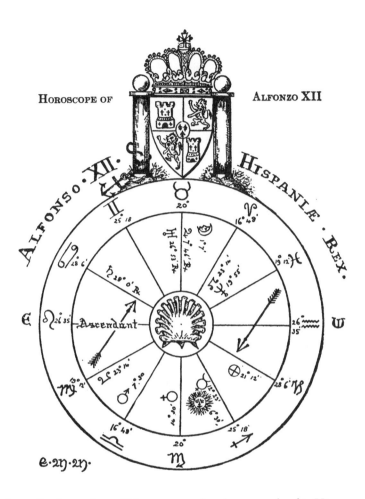

HOROSCOPE OF   ALFONZO **XII**

Astrologically the opal would be accounted unfortunate for this King.

of Alumdena. Ancient philosophy would have depreciated the wearing or giving of an opal by Alfonzo XII of Spain. At this time it must be remembered that cholera was raging throughout Spain—over 100,000 people died of it during the summer and autumn of 1885. It attacked all classes from the palace of the King to the hut of the peasant, some accounts giving the death estimate at 50% of the population. It would be as obviously ridiculous to hold the opal responsible for this scourge as it was to do so in the case of the previously noted plague at Venice.

All that may be said is that in this case the opal was not a talisman of good for King Alfonzo XII of Spain and to those who received
it from his hand, and that in the philosophy of sympathetic attraction
and apathetic repulsion man, stones, metals and all natural objects come
under the same law. We may wonder why the King gave this opal from
one of his relatives to another, but the reputation of the opal as a charm
against cholera (noted previously) must have reached the King who, in
the intensity of his worry, used a charm which according to the ancients
would act in his hands fatally instead of beneficially.

In the month of October, 1908, a French Baron sitting in the stalls
of the London Pavilion during Mr. and Mrs. Marriott's thought-read-
ing exhibition, handed an opal of uncommon form to Mr. Marriott.
Mrs. Marriott seated on the stage with bandaged eyes gave an accurate
description of it, saying further that it was a stone of fortune to the owner
who was about to become the possessor of over half a million of money.
The Baron, who had resided in London for the past 18 years, when inter-
viewed by a representative of the *Evening News* on the following day,
communicated the fact that a few days before, he had, through the death
of a relative in Mexico become heir to property worth over £500,000,
yielding an income of £25,000 per annum. The Baron, who cherished
the opal as his sympathetic luck stone, told the newspaper man that:

> "It is an uncut stone which has been in the possession of my family
> since the twelfth century. We have always had the tradition that it will
> bring good fortune to any direct descendant of the family in the male
> line who holds it.
>
> "A curious stipulation, however, of the tradition is that the person
> who has it must possess qualities which have a sympathetic attraction
> to the stone in order that its beneficent effect may be felt. On a flat sur-
> face of the opal is a word in old Spanish, now only dimly seen, which
> means in English 'good luck.'
>
> "I have treasured the gem as an heirloom, but have thought little
> of the tradition until lately, when a member of the cadet branch of the
> family died and left me the immense fortune I have mentioned to you.
> I can hardly realize all that it means to me as yet. Up to now my income
> has not been much more than £500, and to suddenly find £25 ,000 a
> year at one's disposal is a little staggering.

"There have been one or two previous instances where my ancestors while holding the opal have experienced exceptionally good luck,
but, personally, I have not ever paid much regard to the old tradition.
You may imagine, however, that the gem will be most carefully preserved by me."

"But who can paint
Like Nature? Can imagination boast
Amid its gay creation hues like hers?"
    —THOMSON

The Flame Queen

The Flame Queen—the rarest stone yet won from the barren sun-baked
opal fields of Lightning Ridge, New South Wales, near the borders of
Queensland, Australia—takes its place amongst the famous gems of the
world.

It is a large oval-shaped stone measuring 2.8 inches by 2.3 inches, and
weighing 253 carats. In structure and color phenomena it is unique—the
center slightly in relief whilst the surrounding border stands out boldly as
a frame to a picture. Looking directly on to the stone the inspiration of
the name becomes manifest. The center, a deep flame, burns scarlet, and
two slight depressions almost parallel to each other give the impression
of fire mountains in eruptive action, the lower of which flings two triangular shafts towards the enclosing green frame. Viewed from another
angle the burning center yields as if by magic to a field of cool yet vivid
emerald, and the frame to a royal blue. Another angle shows a bronze
center touched with points of darker hue within a frame of changing
blue and amethyst. The stone is chameleon-like, bewildering in its living beauty.

This stone is the choicest gem in the Kelsey I. Newman collection
of rare opals and precious stones. On the 6th of March, 1916, Mr. Allan
Harris of Brisbane submitted the gem to the Queensland Geological Sur-
vey. In the course of his report Mr. B. Dunstan, the chief Government
Geologist, mentions that the back of the stone "is impressed with what
appears to be a fossil plant called *ginko*, which occurs in the Jurassic rocks

of Queensland but not in association with any opal deposits. The stone is a wonderful specimen and much the largest gem of its class that has ever come under my notice."

This beautiful opal—unlike some other famous gems mentioned in this book—is said to have brought good fortune to all who have been associated with it.

CHAPTER 23

Pearl

PEARL

"Searching the wave I won therefrom a pearl
Moonlike and glorious, such as kings might buy
Emptying their treasury."

—Arnold

The name "pearl" is derived from the Latin *Pilula*, diminutive of *Pila*, a ball, and some of the forms of the word noted are perle, peerle, perl, peril, perill, pearel, peirle, pearle. The pearl is a product of certain salt and fresh water shellfish of the *Aviculidae* family. It is formed by the efforts of the mollusk to rid itself of irritating substances by the iridescent fluid secretion with which he lines his shell. The effect of this irritation is shown in a number of irregular tubercles inside the shell, and within these coverings is the securely protected pearl. Frequently pearls of most beautiful luster and form are found detached from the shell in the fleshy folds of the oyster, and these are said to be the most perfect. It is now quite certain that disease is not the cause, as has so generally been believed.

Amongst the ancient writers so much of the purely symbolic was set down in perfectly plain, matter-of-fact language that it is difficult to make assertions as to what was really known of the material truth. Both Pliny and Discorides poetically state that dew or rain from Heaven fell into the open pearl shells and were transformed by the secretions of the oyster into precious pearls. There is an old legend which tells that the tears of joy shed by the angels for the ultimate destiny of man were the tears that fell into the pearl oyster shell to be transformed into beautiful pearls. Moore delightfully refers to this story:

"Precious the tear as that rain from the sky
Which turns into pearls as it falls in the sea."

The philosopher Anicius Boethius, of the 5th and 6th centuries, A.D., writes that the fresh water pearl mussels of the Scotch rivers, the sky being clear and the weather temperate, open their mouths just a little above water to catch the heavenly dews, which, when swallowed, cause the breeding of pearls. These mussels, continues the philosopher, are so sensitive that the slightest noise causes them to sink to the bottom of the river. He credits them with "knowing well in what estimation the fruit of their womb is to all people." Vishnu, according to Indian mythology, created pearls MOTI by his word, and consequently these gems are foremost in the adornment of Indian deities. The Ramayana, perhaps the greatest poem of ancient India, narrates the story of the death of Maha Bali, telling that pearls sprung from the teeth of the slain god.

In the winter of 1673 the naturalist Sandius sent —on the authority of "Henricus Arnoldi, an ingenious Dane"—a letter, from which the following is extracted, to the newly formed Royal Society of London:

> "Pearl shells in Norway do breed in sweet waters: their shells are like mussels but larger: the fish is like an oyster, it produces clusters of eggs: these, when ripe, are cast out and become like those that cast them: but sometimes it appears that one or two of these eggs stick fast to the side of the matrix and are not voided with the rest. These are fed by the oyster against her will, and they do grow, according to the length of time, into pearls of different bigness, and do imprint a mark both on fish and shell by the situation conform to its figure."

The eminent surgeon, Sir Everard Home, unaware of the letter of Sandius, arrived at the same conclusion independently. He writes that this, "the richest jewel in a monarch's crown which cannot be imitated by any art of man, either in beauty of form or brilliancy of luster, is the abortive egg of an oyster enveloped in its own nacre."

Darwin (*Economy of Vegetation*) writes that pearls are formed "like those calcareous productions of crabs known by the name of 'crabs' eyes' which are always near the stomach of the creature. In both cases the substance is probably a natural provision either for the reparation or enlargement of the shell."

Mr. Kelaart in his reports to the Government of Ceylon (1857–1859), seems to be the first to allude to the part played by parasites in the production of pearls in tropical seas. The researches of Professors Herdman and Hornel confirmed the deductions of Kelaart that the larva of a Cestoid was the identified pearl parasite. Monsieur Seurat, the French naturalist, who made a long study of the pearl oyster of the Pacific, was also convinced that pearl formation was caused by a parasite.

Whatever the cause of the irritability which brings into action the nacreous secretion of the tortured oyster, it is evident that the protective process is a long one. The pearl culture industry of the Chinese and Japanese has shown that it takes twelve months for the irritant to be covered with a coat of a tenth of a millimeter. A new layer is formed over the old one about once a year. Pearlers say that an oyster must be at least four years old before pearls begin to form properly, and that it does not mature for from 7 to 9 years.

The beautiful luster of the pearl Sir Everard Home held to arise from a central cell of bright nacre, the diaphanous substance admitting the light rays. "Upon taking a split pearl," he writes, "and putting a candle behind the cell, the surface of the pearl became immediately illuminated; and upon mounting one with colored foil behind the cell, and by putting a candle behind the foil, the outer convex surface became universally of a beautiful pink color." The examination of a half pearl will show the concentric formation which is like an onion, and the process called "skinning" is often resorted to in the endeavor to gain a more lustrous jewel by removing the outer layer. The translucency of the perfect pearl has not been correctly reproduced by any artificial production.

A curious passage in Jerome Cardan's *De Rerum Varietate* (16th century), repeats an old saying that the luster and polish on pearls arises from doves playing with them. To understand this seemingly absurd story it is necessary to carry our minds far back to the famous Greek oracle at Dodona in Epirus. According to Herodotus the Phoenicians carried off the sacred women from Thebes in Egypt to the Libyan oracle of Zeus Ammon and to Dodona—the legend at Dodona saying that they came in the form of two doves.

The Greek word for "doves" is the same as that for "priestesses," namely, PELEIAI. The connection can be carried further, if necessary, but it is sufficient to establish the tie between women and the doves. The word PELEIAI was freely used for both and came to be employed as an endearing term for wise women just as we today call a woman of talent "Diva." It is a proven fact and an extremely ancient one that pearls worn near the skin of a woman—especially, according to ancient philosophy, near one in whose horoscope the moon was powerfully placed at birth—are improved in luster and tone. So let the "Doves" (or *Peleiai*) be wise and play with their pearls.

Tavernier writes of "the most beautiful pearl in the world" which belonged to Imenheit, Prince of Muscat. After a, lavish entertainment which the Khan of Ormus gave in honor of the Prince, the latter took off a chain which he wore round his neck and to which was attached a small bag. From the bag he drew forth this wonderful pearl of perfect sphericity, so translucent that the light could almost be seen through it. The weight of this gem was 12 carats and so high a value did Prince Imenheit place on it that he refused 2,000 tomans for it from his host, the Khan of Ormus, who coveted it as a present for the King of Persia, and 40,000 crowns with which he was later tempted by an agent of the Grand Mogul. This pearl was discovered off the Persian coast.

Another great pearl which, according to Tavernier, was the most perfect ever discovered, was found at Catifa, a famous fishery in Pliny's time. The great traveler says that the King of Persia obtained it from an Arabian merchant in 1633. It was a pearl of great size and a "pearl of great price," the King giving 1,400,000 livres (about $550,000) for it. It was pear-shaped, and of perfect color and symmetry. The weight is not stated, but it was said to be about 1½ inches in length and 2½ inches in diameter at its greatest part.

The "Hope" pearl of cylindrical form weighs 454 carats. This gem belonged to Mr. Henry Thomas Hope, so well-known in connection with the "Hope" diamond. Another famous pearl of 300 carats once adorned the Imperial crown of Austria. "La Pellegrina," an Indian white circular pearl of 28 carats, said to be the most perfect specimen in the world today, was in the Zosima Museum, Moscow.

Nine large pearls interlinked so as to naturally form a true representation of the Southern Cross were discovered in a pearl oyster off the West Australian Coast by Mr. Kelly, of Roeburn, who was familiarly known as "Shiner" Kelly. The crew of his lugger viewed it with superstitious fear and it was buried for some years. It was afterwards resurrected and exhibited at the Colonial and Indian exhibition, London, in 1886, where it caused some sensation. The pearls which formed the cross were at first thought by many to be joined together by craft, but experts with powerful magnifying glasses speedily dispelled this illusion and proved that nature, not man, was the artist who reproduced the Star Cross of the Heavens—the Cross of Australian Unity—in pearls in a sea oyster.

In the year 1579 a pearl of 250 carats was obtained amongst others by the agents of Philip II, of Spain, from the Island of Margarita in the West Indies. It was said to be worth 150,000 dollars. Marco Polo writes that the King of Maabar wears pearls and gems worth more than a city's ransom.

> "Nobody is permitted to take out of his kingdom a pearl weighing more than half a saggio (a Venetian weight, the sixth of an onze), unless he manages to do it secretly. The King every year proclaims through the realm that if anyone possesses a pearl of great worth and will bring it to him, he (the King), will pay three times as much as its value. Everybody is glad to do this and thus the King gets all into his own hands, giving every man his price."

This King wore a necklace on which 104 pearls and rubies of great size were strung on fine silk, and every day, following the custom of his ancestors, he had to say 104 prayers to the gods. The number is disputed but in an occult sense the Tibetan prayer of Victory over the 104 devils seems to confirm it.

The pearl necklace which Muhammad forced the Hindu King Jaipal to surrender to him (1001 A.D.,) is said to have been made of great pearls. It was valued at 20,000 dinars (more than 500,000 dollars). We read in the Book of Genesis of the terrible famine which affected the peoples of the earth and drove them to seek corn in the land of Egypt where doubtless, owing to the great pull on her stocks, some anxiety was beginning to be felt. The Arabian writer, Ebn Hesham, describes a sepulcher in Yemen which had been discovered after some heavy floods. In this sepulcher lay the embalmed body of an Arabian princess around whose neck were 7 strands of pearls, age-stained and lusterless. There were rings set with precious stones on her fingers and toes, 7 jeweled armlets on each of her arms and 7 jeweled anklets about each ankle. In the tomb treasure was found, and on a tablet at her head she had caused to be written the following inscription, the translation of which by Mr. Forster is reproduced by Mr. William Jones, F.S.A.:

"In thy name, O God, the God of Himyar,

I, Tajah, the daughter of Dzu Shefarr, sent my servant to Joseph,

And he, delaying to return to me, I sent my handmaid,

With a measure of silver, to bring me back a measure of flour:

And not being able to procure it, I sent her with a measure of gold:

And not being able to procure it, I commanded them to the ground:

And finding no profit in them, I am shut up here.

Whosoever may hear of it, let him pity me:

And should any woman adorn herself with an ornament

From my ornaments, may she die with no other than my death."

It would be very unlikely that after understanding these last words of the Princess Tajah (a name which qabalistically would imply "the Sacrifice") any woman would be bold enough to attempt to put on the seven ropes of dead pearls and the other jewels that adorned the mortal remains of the famine-stricken princess.

Turning to later times Benvenuto Cellini tells in his interesting memoirs rather an amusing story of a string of pearls which the Duke of Florence purchased for the Duchess from "that scoundrel Bernardini" for several thousand crowns. Princess Catherine Radziwill whose intimacy with the old Courts of Europe is well known, tells of the love of the Russian Empress Marie Alexandrovna (grandmother of the unfortunate Nicholas II), for pearls which she never tired of buying. She wore ropes of from 25 to 30 which, being of varied lengths, would when worn extend from the top to the hem of her dress. She was reputed to have had some of the largest pear-shaped pearls in the world.

James Bruce, the famous traveler (*Travels to Discover the Sources of the Nile*, 1768–1773), writes that the pinna or wing shell mentioned by Pliny which is found with its fiber-like rope on the bed of the Red Sea yields the beautiful pink-tinted pearl so highly prized in ancient and modern times. Red or rose colored pearls are termed by the natives SOHIT-AMUKTI. Marco Polo mentions that they are found off the island of Chipangu, "big, round and rosy, and quite as valuable as white ones." He also writes that when a dead body is burnt one of these pearls is always put in the mouth, "for such is their custom." Pearls of this tint are accounted as precious objects and were used in Buddhist ceremonies and worship.

Julius Caesar was extremely fond of pearls. Caius Suetonius (*Lives of the Caesars*) tells us that he was a great expert and knew so much about them that he could estimate their exact weights "by his hand alone." The same writer tells us that Caesar's love of pearls was the cause of his expedition against Britain, the pearls he obtained there being, greatly to his chagrin, of poor quality and little luster. Nevertheless, we are told he consecrated a breastplate set with British pearls to the temple of Venus Genetrix. It is recorded that Caesar gave Servilia, the mother of Brutus, a pearl worth nearly £50,000 sterling. Pearls in the time of the Caesars were the rage in Rome and women adorned themselves lavishly with them, a custom which drew violent protests from the philosopher Seneca who, alluding to a lady who wore several pearls dangling from each ear, told her husband that his wife "carried all the wealth of his house in her ears."

In the extravagant intoxication of the rich banquet which Cleopatra VII (Tryphena the Great) gave to the honor of Mark Anthony, it is related that this queen—the last of the Ptolemies—throwing one of her valuable pearls into a vinegar solution, swallowed it. The value of this gem is set down as £80,729 sterling. Its companion afterwards graced the statue of the Pantheon Venus at Rome. Cleopatra was not alone in this act of folly for we are informed that Clodius, son of Æsopus the actor, swallowed a pearl valued at £8,072 sterling. Caligula, the Roman Emperor, added this act also to his many acts of stupidity. He too enjoyed the reputation of a "pearl swallower," which title in the reign of Queen Elizabeth was also coveted by Sir Thomas Gresham who quaffed off a large pearl at a banquet which the Queen attended after visiting the Royal Exchange. The poet Heywood alludes to this act in the lines:

> "Here £15,000 at one clap goes
> Instead of sugar: Gresham drinks the pearl
> Unto his Queen and mistress."

Neither pearls nor diamonds were fortunate for Mary Queen of Scots, yet she wore both in profusion. Her wedding dress at her marriage with Philip of Spain is described as being "richly bordered with great pearls and diamonds," whilst she wore the great diamond which Philip had sent to her by the Marquis de las Traves. Mary's nativity favors few jewels but

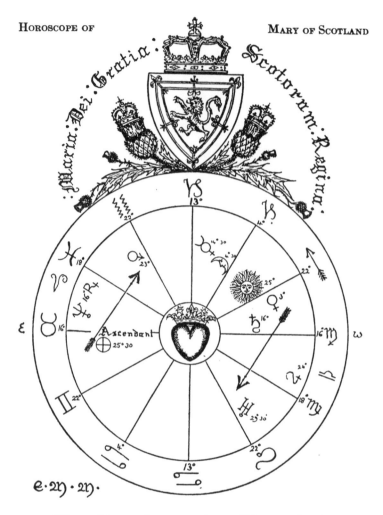

Horoscope of Qyeen Mary indicates pearls would be considered unfortunate

none less than diamonds, pearls and rubies. History relates that, when in the days of her sorrows the Scottish Queen was held captive by the rapacious Earl of Moray, this man who owed her so much sent her exquisite parure of pearls with other costly jewels by his agent, Sir Nicholas Elphinstone to Queen Elizabeth at London.

Madame de Barrera gives the following extract, copy from a letter of Bodutel la Forrest, French ambassador at the English court, describing the pearl parure: "There are six cordons of large pearls strung as pater nosters: but there are five and twenty separate from the rest, much finer

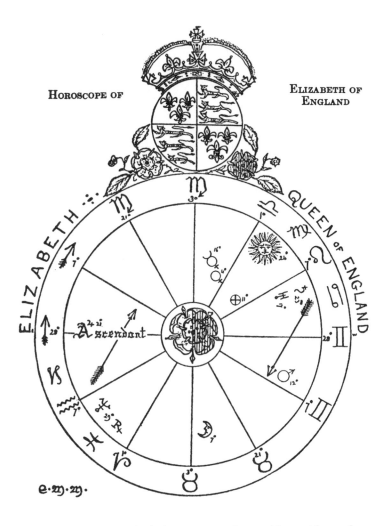

HOROSCOPE OF ELIZABETH OF ENGLAND

Horoscope of Queen Elizabeth demonstrates her problem with pearls

and larger than those which are strung: these are for the most part like black muscades." Elizabeth, after obtaining various expert opinions as to the value of this ornament, eventually purchased it at her own price. But if pearls, fortunate for Scotland, were unfortunate for Mary (for whom Scotland itself was unfortunate), they were doubly so for Elizabeth who had the dark planet Saturn and the subtle Uranus in the sign Cancer at her birth. The two famous diamond rings of Mary and Elizabeth and Elizabeth and Essex are stated to have been the indirect cause of the death of both Mary and Elizabeth.

Old Hebraic legend tells that the manna fell from Heaven, accompanied by showers of pearls and precious stones, and in ancient Judaea it was believed that a pearl wrapped in a bag of leather and tied round the neck of oxen would benefit them and increase their fruitfulness. The Arabs sang that "Nisan's Ram (Sun in Aries) brings pearls to the sea and wheat to the land."

In China the pearl was regarded as the true symbol of ability and so the Chinese character for Pearl (TCHM) was placed on the vases used by artists, poets, scientists and writers, and the term TCHM ONAN is translated as indicating a rare pearl object. Great virtues were ascribed to the pearl by the Chinese and it was, and still is, used medicinally by them chiefly as a remedy for blood disorders, swooning, heart troubles, digestive irregularities and stomach complaints. The ancients used pearls, we are told, as absorbents or antacids and they were given to the weak-minded Charles VI of France in distilled water to cure his insanity. Dissolved in acids they were taken as an absorbent medicine and, as one writer puts it, "for the purpose of displaying the careless opulence and luxury of their possessors."

The Pearl was sacred to the angel Gabriel in the East, and amongst the Muhammadans a great white pearl—the pearl of Paradise—reached from East to West, from Heaven to Earth. This is the Eternal Table of the Koran on which Allah has written all that has been, all that is, and all that is to come. The Arabian Heavenly Home of Glory and the Everlasting Eden of Wonder is, it is related, rich with red pearls.

> "Or where the gorgeous East with richest hand
> Showers on her Kings barbaric pearl and gold."
>
> —MILTON

The benevolent Bishop of Chiapa, Mexico, Bartolome de las Casas, came forth as the protector of the Indians in the cruel times of their oppression. On their behalf he crossed the Atlantic sixteen times, and he tells of the hellish tortures to which they were subjected by their Spanish conquerors: "Nothing," says this good man, "nothing could be more cruel and more detestable." (*Brevissima Relacion de la Destruccion de las Indias*, 1539).

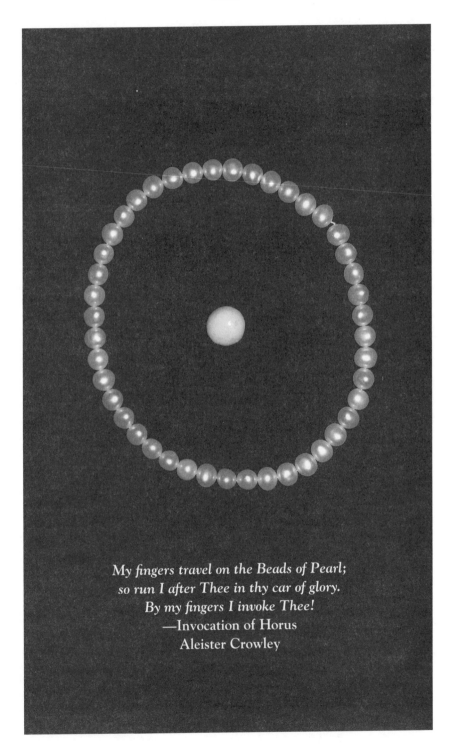

My fingers travel on the Beads of Pearl;
so run I after Thee in thy car of glory.
By my fingers I invoke Thee!
—Invocation of Horus
Aleister Crowley

The story he writes of the Indian pearl divers is a sad one; as soon as the diver came up from the depths the brutal overseer, scarcely allowing him time to breathe the pure air, beat him savagely and compelled him to go down again. His food was poor and scanty, and Mother Earth his bed; his glossy black hair turned prematurely gray, his lungs became diseased, he spat blood freely and the ravenous shark ended his tragic life on earth. The natural result of greed and oppression practically exhausted these fisheries from the neighborhood of which the ancient kings of Mexico drew so much wealth. Indeed, it was the sight of the poor natives adorned with ropes of pearls which excited the cupidity of the first Spaniards who adventured to their shores.

There being no provision made for the protection of the oysters in this fishery, it "gave out" almost entirely towards the end of the 17th century. An idea of the magnitude of these fisheries (which included the ancient grounds between Acapulco and the Gulf of Tehuantepec on the West Mexican coast, and the Caribbean Sea by the islands of Coche, Cubagua, and Margarita) can be gathered from the value of the export to Europe up to the first half of the 16th century. The annual value exported was stated to exceed 800,000 Spanish dollars, those famous "Pieces of Eight" which bring us back to the time of *Treasure Island* and the buccaneers of the Spanish Main.

As much as 700 lbs. weight of pearls was sent to Seville in the year 1587, amongst them, it is stated, being specimens of rare worth and beauty. Fine quality pearls are still found at Panama and the Gulf of Mexico. The poor progress of these fisheries is said to be due to the wretched pay offered to the Indian and negro divers in the past. It is a strange fact that progress and prosperity are gained only by the pursuance of an enlightened policy towards employees, and this is nowhere so clearly indicated as in the history of the pearl.

Pearls from the Persian Gulf are amongst the most esteemed of the present day. The fisheries of the Great Pearl Bank extend along the West from Ras Hassan half way up the Gulf. To the Eastern no pearl is so beautiful and full of color as the pearl from the Persian Gulf. The color is very enduring and improves by being worn next the skin—especially of a person whose jewel it is. The Ceylon fisheries have not been yielding so well of late years, but with wisdom will no doubt regain their old place. The main oyster bank is near Condatchy, about twenty miles from the shore. Twenty men, ten of whom are divers, under a *Tindal* or captain, comprise the crew of each boat. The divers are quick and expert at their work, and although remaining under water seldom more than a minute, have been known to bring to the surface as many as 150 shells.

The pearl diver's greatest dread is the ground shark, and all the time the boats are out the conjurer, termed the "Binder of Sharks" or "*Pillal Harras*," stands on the shore muttering prayers and conjurations. The divers wear also a pearl about their bodies as a charm against their dreaded enemy. The beautiful island of Ceylon—the Taprobane of the old Greeks and Romans and the Serendib of the *Arabian Nights*—is itself shaped like a great drop pearl and is believed by the Indians to be a "part of Paradise."

Perfectly round and fine luster pearls are called by the Ceylonese "*Annees*," next in grade are called "*Annadaree*." Irregular pearls of lesser luster are called "*Kayarel*," generally known amongst us as "Baroques." Pearl-shaped inferior specimens are called "*Samadiem*," those duller and irregular are termed "*Kallipoo*," a poorer grade again is known as "*Koorwell*," and the lowest type is "*Pesul*." Small seed pearls are known as "*Tool*."

Cleopatra's famous pearls no doubt came from the Red Sea fisheries which are believed to have been the property of the Egyptian rulers. The Western Australian fisheries, especially those at Broome and Shark's Bay, are yearly becoming of greater importance and value, although judicious and scientific means should be taken to prevent these valuable fields from sharing the fate of some of the older ones. The fisheries at Thursday Island and Northern Australia are important and the author was told that pearls were discovered in New Guinea through a sailors' row with the natives, who pelted the offending lugger with pearl-bearing shells which, when broken on the decks of the vessel, revealed their precious prizes.

The remarkable Town of the Nymphs near the Japanese city of Ishinomonsky on the Pacific coast obtains its name from the women who support their families by diving for pearls. It is a place of many centuries old and the nymphs begin their strenuous work at the age of 14, continuing until they are 40. Pearl shells abound in Sebiam Bay and the work of the nymphs occupies 10 hours a day in summer time. The length of each immersion is from 2 to 3 minutes. When the baby girl is four years of age, she is taken to the sea and taught to swim and dive. These lessons continue until the time comes for the serious practice of the pearl seek-ers' profession. This work is all done by women whilst the men attend to the training of the children and the duties of the household.

Mention may also be made of the River fisheries of England, Scotland, Wales, Ireland and various parts of Europe where the pearls found are as a rule not of great importance, although it is stated that Sir Richard Wynn of Gwydyr, Chamberlain to Catherine, wife of Charles II, sent a pearl from the river Conway in North Wales as a present to the Queen, which pearl is today in the King of England's crown. In Wales, these river pearl shells are called by the poetic name *Cregin y Dylu*, shells of the Flood.

The gradual replacement of naked divers by those in diving dress may tend to make the yields more effective, but the work is not without its dangers, the toiler beneath the sea having still to meet the challenge of its denizens—the shark, the diamond fish and the deadly octopus.

"The Kingdom of Heaven is like unto a merchantman seeking goodly pearls.

—BOOK OF MATTHEW

The pearl was esteemed as the emblem of purity, innocence and peace, and was sacred to the Moon and Diana. For this reason in ancient times it was worn by young girls and virgins on whom the protection of "chaste Diana" was invoked. Generally as an emblem of chastity the pearl was worn on the neck. As a cure for irritability it was ground to a fine powder and a quantity, seldom more than a grain, was drunk in new milk. In doses of the same quantity mixed with sugar it was recommended to be taken as a charm against the pestilence.

The Hindus included the pearl amongst the five precious stones in the magical necklace of Vishnu, the other four being the diamond, ruby, emerald, and sapphire. The golden pearl was the emblem of wealth, the white of idealism, the black of philosophy, the pink of beauty, the red of health and energy, the grey of thought. Lusterless pearls are considered unfortunate, as also are pearls that have lost their sheen when on a dying person's finger, as sometimes happens.

It is curious how pearls improve in luster when worn by some persons and how they deteriorate when worn by others. A recent writer commenting on this advised that if "pearls turned color temporarily when worn by certain persons they should be put away for a few days and the detrimental effects of constitutional acids will be found to have entirely disappeared." To an extent this is correct, but it is equally certain that if the person by whom the pearls were affected were to continue wearing them they would be destroyed altogether. This is quite in accord with the occult philosophy of the ancient masters who held that only people who had favorable planets in Cancer—the Celestial sign of the Ocean—or in whose nativities the lunar aspects were favorable could wear pearls. The Moon, however, in the sign Capricorn was not considered favorable for wearing pearls, and some writers also include the sign Scorpio.

A half-moon shaped whitish stone of about 25 lbs. weight was oftentimes used by the Ceylonese pearl divers, tied around their waists, when making the plunge for the pearl oyster, and the crew of 20—a lunar number—which made up the Ceylon pearling boat company may have traditional authority, and may be something more than mere coincidence. The Princess of Yemen, previously mentioned, wore seven strands of pearls. Seven is the positive number of the Moon or the Moon's number when going from new to full. This was recognized by ancient nations and it may be well assumed that the symbolic meaning was understood by the advisers to the Princess.

A custom exists in Madagascar which finds a parallel amongst the ancients: it is believed that if at an afflicted birth pearls be buried good will come to the child and will continue to come unless the pearls be unearthed. The Pearl was sacred to the angel Gabriel and Monday was its special day of the week; the Moon was its planet and the zodiacal Cancer its sign. To dream of pearls is considered a favorable omen, being held to indicate wealth and honor gained by personal exertion. To the poor the pearl denotes riches. It is the symbol of happy marriage and popularity.

That pearls are unfortunate is as untrue as that opals or any other gems are. That they are unfavorable to some is as true as that they are favorable to others, but prejudice being narrow and self-centered is hard to kill. A young lady of good family actually told the author that she would never wear pearls because she was unfortunate whenever she wore her necklace. Upon examining this terrible necklace the author saw that the alleged pearls were merely imitation!

As imitation pearls scarcely come within the province of this book it may be sufficient to mention that in the year 1748 Linnaeus wrote to Dr. Haller, the physiologist, telling him that he had ascertained how pearls grow in shells. "I am able to produce in any mother of pearl shell that can be held in the hand, in the course of 4 or 5 years, a pearl as large as the seed of a common vetch." This discovery by the great naturalist was regarded as of such importance by the Swedish Government that they ennobled Linnaeus, rewarded him with a gift of £450, and began to manufacture pearls under his direction with great secrecy.

Linnaeus' method had long been anticipated by the Chinese who used to throw pieces of mother of pearl, grit, etc., into the live oyster. It is said that in a year the coating over a piece of mother of pearl would be sufficient. Of late years the Japanese have acted on these practices with considerable skill, producing by mechanical means some beautiful specimens. Still, beautiful as they are, they are not real pearls. A good deal of pearl "faking" is practiced, and a short time ago a pearl broker in Paris was sentenced to imprisonment for tampering with the color of a pearl. But whenever chemical means are employed in tinting a pearl the false colors invariably fade and leave the specimen worse off than before, more especially if a lady with a "good pearl skin" wears it.

In his book on *Malay Magic*, Mr. W. W. Satek gives the following interesting account of Coconut Pearls, quoting from Dr. Deny's *Descriptive Dictionary of British Malaya*, with acknowledgments to "Nature." "During my recent travels," Dr. Sidney Hickson writes to a scientific contemporary,

> "I was frequently asked by Dutch planters and others if I had ever seen a 'coconut stone.' These stones are said to be rarely found (one in two thousand or more) in the perisperm of the coconut, and when found are kept by the natives as a charm against disease and evil spirits. This story of the coconut stone was so constantly told me, and in every case without variations in its details, that I made every effort before leaving to obtain some specimens and eventually succeeded in obtaining two. One of these is nearly a perfect sphere, 14 mm in diameter, and the other, rather smaller in size, is irregularly pear-shaped.
>
> "In both specimens the surface is worn nearly smooth by friction. The spherical one I have had cut into two halves but I can find no concentric or other markings on the polished cut surface. Dr. Kimmins has kindly submitted a half to a careful chemical analysis and finds that

it consists of pure carbonate of lime without any trace of other salts or vegetable tissue."

On this letter Mr. Thistleton Dyer remarks:

"Dr. Hickson's account of the calcareous concretions occasionally found in the central hollow—filled with fluid—of the endosperm of the seed of the coconut is extremely interesting. The circumstances of the occurrence of these stones or pearls are in many respects parallel to those which attend the formation of tabasheer. In both cases mineral matter in palpable masses is withdrawn from solution in considerable volumes of flint contained in tolerably large cavities in living plants and in both instances they are monocotyledons.

"In the case of coconut pearls the material is calcium carbonate and this is well known to concrete in a peculiar manner from solutions in which organic matter is also present. In my note on Tabasheer I referred to the reported occurrence of mineral concretions in the wood of various tropical dicotyledonous trees. Tabasheer is too well known to be pooh-poohed, but some of my scientific friends express a polite incredulity in the other cases."

The specimen presented by Mr. Skeat to the Cambridge Ethnological Museum is encircled by a black ring which is caused, it is said, by its adherence to the shell of the coconut. These coconut pearls are of much interest and may perhaps be included amongst the mineral curiosities which comprehend tabasheer, apatite, etc. Ancient philosophy would probably associate them with the sign Cancer as is the case with pearls found in seas and rivers. Swedenborg writes that pearls are Truth and the knowledge of Truth, celestial and spiritual knowledge, faith and charity.

CHAPTER 24

Peridot—Ruby

PERIDOT. (See **CHRYSOLITE.**)

PLASMA. This variety of leek-green jasper is derived from the Greek word PLASMA, an image. It was a favorite stone among the ancients who employed it in gem engraving and for important talismans. In the Rhodes collection there is a beautiful oval specimen on which is engraved a nude figure of Hermes holding a caduceus in his left hand, whilst on his right above a purse is perched a cock; a scorpion is on his left side, a little above his knee. He wears the winged cap on his head. Mr. King classes this piece as astrological. It symbolizes the wisdom and rewards of the well-starred subject of Mercury. Plasma was largely used in Abraxas charms by the Gnostics who employed the substance always for special talismans. Astrologically Plasma is under the zodiacal Virgin.

PORPHYRY. The name is derived from the Greek word for purple—PORPHYRA—and we find it written at various periods in many ways, for example: porfurie, porphurye, purphire, porpherie, porphiry. It is a hard purple and white stone, said to have been introduced into Rome by Vitrasisus Pollio in the form of statues of Claudius. The quarries whence the ancients obtained their supplies of porphyry were found at Gebel Dokhan, near the Red Sea, by Wilkinson and Burton. It has always been a favorite stone with sculptors, glyptic artists, and architects, and was chiefly esteemed in the forming of columns. Porphyry was regarded as a stone to promote eloquence in speaking. Astrologically it was placed under "the sign of the Columns"—Gemini.

PRASE. The name is derived from the Greek PRASON, a leek. Leonardus calls it *Prassius*, and he says it is so termed from an herb of its own name. It is also written as prasius, prasium. It is thus described by Marbodus:

"Midst precious stones a place the Prase may claim,
Of value small, content with beauty's fame.
No virtue has it: but it brightly gleams
With emerald green, and well the gold beseems;
Or blood-red spots diversify its green,
Or crossed with three white lines its face is seen."

Other authors, however, endow the prase with a virtue. It was regarded by some as a beauty charm for married women and for the mothers of brides. It resembles the beryl in its clear form, but it is duller. It is translucent and, as its name indicates, leek-green in color. At one time it was believed to be the matrix of the emerald, whence it was called **MOTHER OF EMERALD.** It is under the zodiacal Taurus.

PYRITE

"Named from the fire the yellow pyrite spurns
The touch of man, and to be handled scorns:
Touch it with trembling hand and cautious arm
For, tightly grasped, it burns the closed palm."

The word is found also as pyrit, pirrite, and old writers of the 16th century were especially fond of using pyrit stone. It is derived from the Greek PUR, fire, and is allied to the fire stone family (*Pyrites Lithos*) noted by Isidore of Seville (6th and 7th centuries) in his philosophical fragments from the more ancient writers. He identifies the black pyrites of Pliny in a black Persian stone which, if fractured, and held in the hand, burns. It is assumed from the frequent occurrence of pieces of pyrites in prehistoric mounds that primitive man used the substance for kindling fires.

Later we find it employed before the introduction of flint in wheel lock fire arms when, in the same manner, it threw out sparks of fire when energetically struck on steel. The ancients had a theory that pyrite was the seed or original matter of minerals, and we find it in rocks of every age. To mining people it is known as mundic. Auriferous pyrite which occurs in auriferous countries contains certain quantities of gold, sometimes worth winning, and was known as King of the Pyrites.

The action of water and air makes it troublesome in coal-mining districts. It is then changed into sulfate of iron (vitriol) and fires the mines. Chambers (1866) mentions that "at Quarreltown in Renfrewshire a deep hollow may still be seen where about a century ago the ground fell in, in consequence of a subterranean fire thus kindled." Theophrastus, the great Greek naturalist and philosopher of the 3rd century, before the Christian era, mentions in his work on stones the burning pyrite under the name spinon which, he says, is contained in certain mines and which, if crushed, watered and exposed to the rays of the sun, bursts into flame. The French call this stone *Pierre de Santé* (Stone of Health), because it was said that it is affected by the health of the wearer.

The white iron pyrites, known as **MARCASITE,** is of similar composition to the ordinary pyrite (Iron Disulphide) but it takes on the orthorhombic form of crystallization instead of the usual cube form. This word is also found written as markasit, marquesite. The stone was largely used for jewel ornamentation. Oliver Goldsmith, in *She Stoops to Conquer*, says: "Half the ladies of our acquaintance carry their jewels to town and bring nothing but paste and marcasites back." Eden in 1555 wrote that "Marchasites are flowers of metals by the colors whereof the kyndes of metals are known."

Mr. William Jones mentions a ring in the possession of a clergyman which is made of two hearts surmounted by a crown set with marcasites. Rabbi Chad says that a man on horseback holding a bridle and bent bow engraved on pyrites makes the wearer irresistible in war. These stones are martial according to astrology and are attached to the zodiacal Scorpio.

PYROPE. (See **GARNET**.)

QUARTZ. In 1772 Cronstedt wrote in his work on mineralogy: "I shall adopt the name of Quartz in English as it has already general access in other European Languages." There seems to be little doubt regarding the origin of the word which comes from the German *Quarz*. Professor James P. Dana gives the Quartz varieties under the following heads:

1. *Vitreous*. Distinguished by their glassy fracture.
2. *Chalcedonic*. Having a sub-vitreous or a waxy luster and generally translucent.

3. *Jaspery Cryptocrystalline*. Having barely a glimmering luster or none, and opaque.

To the first belong: amethyst, aventurine quartz, cairngorm, citrine, ferruginous quartz, false or Spanish topaz, milk quartz, prase, rock crystal, rose quartz, smoky quartz.

To the second belong: chalcedony, chrysoprase, sard, carnelian, agate, onyx, catseye, flint, hornstone, chert, plasma.

To the third belong: jasper, heliotrope or bloodstone, Lydian stone, touchstone, basanite, silicified qood, pseudomorphous quartz, etc.

Opal is a near ally to quartz which is a most useful as well as an ornamental substance.

RUBELLITE. (See TOURMALINE.)

RUBICELLE. (See SPINEL.)

RUBY

> "He that has once the flower of the Sunne
> The perfect ruby which we call elixir."
> —BEN JOHNSON

The ruby derives its name from the Latin RUBER, red, and some of its forms at various periods are given by Dr. Murray as rubye, rubie, rubey, roby, rooby, rube, rubu, rybe, rybee, rybwe, ribe, riby. The stone is of the **CORUNDUM** family which includes the sapphire, oriental amethyst, oriental topaz, oriental chrysoberyl, oriental emerald, oriental catseye, oriental moonstone, adamantine spar of hair-brown color and the well-known emery. The term "oriental" is also applied to the ruby and serves to distinguish it from the spinel, ruby garnet and a number of other red stones. The definition "oriental" is applied only to the corundum family and was, according to Dr. G. F. H. Smith, attached to these hard colored stones which in early days reached Europe by way of the East.

The name corundum is derived from a Sanskrit word of doubtful meaning, and the minerals included in it come next in hardness to the diamond. The ruby therefore is a red sapphire, and the sapphire a blue ruby, and it is no infrequent thing to find the two stones combined in one specimen. Mr. Emanuel has drawn attention to the fact that rubies and sapphires are always found in gold-bearing country. It has been stated that whilst sapphires have been found in Australia the red sapphire or ruby has not. This is incorrect. At the Anakie sapphire fields in Central Queensland rubies are also found, and some specimens exhibit blended colors. It is true, however, that rubies have not up to the present been found in Australia in great quantities.

The most celebrated ruby mines in the world are the Mogok mines in Upper Burma. Here the stones are found in calcite deposits occurring in granular limestone on the hill sides and in the clayey alluvial deposits of the river beds. These workings are of very great age and until 1885 were the monopoly of the Burmese Crown, the King being known as Lord of the Rubies. In this country the ruby fields are called "Byon," and the miners "Twin-tsas" (mine eaters). These Twin-tsas were forced to surrender to the monarch all big stones found by them, which stones were carefully guarded in the Royal Treasure House. One of the mine eaters found a large and beautiful gem which, in order to escape the selfish conditions imposed, he divided into two parts; one of these he handed over to the officers of the King, the other he endeavored to conceal. The plot it seems failed, with what result to the unfortunate "Eater" is not told. The weight of these two sections after the cutter had exerted his skill on them was 98 and 74 carats.

A fine Burma ruby called "Gnaga Boh," or the Dragon Lord (the folklore of the East connects rubies and dragons)—weighed when found over 40 carats, losing about half in the cutting. The uncut part of the Great Burmese Ruby (a stone that weighed 400 carats and was split into three parts, two of which were cut) was sold in Calcutta for 7 lakhs of rupees (at the exchange rate of two shillings English for the rupee a lakh would equal £10,000). Marco Polo writes of the great ruby possessed by the King of the Island of Seilan (Ceylon),

> "The finest and biggest in the world… It is about a palm in length and as thick as a man's arm: to look at, it is the most resplendent object upon earth: it is quite free from flaw and is as red as fire. Its value is so great that a price for it in money could not be named. The great Khan sent an embassy and begged the King as a favor to sell this to him offering to give for it the ransom of a city or, in fact, what the King would.

But the King replied that on no account whatever would he sell it for it had come to him from his ancestors."

The great merchant-traveler Cosmas Indicopleustes, of Alexandria, writes in his *Voyages* (1666) of this stone, which "they say is of great size and brilliant ruddy hue, as large as a giant pine cone. When seen flashing from afar—especially if the Sun's rays flood upon it—it is a sight both marvelous and unequaled." Hayton, his contemporary, also writes of this wonderful stone: "At the King of the Island of Ceylon's coronation he places this ruby in his left hand and rides thus with it throughout his city, after which all know him as their King and obey him as such." The Chinese writer Hyuen Tsang also writes of this great stone, as does Odoric. Friar Jordamus discourses not only of this but of the great and wonderful rubies in the possession of the Island King. Andrea Corsali (1515) also writes of the King of Sylen's (Ceylon's) two great rubies—"so shining and sparkling as to seem like flames of fire."

In the Ceylon river beds fine rubies are discovered, and old writers say that many are washed down from the mountain "which they call Adam's Peak." There was superstitious belief in the beautiful Island of Ceylon that rubies are the consolidated tears of Buddha. One of the great medieval Tamul chiefs, Arya Chakravarti, had, it is said, a ruby bowl the size of the palm of a man's hand, which was remarkable for its brilliant color. Colonel Alexander Gardner, Colonel of Artillery in the service of Maharaja Ranyit Singh, describes a visit he made with the Bai or Baron of the Kirghiz to a venerable aged fakir whose worldly possessions seemed to consist of earthen pots of grain placed in a hole in the middle of his hut.

The old philosopher was the reputed possessor of a rare and beautiful ruby. For this the Bai entreated the silent and unmoved fakir, declaring that with it alone could he induce the robber chief he was traveling to see to spare "the lives, property and honor of all the innocent families around." At last the fakir quietly arose, and after a little fumbling produced the gem which, with a dignified gesture, he placed softly in the Bai's hands, giving him his blessing and expressing the hope that the offering might have the desired result, after which he relapsed into silent reverie. He declined money for the gem, asking only that some grain might be sent him so "that he might be able to relieve way-worn and destitute travelers."

The Colonel examined the gem and found cut in high relief on the center of the oblong face of the stone a small Zoroastrian altar. Round this altar were double cordons of letters similar to those appearing on the Scytho Bactrian coins. The Colonel describes the gem as pure and lustrous, of great value, and from 150 to 200 carats in weight. This rare gem was discovered at the time of Timur by an ancestor of the fakir in a cave near the famous shrine of the city of Esh or Oosh on the Bolor Ranges.

A fine ruby of 50 carats which belonged to the King of Vishapoor is mentioned by Tavernier. In China the ruby has always been esteemed and its primary importance as a distinguishing emblem in the cap of the Chief Mandarin had already been noted. A specimen was also placed under the foundations of a building of importance "to give it a good destiny." In the Chinese work CHO KENG LU which relates to various affairs up to the Mongol dynasty, deep red rubies are termed "SI-LA-NI"; scholars translate this word as "from Ceylon." They are also known as "HUNG PAO SHI" (precious red stone) and "CHIN CHU." It has a sacred meaning and talismanic virtue and is attached to the dress set in rare jade and employed as a precious ornament.

Pliny calls rubies "acausti" and says that they are not injured by fire. He relates a practice of the merchants of Ethiopia of placing a ruby in a vinegar solution for two weeks to improve its luster. The effect was, it is said, good for a short period of time but ultimately the stones became soft and fragile. The anthrax or "glowing coals" of Theophrastus is identified as the ruby as we know it today. He gives us an idea of the money value of this stone by stating that a very small specimen would sell for forty golden staters (a gold stater is worth about a 5-dollar gold piece of the United States). Amongst the gems collected in the 18th century by William, third Duke of Devonshire, there is a ruby of about three carats weight, described by Mr. King as of "the most delicious cerise color" on which are cut deeply the figures of Venus and Cupid. The work is of the middle Roman Period and Mr. King deplores the fact that the great value of the gem was in his opinion injured by the inferiority of the workmanship.

A Faun's head on an inferior ruby in the same collection is superior from an art point of view and of greater age. Mr. King mentions a beautiful rose-colored ruby of irregular form on which is a magnificent head of Thetis wearing a crab's shell helmet of most exquisite Greek work. Rabbi Ragiel (Book of Wings) writes that the figure of a dragon cut on a ruby increases the worldly possessions of the wearer, giving happiness and ease.

Old legends say that the ruby mines as well as the emerald mines were guarded by dragons and the symbolic connection between the dragon and the ruby has the virtue of far-reaching antiquity. M. Rochefort in his *Natural History of the Antilles*, says that the Caribbees of Dominica speak of a dragon which lives in a declivity of the rocks and in whose head is a giant ruby so brilliant that the surrounding country is illuminated by it. These people believed that the Son of God came out of the heavens to slay the dragon. St. Margaret is said to have subdued a dragon and to have taken a wonderful ruby from its head.

The Arabian writer Sheikh El Mohdy has amongst his stories one telling of a terrible dragon which inhabited the island of Ceylon and carried in his head a large ruby which shone for many miles amidst the darkness of night. The Indian philosopher Barthoveri said that "the serpent is malefic although it carries a ruby in its head." Dieudonné of Gozon is said to have killed a terrible dragon at Rhodes and to have drawn from its head a wonderful iridescent stone the size of an olive. Some few writers substitute the diamond for the ruby, but whether we take the many-colored stone of Dieudonné (which it has been said was a diamond) or the stones of the Sun, the ruby and the diamond, the import of the legends are similar. The dragon as the symbol of the lower forces whether as the poisonous emanations of stagnant waters or as the Serpent of Eden— the planet Mars and one of his heavenly Houses, Scorpio, or the planet Saturn and his heavenly House, Capricorn—is continually exposed to the benefic rays of the Sun. These rays are personified by the contests between the Sun-Angel Michael and the Dragon and our well-known St. George.

The three skulls, said to be the skulls of the "Three Kings" in the jeweled "Shrine of the Magi" in Cologne Cathedral, have their names Melchior, Gaspar and Balthazar worked on them in rubies, perhaps because the Sun, planet of the ruby, was the accredited planet of Christianity as noted by Albertus Magnus and the Cardinal Dailly. The names of the Magi have also been given as Megalath, Galgalath and Sarasin—Apellius, Amerus and Damascus—Ator, Sator and Peratoras. In their allegories the Rosicrucians follow very nearly the names on the skulls in the 12th century Shrine at Cologne, viz.:

Jasper or Gaspar, the white lord with a diamond
Melchior, the bright lord with a diamond
Belshazzar or Balthazar, the treasure lord with a ruby.

It is said that Henry VIII wore on his thumb a ring in which was set a ruby—some say a diamond—from the tomb of St. Thomas A'Becket. This ruby, known as the "Régale of France," was the talismanic gem of the French King Louis VII who, in accordance with a battle-vow, visited the tomb at Canterbury in the year 1179. Whilst offering his devotions he was asked by the priests at the shrine to give as an offering this beautiful jewel. Being loath to part with his talisman, the King agreed to give one hundred thousand florins in its stead, to which generous substitution the Canterbury fathers humbly agreed. But the precious ruby which dazzled all with its brightness, turning night into day, refused to be thus protected and, flying from the setting of the ring on the King's finger, fixed itself on the Saint's tomb.

Swedenborg recognizes in the ruby a gem of passionate devotion and likens it to the appearance of the Lord's Divine Sphere represented in the celestial Heavens.

In Comtesse d' Anois' fairy story *Chery and Fairstar* there is a narrative of a ruby apple on an amber stem which is known as the "Singing Apple." This apple gave forth a perfume so weirdly sweet that it caused people to laugh or to cry, to write poems or to sing songs; but when it sang itself the hearers were transported with ecstasy. Guarded by a great three-headed dragon with twelve feet, the apple rested in the Libyan desert whence it was secured by Prince Chery in his glass armor, the reflections of which drove the terrified dragon into a cave, the entrance to which was securely shut up by the victor.

The Arabs say that the Angel Bearer of the World stands on a rock of pure ruby, and amongst the Persians the gem was used in magical rites as a charm against the Black Forces. It was the fourth stone of the Nao-Rattan which Iarchus gave to Apollonius, representing Benevolence, Charity, Divine Power, and Dignity. The Burmese value the ruby as an especially sacred stone which to them is a symbol of the last incarnation which precedes the final embrace of Divinity. The beautiful ruby is likened to rich ripe fruit, and its magical power is matured. It has been stated that the ruby is unfortunate for India—a country under the Celestial Capricorn—and one great specimen nearly destroyed a native state,

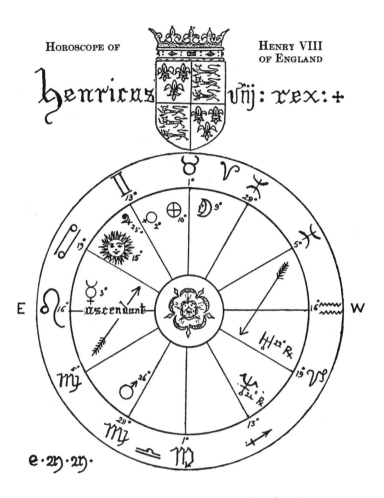

HOROSCOPE OF HENRY VIII OF ENGLAND

The Ruby was considered the fortunate gem for this King.

after which event it was buried with solemn ceremonies in the heart of the Himalayas.

It was an ancient custom to adorn sacred statues with precious stones and the practice has survived into Christian times. Mr. William Jones describes a large shrine in the Liège Cathedral whereon was a figure, more than life size, of St. Lambert. On each hand were three jeweled rings, the most brilliant of which was set with a rare 10-carat ruby. The shrine was of the latter 15th and early 16th centuries. Many similar votive offerings are recorded.

For a ruby to change its color was regarded as a forerunner of misfortune, and it is said that the unhappy wife of Henry VIII, Catharine of Aragon, observing a change in her ruby ring, foretold her own fall. After danger has passed, old writers say, the ruby returns to its color again, if it is the true gem of the wearer.

The ruby is an emblem of passion, affection, power and majesty. It had the reputation of attracting and retaining material love. It was probably for this reason that the amorous Henry VIII of England wore the "Régale of France." It removed obstacles, gave victory, and revealed the hidden places of stolen treasure. It signified vitality, life and happiness, and was an amulet against plagues, poison, sorrow and evil spirits, who dreaded the flashing of the stone from the hand of a good person.

To dream of a ruby indicated to the business man rich patronage and success in trade, to the farmer a successful harvest and to the professional man elevation or fame and success in different degrees. It was always considered more fortunate to wear the ruby on the left hand or left side of the body. The colors of the gem vary from a light rose to a deep red, the most expensive color being that nearest to pigeon's blood. Submitted to a high temperature it turns green but when cooling returns to its original color.

A particularly fortunate and rare variety is the star or asteriated ruby which exhibits a perfect star on its beautifully rounded cabochon surface, coming as it were from a chatoyant interior. Messrs. Jerningham and Bettany in their *Bargain Book* relate how a traveler in Amazonia found in the crop of a bird which he had shot, a large and handsome ruby which he had cut and set in a ring as a souvenir of this uncommon event.

The ruby is under the Celestial sign Leo.

CHAPTER 25

RUTILE — SAPPHIRE

RUTILE

"Fair tresses man's imperial race ensnare,
And beauty draws us with a single hair."

— POPE

The name rutile is derived from the Latin RUTILUS, red, and it appeared under the form rutil in 1803 when it was first applied to the mineral by Dr. A. G. Werner. The mineral occurs in brown, red, yellow and black colors and is composed of oxygen and titanium. In hardness it is about the same as a peridot. The name *Veneris Crinis* (Hair of Venus) was first given to fibrillous rutile in quartz crystal known as sagenite, from a Greek word meaning "a net." The Hair of Venus was suggested by the beautiful hair-like effect which in good specimens is truly Titian. It is also known as the Net of Thetis and the Hair of Thetis. The French call it *"Flèches d'Amour"* (Love's Arrows). The *Veneris Crinis* was worn by the ancients as a charm to favor the growth of hair and to give foreknowledge. Rutile is under the celestial Sagittarius.

SAPPHIRE

"The living throne, the sapphire blaze,
Where angels tremble while they gaze."

— GRAY

The sapphire derives its name from the Greek SAPPHEIROS and the following are some of the many forms of the word: saphyr, saphir, safir, safire, zaphire, safere, saffere, safyre, sapher, saphyre, saphire, saffyr, saffre, safeur, safour, safur, sapheir, saphere, safure, saffure, saffoure, saufir, sapphier, saiffer, sapphyr.

The sapphire which may be said to lead the **CORUNDUM** family is slightly harder than the ruby. The name, which varies but little in ancient languages, was without doubt applied to the blue lapis lazuli—the *Hyacinthus* of the ancients being the true sapphire of our days. Sapphire is the name given to the blue corundum, and the shades of color vary from very light to very dark, the light specimens being anciently termed female, the dark, male. This blue tinge will, however, be detected in several light varieties of the corundum family. The velvety blue sapphire termed the *"bleu du roi"* has held its popularity for ages and is likely to continue to do so, although the pretty light specimens known as "cornflower blue" are fast coming into favor.

Sapphires are found in Ceylon, India and Siam in considerable quantity and some good stones have been found in the United States. Large specimens come from Newton, New Jersey and also from the rich country round Montana. The sapphire fields at Anakie, Central Queensland, bid fair to become one of the biggest in the world, and in a highly instructive report, Messrs. William Rands and B. Dunstan, Government Geologists of Queensland, give a detailed account of the fields. The authors of the report give the following list of minerals found in the sapphire deposits:

> Diamonds
> Sapphire (blue)
> Oriental ruby (red)
> Oriental topaz (yellow)
> Oriental peridot (green)
> Oriental chrysoberyl (yellowish green)
> Oriental amethyst (purple)
> Catseye (smoky, etc.)
> Oriental moonstone (pearly)
> Spinel varieties
> Spinel ruby
> Pleonaste
> Garnet pyrope
> Zircon varieties
> Jargoon (white and yellow)
> Hyacinth (brown and red)
> Quartz varieties
> Rock crystal (colorless)
> Amethyst (purple)
> Cairngorm (smoky)

Chalcedony varieties
Carnelian (red and yellow)
Jasper varieties: black (Lydian Stone), red and brown
Rutile (in quartz pebbles)
Topaz (white)
Magnetite
Titanic iron
Magnesite
Tourmaline
Hornblende

The report emphasizes the facts that "the field is a large one, that the extent of sapphire wash is second to none in the world and that a constant supply of stones could be maintained." It seems that these Australian gems have not met with the fair treatment so necessary in the development of the fields, and in their report Messrs. Rands and Dunstan submit an extract from a letter received from an important firm of lapidaries and gem merchants in Geneva:

"Fine sapphires equal to those from Burma have been found amongst the Australian gem stones. Most of these are sent to Germany by dealers where they are sorted. The best gems are afterwards sold separately under another name, and the inferior lots sold as Australian."

Large sapphires are more frequently found than large rubies and Dr. Chambers mentions one discovered in 1853 in the alluvium a few miles from Ratnapoora, which was valued at over £4,000 sterling. A large specimen, three inches long, is mentioned by Professor J. D. Dana as being in the possession of Sir Abram Hume. In the Green Vaults at Dresden several great specimens are shown. The large "*Saphir merveilleux*" which Mr. Hope exhibited at the London Exhibition in 1851—known as the "Hope Sapphire"—was blue by daylight and amethyst color by nightlight. This gem was last said to be in the Russian Treasury. This sapphire has nothing in common with the blue cobalt-colored artificial spinels known as "Hope Sapphires."

Dr. G. F. H. Smith mentions several large stones, the most notable being one of 950 carats which was reported to be in the King of Ava's treasury in 1827. The weight of the Rospoli rough sapphire in the Jardin des Plantes is 132 carats. The Duke of Devonshire has a fine sapphire of 100 carats, brilliant cut above the girdle of the stone, and step cut below. From the earliest times the sapphire had the reputation of a holy gem. Solinus says that "it feels the air and sympathizes with the heavens, shining not the same if the sky be bright or obscured." The ancients held the gem sacred to Phoebus, not as a personification of the Sun, but rather as explained by Dr. Alexander S. Murray (Department of Greek and Roman Antiquities in the British Museum) as follows:

"From the sun comes our physical light, but that light is at the same time an emblem of mental illumination, of knowledge, truth and right, of all moral purity: and in this respect a distinction was made between it as a mental and a physical phenomenon—a distinction which placed Phoebus Apollo on one side and Helios on the other. Accordingly Phoebus Apollo is the oracular god who throws light on the dark ways of the future, who slays the Python—that monster of darkness which made the oracle at Delphi inaccessible. He is the god of music and song which are only heard where light and security reign and the possession of herds is free from danger."

This is the ideal of the sign Aquarius, astrologically considered, and, students of the old science well know what Solinus implies when he says that the gem of the sign Aquarius "feels the air and sympathizes with the heavens," for this sign of "air," of fine ethereal forces, of "outer airs," of fine subtle substances, etc., is also the sign of Heaven and the Heavens.

The great physician Galen used the sapphire "for expelling the hot humors of the body," which unfavorable health condition is included in astrological philosophy on the evils of the sign Aquarius. The sign also, as the astrologer Raphael says, "has particular rule over the eyesight, and the Sun conjoined with Saturn therein is a sure sign of blindness." Ancient writers say that he who gazes into a sapphire will charm away all threatened injury to his eyes, and Marbodus recommends that a sapphire "dissolved in milk" takes the sting from "dimmed eyes."

For removing foreign bodies from the eye, specks of dust, sand, etc., it was recommended that a sapphire be held a while on the closed eyelid and then drawn gently and slowly several times across from the nose to the corner of the eye. It is one of the old principles in medicine, astrologically administered, that the cause of the disease can also be used as a cure, whilst another rule advises the virtue of opposites. In this latter connection it was said that a sapphire placed near the heart would fortify that organ—the sign of Heaven "ruling" the heart is Leo, and Aquarius is exactly opposite to Leo in the Zodiac. In homeopathic medicine aconite in proper proportion is administered to reduce fevers and inflamed conditions. Astrologically, aconite is a herb of Saturn. Saturn is, like the herb, cold and contracting whilst Mars is warm and expanding.

The blood and mental faculties are liable to disorder in certain people born with Aquarius rising at birth or with the Sun therein: and the sapphire was the panacea which also, it was said, stopped bleeding of the nose if held against the temples. In old pharmacies the sapphire held a place of importance and its reputed curative virtue led to its employment as a charm against swellings, boils, ruptures, profuse perspirations, poisons, melancholy, flatulence and other bodily disharmonies. It was also employed as a charm against enchantment, danger, treachery, quarrels between friends, evil suggestions and undue influence. Porta in his work on *Natural Magic*, 1561, writes of the value of the sapphire in all magical and religious ceremonies, protecting the wearer from the Larvae of the lower spiritual world and from the snakes and poisonous reptiles of the world of matter. It was considered intensely powerful as a destroyer of poisonous insects which it was said to kill if placed at the mouth of a vessel in which they were imprisoned.

Boetius (*De Natura Gemmarum*) writes that the sapphire was worn by priests as an emblem of chastity, for none of evil thoughts, bad minds or vicious habits dare wear this gem of pure heavenly love which was used of old by those consulting the sacred oracles. In his messages to the Bishops of the 12th century Pope Innocent III asked that they should have their pure gold rings set with "that stone which is the true seal of secrecy." When the Roman Catholic church received her novices into the Sisterhood a sapphire ring blessed by a Bishop was given as a holy symbol of the mystical marriage. In the famous Pulsky Collection—mentioned by Mr. C. W. King—there is a wonderful intaglio on a fine sapphire of Pope Paul III by the great Alessandro Cesati, three-quarters of an inch square.

St. Jerome (4th and 5th centuries) wrote that the sapphire saved its wearer from captivity and pacified his enemies, also that it gained the favor of princes. Some old authors recommend the sapphire as a stone for the hands of Kings. It is a stone rather of Democracy. Perhaps, however, the symbolic idea was that the King as the servant of the people could adorn his hand with no more fitting emblem.

It is traditionally reported that the ring of King Solomon was a sapphire, which stone was believed by some of the masters to be the special talisman of the Jews. One kept in the Holy of Holies as a holy emblem is said to have been saved and concealed for the people of Israel when Titus sacked Jerusalem. Moses was born with the Sun rising in the ascending Aquarius, hence the adoption of either the sapphire as we know it today or the lapis lazuli as a national gem is perfectly natural.

The sapphire in the signet of Constantine, weighing 53 carats, which now lies amongst the treasures in the Rinuccini Cabinet at Florence, is cut in intaglio with a portrait of the Emperor in the guise of Nimrod attacking a great boar with his spear in the Caesarean plains. As a gem of heavenly and beautiful thoughts the sapphire was regarded as a scare against devils, evil forces, witchcraft, sorcery and all forms of villainy. The Buddhists symbolically say that a sapphire opens a closed door, brings prayerful feelings and sounds the sweet bells of peace. It is a stone of truth, constancy, friendship, goodness and angelic help; it warns against hidden dangers and heightens the imagination and psychic forces. It rebels against intoxication and refuses to adorn the hand of a drunkard; it helps hopes and wishes that are truly just and right. It was the third stone of the Nao-Rattan and the fourth of the seven rings which Iarchus brought down from the angelic spheres as a gift to Apollonius of Tyana. It was the fourth stone of the magical necklace of Vishnu, and according to the Ramayana sapphires fell from the eyes of the slain god Maha Bali.

An Irish Countess lent for exhibition to the South Kensington Loan Collection in 1872 the sapphire ring which Lady Scroope threw from the window of the death chamber of Queen Elizabeth to Sir Robert Carey who was waiting below for this signal of the Queen's passing in order to convey the news post haste to James. In the Sepher of Solomon "which was set together in the desert by the Children of Israel in the Holy Name of God, following the influences of the stars," a charm for favoring desires, for procuring invisibility, and certain benefits was a light colored sapphire on which was engraved a mermaid holding a twig in one hand and a mirror in the other. The time for the construction of this talisman (which was to be set in a ring and worn inwards for escaping the eyes of others) was when the moon, well-aspected, was passing through the 5th, 6th and 7th degrees of the sign Aquarius.

Another charm from the same source is the figure of a young man crowned, a circle round his neck, his hands raised in prayer, seated on a four-legged throne supported on the back of their necks by four men standing. The charm is to be cut on a "cornflower" sapphire for purifying the mind and obtaining favors from rulers, scholars, priests and people of wisdom. It was to be constructed when the well-aspected moon was passing through the 1st, 2nd, 28th and 29th degrees of Aquarius. In the *Book of Wings*, a charm advised for gaining wealth and prophetic foresight is an astrolabe cut on a sapphire, especially when the moon, well-aspected, passes through the 1st, 2nd, 28th and 29th degrees of Aquarius. Another for health, protection from poison, poisonous airs, and tyranny was the bearded head of a man or a ram engraved on a sapphire, constructed when the well-aspected moon was passing through 8th, 9th, 25th and 26th degrees of Aquarius.

Dreaming of sapphires is said to denote protection, social success, and favor generally. The asteriated or star sapphire, displaying like the star ruby an opalescent star, is a valued charm for procuring the love of friends, for constancy and harmony.

All shades of blue and green sapphires are under the zodiacal Aquarius. White sapphires (called leucos sapphires) are under the sign Pisces. Yellow sapphires are under the sign Leo. Amethyst sapphires are under the sign Sagittarius.

CHAPTER 26

Sardonyx — Succinite

SARDONYX. (See **ONYX.**)

SCHORL. (See **TOURMALINE.**)

SELENITE

"This stone, a remedy for human ills,
Springs, as they tell, from famous Persia's hills."
—Marbodus

The word selenite is derived from the Greek SELENE, the moon, and is found also written as silenite, silonite, silenitis. The stone, which is a crystallized variety of gypsum, is in pearly white, green, yellow and gray colors. Marbodus compares it with soft grass or verdant jasper, and Malpleat, in 1567, says it is like a fresh and flourishing green herb. The moon-like lusters whether in pearl-white or light green are the most esteemed, and Pliny writes that it is frequently employed in the construction of beehives to enable the curious to watch the little insects at their wonderful work. The ancients employed it in much the same way as we do glass, and it formed an item of considerable trade importance between Rome, Spain, Cyprus, Africa, Cappadocia and other parts of the ancient world.

Slightly coarser varieties were used by Tiberius to cover his hothouses, for it is susceptible of being split into comparatively thin sheets. A finer variety of very great value was at one time to be seen in the palace at Peking. Dr. John Goad, who wrote the *Astro-Meteorologia*, a book on the natures and influences of the celestial bodies, mentions the selenite which Pope Clement VIII had amongst his treasures. It was a natural moon dial, of which Cocheram said in 1623, "it decreaseth and encreaseth as the moon groweth." This Dr. Goad was a famous scholar who, wrote Cooper, "gained a reputation for his astrological knowledge founded on reason and experiment."

The Greeks called the stone *Selenitis Lithos*, because they said it waxed and waned with the moon, a belief quaintly expressed by Trevisa in 1398 as follows: "Selenites is a stone of Perse, grene as grasse. It shineth with a white specke and followeth the moon and waxyth and waneth as the moon doeth." Some old stories tell of a belief that little Moon men which Howell, a 17th century writer, calls "Selenites or Lunary Men," flung these stones deep in the earth.

The selenite was regarded as a love attractor and a stone to restore harmony between quarrelsome lovers. If engraved with a figure of Diana with bow and arrow when the moon was passing through the 3rd, 16th and 17th degrees of Cancer it increased, say old writers, the power of imagination and helped the wearer to realize future movements. If the selenite be burned and carefully powdered it is said to be of great use in cleaning pearls (which also are moon-ruled according to astrology). The selenite is under the sign Cancer like the moonstone, with which it is frequently confounded.

SERPENTINE or **HYDRINUS.** The name serpentine appears at different periods as serpentyn, serpentyne, sarpentene, sarpentin, scharpentyn. It is derived from the Latin SERPENS, and its more ancient term hydrinus indicates exactly the Sea Serpent family (*Hydride*), so well known to ancient and modern writers.

Precious serpentine is translucent—or about so—and of a rich oily green color. Common serpentine is opaque. The precious serpentine is called "noble," the impure "common." The colors are dark oily green, light green, olive green, black green, brown yellow, green yellow, sometimes almost white. The serpentine is identified with the THARSHISH stone, the 10th stone of the High Priest's Breastplate. It was known as "ophite stone" by Dioscorides and Pliny, and Agricola writing in the 16th century calls it "*Lapis Serpentinus*." Other writers called it "serpentinum," hence the modern name "serpentine." In Italy, especially amongst artists, some specimens of the stone are known as "ranochia," because of its similarity to a frog's skin.

It was recommended of old as a cure for rheumatism and rheumatic pains in the limbs, and for that purpose specimens were carried on the body next the skin, attached to the arms or legs. It was believed to cure dropsy and all moist complaints, especially if the sufferer held a specimen in each hand whilst resting in the sunlight. The wearer was also warned not to overdo this sunbathing with serpentine in his hands because of its affinity with all natural bodily fluids. It was said to be a charm against serpent bites or stings and to scare away poisonous insects and reptiles of the sea and land.

Serpentine was much esteemed by the ancients for its healing virtues and peculiar beauty. They effectively employed it in the manufacture of vases, pillars, boxes, etc., and for the making of special charms and talismans. The figure of a goat with a fish's tail cut on a serpentine when the moon, well-aspected, was passing through the 3rd and 4th degrees of the sign Capricorn, was a charm against rheumatism, skin troubles, gout, stiff limbs, accidents to the limbs, falls or hurts.

The serpentine was largely used by the ancient Egyptians in the making of sacred scarabs, and the Persians favored it especially for shaping into cylinders of authority, one of which is described by Mr. C. W. King, as follows: "A King contending with two andro-sphinxes, Ormuzd hovering above on the Tree of Life"—a very symbolic cylinder.

The serpentine or hydrinus is under the celestial Capricorn.

SOAPSTONE or **STEATITE.** Steatite derives its name from the Greek word STEAR, fat, which well describes the greasy feel of this soft magnesian rock—a massive variety of talc. It was extensively used by the ancient Egyptians who cut it into scarabs which in many cases they first burnt and then coated with a vitreous blue or green glaze. The substance is extremely soft and can easily be cut with a knife. Soapstone figures are cut from a variety known as pinite—the agalmatolite or pagodite of China, called by them HOA-CHI. Many of these are very beautifully cut, a number being lucky figures presented in the guise of gods and goddesses, flowers, fruits, etc. This custom reminds of the "household gods" of the ancients. A kind of soft steatite earth is still eaten by the savages of New Caledonia and other places.

All varieties of steatite are under the zodiacal Taurus.

SPHENE or **TITANITE.** Sphene derives its name from the Greek SPHEN, a wedge. As the name indicates the form of the crystals is wedge-shaped. The luster is very brilliant but the stone is scarcely as hard as the opal and therefore is little used in jewelry.

Sphene is under the zodiacal Sagittarius.

SPINEL or **BALAS RUBY.** Spinel, which derives its name from the Greek word SPINOS, a spark, is found written in a variety of ways, chief amongst which are spinell, spinele, spinel. Its colors are red, brown, green, yellow and blue. The red varieties are clear and glittering and the dark generally more dense or opaque.

The name spinel is applied to those of	bright red color
The name balas is applied to those of	rose red
The name rubicelle is applied to those of	orange red
The name almandine ruby is applied to those of	violet
The name chloro spinel is applied to those of	green
The name ceylonite or pleonaste is applied to those of	black
The name sapphirine is applied to those of	blue

Spinel and balas are often intermixed and both terms are accepted as denoting this aluminate of magnesium, whose hardness is just a little inferior to the corundum and whose crystalline form is isometric, like the diamond. The spinel, however, is non-electric, no matter if submitted to heat or friction, whilst the ruby (corundum), and garnet are highly so. Hence it is not a difficult matter to distinguish these stones from each other even if their outward similarities tend to confuse the eye. The spinel, submitted to trial by heat, first changes from red to brown; if left to cool it becomes dark; then it changes to green; then, as if exhausted, it seems to lose its color which, however, slowly reappears in its red expression.

The word balas has been written as balace, baless, balays, balais, balass. It is derived from the Arabic BALAKHSH which, says Albertus Magnus, is the female of the real ruby "and some say it is his house." That prolific writer on precious stones, Andrea Bacci (16th and 17th centuries), echoes older thought also when he writes that "Balas is derived from PALATIUS, a palace, which is the palace where the ruby lives." He echoes the symbolic ideas of the old Greek writers who said that the true ruby resided in a palace—clearly showing that they knew the difference between rubies and spinels. Marco Polo's remarks are as follows:

"In this Provence (Badachschan), those fine and valuable gems the Balas rubies are found. They are got in certain rocks among the mountains and in the search for them the people dig great caves beneath the earth just as is done by miners for silver. There is but one special mountain that produces them and it is called Syghinan. The stones are dug on the King's account and no one else dares dig on pain of death as well as of seizure of worldly possessions, nor may any take the gems out of the Kingdom. The King collects them all and sends them to other kings as tribute or as presents. He so acts in order to keep the Balas at a great value for if he allowed all persons to mine for them the world would be filled with them and they would be valueless."

In Persia there is a story which tells that they were found in a destroyed mountain after an earthquake. The Indians know the stone as the "pomegranate ruby" (*Lal Rumani*), and the King of Oude is said to have had a remarkable and beautiful specimen as big as the egg of a pigeon, which was known as "*Lal-i-jaladi.*" The beautiful heart-shaped balas which is set in the British Crown under the Black Cross known as the "Black Prince's Ruby," is said to have been obtained in Spain by Prince Edward when he was aiding Don Pedro of Castillo to hold his throne. It is reported that this was the gem worn by King Henry V at the Battle of Agincourt.

This may have been the "fair great ruby" which Sir James Melville says Queen Elizabeth valued so highly. Elizabeth was very fond of spinels, of which she possessed some splendid specimens, as shown in the still extant inventories of the personal effects of the Queen. An inspection of her nativity will show that they were gems of good omen for her. Madame de Barrera gives an extract from Robert de Berquen's *Merveilles des Indes Orientales et Occidentales* wherein it is stated that

"Josephus Barbaro, a Venetian gentleman, says in a report made to the Signori of Venice that when he was ambassador for the Republic at the court of Yussum Cassan, King of Persia, on a certain day of the year 1472 when he was received in solemn audience, that prince showed him a handkerchief filled with the rarest and most inestimable precious stones. Among others there was a table-cut Balass ruby, of a beautiful shape, of at least a finger's breadth, weighing two ounces and a half, and of a most peerless color: in fact, it was a most perfect paragon, so exquisite that when the King asked what he valued it at, he replied that he thought a city or even a kingdom would scarcely pay for it."

Spinels and corundum are always found together, and Dr. G. F. H. Smith comments on the fact that although harder stones, rubies in the river gravels are usually water-worn whilst spinels are found in perfect crystals. The ancient zoologist Elianus repeats an old story that a stork brought a spinel as a present to the woman-nurse Heraclis for healing his wounded leg.

Here again it is necessary to look beneath the fable for true understanding of it. The stork is one of the birds of Jupiter and its legs are astrologically under the zodiacal Sagittarius (the house or mansion of Jupiter). The woman symbolizes the moon and in her name the afternoon sun is concealed. The nurse is under Virgo, the sign to which the spinel is attached. The 4 toes of the stork symbolize the negative or afternoon sun, the 3 front toes webbed to the first joint, Jupiter. Again, the stork has no voice and tells no secrets. Hence we have a cryptic prescription illustrating the method employed by the ancient medical brethren to convey their meaning to each other. The spinel is here an active mineral employed in the treatment, together with the moon and negative or afternoon sun, of certain afflictions of the legs. Even today it is a custom amongst medical men to preface their prescriptions with the symbol of Jupiter. The stork is also greatly esteemed as a bird of good fortune and happy omen, and in many countries it is protected against destruction.

The spinel was esteemed as a perfect health stone and was especially valued as a charm to be worn over the solar plexus. It was a fortunate gem for doctors of medicine, scholars, writers, clerks, secretaries, manufacturers, business people, hospital attendants, nurses, etc. It raised the thoughts and purified the imagination. A specimen placed at each corner of a house was considered a protection against calamity, and rough pieces placed at the 4 angles of a garden, orchard or corn field were said not only to protect the products from storms and lightning, but also to carry the symbolic influence of rich returns for the farmer.

The spinel or balas, rubicelle, almandine ruby and the sapphirine are under the Zodiacal Virgo. The chloro-spinel and the pleonaste are under the zodiacal Capricorn.

SPODUMENE. Spodumene derives its name from the Greek word SPODIOS, ash-colored. It is a stone resembling feldspar, but has a luster more pearl-like. In general appearance spodumene is of a pale yellow tint, sometimes gray or as its name suggests, ash-colored. It is about the hardness of quartz. The emerald green variety, which is exceedingly rare, is called **HIDDENITE,** after its discoverer, Mr. M. G. Hidden, and it is said by Professor Dana to rival the emerald as a gem. It was discovered in 1881 in North Carolina, which seems to be the only place of its occurrence. Comparatively few specimens have been distributed and amongst them no stones of any considerable size. A pretty example of 2½ carats is in the Natural History section of the British Museum.

Perhaps the most beautiful examples of this mineral were discovered in the San Diego district of California in 1903 and named **KUNZ-ITE,** after Dr. G. F. Kunz. These stones range in color from pale violet to deep lilac and large specimens have already been unearthed, that in the British Museum weighing 60 carats. Dr. G. F. H. Smith remarks that under the influence of radium kunzite is phosphorescent, thus presenting some difference from spodumene in general. In analysis it is shown that spodumene contains 7.5 per cent of lithium. It would be, in harmony with ancient philosophy, under the zodiacal Libra, although the variety hiddenite may be connected with the zodiacal Taurus. All varieties of spodumene would be regarded as powerful eye charms and as beneficial to the kidneys and lumbar regions.

SUCCINITE (See **GARNET.**)

CHAPTER 27

TITANITE — TOPAZ

TITANITE. (See **SPHENE.**)

TOPAZ

"The flaming topaz with its golden beam."
—GLOVER

At various times the word has been rendered tupase, tupace, topace, topas, thopas, topaze, topasie, topazius, topasius. In the traditional derivation of the word a mystery is concealed. Pliny says that the stone was found in an island difficult for mariners to locate on account of the fogs and mists surrounding it, and Marbodus seems to indicate the true topaz when he says:

"From seas remote the yellow topaz came.
Found in the island of the self-same name."

The island was known as Topazios, which owes its origin to the Greek word meaning "to divine, guess, conjecture." The misty island is the celestial Scorpio which is accounted in astro-philosophy the death sign and the sign of the serpent, the wounder of the heel of man. It also concerns the goods of the departed, their abode in the world to come, etc., hence the Island of the Mists, the place of guess, conjecture or philosophical speculation which the traveler in the flesh can dimly see through the strange cloudy lights of the spirit. The name was originally given to the stone known to us as the chrysolite which gem is now identified with the occult sign of the Fishes employed in the mysteries in ancient and modern times. The classification as we at present know it is of very ancient date, and specimens of the modern topaz have been found adorned with various intaglios of proven antiquity.

Although it has been stated that Thomas A' Becket wore a topaz ring, there is no doubt that Adam Sodbury, Abbot of Glastonbury, was correct when he says it was a peridot, for the peridot or chrysolite was the stone of the Churchmen and intimately associated with the mystic sign of Christianity—Pisces, the Fishes. The old Abbot wrote that "a gold ring in which was set the stone peritot (an old form of peridot) encircled the finger of our Martyr St. Thomas when he was killed by the swords of evil men." At that time it is certain that the topaz and the peridot were the stones known as such today and as such they had been known for many centuries before.

The Sanskrit word TOPAS, meaning heat, may well describe the topaz, the color of which can be changed readily by heat, and which, under heat pressure and friction, exhibits strong electric phenomena.

Scorpio, as before remarked, is the sign of the snake or serpent so intimately connected with the mysteries of life and death, and the topaz is remarkable for its cleavage, for when struck with a hammer it breaks into flakes like the backbone of a serpent. The topaz was considered as of wonderful potency in the treatment of sexual disorders, which astrologically are considered as disorders of the sign Scorpio. It contains from 55 to 58 per cent of alumina, which substance has been used in modern times by Dr. Richard Hughes, Dr. Teste, Dr. Peters, Dr. Marcy and others in troubles of the sexual system and the mucous membranes. The drug has been used homeopathically in such morbid conditions and in chronic pharyngitis and diseases of the nose and throat. The nose is ruled by Scorpio in astrological deductions, and the throat by Taurus, its opposite sign.

Alumina is most strongly expressed in corundums, which include the Oriental topaz, next the chrysoberyl, next the spinel, and next the topaz, but there are certain characteristics of the topaz which in some way render it distinct from other gems, and these would have been considered by the hermetic schools whence such philosophy originated. Amongst mineralogists the topaz is known as topaz rhombicus. It is found in colors golden, yellow, reddish, white, greenish, wine color and blue. A charming pink is produced artificially by subjecting the real stone to heat, the best results being procured from a golden-brown variety. This process was first discovered by M. Dumelle, a Paris jeweler, in the year 1750. The color thus obtained is doubtless permanent, the shade being manifest when the stone cools. Great care must be observed in this simple experiment because the stone is so sensitive that unless properly handled it is likely to split under the various degrees of heat and cold.

Translucent achromatic topaz is called *Pingos d'Agoa* (drops of water) by the Brazilians, and *Gouttes d'Eau* by the French. In England the variety is called Minas Novas, after the Minas Novas in the State of Minas Geraes in Brazil where it is extensively found. In Portugal this type of topaz is called the "diamond of slaves." The large British Museum specimen of this white topaz which, according to Mr. Emanuel, weighs over 12 lbs. (avoirdupois,) was sold for three shillings by a marine store dealer who used it to hold open his door. The great blue Queensland topaz in the possession of Queen Mary of Great Britain is said to have been discovered by a shepherd who, thinking it was a common stone, threw it at a howling dog during the night and wakened in the morning to discover the precious nature of his missile.

The topazion statue of 4 cubits high which Pliny mentions as having been made by the order of Ptolemy Philadelphus to the memory of his sister-wife Arsinoe has puzzled investigators. It has been set down as indicating a statue of jasper, agate, prase, chrysoprase or rock crystal of the citrine or the smoky quartz varieties. Probably this latter suggestion is right but the real meaning will no doubt lie in the sign Scorpio, which was known in old Egypt as the Eagle (the symbolic badge of the Ptolemaic dynasty), and was the sign of material death and spiritual life. The Emperor Hadrian is said to have had a large topaz ring on which was engraved:

"*Natura deficit.*
Fortuna mutatur,
Deus omnia cernit."

Tavernier writes of a great topaz in the possession of the Grand Mogul weighing 157 carats and worth about 100,000 dollars. Runyeet Singh's topaz, half the size of a billiard ball, was worth 200,000 rupees. The Great Braganza, 1,680 carats, which adorned the crown of Portugal and was supposed to be a diamond, is a white topaz. One of the pleasures of the giant Emperor Maximilian, of whose strength so many stories are told, was to crush topazes to powder in his fingers. Why he indulged in this form of sport is unknown; probably he found it recreation after killing an ox at a blow or knocking out the teeth of an unfortunate horse. Mr. King mentions a head of Maecenas on topaz attributed to Solon at Florence, and another—wrongly attributed to Dioscorides—of a girl's head in the Marlborough collection. The topaz was called "Stone of Strength" by Pliny for the martial Scorpio is the wrestler's sign and the sign of strong people.

The power of the topaz was said to increase as the moon increased, especially if the night orb was at new or full in the sign Scorpio. It banished the terrors of the night, protected the wearer during epidemics, soothed the wild passions and gave a glimpse of the beyond. It banished the fear of death and secured a painless passing from this life to the next; it gave strength to the intellect and enabled the wearer to receive impressions from astral sources. It preserved from miasmatic conditions and lost its color when in the presence of poisons. The power attributed to it of quenching boiling water is symbolic of the fiery Mars, planet of power in the watery Scorpio.

It was also said by the old masters that the topaz preserved against drowning, and a curious illustration of this belief came recently under the writer's notice. He advised the wife of a well-known Australian to purchase a very beautiful topaz, which was mounted under his direction as a charm of the sign Scorpio. During the late war this lady and her daughter had need to travel to England. The voyage was about half accomplished when the vessel began to sink. The boat in which the lady and her daughter were capsized and all the struggling passengers were thrown into the sea. She seized a piece of wreckage and supported her daughter and herself until they were both dragged into a boat some considerable time after. The lady had clutched the topaz charm from her neck and was holding it tightly in her hand while struggling in the water. Just as they got into the boat she felt someone give a heavy blow on her hand and take the gem from her. She grieved for the loss of her beautiful topaz charm which she regarded as the symbol of her own and her daughter's salvation.

Leonardus said that the topaz was a charm against asthma and Rabbi Benoni calls it the emblem of strength and the easer of hemorrhage. In the *Book of Wings*, it is recommended that to secure favor with kings, princes, nobles and important personages a topaz engraved with the figure of a flying falcon should be worn. This charm was to be constructed as a charm of power when the well-aspected moon was passing through the 5th, 6th and 7th degrees of the heavenly Scorpion. Another topaz charm given is for acquiring riches: this takes the form of a man holding a lamp. It had to be mounted in gold and constructed when the increasing moon, in good aspect to the direct Jupiter and the Sun, was passing through the 5th, 6th, 7th, 26th and 27th degrees of Scorpio.

In a dream the topaz is a symbol of movement, protection from harm, poisons, etc. The symbolic dream introducing this stone is a symbolic message from the departed. The topaz and its varieties are under the celestial Scorpio.

CHAPTER 28

TOURMALINE—ZIRCON

TOURMALINE

"This black thing, one of the prettiest of the very few pretty black things in the world, is called Tourmaline."

—RUSKIN

The tourmaline, written in the 18th century in England as tumalin, is derived from the Ceylonese TURMALI or TORAMALLI. The first specimens to arrive in London were known as "Brazilian emeralds," and they came from Brazil in the 17th century only to meet with an unfavorable reception. In the beginning of the 18th century Dutch merchants began to bring from Amsterdam specimens obtained by them from Ceylon. The Dutch cutters, observing how straw and other particles were attracted to specimens which had been lying in the sunlight, called the stone in consequence *Aschentrekker* (ash attractor). The Germans called it *Azchenzieher*, and the French *Tire-cendre*.

The Swedish scholar Linnaeus experimented with the tourmaline, calling it the "Electric Stone." M. Lemery, the French Professor, called it the "Magnetic." The experiments of Aepinus and Lehmann were concerned with the positive and negative energies exhibited by the Tourmaline. These 18th century scholars held that its power of repulsion exceeded its power of attraction. This sensitive stone is affected by weather changes, and it exhibits considerable power when heated—the electricity then developed being termed pyroelectric. Professor W. Goodchild, M.B., etc., details an interesting experiment in dealing with the physical properties of gemstones:

"A crystal of tourmaline, in heating to 150° C., becomes positively electrified at one terminature and negatively at the other. If now it be suspended by a non-conducting thread it will act as a magnet: on cooling, the charges on the poles reverse, positive becoming negative. If a crystal with such a charge be dusted with a fine mixture of sulfur and red lead, the yellow sulfur will be attracted to the portions charged with positive electricity, while the red lead goes to the negatively charged portions."

This experiment serves to illustrate the attraction of the mind (represented by yellow sulfur), towards the positive pole, and matter (represented by red lead), towards the negative pole, as noted in the philosophical researches of the old alchemists. If in a heated state the tourmaline be shattered, all the little pieces will exhibit the forces of attraction and repulsion so marked in this strange stone. It has been suspected, not without reason, that tourmaline specimens were used by some of the Eastern students of alchemy who held primarily that the substance of the Philosopher's Stone is Mercurial and that it should be treated with heat, for by that means alone would its use be shown, warmth coming from the Heavens to bless Man, Nature, and the Kingdoms of Nature.

The tourmaline is remarkable also for the variety of its colors, indicated by various and not always appropriate names. **SCHORL,** the black variety spoken of by Ruskin, was so called according to De Costa (1761) by the German miners. The same writer says "our English miners call them 'bockle' and 'ball'." The name appears as shin, schirl (so spelled by De Costa), schoerl, shorl. In the 16th century it was known in Germany as schrul, but later in the 18th century it appears as schorl. The name is now becoming unpopular, the simple term black tourmaline being preferred. The colorless variety is termed **ACHROITE,** from a Greek word meaning colorless; pink and rosy red are termed **RUBELLITE;** indigo blue, **INDICOLITE;** blue, Brazillian sapphire; green, Brazilian emerald; yellow-green, Brazilian peridot; honey-yellow, Ceylon peridot; red violet, **SIBERITE.**

The brown variety is usually known as brown tourmaline, although it has been known and still is known as Brazilian topaz or Ceylonese topaz. It is not so hard as the topaz, however, ranging in the scale somewhere between quartz and zircon. The refractive powers are likewise not in agreement, and in methylene dioxide the topaz (stone of Mars) sinks, whilst the tourmaline (stone of Mercury) floats. There are also amber-colored, cinnamon, lilac, gray, blue-gray, water-green and many beautiful parti-colored specimens.

It is believed by some students that this gem was known to the ancients by the name lyncurium, which Mr. King believes to be a species of jacinth, Dr. Brotero an orange-colored hyacinth. Professor Ajasson, believing the name to refer to tourmaline, suggests that LYN may be derived from the Sanskrit word LANKA, the name of Ceylon, a place where the stone is plentifully found. The general opinion now is that the stone described by Pliny under the name of lychnis is our tourmaline. Pliny writes in his 37th Book on *Natural History* of the power of the lychnis of drawing straws and fluff towards it when heated by the sun or by the friction of the hand.

The peculiar attractive and repulsive properties of the tourmaline may be compared with the mysteries contained in the caduceus of the wise and ever-restless Hermes. The symbolical snakes which adorn the rod represent knowledge received and knowledge imparted in the hermetic scheme of the Rosicrucians. The tourmaline is symbolical of wisdom, strength of mind, eloquence, learning and the power of knowledge. It is the stone for the author, poet, editor, and teacher. To dream of it means—in harmony with ancient philosophy—success through knowledge in all walks of life.

The tourmaline in all colors is under the zodiacal Gemini.

TURQUOISE

"The fair Queen of France
Sent him a turquoise ring and glove,
And charged him as her knight and love
For her to break a lance."

          —SIR WALTER SCOTT

"Turquoise" has been written in a remarkable number of ways, amongst them being turky, torkey, turquay, turkey stone, turkie, turkeis, turkese, turkise, turkes, turkas, turkis (as used by Tennyson), turkoise, turkez, turqueis, turques, turchis, turquesse, torchas, turcasse, turquez, toorkes, turkesse. The Venetians call it turchesa, the French turquoise, the Germans turkis. Andrea Bacci (*De Gemmis et Lapidibus pretiosis*, etc., 1605) says that this stone is called turcicus, "Either on account of its admirable loveliness or for the reason that it is obtained from the Turks." The name

Specimen of Rough Turquoise, Victoria, Australia.

as we have it does not seem to go further back than the 13th century when Saxo, agreeing with Albertus Magnus, writes of it and praises its virtues as a preventive of accidents to the eye.

The old Persians called it PIRUZEH, the Triumphant, and the Arabians, whose special luck stone the turquoise is, engrave on specimens the name "Allah" with a verse from the Koran, or with some magical sign inserted in pure gold. It is known to the Mexicans as CHALCHIHUITL. This stone is identified with the callais of Pliny, who relates symbolically that it was shot down by means of slings from unapproachable rock lands. The symbol has relation to the power of this stone of the Heavenly Archer over seemingly terrifying obstacles when firmly directed by the compelling will.

The turquoise is favored by Eastern occult students who employ it largely in the composition of amulets and charms. It was said to have sprung up like an eye from its matrix, and is identified with the Antares in the Archer of the Heavens. These stars were indicated as affecting the eyes in the same degree as the Pleiades and the Asselli of Taurus and Leo. In modern Egypt a turquoise is applied to the eye as a remedy for cataract and other ophthalmic troubles, specimens thus employed being usually engraved with the sacred name of Allah.

The turquoise is especially the stone of horses, mules and camels, and from most ancient times specimens have adorned their trappings.

Leonardus said that so long as a horseman carried a piece of turquoise with him whilst riding he would never have an accident, nor would his horse be fatigued, for it was believed that the stone would draw the pain of the accident to itself. Boetius de Boodt says that when riding to his house along an uncertain road on a dark night he fell with his horse down a declivity but neither he nor his animal suffered hurt. His turquoise, however, was shattered. The stone was carried by jockeys, huntsmen and horsemen generally as a symbol of the special protection of Jupiter.

In the Middle Ages the turquoise was much worn by young girls who regarded it as a religious jewel for the protection of their virtue and for the uplifting of their thoughts. In the most ancient science the sign Sagittarius—the house or mansion of the planet Jupiter—is the sign of sport, horses, dreams, high philosophy, religion (not in the sense of creed), the true lamp of life, long voyages, publications (not newspapers), etc. Thus the turquoise—as the stone of Sagittarius—was a stone of dreams, the horse, philosophy, religion, etc., and its grand symbolic purpose was to help the spiritual person to resist the weakness, evils and temptations so intermixed with material life. The turquoise was said to be a charm against the evil eye and evil thoughts.

The Arabs say that the stone is sensitive to weather changes and that its color is affected by the state of the atmosphere. They knew Jupiter as the "Cloud Gatherer," "The Thunderer," "The God of the Murky Cloud," etc., and they connected the turquoise with his powerful works. The planet Jupiter strong at birth is held to indicate riches and worldly advantage. The old Arabian writers note a form of magic for inducing wealth and monetary advantages, performed in the hour of Jupiter. During this ceremony a turquoise was held in the right hand and the desires spoken into the stone at which a steady gaze was directed.

Carelessness has led to error amongst writers. A 16th century author confuses the topaz with the turquoise, describing the latter as a "gem of yellow color" and recommending it as a charm against the bites of reptiles and stings of insects—qualities ascribed by the old masters to the topaz, gem of the sign of the Scorpion. Another writer repeats the error, saying that "this yellow stone reduced to a powder is helpful in case of stings from scorpions and fearful and venomous reptiles."

The turquoise was held in esteem for diseases of the hip—a part of the body astrologically under the sway of Sagittarius. In this connection the stone was reduced to a paste and bound flat to the part affected, whole specimens being bound above and below the seat of the trouble. The turquoise contains a high percentage of phosphoric acid, which is employed in modern homeopathy for affections of the lungs, astrologically under the sign Gemini and therefore opposite to the sign Sagittarius. The ancients advised the turquoise as a lung medicine, not to be taken internally. The sign Sagittarius is also the sign of prophecy, and the turquoise set in the foreheads of the statues of Buddha and other images symbolizes the knowledge of things to come. The golden bow and the turquoise arrow of the Tibetan legend have especial reference to the Sun in the sign Sagittarius. Dr. Kunz, quoting from Dr. Berthold Laufer of the Field Museum, Chicago, refers to this legend as follows: "A powerful saint touching the bow and arrow of a blacksmith transforms the bow into gold and the arrow into turquoise."

The bow represents the solar rays and the arrow the Heavens, hence it is little wonder that the turquoise was termed the "gem of the Gods." The turquoise was also recommended for diseases of the throat and heart—as phosphoric acid is today in homeopathy. In harmony with an ancient astro-philosophy known as "Planetary Interchanges," the turquoise was considered an ideal lovers' gift—unless the stone was otherwise than fortunate in the horoscope of the recipient—and a gift of friendship.

The changes of color in a turquoise have been long noted, and the lines of the poet Donne are frequently quoted:

"As a compassionate turquoise that doth tell
By looking pale the wearer is not well."

Boetius tells a story of a wonderful turquoise possessed by a Spanish gentleman which so lost its color after his death that it appeared "more like a malachite than a turkois." Boetius then says that his father bought it for very little at the sale of the Spaniard's effects and gave it to him. He relates that he had hardly worn it for a month when "it resumed its pristine beauty and daily appeared to increase in splendor." Mr. Harry Emanuel gives a somewhat similar story concerning a turquoise that lost its luster with the death of its owner "as if mourning for its master," regaining it in its "former exquisite freshness" when worn by its new owner.

A case of this kind came under the writer's notice: The wife of a well-known pastoralist of New South Wales had a bangle of turquoises cut into the shape of Egyptian scarabs. While traveling in Japan she became ill and the stones changed from a soft blue to a dull green, regaining their former beauty when the lady regained her health. One of the oldest firms of jewelers in the city of Melbourne, Australia, was worried to find that an exquisite Persian turquoise entrusted to them to mount in a tiara with diamonds was changing color whilst in the hands of their chief "setter." This craftsman had been complaining for some days of indisposition. Strangely enough, the gem regained its beautiful color on being entrusted to another and healthier workman.

The connection of the turquoise with weather changes is not confined merely to Oriental peoples. The Pueblo and Apache Indians employ it as a rain-stone, which they say is always found concealed at the foot of the rainbow. They place pieces of turquoise on their bows and fire arms as directing charms for trueness of aim.

This stone is also called the "gem of liberty and benevolence," and an old Eastern proverb says: "A turquoise given with the hand of love carries with it true fortune and sweet happiness." Another Eastern belief runs that the turquoise turns pale when danger threatens the giver. Felton in his *Secrete Wonders of Nature*, 1569, states that "the turkeys does move when there is any peril prepared to him that weareth it." Dr. E. A. Wallis Budge identifies Tcheser of the 3rd dynasty (3900 B.C.) who built the "Step Pyramid" at Sakkarah as the Memphian King who worked the turquoise mines of Sinai. His name is still perpetuated on a rock at Wadi Magharah. It was at this place that Major C. MacDonald found turquoise in 1849, and Professor Flinders Petrie in 1905. Professor Petrie also discovered evidences here of very ancient mining operations. Archaic specimens of worked turquoise are still being found in Egypt. The color appealed to the sons and daughters of Khem who imitated it to a very great extent in their scarabs, beads, ornaments and other articles of adornment.

In the Vatican collection there are valuable intaglios and cameos cut in this stone which in some instances retain their heaven-blue color to this day. Mr. King mentions a laureated head of Augustus and the head of a Gorgon in the Fould collection, "the original azure converted into a dull green by the action of the earth." In Persia the stone was always highly esteemed and the most perfect specimens are held by the Royal House. The Khorassan mines near Nishapur are still famous for the remarkable beauty of the stones won from them. So fashionable was the gem in Europe in the 17th century that no true gentleman would consider his dress complete unless his hand was adorned with a ring of turquoise, for it was (as a true stone of the Archer) symbolic of the fairness and high sense of justice of the wearer. The famous turquoises in the Royal Jewels of Spain were brought from New Mexico somewhere about this period also.

Sir Walter Scott in *Marmion* sings of the turquoise ring and glove which the French Queen sent to the Scottish King James IV, with 14,000 crowns of France, begging him for the love she had for him to raise an army for her sake. It is a curious fact that the turquoise was the death stone of James IV who was killed at Flodden Field by an arrow from an *archer's* bow. The turquoise was to him a symbol of error and fatality. Henry VIII sent the dying Cardinal Wolsey a ring of turquoise by Sir John Russel, bidding him say to his fallen favorite that he, the King, "loved him as well as ever he did and grieved for his illness." For a talisman of liberty and freedom Marbodus advises that a perfect turquoise be engraved with a man standing under a beetle. It should be then set in a brooch of gold and blessed and consecrated; "then the glory which God hath bestowed shall manifest." An astrological charm for wealth and prosperity takes the form of a centaur firing an arrow upwards, to be engraved on a turquoise, preferably in the hour of Jupiter with the Moon in good aspect to Jupiter passing the 3rd and 4th degrees of Sagittarius.

True turquoise, termed "*de vieille roche,*" or oriental turquoise, differs from the fossil turquoise or odontolite, called "*de nouvelle roche,*" or occidental turquoise. Fossil turquoise can be easily marked by a steel instrument, while true turquoise acts as flint to steel. A drop of hydrochloric acid causes effervescence in fossil turquoise, which when submitted to fire gives out an animal odor. Fine turquoises are of that heavenly blue color known as "turquoise blue," and they present a waxy appearance. The variety known as variscite, supposed to be the callaina of Pliny, is a soft green stone found in various forms in prehistoric graves near *Mane er H'rock* or Fairy Rock in Brittany, in the State of Utah in the United States of America, and other places.

The turquoise is under the zodiacal Sagittarius.

CHAPTER 29

STONES IN MAGIC AND AS SYMBOLS

Gems in Heraldry

"Sweet mercy is nobility's true badge."
   — *Titus Andronicus*

Without doubt the science of Heraldry was evolved from ancient astrological philosophy. Various distinctive badges, shields and tokens were employed by the peoples of the past, but the system as known today did not properly evolve much before the 13th Century. In the present book, that section of Heraldry known as Blazoning by Planets and Precious Stones deserves some passing notice. By Blazoning the Sovereigns and Peers were distinguished, the former by the Planets and the latter by precious stones, as shown in the following table:

Tincture	Planet	Precious Stone
Or	Sun	Topaz
Argent	Moon	Pearl
Sable	Saturn	Diamond
Gules	Mars	Ruby
Azure	Jupiter	Sapphire
Vert	Venus	Emerald
Pupure	Mercury	Amethyst
Tenny	Caput Draconis (Moon's North Node)	Jacinth
Sanguine	Cauda Draconis (Moon's South Node)	Sardonyx

The planetary gem grouping is not quite accurate according to astrological science, and the errors can be referred to the early chroniclers. For example, the ruby is given to Mars and the topaz to the Sun, whereas the ruby is a stone of the Sun and the topaz a stone of Mars. Mars is

411

termed Warlike and Violent in old works, whilst the Sun is the emblem of Faithfulness and Constancy. At the coronation of a British Sovereign a ruby ring emblematical of Faithfulness and Constancy is placed on his finger. Thus it is in harmony with the royal sign Leo—the sign of the Sun—and the Monarch who is astrologically ruled by the Sun.

The pearl is correct for the Moon; the diamond is not a stone of Saturn; the sapphire is not a stone of Jupiter; the emerald is correct for Venus; the amethyst is not a stone of Mercury. The assigning of jacinth and sardonyx to the North and the South Nodes of the Moon has not the support of astrological science.

Magical Squares of Abra Melin the Mage

"The Wisdom of the Lord is an inexhaustible fountain, neither hath there ever been a man born who could penetrate its veritable origin and foundation."

—*The Second Book of the Sacred Magic*

In that remarkable ancient magical work, *The Book of the Sacred Magic of Abra Melin the Mage,* skillfully translated by a past Rosicrucian adept, Monsieur le Comte Macgregor de Glenstrae, are a number of symbolic Name Squares which were variously employed by the old masters who so well knew the use of them. For the finding of certain treasures which are not "magically guarded" ("magically" may here be accepted in a wide sense) the following symbolic power figures were employed:

For **JEWELS**: This square, the Comte notes, is a square of 36 squares, and the name BELIAL that of one of the four great chiefs of the Evil Spirits.

B	E	L	I	A	L
E	B	O	R	U	A
L	O	V	A	R	I
I	R	A	V	O	L
A	V	R	O	B	E
L	A	I	L	E	B

For **PEARLS**: A square of 16 squares.

I	A	N	A
A	M	E	N
N	E	M	A
A	N	A	I

For **DIAMONDS**: A square of 49 squares.

B	I	C	E	L	O	N
I	R	O	L	A	T	O
C	O	R	A	M	A	L
E	L	A	M	A	L	E
L	A	M	A	R	O	C
O	T	A	L	O	R	I
N	O	L	E	C	I	B

For **RUBIES**: A border of 12 squares from a square of 25 squares. The Comte translates SEGOR as "to break forth" or to "shut in," according as the root begins with S or SH.

S	E	G	O	R
E				
G				
O				E
R			B	S

For **BALASSIUS RUBIES**: Twenty squares from a square of 49 squares.

H	E	T	I	S	E	R
E						
T						
I						
S						
E	C	I	N	E	S	E
R						H

For **EMERALDS:** A square of 49 squares. ASTAROT is set down in the Comte's notes as one of the 8 Sub Princes of the Evil Spirits.

A	S	T	A	R	O	T
S	A	L	I	S	T	O
T	L	A	N	B	S	R
A	I	N	O	N	I	A
R	S	B	N	A	L	T
O	T	S	I	L	A	S
T	O	R	A	T	S	A

To find stolen jewels, the following is given: The square consists of 22 squares taken from a square of 49 squares.

K	I	X	A	L	I	S
I	R	I	N	E	Q	I
X						
A						
L				M		
I	Q					
S						K

These and many similar figures were used by the Hermetic philosophers in their occult scientific practices. They can be nothing but interesting curiosities to the majority who are ignorant of the trials, sufferings and disappointments of those brave and faithful Fraters and Sorores who regarded no sin so great as ingratitude and no tendency so foolish as incredulity. "For," says Abra Melin, "you must have Faith. Neither should you dispute concerning that which you understand not. God out of nothingness hath created all things, and all things have their being in Him. Watch, labor and you will see."

Psychology of Botany, Minerals and Precious Stones

In the year 1907, a remarkable book bearing the above title, written by a gifted student who preferred to veil his identity under the pen name of Charubel, was published by R. Welch, Esq., 92 Shuttle St., Tyldesley, England. This work is now difficult to obtain. The author insists on a direct sympathy between the human soul and surrounding nature, and his work illustrates his method of linking together these eternal immortal powers so that the human can draw from these elements exactly that force he needs.

The Psychological Properties of Precious Stones includes his occult researches into hidden properties which he presents in certain order. The stones mentioned are the topaz, amethyst, coral, rock crystal, emerald, diamond, ruby, turquoise, sapphire, red garnet, carbuncle. He writes:

"The realm of precious stones abounds with wonders which transcend everything I may have hitherto been made conversant with. Hence, I am very much fascinated with these lustrous specimens of a chemistry which transcends the skill of the ingenious to identify or to produce the same. It is true that so far as appearance goes, modern skill can produce from a kind of paste what resembles the genuine stone, but he can no more produce a living stone than he can make a living tree. The true stone has a life and it is in this life that its true virtue consists."

The Topaz

The virtues of the topaz, writes Charubel, are to be appreciated by "fair people with weak or fragile constitutions, inclined to become despondent, of cold habits. A help to those who are out of sight or in the shade. It begets hopefulness in the hopeless. Strengthens and fortifies the soul against evil, wicked persons." The seal of the topaz is according to our author:

The sacred name by which it is invoked is SOO-MAH-THU-EL-DI-VOO-MATH-EL.

The Amethyst

The virtues of the amethyst are set down as a cure for false vision, bad memory, color-blindness, intoxication, etc. The seal is given as:

The sacred name by which the life of the amethyst is invoked is given as AVRUTHEL.

The Coral

The virtues of the coral, according to Charubel, benefit decrepit persons and those prematurely old. It quickens the senses, is good in defect of the eyesight from gradual loss of energy in the optic nerve, and it strengthens the mental faculties.

The seal is given as:

and the sacred name of invocation AG-ATH-EL.

The Rock Crystal

The virtues of the rock crystal include, writes Charubel, safeguard against deception or imposition. "It is for the pure in heart and those who think of a better life."

The seal is given as:

and the sacred name of invocation EV-AG-EL.

The Emerald

The virtues of the emerald are for those "who aspire to wisdom and seek enlightenment, and for those who seek the good of life," etc.

The seal is given as:

and the sacred name of invocation as AM-VRADEL.

The Diamond

The diamond is for

> "Kings, Monarchs, Presidents and people of high standing, etc., State Authorities and the advanced Occultists. The diamond is a gem by the virtue of its homogeneity and belongs to the domain of the true life. The diamond is *sacred*: one of the most *sacred*: yes, the most *sacred* of all gems. I am not allowed to give word and seal for this gem."

The Ruby

Charubel hails the ruby as "the most precious of gems, a balm in the hour of trial, grief, bereavement, disappointment, a soother of agitation and disburdener of the oppressed soul."

The seal of the ruby is given as:

and the sacred word of invocation as DER-GAB-EL.

The Turquoise

The turquoise is set down as the "Sympathetic Stone, an invaluable treasure to the thoughtful and meditative, a connector of souls, a developer of Inner Powers."

The seal is given as:

The sacred word of invocation is HAR-VAL-AM.

The Sapphire

The sapphire is written down as "a cure for doubt and despondency, a reviver of blighted hopes, which robs the future of its dread and renders the Valley of Death redolent with sunshine."

The seal is given as:

The sacred word of invocation is TROO-AV-AL.

The Red Garnet

The red garnet is hailed as the stone of inspiration and a remedy, for diabolical influences, etc.

The seal is given as:

and the sacred word of invocation as AR-HU-GAL.

The Carbuncle

The carbuncle "physically strengthens and vivifies the vital and generative forces in human nature, those that lack energy, sufferers from anemia, and those wanting in animal courage. It sharpens business propensities and is invaluable to the dull, lethargic, sluggish, lymphatic, and people of cold habits."

The seal is given as:

and the sacred word of invocation is APH-RU-EL.

Gems of Countries

Old philosophy allots a particular talismanic gem to every country in the world. Those of the following countries are:

Abyssinia	Lapis Lazuli
Afghanistan	Catseye
Albania	Dark Onyx
Algeria	Banded Agate
Arabia	Flint
Argentina	Spodumene
Australia	Opal
Austria	Opal
Bavaria	Topaz
Belgium	Marble
Brazil	Jasper Bloodstone
Bulgaria	Striped Onyx
Burma	Malachite
China	Pearl
Denmark	Hematite
Egypt	Jasper Opal
England	Diamond
France	Ruby

Germany	Hematite
Greece	Dark Onyx
Holland	Pearl
Hungary	Carbuncle
India	Catseye
Ireland	Emerald
Italy	Sardonyx
Japan	Jade
Judea	Topaz
Mexico	Onyx
Morocco	Banded Agate
New Zealand	Nacre
Norway	Topaz
Nubia	Crystal
Palestine	Limonite
Persia	Mocha Stone
Poland	Emerald
Portugal	Chrysolite
Prussia	Sapphire
Rumania	Lapis Lazuli
Russia	Chrysoberyl-Alexandrite
Scotland	Chalcedony
Sicily	Carnelian
South Africa	Pearl
Spain	Turquoise
Syria	Limonite
Sweden	Sapphire
Switzerland	Jasper
Turkey	Jacinth
Transvaal	Cairngorm
United States of America	Tourmaline
Wales	Marble

CHAPTER 30

THE INEVITABLE LAW OF TRANSMUTATION

"Each change of many color'd life he drew.
Exhausted worlds and then imagin'd new."

— JONSON

Transformation, under the various forms of transfiguration, transmutation and change, forms the subject of many fascinating stories which adorn the pages of romance, mythology, science and symbology. It may be said to exhibit itself as the dominant force in the world of matter—the changeful, restless world with which we change and to which, while dressed in its elements, we are held. The disobedience of Lot's wife changed her material form into a pillar of salt; the fated Niobe was transformed into a rugged rock which forever was bathed by her tears; the glance of Medusa turned her victims into stone, her blood turned trees into coral; the stone which Rhea duped Cronus into swallowing in the belief that it was one of his children—indeed, the whole legend concerning the devouring of his offspring by the old god—is illustrative of the process of nature which forever consumes that which it produces. Nature is a veritable alchemist, a royal transmuter, turning the precious into the base and the base into the precious, regardless of dignity, rank or name.

Parable and symbol have ever been the ornate coverings beneath which lie securely hidden from the superficial gaze the secrets with which searching man has played for ages. The work of these intrepid scientists had, at certain periods of the world's history, to be carefully concealed from the vulgar and intolerant mind which was continually endeavoring to bind the thoughts of men within the slavery of a fixed dogma. The true meaning of this dogma was indeed far better known and understood by the faithful searchers into the mysteries of nature than by all the narrow agents seeking to suppress them. But they were compelled to wait till the champions of liberty in the material world had swept back the devils of intolerance which darkened the way to spiritual and material freedom.

The waiting for the right time to present their discoveries to the people did not suspend their researches—it rather advanced them. Nearly 600 years before the Christian era the poetical philosopher Xenophanes wrote of fossil fishes, shells and other petrifaction found on high mountains and in quarries, which he instanced as indicating changes on the earth's surface, certain lands sinking beneath the sea and certain lands rising out of it. The earlier examinations of these remains were considered as evidence of a subtle tractable power inherent in the earth. Plato, Aristotle, and Zeno taught that God entered His Spirit into eternal matter, producing the earth, thus eternally filled with the potential Spirit.

That many-sided genius of the 15th and 16th centuries, Leonardo da Vinci, was rightly regarded by Dmitri Merejkowski as "The Forerunner," in his historical story of that name. Leonardo was most precise in his remarkable deductions on fossilization, which, he wrote, occurred from the accumulation of mud in the cavities of shells discovered in rivers which were at an ancient period beneath the sea near the coast.

Nature's wonderful workings are exhibited in the metamorphoses of the various stones. This process is noticed in the silicification of wood, shells, coral, etc. It is observed in the incrustation of one substance on another, the expulsion of one mineral matter by some chemical agency, by the gradual yielding of original substance to new and foreign invaders and by the occurrence of one mineral in the form of another, etc. So far as is considered necessary this subject has been already dealt with.

And so Nature is continually proving to man that all is change and that dissolution is impossible. Continually, lower forms are giving place to higher, and the work of the world goes on with the persistent regularity of a huge machine. "Nothing is lost," says chemistry, and even the voice of man, the cries of animals, sounds of breaking rocks, the restless sea, the moaning of the winds amongst the trees, etc., can now be easily impressed on the modern phonograph plates which provide a material working body. Every action can be recorded and reproduced by the photographic camera; even the air can be harnessed to convey a desire. Everything in the Universe, from the stars of Heaven to the atom, or to the minutest subdivision of the atom, is mathematical, law abiding, and under the mysterious and controlling Force which we reverence as God the Infinite.

Nature claims her own, the material goes to the material, "dust to dust," and earth processes turn the visible parts of animals and plants, etc., into its identical crystal form. And the controlling powers about which these perceptible forms materialize, seek the realms of finer forces to which they truly belong. Rightly say the venerable philosophers whose inspired utterances have taught us so much, "The Spirit strips itself to go up and clothes itself to go down." The writer has tried to make this palpable truth clear in these pages, and trusts that the links in the ancient chain are now left in a little better repair than they were, and that the power within the stone will be better appreciated and better understood.

The order of the Infinite Universe is exact and sincere. From its inception the work, trials and struggles of the smallest atom are determined and Mind is compelled to express itself. The exact point of union between the visible and the invisible forces has been long known to the hermetic scientists and philosophers whose thoughts are echoed by Wilks, the English poet of Geology, in the following lines:

> "God is a God of order, though to scan
> His works may pose the feeble powers of man."

FINIS

"It seems she hangs upon the cheek of night
Like a rich jewel in an Ethiope's ear."
— *Romeo and Juliet*

Those who labor for the world belong to the world, no matter which little part of it may be claimed as their birthplace. This applies to the humblest as well as to the greatest, as in a play the excellence of individual players contributes to the artistic harmony and influence of the entire production. So it is that William Shakespeare, the inspired master of the "spacious times of great Elizabeth," breaks through the narrow limits of sea-girt England and encompasses the whole world of women and men, detaches his immaterial self from the period of his earth life and endures—a perpetual source of pleasure, philosophy, wisdom and music. Throughout his works William Shakespeare mentions seventeen distinct stones of adornment, viz: agate, amber, carbuncle, chrysolite, coral, crystal, diamond, emerald, flint, jet, lapis lazuli, marble, opal, pearl, ruby, sapphire, turquoise.

AGATE

In Act I, Scene 4 of *Romeo and Juliet*, Mercutio tells of Queen Mab—

"She is the fairies' midwife, and she comes
In shape no bigger than an agate stone
On the forefinger of an alderman."

In Act III, Scene 1 of *Much Ado about Nothing*, Hero says that

"Nature never framed a woman's heart
Of prouder stuff than that of Beatrice,"

who would swear that if a man were tall he would be like

"A *lance ill-headed;*"
"*If low, an agate very vilely out.*"

In Act II, Scene 1 of *Love's Labors Lost*, Boyet tells the Princess of France that Navarre's heart is

"*Like an agate, with your print impressed.*"

In *King Henry IV*, Part 1, Act II, Scene 4, Prince Hal says to Francis:

"*Wilt thou rob this leathern jerkin, crystal button, knott-pated, agate-ring, puke-stocking, caddie-garter, smooth tongue, Spanish-pouch ...*"

Falstaff in Part 2, Act I, Scene 2, of the same play complains to his page that he was never

"*manned with an agate till now.*"

(These quotations all serve to show how popular the agate was as a ring stone in Shakespeare's time.)

AMBER

Hamlet, in answer to a question (ACT II, Sc. 2), tells Polonius that the "satirical rogue" whose book he is reading says that old men's eyes are

"*purging thick amber and plum-tree gum,*"

a thought no doubt suggested by the ancient myth of the "weeping sisters."

Petruchio asks his "Mistress Kate":

> *"Will we return unto thy father's house*
> *..... With amber bracelets, beads, and all this knavery?"*
> (*Taming of the Shrew*, ACT IV, Sc. 3.)

Says Dumain in *Love's Labors Lost* (ACT IV, Sc. 3):

> *"Her amber hair for foul hath amber quoted"*

and Biron—

> *"An amber-colored raven was well noted."*

CARBUNCLE

Dromio of Syracuse in Act III, Sc. 2, of the *Comedy of Errors*, speaks of

> *"Her nose all o'er embellished with rubies, carbuncles, sapphires."*

In the first Act of *Coriolanus*, Scene 4, Titus Lartius says of Marcius:

> *"Thou art lost, Marcius;*
> *A carbuncle entire, as big as thou art.*
> *Were not so rich a jewel."*

Iachimo, the soothsayer, (*Cymbeline*, ACT V, Sc. 5) tells that—

> *"He, true knight,*
> *No lesser of her honor confident*
> *Than I did truly find her, stakes this ring:*
> *And would so, had it been a carbuncle*
> *Of Phoebus' wheel, and might so safely, had it*
> *Been all the worth of 's car."*

Hamlet speaks to the Players (*Hamlet*, Act II, Sc. 2) of Pyrrhus:

> "With eyes like carbuncle, the hellish Pyrrhus
> Old grandsire Priam seeks."

Again the poet uses the "carbuncle of Phoebus' wheel" in *Antony and Cleopatra*, Act IV, Scene 8:

> "He has deserved it, were it carbuncled
> Like holy Phoebus' car."

CHRYSOLITE

The fated Moor says of his poor murdered Desdemona in the last scene of the last act of *Othello*:

> "Nay, had she been true,
> If Heaven would make me such another world
> Of one entire and perfect chrysolite
> I'd not have sold her for it."

CORAL

Says Lucentio in Act I, Scene 1, of the Taming of the Shrew:

> "I saw her coral lips to move
> And with her breath she did perfume the air:
> Sacred and sweet was all I saw in her."

The charming Ariel in *The Tempest*, (Act I, Sc. 2) sings:

> "Full fathom five thy father lies:
> Of his bones are coral made:
> Those are pearls that were his eyes:
> Nothing of him that doth fade
> But doth suffer a sea-change
> Into something rich and strange."

CRYSTAL

"But in that crystal scales let there be weighed
Your lady's love against some other maid,"

says Benvolio to Romeo. (*Romeo and Juliet*, Act I, Sc. 2.)

In *Love's Labors Lost* (Act II, Sc. 1), Boyet tells the Princess of France:

"Methought all his senses were locked in his eye.
As jewels in crystal for some prince to buy."

In Act IV, Scene 3, of the same play, the King says:

'Ay, me! says one: 'O, Jove!' the other cries:
One, her hairs were gold, crystal the other's eyes."

In Act III, Scene 2 of *A Midsummer Night's Dream*, the awakening Demetrius sings Helen's praises:

"O Helen, goddess, nymph, perfect, divine!
To what, my love, shall I compare thine eyne?
Crystal is muddy."

In Act II, Scene 1, of *King John*, Queen Eleanor says of the sad sensitive Arthur:

"His mother shames him so, poor boy, he weeps,"

Constance retorting:

"Now shame upon you whether she does or no!
His grandam's wrongs, and not his mother's shame,
Draws those heaven-moving pearls from his poor eye,
Which Heaven shall take in nature of a fee:
Ay, with these crystal beads Heaven shall be bribed
To do him justice and revenge on you."

Bolingbroke in *Richard II* (Act I, Sc. 1) says:

> *"Since the more fair and crystal is the sky,*
> *The uglier seem the clouds that in it fly."*

Says Bardolph in *Henry V* (Act II, Sc. 3):

> *"Go clear thy crystals."*

At the opening of *King Henry VI*, Bedford has the famous lines:

> *"Hung be the heavens with black, yield day to night,*
> *Comets, importing change of times and states,*
> *Brandish your crystal tresses in the sky."*

In Act V, Scene 4, of *Cymbeline*, the ghost father Sicilius says:

> *"Thy crystal window ope: look out."*

Two Gentlemen of Verona, Act. 2, Scene 4:

> *"But that his mistress*
> *Did hold his eyes locked in his crystal looks."*

The poetic use of crystal has its basis in ancient mystical philosophy, which is partly noticed in the section under **CRYSTAL**.

DIAMOND

Shakespeare alludes to the diamond twenty-one times, most of all in Cymbeline.

Imogen gives Posthumus as a pledge of affection her diamond ring:

> *"This diamond was my mother's: take it, heart."*

The diamond is mentioned four times as an important part of the plot in the bargain between Posthumus and Iachimo:

> "If she went before others I have seen, as that diamond outlusters many I have beheld, I could not but believe that she excelled many: but I have not seen the most precious diamond that is, nor you the lady."
> POSTHUMUS: "I praised her as I rated her: so do I my stone."
> "I shall but lend my diamond till you return."
> IACHIMO: "My ten thousand ducats are yours: so is your diamond too: if I come off."

In Act II, Scene 4, poor Posthumus says:

> "All is well yet,
> Sparkles this stone as it was wont?"

alluding to the ancient belief that the diamond turned dull when lovers proved unfaithful.

> ".... The stone's too hard to come by."
> Iachimo: "I beg but leave to air this jewel: see! it must be married
> To that your diamond."

In Act V, Scene 5, Cymbeline asks Iachimo:

> "That diamond upon your finger—say,
> How came it yours?"

The diamond is mentioned three times in *Pericles*:

> MAISA: "To me he seems like diamond to glass."
>   (ACT II, SC. 3.)

> HELICANUS: "Whom if you find, and win unto return,
> You shall like diamonds sit about his crown."
>   (ACT II, SC. 4.)

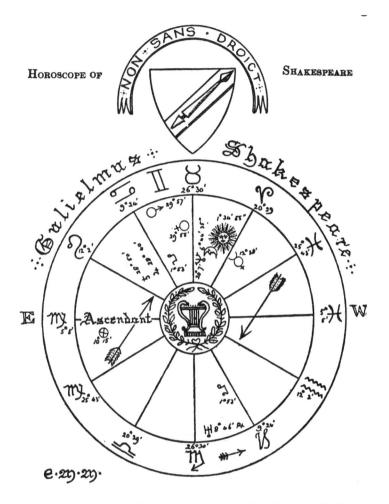

"To me he seems like diamond to glass."—Pericles, Act II, Sc. 3

CERIMON: "She is alive: behold
Her eyelids, cases to those heavenly jewels
Which Pericles hath lost,
Begin to part their fringes of bright gold:
The diamonds of a most praised water
Do appear, to make the world twice rich."

(ACT III, SC. 2.)

The diamond is mentioned three times in *King Henry VI*:

> SUFFOLK: *"So farewell Reignier: set this diamond safe*
> *In golden palaces, as it becomes."*
>> (PART 1, ACT V, SC. 3)

> THE QUEEN: *"I took a costly jewel from my neck*
> *A heart it was, bound in with diamonds,*
> *And threw it towards thy land."*
>> (PART 2, ACT III, SC. 2.)

> KING HENRY: *"My crown is in my heart not on my head:*
> *Not decked with diamonds and Indian stones*
> *Nor to be seen: my crown is called content*
> *A crown it is that seldom kings enjoy."*
>> (PART 3, ACT III, SC. 1.)

In the *Comedy of Errors*, the diamond is twice mentioned:

> THE COURTESAN: *"Give me the ring of mine you had at dinner,*
> *Or for my diamond, the chain you promised."*
>> (ACT IV, SC. 3.)

> THE COURTESAN: *"Sir. I must have that diamond from you."*
>> (ACT V, SC. 1.)

In Act III, Scene 3, in *The Merry Wives of Windsor*, Falstaff says to Mistress Ford:

> *"I see how thine eye would emulate the diamond."*

The Princess in *Love's Labors Lost*, Act V, Scene 2, speaks of a

> *"Lady walled about with diamonds."*

In *Timon of Athens* Act III, Scene 6, the Fourth Lord says:

"One day he gives us diamonds, next dry stones."

In *The Merchant of Venice*, Act III, Scene 1, Shylock exclaims,

"A diamond gone, cost me two thousand ducats in Frankfort."

In *Macbeth*, Act II, Scene 1, Banquo presents the King's diamond with the words:

"This diamond he greets your wife withal."

In *King Lear*, Act IV, Scene 3, the gentleman tells Kent:

"You have seen
Sunshine and rain at once: her smiles and tears
Were like a better way: those happy smilets,
That played on her ripe lip, seemed not to know
What guests were in her eyes: which parted thence
As pearls from diamonds dropped."

EMERALD

Emerald is mentioned but once—in Act V, Scene 5, of *The Merry Wives of Windsor*, when Mistress Quickly says:

"And 'Honi soit qui mal y pense' write
In emerald tufts, flowers purple, blue and white:
Like sapphire, pearl and rich embroidery
Buckled below fair knighthood's bending knee."

FLINT

TALBOT: *"God is our fortress in whose conquering name
Let us resolve to scale their flinty bulwarks."*

> (*King Henry VI*, PART 1, ACT II, Sc. I.)

GLOUCESTER: *"Uneath may she endure the flinty streets."*
DUCHESS OF GLOUCESTER: *"The ruthless flint doth cut my tender
feet."*

> (*Henry VI*, PART 2, ACT II, Sc. 4.)

QUEEN MARGARET: *"Because thy flinty heart more hard than they
..."*

> (*Henry VI*, PART 2, ACT III, Sc. 2.)

YORK: (*aside*): *"Scarce can I speak my choler is so great:
Oh, I could hew up rocks and fight with flint
I am so angry at these abject terms."*

> (*Henry VI*, PART 2, ACT V, Sc. 1.)

YORK: *"Women are soft, mild, pitiful and flexible:
Thou stern, obdurate, flinty, rough, remorseless."*

> (*Henry VI*, PART 3, ACT I, Sc. 4.)

RICHARD: *"Then Clifford were thy heart as hard as steel
As thou hast shown it flinty by thy deeds
I come to pierce it or to give thee mine."*

> (*Henry VI*, PART 3, ACT II, Sc. 1.)

LUCIUS: *"Searching the window for a flint I found
This paper, thus sealed up."*

> (*Julius Caesar*, ACT II, Sc. 3.)

BRUTUS: *"O Cassius, you are yoked with a lamb
That carries anger as the flint bears fire."*

> (*Julius Caesar*, ACT IV, Sc. 3)

ENOBARBUS: *"Throw my heart*
Against the flint and hardness of my fault."
            (Antony and Cleopatra, ACT IV, Sc. 9.)

THERSITES: *"There were wit in this head, an 'twould out: and so*
there is, but it lies a coldly in him as fire in a flint, which will not
show without knocking."
            (Troilus and Cressida, ACT III, Sc. 3.)

DEMETRIUS: *"But be your heart to them*
As unrelenting flint to drops of rain."
            (Titus Andronicus, ACT II, Sc. 3.)

MARCUS: *"My heart is not compact of flint nor steel."*
            (Titus Andronicus, ACT V, Sc. 8.)

GOWER: *"Make raging battery upon shores of flint."*
            (Pericles, ACT V, Sc. 4.)

POET: *"The fire i' the flint shows not till it be struck."*
            (Timon of Athens, ACT I, Sc. 1.)

TIMON: *"What, dost thou weep? Come nearer. Then I love thee.*
Because thou art a woman and disclaim'st
Flinty Mankind."
            (Timon of Athens, ACT IV, Sc. 3.)

FRIAR LAWRENCE: *"Here comes the lady: oh, so light a foot*
Will ne'er wear out the everlasting flint."
            (Romeo and Juliet, ACT II, Sc. 6.)

GLOUCESTER: *"I would to God my heart were flint, like Edward's."*
            (Richard III. ACT I, Sc. 8.)

BELARIUS: ". . . *Weariness*
Can snore upon the flint, when resty sloth
Finds the down pillow hard."

    (*Cymbeline*, ACT III, SC. 6.)

FIRST PRIEST: "... *For charitable prayers,*
Shards, flints and pebbles should be thrown on her."

    (*Hamlet*, ACT V, SC. 1.)

BASTARD: "*Till their soul-fearing clamors have brawled down*
The flinty ribs of this contemptuous city."

    (*King John*, ACT II, SC. 2.)

KING RICHARD: "*Go to Flint castle: there I'll pine away;*
A King, woe's slave, shall kingly woe obey."

    (*Richard II*, ACT III, SC. 2.)

QUEEN: "*This is the way*
To Julius Caesar's ill-erected tower,
To whose flint bosom my condemned lord
Is doomed a prisoner by proud Bolingbroke."

    (*Richard II*, ACT V, SC. 2.)

KING RICHARD: "*How these vain weak nails*
May tear a passage through the flinty ribs
Of this hard world."

    (*Richard II*, ACT V, SC. 5.)

KING HENRY: "*He hath a tear for pity and a hand*
Open as day for melting charity:
Yet notwithstanding, being incens'd, he's flint."

    (*Henry IV*, PART 2, ACT IV, SC. 4.)

OTHELLO: *"The tyrant custom, most grave senators,*
Hath made the flinty and steel couch of war
My thrice-driven bed of down."

> (*Othello*, ACT I, Sc. 3.)

HELENA: *"Which gratitude*
Through flinty Tartar's bosom would peep forth,
And answer 'Thanks.'"

> (*All's Well that Ends Well*, ACT IV, Sc. 4.)

DUKE: *"Pluck commiseration of his state*
From brassy bosoms and rough hearts of flint."

> (*Merchant of Venice*, ACT IV, Sc. 1.)

VIOLA: *"My master, not myself, lacks recompense,*
Love make his heart of flint that you shall love;
And let your fervor like my master's, be
Placed in contempt! Farewell, fair cruelty."

> (*Twelfth Night*, ACT I, Sc. 5.)

HOLOFERNES: *"Fire enough for a flint, pearl enough for a swine."*

> (*Love's Labors Lost*, ACT IV, Sc. 2.)

VOLUMNIA: *"Oh, stand up blest,*
Whilst, with no softer cushion than the flint,
I kneel before thee."

> (*Coriolanus*, ACT V, Sc. 3)

JET

GLOUCESTER: *"What color is my gown of?"*
SIMPCOX: *"Black, forsooth: coal black as jet."*
KING: *"Why then, thou know'st what color jet is of?"*
SUFFOLK: *"And yet, I think, jet did he never see."*

> (*Henry VI*, PART 2, ACT II, Sc. 1.)

TITUS: *"Provide two proper palfreys, black as jet,*
To hale thy vengeful waggon swift away."

           (*Titus Andronicus,* ACT V, SC. 2.)

SALARINO: *"There is more difference between thy flesh and hers*
than between jet and ivory."

           (*Merchant of Venice,* ACT III, SC. 1.)

LAPIS LAZULI

EVANS: *"What is 'lapis,' William?"*
WILLIAM: *"A stone."*
EVANS: *"And what is a 'stone,' William?"*
WILLIAM: *"A pebble."*
EVANS: *"No, it is 'lapis': I pray you, remember in your prain."*
WILLIAM: *Lapis.*
EVANS: *"That is a good William."*

           (*The Merry Wives of Windsor,* ACT IV, SC. 1.)

MARBLE

CARD. WOLSEY: *"When I am forgotten, as I shall be:*
And sleep in dull, cold marble."

           (*Henry VIII,* ACT III, SC. 2.)

KING HENRY: *"Her tears will pierce into a marble heart."*

           (*Henry VI,* PART 3, ACT III, SC. 2.)

GLOSTER: *"He plies her hard: and much rain wears the marble."*

           (*Henry VI,* PART 3, ACT III, SC. 2.)

SICILIUS: *"Peep through thy marble mansion."*
SICILIUS: *"The marble pavement closes."*

           (*Cymbeline,* ACT V, SC. 4.)

Lavinia: *"The milk from her did turn to marble."*
> (*Titus Andronicus*, Act II, Sc. 3.)

Othello: *"Now by yond marble heaven,*
In the due reverence of a sacred vow
I here engage my words."
> (*Othello*, Act III, Sc. 3.)

Hamlet: *"O, answer me! why the sepulchre*
Wherein we saw thee quietly inurn'd,
Hath oped his ponderous and marble jaws.
To cast thee up again."
> (*Hamlet*, Act I, Sc. 4.)

Duke: *"And he, a marble to her tears, is washed with them, but relents not."*
> (*Measure for Measure*, Act III, Sc. 1.)

Mariana: *"Let me in safety raise me from my knees:*
Or else forever be confixed here,
A marble monument!"
> (*Measure for Measure*, Act V, Sc. 1.)

Macbeth: *"I had else been perfect,*
Whole as the marble."
> (*Macbeth*, Act III, Sc. 4.)

3rd Gentleman: *"Who was most marble there, changed color."*
> (*The Winter's Tale*, Act V, Sc. 2.)

Andriana: *"If voluble and sharp discourse be marred,*
Unkindness blunts it more than marble hard."
> (*Comedy of Errors*, Act II, Sc. 1.)

OPAL

CLOWN: "*Now, the melancholy god protect thee: and the tailor make thy doublet of changeable taffeta, for thy mind is a very opal.*"
(*Twelfth Night*, ACT II, SC. 4.)

PEARL

ARIEL: "*Those are pearls that were his eyes.*" (See **CORAL**).
(*Tempest*, ACT I, SC. 1.)

MACDUFF: "*I see thee encompass'd with thy kingdom's pearl
That speak my salutation in their minds.*"
(*Macbeth*, ACT V, SC. 8.)

CONSTANCE: "*Those heaven-moving pearls.*" (See **CRYSTAL**.)
(*King John*, ACT II, SC. 1.)

OTHELLO: … "*Of one whose hand,
Like the base Indian, threw a pearl away
Richer than all his tribe.*"
(*Othello*, ACT V, SC. 2.)

KING: "*Hamlet, this pearl is thine:
Here's to thy health.*"
(*Hamlet*, ACT V, SC. 2.)

LEAR: "*As pearls from diamonds dropped.*" (See **DIAMOND**.)
(*King Lear*, ACT IV, SC. 3.)

QUICKLY: "*Like sapphire, pearl and rich embroidery.*" (See **EMERALD**.)
(*Merry Wives of Windsor*, ACT V, SC. 5.)

VALENTINE: "And I, as rich in having such a jewel
As twenty seas, if all their sand were pearl.
The water nectar and the rocks pure gold."

> (Two Gentlemen of Verona, ACT II, Sc. 4.)

PROTEUS: "A sea of melting pearl which some call tears."

> (Two Gentlemen of Verona, ACT III, Sc. 1.)

PROTEUS: "But pearls are fair: and the old saying is,
Black men are pearls in beauteous ladies' eyes."
JULIA (aside): "'Tis true: such pearls as put out ladies' eyes:
For I had rather wink than look on them."

> (Two Gentlemen of Verona, ACT V, Sc. 2.)

LORD: "Or wilt thou ride? thy horses shall be trapped,
Their harness studded all with gold and pearl."

> (Taming of the Shrew, INDUCTION, Sc. 2.)

GREMIO: "In ivory coffers I have stuffed my crowns:
....Fine linen, Turkey cushions bossed with pearl."

> (Taming of the Shrew, ACT II, Sc. 1.)

TRANIO: "Why, sir, what 'cerns it you if I wear pearl and gold?"

> (Taming of the Shrew, ACT V, Sc. 1.)

TOUCHSTONE: "Rich honesty dwells like a miser, sir, in a rich house:
as your pearl in your foul oyster."

> (As You Like It, ACT V, Sc. 4.)

MARGARET: "I saw the Duchess of Milan's gown that they praise so.
By my troth 's but a night-gown in respect of yours: cloth o' gold,
and cuts, and laced with silver, set with pearls, down sleeves, side
sleeves, and skirts, round underbone with a bluish tinsel."

> (Much Ado About Nothing, ACT III, Sc. 4.)

HOLOFERNES: *"Pearl enough for a swine."* (See **FLINT**.)
       (*Love's Labors Lost*, ACT IV, Sc. 2.)

MARIA: *"This and these pearls to me sent Longaville."*
PRINCESS: *"What, will you have me or your pearl again?"*
       (*Love's Labors Lost*, ACT V, Sc. 2.)

LYSANDER: *"Tomorrow night when Phoebe doth behold*
Her silver visage in the watery glass,
Decking with liquid pearl the bladed glass
A time that lovers' flights doth still conceal,
Through Athens' gates have we devised to steal."
       (*A Midsummer Night's Dream*, ACT I, Sc. 1.)

FAIRY: *"I must go seek some dewdrops here*
And hang a pearl in every cowslip's ear."
       (*A Midsummer Night's Dream*, ACT II, Sc. 1.)

OBERON: *"And that same dew which sometime on the buds*
Was wont to swell like round and orient pearls,
Stood now within the pretty flowerets' eyes."
       (*A Midsummer Night's Dream*, ACT IV, Sc. 1.)

SEBASTIAN: *"This is the air: that is the glorious sun:*
This pearl she gave me, I do feel't and see't
And though 'tis wonder that enwraps me thus,
Yet 'tis not madness."
       (*Twelfth Night*, ACT IV, Sc. 8.)

FALSTAFF: *"Your brooches, pearls and ouches."*
       (*Henry IV, Part 2*, ACT II, Sc. 4.)

KING HENRY: *"I am a king that find thee, and I know*
'Tis not the balm, the scepter, and the ball,
The sword, the mace, the crown imperial,

The intertissued robe of gold and pearl,
The farced title running 'fore the King,
The throne he sits on nor the tide of pomp
That beats upon the high shore of the world."

(Henry V, Act IV, Sc. 1.)

CLARENCE: *"Methought I saw a thousand fearful wrecks:*
Ten thousand men that fishes gnawed upon:
Wedges of gold, great anchors, heaps of pearl,
Inestimable stones, unvalued jewels,
All scattered in the bottom of the sea:
Some lay in dead men's skulls: and, in those holes.
Where eyes did once inhabit, there were crept
As 'twere in scorn of eyes, reflecting gems."

(King Richard III, Act I, Sc. 4.)

"The liquid drops of tears that you have shed
Shall come again, transformed to orient pearl."

(King Richard III, Act IV, Sc. 4.)

CLEOPATRA: *"How goes it with my brave Mark Antony?*
ALEXAS: *Last thing he did, dear Queen,*
He kissed—the last of many doubled kisses—
The orient pearl. His speech sticks, in my heart."
CLEOPATRA: *"Mine ears must pluck it thence."*
ALEXAS: *'Good friend,' quote he,*
'Say the firm Roman to great Egypt sends
This treasure of an oyster.'"

(Antony and Cleopatra, Act I, Sc. 6.)

CLEOPATRA: *"I'll set thee in a shower of gold and hail*
Rich pearls upon thee."

(Antony and Cleopatra, Act II, Sc. 2)

TROILUS: "Her bed is India: there she lies, a pearl."
(*Troilus and Cressida,* ACT I, SC. 1.)

TROILUS: "Why, she is a pearl,
Whose price hath launched above a thousand ships,
And turned crowned kings to merchants."
(*Troilus and Cressida,* ACT II, SC. 8)

AARON: "I will be bright and shine in pearl and gold,
To wait upon this new-made empress."
(*Titus Andronicus,* ACT II, SC. 1.)

LUCIUS: "This is the pearl that pleased your empress' eye.
And here's the base fruit of his burning lust."
(*Titus Andronicus,* ACT V, SC. 1.)

RUBY

FAIRY: "The cowslips tall her pensioners be:
In their gold coats spots you see:
Those be rubies, fairy favors,
In those freckles live their savors."
(*A Midsummer Night's Dream,* ACT II, SC. 1.)

MACBETH: "You make me strange
When now I think you can behold such sights.
And keep the natural ruby of your cheeks,
When mine is blanched with fear."
(*Macbeth,* ACT III, SC. 4.)

MARK ANTONY: "Over thy wounds now do I prophesy—
Which like dumb mouths do ope their ruby lips,
To beg the voice and utterance of my tongue."
(*Julius Caesar,* ACT III, SC. 1.)

DROMIO: *"Embellished with rubies, carbuncles, sapphires."* (*See* CARBUNCLE.)

> (*Comedy of Errors,* ACT III, SC. 2.)

SAPPHIRE

MISTRESS QUICKLY: *"Like sapphire, pearl and rich embroidery."* (See **EMERALD**.)

> (*Merry Wives of Windsor,* ACT V, SC. 5.)

DROMIO: *"Embellished with rubies, carbuncles, sapphires."* (*See* **CARBUNCLE**.)

> (*Comedy of Errors,* ACT ILL, SC. 2.)

TURQUOISE

SHYLOCK: *"Thou torturest me, Tubal: it was my turquoise:*
I had it of Leah when I was a bachelor: I would
not have given it for a wilderness of monkeys."

> (*Merchant of Venice,* ACT III, SC. 1.)

UNION

In Hamlet, Shakespeare mentions the pearl twice under the name UNION.

KING: *"The King shall drink to Hamlet's better breath;*
And in the cup an union shall he throw,
Richer than that which four successive kings
In Denmark's crown have worn."
HAMLET: *"Drink off this potion. Is thy union here?"*

> (ACT. V, SC. 2.)

Forms, Compositions, Characteristics, Zodiacal Classification, and Places of Origin

AMBER

Hardness: 2–2.5

Luster: Resinous.

Chemical Composition: Carbon 78.96. Hydrogen 10.51. Oxygen 10.52.

Specific Gravity: 1.10–1.13.

Properties: Becomes highly electric by friction. When submitted to heat, organic compounds escape and leave a black residue.

In the Zodiac: Amber is under the heavenly Taurus.

Where found: Chiefly on the Baltic coast. On the Danish coast. Parts of Asia, etc.

BERYL

Emerald, Aquamarine

Crystalline System: Hexagonal.

Hardness: 7.5–8.

Luster: Vitreous or Resinous. Transparent to translucent.

Refraction: Weakly double.

Chemical Composition: Silicate of aluminum and beryllium.

Chemical Symbol: $Be_3 Al_2 (SiO_3)C$.

Specific Gravity: 2.63–2.75.

Dichroism: Distinct.

Properties: Exhibits frictional electricity. The emerald clouds before the blowpipe flame without fusing but under intensified heat the edges curve. With borax the stone melts into a pale green bead. It resists acids but is affected by microcosmic salt. The stone is so fragile when taken out of the mine that friction crumbles it.

In the Zodiac: All varieties of beryls are under the Heavenly Taurus.

Where found: Generally all over the world. Chiefly in Ekaterinburg, Brazil, India, United States, Australia.

CHRYSOBERYL

Alexandrite, Oriental Chrysolite, Cymophane or Chrysoberyl, Catseye

Crystalline System: Orthorhombic.

Hardness: 8.5.

Luster: Vitreous. Transparent to translucent.

Refraction: Double.

Chemical Composition: Alumina 80.2. Glucina 19.8.

Chemical Symbol: Be Al_2O_4.

Specific Gravity: 3.7–3.86.

Dichroism: Strong in alexandrite. Distinct in chrysoberyl.

Properties: Crystals exhibit remarkable twinning at times. Chrysoberyl is highly electric and when submitted to frictional agitation holds electricity for a longtime. Not affected by acids. Under the blowpipe it is unaltered and infusible, but it fuses tardily with borax or microcosmic salt. The alexandrite variety which, as Professor J. G. Dana says, bears the same relation to ordinary chrysoberyl as emerald to beryl, displays curious changes of color from leafy green to raspberry red in real and artificial lights.

In the Zodiac: Chrysoberyl is under the Heavenly Pisces; alexandrite is under the Heavenly Aquarius.

Where found: Ceylon, Brazil, Russia, Ireland, Australia, etc.

CORUNDUM

Sapphire, Ruby, Oriental Amethyst, Oriental Emerald. etc.

Crystalline System: Rhombohedral.

Hardness: 9.

Luster: Transparent to translucent.

Refraction: Moderately double.

Chemical Composition: Aluminum 53–53.2 Oxygen 46.8.

Chemical Symbol: Al_2O_3.

Specific Gravity: 3.90–4.16.

Dichroism: Strong.

Properties: Submitted to friction exhibits electrical properties which withdraw very slowly. Acids do not affect corundum, but under the blowpipe in borax or microcosmic salt it gradually melts to a transparent globule. Radium influences the color strongly, so much indeed as to impart it in achromatic specimens. The stone is variously affected by heat. Treated by Sir William Crooks by exposure to high tension electric currents in a similar way to the diamond, the ruby phosphoresced with an intense red light, and the sapphire with an intense blue.

Dr. T. Coke Squance of Sunderland, well-known in connection with radio-therapeutic research, has succeeded in transforming a faint pink sapphire into a fine ruby. During the process of transformation the luster of the stone was so intensified that it nearly assumed the brilliancy of a diamond. Dr. Squance observed that both radium and Xrays cause a diamond to glow with a green light. "Besides the diamond," he says, "a mineral called kunzite glows with a lovely red hue. I submitted a sapphire to the radium rays for a long period and it turned to a glorious red. In fact, it had become a ruby. I have similarly transformed other stones, a faint green sapphire, for instance, turning into an oriental emerald." Sir William Crooks noted the sage-green color of the diamond under radium, but found that the color could easily be removed by mechanical means.

In the Zodiac: Blue and green sapphires are under the Heavenly Aquarius; white are under the Heavenly Pisces; yellow or oriental topaz and rubies are under the Heavenly Leo. Oriental amethyst is under the Heavenly Sagittarius.

Where found: Ceylon, China, Burma, Russia, East Indies, United States of America, Australia (chiefly Queensland), etc.

DIAMOND

DIAMOND, BOART

Crystalline System: Isometric.

Forms: Octahedron, dodecahedron. Crystals frequently twinned.

Hardness: 10. Scratches every other stone.

Luster: Adamantine. Transparent and when dark, translucent.

Refraction: Single.

Chemical Composition: Pure carbon.

Chemical Symbol: C.

Specific Gravity: 3.50–3.55.

Properties: Exhibits positive electricity when rubbed, but is itself a non-conductor of electricity. When intensely heated it burns, yielding carbonic anhydride. When heated so as to exclude chemical combination it dilates and forms into a black concretion. It displays phosphorescence under radium, when submitted to strong sunlight and, when put in a vacuum tube, to a high tension electric current.

Dr. G. F. Herbert Smith found that "some diamonds fluoresce in sunlight, turning milky, and a few emit light when rubbed." Dr. Kunz proved that diamonds phosphoresce when exposed to the rays of radium, polonium, or actinium, even when glass is interposed. These phenomena formed special object of experiment with the late Sir William Crooks, who showed that exposed to high tension electric currents in greatly rarified atmosphere, the diamond phosphoresced with an intense green light. Prismatic colors are radiated by this gem.

In the Zodiac: The Diamond is under the Heavenly Aries, Leo and Libra.
Where found: India, Borneo, Brazil, South Africa, Siberia, Australia, United States of America.

GARNET

ALMANDINE, PYROPE, HESSONITE, (GARNET HYACINTH), UVAROVITE
Crystalline Form: Isometric.
Hardness: 6.5–7.5.
Luster: Vitreous.
Refraction: Single.
Chemical Composition: Silica alumina, red iron oxide, lime magnesia, manganese, protoxide.
Chemical Symbol: Dr. Smith has the following formulae:
Hessonite: $Ca_3 Al_2 (SiO_4)_3$.
Pyrope: $Mg_3 Al_2 (SiO_4)_3$.
Almandine: $Fe_3 Al_2 (SiO_4)_3$.
Andradite: $Ca_3 Fe_2 (SiO_4)_3$.
Specific Gravity: 3.4–4.3.
Properties: Exhibits positive electricity by friction. With the exception of uvarovite, all varieties of garnets fuse before the blowpipe flame. The stone generally does not contain water.
In the Zodiac: The almandine is under the Heavenly Sagittarius; the pyrope, Aquarius; hessonite, Virgo; uvarovite, Aquarius.
Where found: Generally all over the world.

OPAL

Crystalline System: None.
Form: Amorphous.
Hardness: 5.5–6.5.
Luster: Waxy to sub-vitreous.

Refraction: Single.

Chemical Composition: Silica 91.32. Water 8.68.

Chemical Symbol: $Si\ O_2$, $n = Si\ O_2\ n\ H_2O$.

Specific Gravity: 1.9–2.3.

Properties: No electrical properties. Opal exhibits characteristic color reflections known as Opalescence. It is susceptible to heat and weather changes, exhibiting greater brilliancy on hot than on cold days. The opal has never yet been successfully imitated, and certain peculiar properties yet remain to be investigated. Professor Frank Rutley F. G. S., emphasizes the fact that "the nature of the Silica (Hydrous Silica) is not yet definitely determined." It is infusible before the blowpipe, but turns opaque.

In the Zodiac: The opal is under the Heavenly Leo, Libra and Aquarius. Leo favors red and fire opal; Libra, light translucent, pure colors, etc.; Aquarius, dark, black opal, etc.

Where found: Hungary, Honduras, Mexico, United States. The finest opal is now found in Australia, principally at Lightning Ridge, White Cliffs, Stuart's Range, Charleville, etc.

Mr. Conrad H. Sayce gives (*Australasian*, March issue, 1920) an analysis of Stuart's Range opal, bearing earth which contains about 35 per cent each of alumina and sulfur trioxide. He opines that this may account for the harmful effect it has on the men's eyes and lungs.

PEARL

Hardness: 3.5–4.

Luster: Translucent.

Chemical Composition: Carbonate of lime and organic matter.

Specific Gravity: 2.65–2.89.

Properties: Affected by acids. Benefitted by some skins, adversely affected by others. Destroyed by fire.

In the Zodiac: Pearls are under the Heavenly Cancer.

Where found: Persian Gulf, Ceylon, Red Sea, South America, New Guinea, Thursday Island, Australia, etc.

PERIDOT

CHRYSOLITE, OLIVINE

Crystalline System: Orthorhombic.

Hardness: 6–7.

Luster: Vitreous. Transparent to translucent.

Refraction: Double.
Chemical Composition: Silicate of magnesium and iron.
Chemical Symbol: (Mg, Fe)$_2$ SiO$_4$.
Specific Gravity: 3.3–3.5.
Dichroism: Distinct.
Properties: Friction induces electricity in the stone which is infusible before the blowpipe, but is affected, whitening and forming with borax, a yellow bead. Decomposes in hydrochloric acid.
In the Zodiac: The peridot is under the Heavenly Pisces.
Where found: United States, Ireland, Australia, (Queensland particularly), etc. A large number of meteorites contain peridots.

QUARTZ

ROCK CRYSTAL, AMETHYST, CAIRNGORM, CHRYSOPRASE, CATSEYE, PLASMA, JASPER, CARNELIAN, AGATE, ONYX, SARDONYX, MOSS AGATE
Crystalline System: Rhombohedral.
Hardness: 7.
Luster: Vitreous. Splendent to dull and resinous.
Refraction: Double.
Chemical Composition: Silicon 46.67. Oxygen 53.33.
Chemical Symbol: Si O$_2$.
Specific Gravity: 2.5–2.8. In pure crystals 2.65.
Dichroism: Distinct.
Properties: Generates positive electricity by friction. It is infusible under the blowpipe, but effervesces with carbonate of soda. Although it resists the common acids it may be dissolved in hydrofluoric.
In the Zodiac: Rock crystal is under the Heavenly Pisces; amethyst is under the Heavenly Aries; cairngorm under the Heavenly Scorpio; chrysoprase under the Heavenly Cancer; catseye under the Heavenly Capricorn; plasma under the Heavenly Virgo; jasper under the Heavenly Virgo; bloodstone under the Heavenly Leo; carnelian under the Heavenly Leo; agate under the Heavenly Scorpio; onyx under the Heavenly Capricorn; sardonyx under the Heavenly Leo; moss agate under the Heavenly Taurus.
Where found: Distributed plentifully about the world. Rock amethyst is found in the United States, Brazil, India, Ceylon, Ekaterinburg, Australia, etc. Mr. R. J. Dunn, late Victorian geologist, discovered large quantities of rose quartz in South Africa. It is also found in the United States,

Russia, Australia and other places. Catseyes are found in Ceylon and India. Cairngorm is found in Scotland, United States, Australia, etc. Chrysoprase is found in the United States and other places.

SPINEL
SPINEL RUBY, BALAS RUBY, RUBICELLE, PLEONASTE OR CEYLONITE
Crystalline System: Isometric.
Hardness: 8–8.5.
Luster: Vitreous.
Refraction: Single.
Chemical Composition: Alumina 72. Magnesia 28.
Chemical Symbol: $Mg\,Al_2\,O_4$.
Specific Gravity: 3.5–4.0.
Dichroism: None.
Properties: Does not display electricity when submitted to friction or heat, but under heat the red spinel changes to brown. On cooling it becomes green, after which it is nearly colorless; then it resumes its pristine hue. Spinel crystals also change into hydrotalcite, a soft pearl-like stone of similar chemical composition. Infusible alone under the blowpipe but yields slowly with borax. It is soluble in concentrated sulfuric acid.
In the Zodiac: Spinel, balas, almandine, ruby and sapphirine are under the Heavenly Virgo. The chloro-spinel and the pleonaste are under the Heavenly Capricorn.
Where found: United States, Canada, Burma, Siam, Ceylon, Australia, etc. It is discovered in granular limestone, in gneiss and rocks of volcanic origin.

SPODUMENE
KUNZITE, HIDDENITE
Crystalline Form: Monoclinic.
Hardness: 6.5–7.
Luster: Pearly. Translucent to sub-translucent.
Refraction: Double.
Chemical Composition: Silicate of aluminum and lithium.
Chemical Symbol: $Li\,Al\,(Si\,O_3)_2$.
Specific Gravity: 3.5–3.20.
Dichroism: Strong.

Properties: Electrical. Unaffected by acids. Under the blowpipe flame expands and melts into a clear or opaque glass, indicating lithia by coloring the flame red. Kunzite exhibits phosphorescence under radium.

In the Zodiac: Spodumene and kunzite are under the Heavenly Libra. Hiddenite may be under the zodiacal Taurus.

Where found: United States of America, Madagascar, Brazil, Sweden, etc.

TOPAZ

Crystalline Form: Orthorhombic.

Hardness: 8.

Luster: Vitreous. Transparent to translucent.

Refraction: Slightly double.

Chemical Composition: Silicate of aluminum.

Chemical Symbol: $[Al (F, OH)]_2 Si O_4$. (Penfold and Minor.)

Specific Gravity: 3.4–3.65.

Dichroism: Distinct.

Properties: Becomes strongly electric by friction, heat and pressure. Infusible alone before the blowpipe flame, but with borax melts into a bead. Changes color when heated.

In the Zodiac: The Topaz is under the Heavenly Scorpio.

Where found: Brazil, Ceylon, Mexico, United States, Australia, etc.

TOURMALINE

Crystalline Form: Rhombohedral.

Hardness: 7–7.5.

Luster: Vitreous.

Refraction: Double.

Chemical Composition: Varied, but all varieties include silicate of alumina, boric acid, iron, magnesia, lime and soda, sometimes lithium in small quantity, with fluorine and trace of phosphoric acid.

Chemical Symbol: Professors Penford and Foote refer all varieties of Tourmaline to $(H_6 Na_6 Mg_3 Al_2)_3 (Al, Fe)_6 (B, OH)_4 Si_8 O_{38}$.

Specific Gravity: 2.39–3.3.

Dichroism: Strong.

Properties: Becomes charged by heat and friction with positive and negative electricity. Before the blowpipe flame the darker varieties fuse easily but the lighter more tardily.

In the Zodiac: The tourmaline family is under the Heavenly Gemini.

Where found: Brazil, Russia, California and other parts of the United States, Ceylon, Australia, etc.

TURQUOISE
Crystalline Form: None.
Hardness: 6.
Luster: Waxy.
Chemical Composition: Dr. Smith gives the composition as a complex phosphate of aluminum, iron and copper.
Chemical Symbol: Dr. Smith gives Penfold's formula as [Al (OH)$_2$ Fe (OH)$_2$, CU (OH), H]$_3$ PO$_4$, approaching nearly to H$_5$ Al$_2$ PO$_8$.
Specific Gravity: 2.6–2.8.
Properties: Infusible before the blowpipe flame, but changes its color to brown. Dissolves in hydrochloric acid. Is affected by acids, oils, the health of the wearer, etc.
In the Zodiac: Turquoise is under the zodiacal Sagittarius.
Where found: Chiefly in Persia where the best specimens are found. Also found in Mexico, Russia, United States, Australia, etc.

ZIRCON
ZIRCON, JARGOON, HYACINTH OR JACINTH
Crystalline System: Tetragonal.
Hardness: 7.5
Luster: Adamantine. Transparent to opaque.
Refraction: Strongly double.
Chemical Composition: Silica 33. Zirconia 67.
Chemical Symbol: ZR Si O$_4$.
Specific Gravity: 4.6–4.86.
Properties: Exhibits frictional electricity. The zircon is infusible before the blowpipe flame but colored specimens lose their colors. With borax zircon melts under the blowpipe into a transparent bead. Heated with lime the zircon is transformed into a straw-colored stone which so closely resembles the yellow diamond that it is sold to travelers by some unscrupulous Eastern dealers as the more costly gem. Scientists have not yet been able to explain the constitution and distinct characters of the zircon satisfactorily.

Professor Sir A. H. Church has made a technical study of the zircon for over half a century, and is universally accepted as its most authoritative student. In his researches he found that in certain varieties of zircon the green and yellow stones, ground on copper wheel with diamond dust, exhibit a sparkling orange light, and the intermediate golden types radiate orange tints in the flame of a Bunsen burner. Students are seeking for the unknown element which, blended with zirconium, defies detection.

The zircon is very little affected by acids, except sulfuric acid after very long steeping. It is also peculiar that when first heated the stone exhibits strong phosphorescence, but as its color leaves it, its specific gravity is magnified and it will not again phosphoresce when reheated after cooling.

In the Zodiac: All varieties of zircon are under Heavenly Virgo.

Where found: In almost every part of the world.